AF600358

Alton's Paradox

SUNY series in Latin American Cinema

Ignacio M. Sánchez Prado and Leslie L. Marsh, editors

Alton's Paradox

Foreign Film Workers and the Emergence of Industrial Cinema in Latin America

Nicolas Poppe

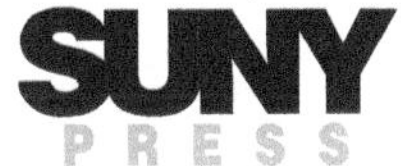

Published by State University of New York Press, Albany

Printed in the United States of America

For information, contact State University of New York Press, Albany, NY
www.sunypress.edu

Library of Congress Cataloging-in-Publication Data

Name: Poppe, Nicolas, author.
Title: Alton's paradox : foreign film workers and the emergence of industrial cinema in Latin America / Nicolas Poppe.
Description: Albany : State University of New York, [2021] | Series: SUNY series in Latin American cinema | Includes bibliographical references and index.
Identifiers: LCCN 2021016712 (print) | LCCN 2021016713 (ebook) | ISBN 9781438485034 (hardcover : alk. paper) | ISBN 9781438485058 (ebook)
Subjects: LCSH: Motion picture industry—Latin America—History—20th century. | Foreign workers—Latin America—History—20th century.
Classification: LCC PN1993.5.L3 P67 2021 (print) | LCC PN1993.5.L3 (ebook) | DDC 791.4309809/04—dc23
LC record available at https://lccn.loc.gov/2021016712
LC ebook record available at https://lccn.loc.gov/2021016713

10 9 8 7 6 5 4 3 2 1

For Erin

Contents

Illustrations

Acknowledgments

As I grew into my teens, I eventually realized that the only time of the day I could be by myself at home was late into the night. Growing up without cable in San Antonio, Texas, my minimal options for entertainment forced me to be creative. During the school year, this was less of a worry, as I would usually watch the *Late Show with David Letterman* or *Saturday Night Live*. Or, maybe, reruns of *Cheers* or a syndicated show such as *Xena: Warrior Princess*. In the summer, I was dulled not only by the oppressive summer heat, but also an excess of free time. Reading proved difficult; I fell asleep. Playing video games eventually bored me as much the shows I had already seen. Listening to the BBC World Service on Texas Public Radio (KSTX 89.1) opened the world to me. But some of the shows, well, were directed to different audiences. What almost always proved to be a good bet for some good entertainment, especially on the weekends, were movies on Univisión (KWEX 41) and Telemundo (KVDA 60). Even though I did not yet speak Spanish, the strange plots of late-night movies such as *Asalto en Tijuana* (Assault in Tijuana, dir. Alfredo Gurrola, 1984) and *Nacido para matar* (Born to Kill, dir. Juan Manuel Herrera, 1986) were easy enough to follow. The sex and violence of Mexploitation and *narcocine* usually caught my eye, but occasionally I would watch an older movie such as *Una carta de amor* (*A Love Letter*, dir. Miguel Zacarías, 1943) and *El Profe* (*The Professor*, dir. Miguel M. Delgado, 1971). Not that I would have known who Jorge Negrete or Cantinflas, the films' stars, were. Not at first, at least. These may have not been the exact films I watched, although they were shown in San Antonio in the mid-1990s, but they were the kind of movies I first experienced in Spanish. And I more than kind of liked it.

I did not know that you could study cinema until I began writing my dissertation at the University of Texas at Austin. This seems improbable to me even today, but either through lack of exposure or understanding, I had never really considered the possibility. A chance conversation led to a meeting with Leo Zonn, a cultural geographer whose generosity not only turned my dissertation on its head, but also my career. In Nicolas Shumway, I was lucky to have an intellectual mentor who urged me to "ruin my dissertation however I [saw] fit." My project, which examined the representation of Buenos Aires as place in different modes of cultural production in the 1920s and 1930s, was not the dissertation Professor Shumway might have wanted it to be, but it set the course for my last ten years of writing and teaching, if not my entire scholarly career. Like so many others working in today's academia—so marked by precarity and casualization that more than a generation of scholarship, some of which would have been truly brilliant, has already been lost—my path has been rather more circuitous than I would have imagined that day I decided to write on the movies. At Denison University, I was fortunate to have as colleagues two other visiting assistant professors: Phillip Penix-Tadsen and Ana María Mutis. I will always admire and deeply appreciate their friendship, grace, and intellectual acuity. Their camaraderie got me through some dark times. In my next position, at Ball State University, I was encouraged to grow into my potential by Lisa Kuriscak and Chris Luke. Without their support, I am not sure if I would have continued my search for a real academic home. But I miss them dearly.

In my six years at Middlebury College, I have come to feel as if I am not only in my place, but also at home. I am especially grateful for my wonderful colleagues in Luso-Hispanic Studies, as well as our excellent students. Without Brandon Baird, Enrique García, Mario Higa, Fernando Rocha, and Patricia Saldarriaga, this book would have been much more difficult to write. This project benefited greatly from varying kinds of work done by my brilliant undergraduate research assistants Miles Meijer, James Scott, Soyibou Sylla, Melisa Topic, and Greyson Zatzick. I am also lucky to teach at an institution in which film and media studies is so vibrant. My colleagues Christian Keathley, Jason Mittell, David Miranda-Hardy, Ethan Murphy, and Louisa Stein in Film and Media Culture not only have pushed me to learn new ways of approaching teaching and writing about movies, but also new ways of thinking about film and media. Economic historians Leticia Arroyo Abad and Amanda Gregg were important sounding boards for ideas, some of which would undergird this book. *Alton's Paradox* is what it is because I was fortunate enough to have institutional support for my research. I am a different scholar now than I was (or could have become) as a direct result of money invested by Middlebury College in research leaves, startup funds, professional development funds, and other kinds of grants. If funding for higher education had not been decimated throughout my life, cynically and systematically, we would see more young scholars throughout academic disciplines with the opportunity to grow into their intellectual potential. We might then live in a society that more greatly appreciates the exploration of the meaning of our human experience, as well as confronts the damage we have inflicted upon our environment. We can only hope for change. With deep budget cuts looming in response to the COVID-19 pandemic, I am fearful that few of us will have the opportunity to work on the kind of scholarship that makes possible books like *Alton's Paradox*.

Support from Middlebury College made possible archival research without which this book would have been impossible. I am deeply grateful to archivists and librarians, cinephiles and collectors whose generosity made available materials woven into this book, as well as other projects of mine (past, present, and future). More specifically, I want to recognize the contributions of the following institutions and people: in Buenos Aires, Celeste Castillo at the Museo del Cine Pablo C. Ducrós Hicken and Adrián Muoyo of the Biblioteca INCAA-ENERC; in Los Angeles, Jan-Christopher Horak and Maya Smukler of the UCLA Film & Television Archive and Kristine Krueger of the Academy of Motion Picture Arts and Sciences's Margaret Herrick Library; in Mexico City, Raúl Miranda of the Centro de Documentación Cineteca Nacional México, Antonia Rojas Ávila and Hugo Villa Smythe of the Filmoteca de la Universidad Autónoma de México, and the director Sebastián del Amo. Emiliano Aguilar and Oswaldo Mejía Mendiola conducted important research assistance in Buenos Aires and Mexico City, respectively. I also want to thank the archivists at the New York State Archives' Motion Picture Scripts Collection, Stanford University's Media & Microtext Center, and the University of Texas at Austin's Nettie Lee Benson Latin American Collection, especially those in Rare Books and Manuscripts. This book, as well as my research more generally, has been deeply impacted by important digital humanities projects such as Media History Digital Library, Colecciones Digitales of the Biblioteca Nacional Mariano Moreno de la República Argentina, Hemeroteca Digital of the Biblioteca Nacional do Brasil, CineChile.cl, and Memoria Chilena of the Biblioteca Nacional de Chile. My appreciation extends from those who directed the projects to the individuals who scanned the documents I consult, from those who fought to obtain funding to those who keep everything running online.

This book would have also been impossible had it not been for the guidance, inspiration, and support of so many colleagues. Like many scholars of my generation, I am particularly indebted to Ana M. López. Her scholarship will always serve as a benchmark, and her mentorship has been invaluable to me and many others. Whether it be via email or between panels at a conference, I am deeply grateful to Rielle Navitski, Nilo Couret, Alejandro Kelly Hopfenblatt, Colin Gunckel, Andrea Cuarterolo, Jason Borge, Rafael de Luna Freire, Jeffrey Middents, Kathleen Newman, Isabella Goulart, Georgina Torello, Adela Pineda Franco, Jacqueline Avila, John Koegel, Arcelia Gutiérrez, Ana Almeyda Cohen, Olivia Cosentino, and Laura Isabel Serna. David Wilt, whom I hope to meet one day, made possible this book's contributions to Mexican film history. Without the friendship of fellow Longhorns Brian Price, Anna Nogar, and Ryan Schmitz, who continue to challenge and support me to today, this book would not exist. Nor would it exist without the mentorship of Lilian Contreras-Silva and Ginger Ochoa. Two wonderful, strong women, they are always present in my life, no matter how long it has been since I have last seen them. I am also deeply thankful to Ignacio M. Sánchez Prado and Leslie L. Marsh, editors of the SUNY series in Latin American Cinema. Their work has made possible growth in our all too frequently ignored field. Cultivating the work of authors like me is the indefatigable Rebecca Colesworthy. Her labor is a true gift. I am also deeply appreciative of those at SUNY Press who have worked to transform a series of computer files into a physical object (and e-book): copyeditor Alan Hewat, cover designer Amane Kaneko, compositor Sue Morreale, editorial coordinator Catherine S. Blackwell, editor-in-chief James Peltz, production editor Ryan Morris, and promotions manager Michael Campochiaro.

Alton's Paradox is a book whose most important figures make the most fleeting of appearances. My sons Sebastian, Lucas, and Isaac Poppe make me want to become the best version of myself, not only as a father but also as a man. Their names may appear only on this page, but they imbue this entire book. I simply do not have the words to express what the support and love of my wife, Erin Jones-Poppe, mean to me. You, Erin, made this book possible.

1

Alton's Paradox

Writing in mid-1934 from Buenos Aires for the Hollywood-published monthly *International Photographer*, the cinematographer John Alton examines recent industrial developments in "Motion Picture Production in South America," paradoxically arguing that "[t]he possibilities are enormous, but not until foreign technicians will take the matter in their hands and with foreign organization will there be local industry."[1] Alton's concern was not born merely out of self-interest, as he had been working in Argentina since contributing to the launch of the Lumiton studios in 1932, but it was also of professional relevance for the magazine's readership, which consisted of film technicians in Hollywood and beyond. Initially using as its epigraph the Abraham Lincoln (mis)quote, "Capital is the fruit of labor, and could not exist if labor had not first existed. Labor, therefore, deserves much the higher consideration," *International Photographer* served as Los Angeles house bulletin of the International Photographers of the Motion Picture Industries. It was "a voice of an ENTIRE CRAFT."[2] With pieces on aesthetics and technology, but also, at least initially, Hollywood's abusive labor practices, *International Photographer* also kept its readers up to date on members' work throughout the globe.[3] Alton—one such cosmopolitan figure, whose own convoluted personal history led him to live in Argentina for much of the 1930s before moving back to Los Angeles, where he would later became known as the visual stylist of film noir, a quintessentially American film genre of the 1940s and 1950s that would quickly become internationalized—insists that national cinemas like that of Argentina should mirror other forms of industrial development through relying on foreign capital, both human and monetary.

By signaling the complex interrelation between "local" and "foreign," Alton alludes to a central tension of the early sound period in world cinema, particularly in Latin America. The arrival of sound film technologies transformed how cinema was practiced in production, distribution, and exhibition. Drastically reshaping film markets—not only was production severed for years, if not decades, after its introduction in places such as Bolivia, Venezuela, and Colombia, but distribution and exhibition in countries throughout Latin America were fundamentally reorganized—sound film did little, however, to challenge the dominance of Hollywood and, to a lesser extent, European cinemas. Working with established, well-organized distribution networks, particularly those of U.S. studios with their own agencies in metropolises such as Havana, Mexico City, Santiago, Buenos Aires, São Paulo, and Rio de Janeiro, but also smaller cities such as Panama City, Lima, and Caracas, local exhibitors worked with foreign companies like Western Electric and RCA to wire their theaters in order to continue to show the latest popular releases.[4] Local filmmakers, for their part, were forced to acquire (or imitate) imported advanced technologies such as cameras, microphones, and sound-on-film systems; to learn how to use new, frequently intricate sound film equipment; and to revamp the ways in which they told their cinematic stories. If local filmmakers were to adjust to the new world of the talkie and (re)establish national cinemas, they had to constantly interact with distinct foreign entities. Thus, they were obliged to confront Alton's paradox: in order to create national film industries that not only competed with Hollywood, but also produced films that resonated meaningfully with local audiences, they needed to learn how to employ and incorporate foreign capital.

"The cinema appears in Latin America as another foreign import," as Paulo Antônio Paranaguá states.[5] Later expanded upon by a number of scholars, but most notably by Ana M. López, the cinema has always been inextricably enmeshed within transnational flows of capital.[6] Along with the cinematic apparatus itself, technicians, representatives, and an assemblage of other workers arrived in Latin America as part of broader processes of industrialization and modernization that were entangled with the cinema from its very beginnings. Initially tied to exhibitions such as the Lumière's Cinématographe in Rio de Janeiro (July 8, 1896) or Edison's Vitascope in Buenos Aires (July 20, 1896), these foreign workers imported economic, cultural, and social capital.[7] Appropriated materially through the importation of cinematic technology and symbolically through contracting technological and technical experts, foreign capital has always marked Latin American cinema. Despite these contributions, foreign film workers have been largely overlooked by traditional film historiographies, whose approaches are excessively bound by nationness. National cinema in Latin America, as a notion expressed in film periodicals from the 1930s, initial critical approximations in the 1940s and 1950s, and scholarly interventions today, is often construed as both being structured (by shared cultural, historical, political, and social understandings) and structuring (particularly of national identity, usually in opposition to Hollywood). Rather than playing protagonists in film histories, even those less interested in presenting totalizing narratives of national cinema than in recovering its *petites histoires,* foreign film workers play at the margins of the frame, if they are on screen at all. Genesis amnesia also clouds our understanding of their function in film history.[8] The national cinemas of Latin America have come to be understood as almost natural, even organic, having developed in specific ways according to some underlying local logic or order. Their uncertain origins have been forgotten. The

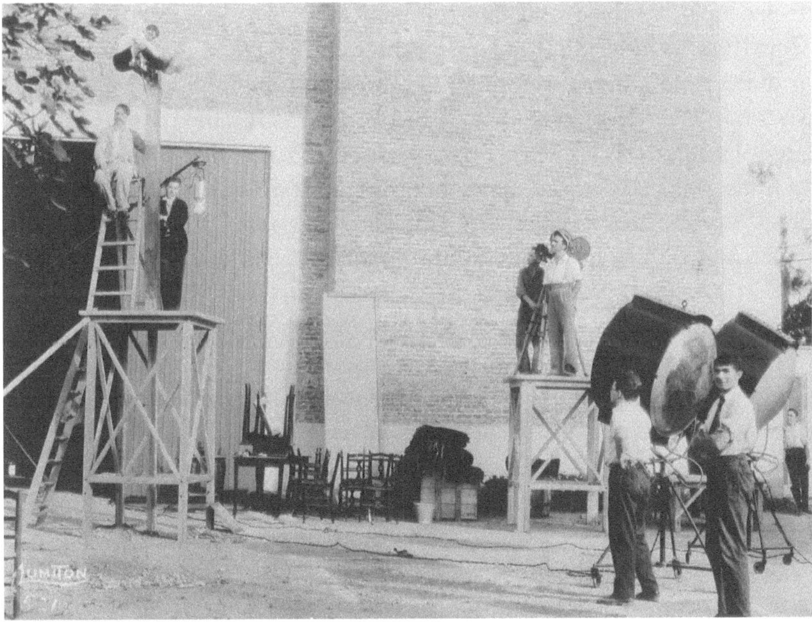

Figure 1.1. John Alton shooting a scene for *Los tres berretines*. Luis Arata, one of the film's stars, sits upon a ladder. Courtesy of the Museo del Cine Pablo Ducrós Hicken.

contingency and incoherence of history is eschewed, often for thematic or ostensibly theoretical approaches that cannot account for the heterogeneity of Latin American cinema of the 1930s and early 1940s. Foreigners, of course, are often among the first to be lost to oblivion. Hardly ever the focus of critical attention, these foreign film workers nonetheless played important roles in the history of Latin American cinema, as well as the stories of Latin American cinemas.

One such secondary character was John Alton. Initially reported by the *porteño* trade publication *Revista del Exhibidor*, Alton arrived in Argentina on the steamship *L'Atlantic* on April 20, 1932.[9] The report states, "He will remain in our country, according to the contract signed to the effect, for a space of six months, if the contract is not extended. He will direct two or three films in said time." Several months later, *International Photographer* echoed these words, asserting, "Word from John J. Alton, now in Buenos Aires, brings the interesting information that he has signed a six months' contract with Dr. Enrique Sussini [*sic*] of the S. A. Lumiton Studios of the making of motion pictures in the Argentine."[10] Contracted for his experience not as a director but as a cameraman, Alton helped to shoot the production company's first feature, *Los tres berretines* (The Three Whims, dir. Equipo Lumiton, 1933). His experience working in difficult conditions was surely an asset, as Domingo Di Núbila later described the transition to sound in his landmark national film history: "In order to clearly appreciate the evolution of Argentine cinema through its films, it is necessary to remember that the starting line, from the point of view of cinematographic arts, was kilometer zero."[11] Like other Latin American countries, Argentine film production had not yet become fully modernized. Still preindustrial, its sporadic films were improvisational in their production, as well as their distribution and exhibition. Referring to the place from which distance is measured in a country, and as many local sources argued in the 1930s, Argentine filmmakers needed foreign film workers such as John Alton to operate the technology purchased abroad; to adapt to difficult, effectively preindustrial conditions; to apply aesthetic and diegetic techniques practiced in Hollywood and European cinemas; and to train local film workers, among many other responsibilities.[12] Through employing his cultural and social capital, Alton helped to make possible what may not have otherwise come to fruition, such as Mario Soffici's 1938 social folkloric drama *Kilómetro 111*.[13] Argentine cinema traveled quite a distance in the 1930s.

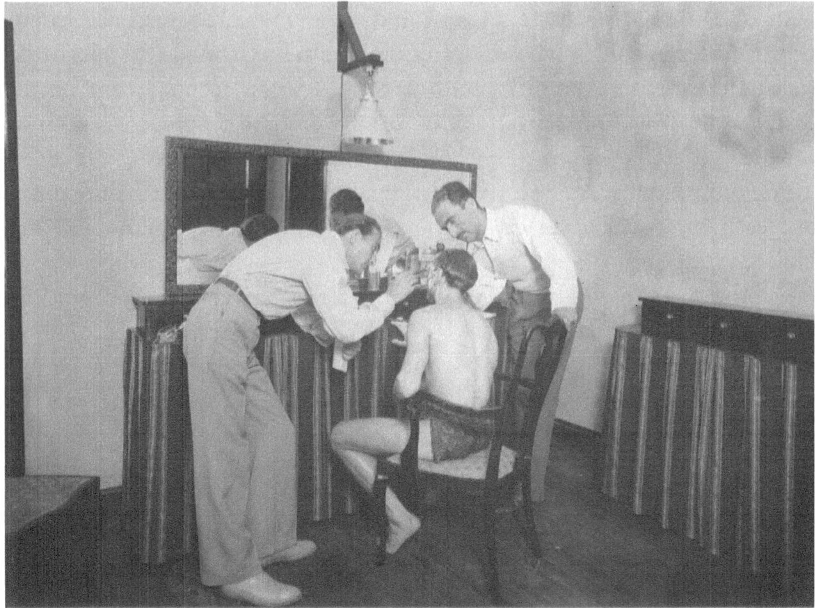

Figure 1.2. Alton supervises the makeup of Miguel Ángel Lauri during the filming of *Los tres berretines*. Courtesy of the Museo del Cine Pablo Ducrós Hicken.

After his first three years in Argentina, a period of experimentation and expression, Alton became the technical director of what was becoming the country's most important film studio, Argentina Sono Film.[14] In addition to applying his technical expertise, Alton oversaw the acquisition of new technologies by Argentina Sono Film and the installation of the studio's new, modern laboratory and, in so doing, aided in its transformation into Latin America's first industrial film studio.[15] Situated in specific conditions paralleling but not fully corresponding to each other, Latin American filmmakers reassessed how they understood and practiced their craft after the arrival of sound film technologies. With production costs precipitously rising, and distribution networks yet to be established that would more immediately and lastingly benefit production companies, local filmmakers were forced to invest in film technologies (and heavily so) in order to compete with imports from Hollywood and Europe. These technologies ranged from film stock to processing equipment, lenses for 35 mm cameras to incandescent lamps, microphones to

Moviolas, among other equipment and goods, which sometimes led to the rise of companies whose locally made products sought to substitute for more expensive, or difficult to acquire, foreign technologies. Levels of technological capitalization varied, and were tied to processes such as broader industrialization of the economy and involvement by the state. Throughout Latin America, each incipient industry reacted differently, but each was obliged to do business with firms from Europe and the United States.

The technological changes caused by the arrival of sound precipitated structural shifts in Latin American film industries, but also, more narrowly, in their modes of production. If silent films in the period were generally financed by producers closely tied to the project, usually without a strategic plan for distribution or additional future projects, the substantial new costs of sound film were prohibitive. Effectuated

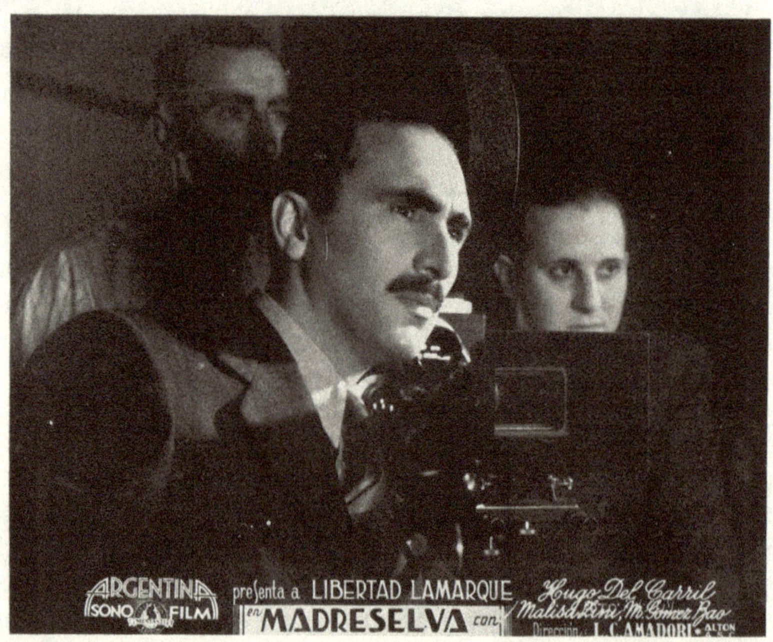

Centre is John J. Alton, A. S. C., directing photography on the just completed "Madreselva," "first million peso" production of Argentina for Argentina Sono Film. Directed by Luis Cesar Amador.

Figure 1.3. From the American Society of Cinematographers collection of the Margaret Herrick Library, Academy of Motion Picture Arts and Sciences.

by the demand for greater capitalization, particularly from investors not directly associated with the production of a film, local filmmaking became increasingly modernized and industrialized. Following the lead of Hollywood studios, but in distinctive ways depending on local contexts, Latin American film industries moved toward the producer-unit system, in which labor serving a studio became ever more specialized in order to produce more, and higher quality, films year by year. Similar to Hollywood, but in quite different ways from Argentina to Mexico, for example, labor force activities and financing reinforced and challenged emergent production systems. Leading to more production efficiency, as the number of films in these countries grew steadily, but always tethered to the use of available technologies, unit production allowed Latin American studios, especially those in Argentina, Brazil, and Mexico, to produce commercial films that were able to compete with Hollywood's.[16] Although there is perhaps greater continuity in Latin America from the silent period to classical cinema in terms of film style and narrative than is generally acknowledged, industrialization resulted in greater commercialization of the film diegesis. This is not to say that producers of silent films did not hope that their films would become huge hits, but rather that labor specialization allowed production companies to cultivate the commercial potential of a film's storyworld from script development to recutting after a sneak preview or initial screening.

Through their knowledge of more advanced technologies and progressively specialized roles—whether they were glamor lighting strategies or ways to narratively structure a gag—foreign film workers contributed to the assembling of the films on which they worked. Traced initially in contemporaneous film periodicals and later inscribed in national film histories, special emphasis in Latin American film historiography has been given to those used to sell the movies: stars and directors. Even though they are central to how we experience movies, stars and directors were not the sole creators of Latin American cinema in the early sound period. It has proven easier to discuss the comic genius of Pepe Arias in *El pobre Pérez* (*Poor Pérez*, 1937) or the melodramatic directing style of Luis César Amadori in *Madreselva* (*Honeysuckle*, 1938) than the cinematography of John Alton in those two Argentina Sono Film productions, but his genre lighting of both helped establish spectators' experience of their diegeses. Enmeshed within actors' performances and directors' authorship is the labor of countless other workers like Alton whose contributions, however big or small, are projected onto screen. Ignored in marketing to

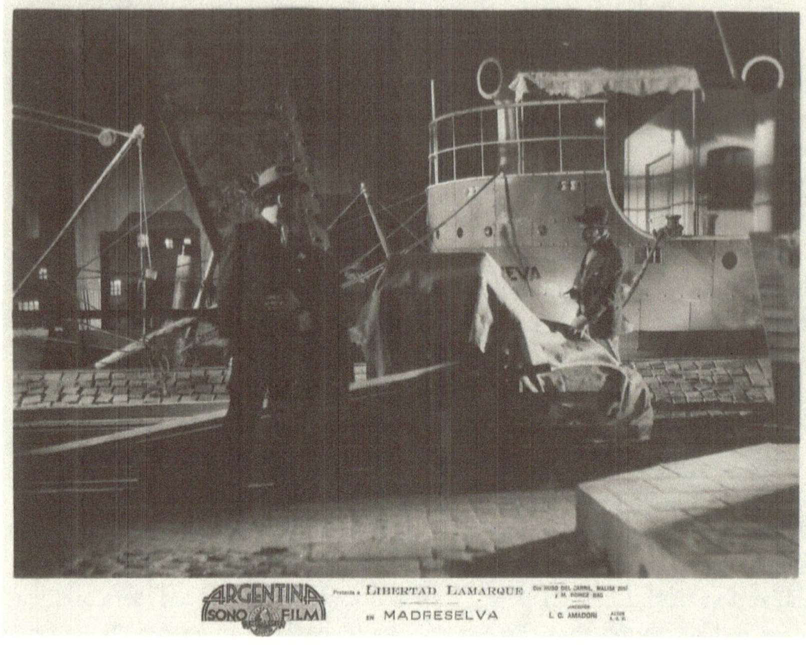

Figure 1.4. Opening sequence of *Madreselva*. Courtesy of the Museo del Cine Pablo Ducrós Hicken.

differentiate national films, and folded into readings used to differentiate and distinguish national cinema of the classical period, the recovery of these contributions allows us to better understand the complexities of commercial cinemas too frequently disregarded by critics, despite their long-lasting popularity in Latin America and beyond.[17]

The transition to sound also altered local and regional film cultures by changing spectators' relationships to the moving image and, newly, sound. Structured by Hollywood, whose control over these markets was largely unaffected due to the strength of its distribution networks and the power and popularity of its stars, these film cultures were constituted by moviegoers whose complex relationships to their own emerging cinemas revealed cultural, economic, and social anxieties. Transformed, often in nuanced ways, these film cultures were forced to renegotiate their relationships with the films they loved (and hated and were indifferent toward). Further estranged by language—no longer were production companies and distributors able to adapt intertitles, and possibly even the narrative structure of a film, to better appeal to the taste of a local market—spectators watched their favorite stars in English (a language most did not speak) or in translation (subtitling and, later, dubbing were common by the mid-1930s), or they encountered (trans)national stars from other forms of mass media, especially the radio, on-screen for the first time. The reactions of local and regional film cultures to the new identity and language politics instigated by sound cinema would shape the emergence (and disappearance) of the first three major industries in Latin America: Hollywood's Spanish-language production, Mexico, and Argentina.

Alton's paradox invites us to rethink the organization of Latin American film industries from the transition to sound to the early classical period. By focusing attention on the contributions of specific workers, my aim is not to argue that the various film industries throughout the region would not exist if it were not for foreign labor, but rather that what came to be known as national cinemas incorporated foreign film workers who employed capital necessary for these industries to emerge. Whether contracted for a determined time to perform a specific task or employed much more incidentally and indeterminately, these foreign film workers plied their trade within contexts specific to different levels of industrial development in different nations. John Alton was not necessary to the rise of Argentine national cinema, but, at the risk of being overly reductive, he was there. Had he worked in Brazil, his contributions to Latin American cinema would have been vastly different. My approach is at once historical and theoretical, trying to recover traces left behind by foreign film workers inscribed within national cinemas, while questioning the meaning of these marks, which, contradictorily, seem at once to be indelible and evanescent. Like capital—or, perhaps, as an expression and form of capital—national cinema is the fruit of this labor; consequently, this labor deserves more consideration. To approach the role of foreign labor in this particular expression of industrial development, as well as its relationship to forms of foreign capital, I discuss the contours of labor markets as well as the the participation of individual foreign film workers. My approach is also dialogic and formal, as I examine the ways in which these foreigners and their work were written about in periodicals, especially in daily newspapers and specialized film magazines, and how their work is imprinted within their films. By doing so, I posit the establishment of an uneven and disjointed interconnectedness of Latin American commercial cinemas, which to this day exist somewhere between the national and transnational.

Alton's Paradox begins with the world's first large-scale Spanish-language film industry: Hollywood. Shot primarily in Los Angeles, New York, and Joinville (France), I argue that Hollywood's Spanish-language film production represented the first, albeit largely incoherent, expression of Latin American industrial cinema. The *films hispanos,* as they were sometimes called, began as multilinguals (also known as multiple language versions [MLVs] or foreign language versions [FLVs]) and eventually became original features. Initially, I introduce the complex labor market in which these films were produced by U.S. studios in order to monologically replicate their industrial model and, by extension, maintain their pre-sound dominance of Latin American film markets. By the late 1930s, these productions had been abandoned by Hollywood studios due to their high costs, which were particularly onerous in comparison with the costs of subtitling and dubbing, and their lack of commercial success, in no small part due to their cultural and linguistic heterogeneity. With studios' focus on talent, especially performers already working within other forms of mass media and popular entertainment, I examine the work of a star. Nearly forgotten today, in no small part due to his films being almost totally inaccessible, the Mexican baritone José Mojica was one of the most famous performers in Latin America in the 1930s. Through formal analysis of his work for Fox Film, especially *El rey de los gitanos* (*King of the Gypsies*, dir. Frank Strayer, 1933) and *La cruz y la espada* (*The Cross and the Sword*, dir. Strayer, 1934), I show how Mojica was audiovisually fashioned into a transnational star designed to appeal to audiences from California to Chile. Even though most of Mojica's films are presumed lost, I use materials from a wide array of critical sources to paratextually reconstruct textures of his work and star text.

Focusing on Mexico, which by 1943 had become the dominant regional film industry in Latin America, the book's second section studies the ways in which film workers from abroad shaped modes of production that were entangled within distribution and exhibition practices. In addition to an introductory section detailing the distinct industrial and labor dynamics in which these foreign workers plied their trades, and how they were caught up in transnational flows of labor that included Mexicans who had previously been working abroad, I closely examine films of cinematographer Alex Phillips and the director Juan Orol in the early sound period. As the Mexican film industry emerged due to increased capitalization and, more notably, the intervention of the state, the professional obligations of workers' roles were consolidated and defined.

I examine how these two roles (cinematographer and director), specifically, reflected the structure of the Mexican film industry and structured cinematically what spectators came to know as the *Época de oro*. Through studying the Canadian Russian cinematographer Alex Phillips's collaborations with the directors Arcady Boytler and Fernando de Fuentes, in analyses of films such as *La mujer del puerto* (*Woman of the Port*, 1933) and *Doña Bárbara* (1943), I argue that Phillips's films reveal tendencies that were present—and in tension—throughout the early sound period: the use of lighting strategies serving generic conventions that had been established primarily (but not exclusively) in Hollywood, as well as the implementation of his own, personal style within narrative and professional constraints. I detail Phillips's style (or, really, styles) within the framework of these collaborations, and also within the specific limitations of the role of the cinematographer in the emerging Mexican film industry of the 1930s and early 1940s. Continuing to eschew the more auteurist approach of critics such as Charles Ramírez Berg, I explore the explicit and implicit heterogeneity of the films of Juan Orol, a peripatetic figure born in Spain and partially raised in Cuba, who would eventually become the "*Rey del churro* (King of the B-movie)" and subject of Sebastián del Amo's 2012 biopic *El fantástico mundo de Juan Orol* (*The Fantastic World of Juan Orol*).[18] Although Orol was known as a kind of "one man orchestra" in his films, assuming numerous roles in their production, I focus on his work as the director of melodramas that contributed greatly to the emergence of one of the most important cinematic modes of the *Época de oro* of Mexican cinema. I am especially interested in the ways Orolian melodrama, which was ostensibly targeted at female audiences, but which also frequently used to draw men into the cinema, structures narrative excess in six films of the mid-1930s.

I also examine the emergence of the sound film industry in Argentina. Within its distinctive context, as reflected in film production, distribution, and exhibition, those attempting to create the Argentine film industry incorporated foreign film workers in very different ways during the early sound period. So as to approach how industrial and labor conditions there differed from those in the United States and Mexico, I examine two very different kinds of foreign film workers in Argentina: a studio head and a working filmmaker. After founding Argentina Sono Film in 1932, a studio that would dominate the domestic industry for four decades, the Italian immigrant Ángel Mentasti acted as studio head until his death in 1937, producing many of the most important films of the early sound period.

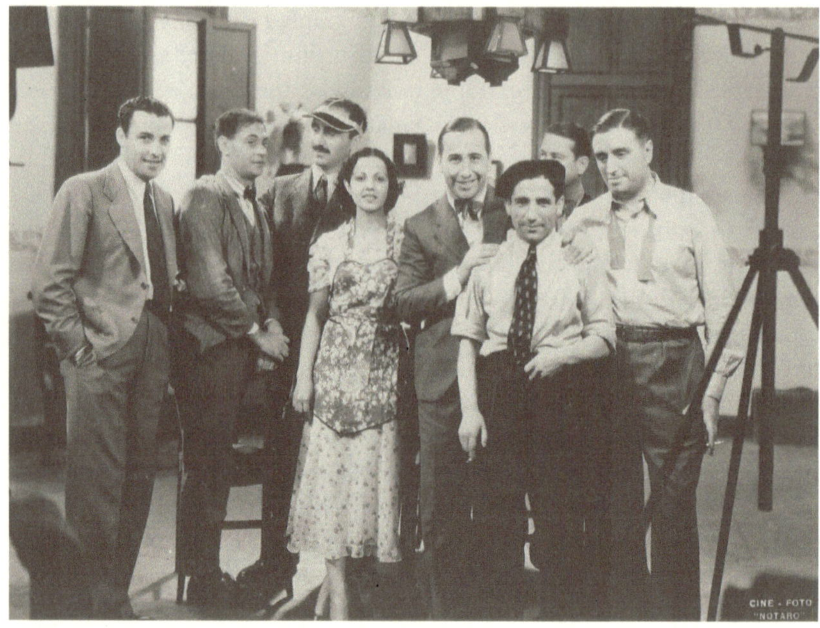

Figure 1.5. Between scenes on the set of *Loco lindo*. From left: Agustín Irusta, Luis Sandrini, John Alton, Anita Jordán, Miguel Paulino Tato (Néstor), Gumer Barreiros, and Arturo S. Mom. Mentasti might not be in the photograph, but his presence would have been undeniable. Courtesy of the Museo del Cine Pablo Ducrós Hicken.

In so doing, Mentasti not only shaped new modes of production and new distribution strategies, but indelibly marked the images and sounds forming the narratives of Argentine national cinema. Unlike Mentasti, who came to be known to wield great power within the industry, the next chapter centers on a jack of all trades, the Chilean actor, director, and screenwriter Tito Davison, and examines his time in Argentina. With experience in Hollywood, where he participated in Spanish-language film production and wrote for magazines such as *Cine-Mundial* (distributed monthly throughout the Spanish-speaking world) and *Ecran* (the most important Chilean film magazine of the time), Davison's credits in Argentina ranged widely (dialogue director, director, editor, and writer). Focusing primarily on his writing and directing, I argue that Davison's contributions to the Argentine film industry are intertwined within broader economic factors. If Davison arrived in Buenos Aires as the industry was in sharp ascent due to success in domestic and international markets, his exit was precipitated by the effects of Argentina's uncertain geopolitical situation as a neutral country in World War II. He would then make his way to Mexico City where, eventually, he would become a prolific director.

The book's coda returns to Alton's paradox both to illuminate the role of foreign workers in other Latin American film industries during their early sound periods and to challenge competing notions of both national and transnational cinema. Moving beyond Hollywood, Mexico, and Argentina, the coda delineates the distinctive labor forces in Latin American film industries that led to the emergence of individual, uneven national cinemas. Examining the diverse artistic, cultural, and industrial forces at work in countries such as Brazil, Chile, Peru, and Uruguay, I show that interrelated but nationally distinct labor networks led to the negotiation of different cinematic, industrial, and organizational strategies. Through these negotiations with different forms of capital, foreign and local filmmakers created commercial films that were distributed and exhibited domestically, regionally, and, at times, globally. Using these Latin American networks as a point of departure, I return to Alton's paradox to question how we can move beyond reading the period simultaneously through the lenses of national rootedness and transnational detachment in order to account for each industry's peculiarities.

By contextualizing the incorporation of foreign workers into emergent local film industries and, more specifically, examining the diverse ways in which individual foreign workers contributed to distinct incipient national cinemas, I hope not to retrace ordered lines of inquiry, but rather to follow scrawls, however faint, that were left behind. Caught within broader processes of industrialization in Latin America, which incorporated other mass media forms as well (including the radio and recording industries), the cinema (wherever and whatever it was) was merely one sector in which foreign workers in Latin America confronted Alton's paradox. It was, however, a central space for shaping new subjective experiences and anxieties from the 1930s and 1940s to today. Because of this, it is necessary to seek out nuances in the ways in which we have come to understand it. It is not that I do not engage those notions of classical cinema that define it as the systematization of industrial processes that creates neatly packaged commercial movies (or national cinema) to elicit a reflective and refracting idea of nationhood, but rather that I want to examine the films produced by specific workers, textually and historically, both in terms of their initial release and their subsequent critical reception. Through a chronological rather than thematic approach, I uncover some of the particularities of a rich period that is underrepresented in Latin American film history. Leveled later into an *Época de oro,* if not totally forgotten, the films of the early sound period helped to create the enduring uneven and disjointed interconnectedness of Latin American commercial cinemas.

2

Hollywood, City of Dreams

The First Spanish-Language Film Industry

On June 20, 1930, the cinema spoke Spanish for the first time in Uruguay.[1] Some nine months after the arrival of the talkie to the country, a Spanish-language movie debuted in the Cine Ariel. It was not the country's first—Juan Etchebehere's *Dos destinos* (Two Destinies) would open on July 27, 1937—nor was it imported from across the River Plate, as Luis Moglia Barth's *Tango!*, the first Argentine sound film, would later arrive at the Rialto, Continental, Avenida, and Renacimiento theaters on June 30, 1933. Nor was it a Spanish or Mexican film; *montevideanos* would have to wait to catch José María Castellví's musical *Mercedes* at the Estudio Auditorio on July 4, 1934, and Miguel Contreras Torres's historical melodrama *Tribú* at the Azul on March 8, 1936.[2] The first talkie to premiere *en español* in Montevideo was produced in Hollywood: *El cuerpo del delito*, the Spanish-language version of *The Benson Murder Case* (dir. Frank Tuttle, 1930).[3] By the early 1940s, eighty-five of these films would come to be shown in Montevideo.[4] So, too, would many shorts. *El cuerpo del delito* was co-directed by Cyril Gardner (a peripheral Hollywood figure who worked as an actor, director, and editor) and A. Washington Pezet (a playwright whose father served in Peru's diplomatic mission in the United States), the film featured actors, such as Antonio Moreno, Ramón Pereda, María Alba, and Barry Norton, who would contribute to the cinema in Hollywood, Mexico, Puerto Rico, and Spain.[5] Now presumed lost, *El cuerpo del delito* was Paramount Pictures' first foray into Spanish-language film production, but it would not be its last.

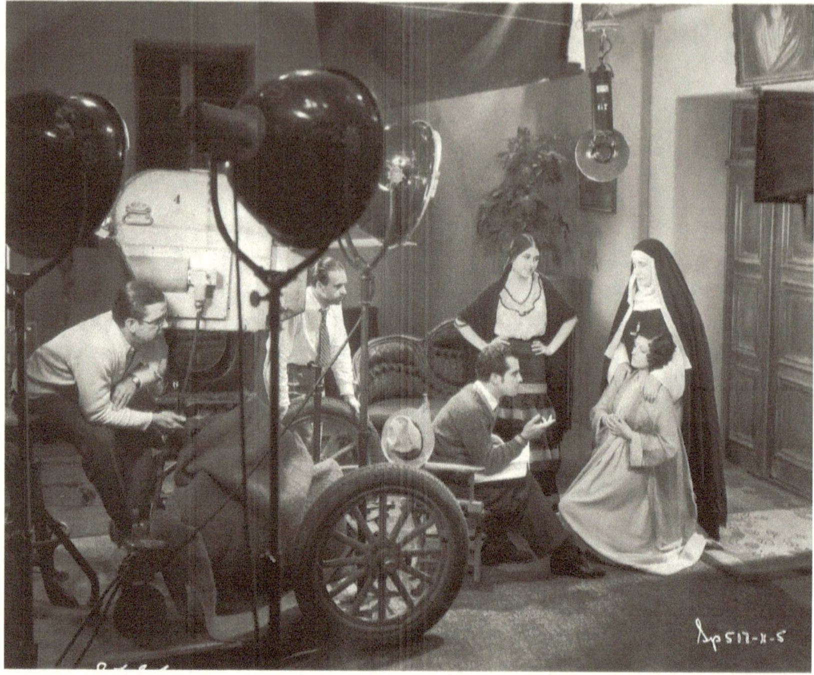

Figure 2.1. Ramón Novarro, center, directing Conchita Montenegro and Leonor de Samaniego, dressed in nun's habit, in *Sevilla de mis amores* (vers. *Call of the Flesh*, 1930). Actress Rosita Ballesteros, director's assistant Carlos Borcosque, and cinematographer Merritt B. Gerstad look on. From the core collection production files of the Margaret Herrick Library, Academy of Motion Picture Arts and Sciences.

Hollywood gave the world its first large-scale Spanish-language film industry. With its market dominance potentially threatened by the arrival of sound film technologies, as studios could no longer count on silent-era practices of quickly adapting their movies for local taste, Hollywood "sought new ways to connect with consumers in international markets such as that of Latin America. Though dubbing and subtitling would eventually become the industry standard by overcoming initial technological and cultural limitations, the fledgling sound film industry aimed to overcome the new language barriers imposed by sound via multilinguals."[6] Also known as multiple-language versions (MLVs) or foreign language versions (FLVs), multilinguals were films shot in different languages more or less simultaneously. Universal Pictures' *Drácula* (dir. George Melford, 1931), perhaps the best-known Spanish-language multilingual today, was famously shot at night after the cast and crew of the English-language *Dracula* (dir. Tod Browning, 1931) had left the studio.[7] Counterparts to the cinematic iterations were Spanish-language original features such as *Hollywood, ciudad de ensueño* (Hollywood, City of Dreams, dir. George Crone, 1931).[8] Mainstays of fleeting independent production companies from the very beginning, Spanish-language originals eventually were taken up by major Hollywood studios.[9] The vast majority of these films were produced between late 1929 and 1931. Monologically replicating their industrial model, Hollywood studios created a new labor market. With technical infrastructure already in place, studios focused on performers, bringing talent from the stage to the set. These actors, some more newly formed than others, were brought to Hollywood (and its satellites) from throughout the Spanish-speaking world, but many of them had already established themselves and their careers in the United States.[10] The films of this initial period were ostensibly rejected by audiences throughout the Spanish-speaking world for their inauthenticity and cultural heterogeneity, but many of them were major hits.[11] "In part, confusion over the real reasons for the sudden reversals of policy on Spanish films by the major studios reflects the uncertainty and lack of coherent and reliable sources of information from which studios themselves suffered throughout the period."[12]

Even though much of Hollywood abandoned Spanish-language production, choosing instead to explore the cheaper production alternatives of subtitling and dubbing, Fox Films and, to a lesser extent, Paramount invested in developing stars.[13] "From 1932 to 1935, just as other studios eliminated most foreign-language production, Fox Films expanded its Spanish production slate. During this period, Fox moved toward a greater number of original productions and, above all, granted more authority to the Spanish-speaking stars and writers it employed to work on these projects."[14] Eventually, the labor market for Spanish-language production became more complex than it may initially seem. Not only employing actors and screenwriters, studios also began hiring more technical advisors from throughout the Spanish-speaking world. More than translators, these advisors sought to produce a more culturally and linguistically authentic cinematic experience. In this period, Fox's Spanish department produced two versions and twenty-two originals featuring performers and stars such as Catalina Bárcena, José Crespo, Mona Maris, José Mojica, Conchita

Montenegro, Rosita Moreno, Gilbert Roland, Raúl Roulien, and Berta Singerman. It also employed figures who often drifted between technical supervision and screenwriting, such as Paul Pérez, Enrique Jardiel Poncela, Miguel de Zárraga, Julio López Rubio, and, most notably, Gregorio Martínez Sierra, the famous Spanish playwright. Likely due to cost-cutting measures after its merger with Twentieth Century, Fox shuttered the Spanish department by mid-1935.[15] Paramount, for its part, produced films starring Imperio Argentina and Carlos Gardel. Florián Rey, Argentina's husband, worked as a dialogue director, scene supervisor, and, finally, director on her films. On his own projects, Gardel brought in Alfredo Le Pera to work as screen- and songwriter. Unlike their Fox counterparts, Argentina's and Gardel's contributions to Hollywood's Spanish-language film industry were not produced in Los Angeles, but rather in Joinville and, in Gardel's case, in New York.[16] They were relatively brief, however, as Gardel tragically died in a plane accident in Medellín on June 24, 1935, and Argentina returned to her adopted country, Spain, to film *Nobleza baturra* ([Aragonese] Rustic Chivalry, dir. Rey, 1935).

By 1935, major Hollywood studios' Spanish-language production may have ceased, but they continued to irregularly coproduce and distribute

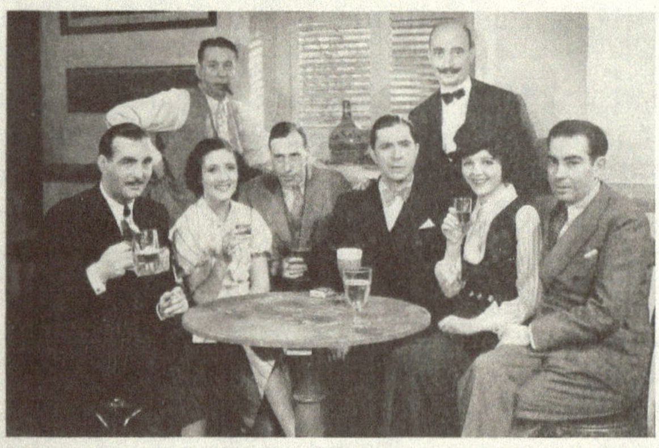

Viendo Filmar a Veinte Minutos de Nueva York

De izquierda a derecha, de pie: el director de cine Louis Gasnier, el excelente compositor y ejecutante Castelano (disfrazado con un bigotito postizo); sentados: Vicente Padula, Anita Campillo, el jefe de redacción de CINE-MUNDIAL, Francisco J. Ariza; Carlos Gardel, Mona Maris y Alfredo Le Pera.

no es víctima de ninguna rabi
está satisfecho con la colabor
han dado, los novatos escucha
consejo de un veterano, los f
necesitan lanzar gritos ni tirars
cuando álguien sale del redu
que la cámara abarca. Y, en
grupo (que no es exiguo, pues
tres docenas de personas) resu
organizado como simpático.

La escena, en Buenos Air

El local donde están repre
actores es muy reducido. Se s
ducir un cafetín bonarense. A
del asiento donde CINE-MU
arrellanó, están las cámaras,
encargado de los efectos sonoro

Figure 2.2. Cast and crew of *Cuesta abajo*, including Carlos Gardel, with Francisco J. Ariza, chief editor of *Cine-Mundial*, August 1934.

independent films *en español* until 1939.[17] Even though some talent previously involved in Spanish-language film production left to participate in emerging film industries elsewhere, many familiar cast and crew members worked on these films. Integrating at times well-known Mexican actors such as Fernando Soler, Arturo de Córdova, and Andrea Palma, these films often revolve around Spanish-speaking communities in the United States, especially in Los Angeles. With few extant films, relatively little is understood of the period, but it is a moment of Latinx cultural heritage in need of much further study. Important ventures included Cantabria Films' *La vida bohemia* (*Bohemian Life*, dir. Josef Berne, 1937) and *Verbena trágica* (Tragic Festival, dir. Charles Lamont, 1939), both distributed by Columbia, and five star vehicles distributed by Paramount that sought to exploit Tito Guízar's success post-*Allá en el Rancho Grande* (*Over on the Big Ranch*, dir. Fernando de Fuentes, 1936).[18]

Scholarship on this first, somewhat incoherent expression of Latin American industrial film production has been tackled most substantively in the early 1990s and the 2010s. In addition to "Hollywood or Bust!," a brief chronicle of this curious moment of film history, Juan B. Heinink and Robert G. Dickson provide readers with an exhaustive list with productions details relating to Spanish-language films produced by Hollywood studios in their foundational *Cita en Hollywood*.[19] Subsequently, other works were published such as Heinink and Dickson's edition of film journalist Florentino Hernández Girbal's *Los que pasaron por Hollywood* (originally written in the mid-1930s), Jesús García de Dueñas's encyclopedia *¡Nos vamos a Hollywood!*, and Álvaro Armero's edited volume *Una aventura americana: españoles en Hollywood*.[20] Twenty years later, these movies were taken up again by Lisa Jarvinen in *The Rise of Spanish-Language Filmmaking: Out from Hollywood's Shadow, 1929–1939*.[21] Along with Jarvinen's history, Colin Gunckel's *Mexico on Main Street: Transnational Film Culture in Los Angeles Before World War II* has helped to awaken growing scholarly interest in the reception of Hollywood's Spanish-language movies by local film cultures. Recently, two edited volumes have contributed to this scholarship: *Cinema between Latin America and Los Angeles: Origins to 1960* (eds. Gunckel, Jan-Christopher Horak, and Jarvinen) and *Hollywood Goes Latin: Spanish-Language Cinema in Los Angeles* (eds. María Elena de las Carreras and Horak).[22] Each arising "as an outgrowth of an initiative at UCLA Film & Television Archive to recuperate the Spanish-language cinema culture of Los Angeles as it existed from at least the 1930s through the 1960s" and the Getty Foundation's "Pacific Standard Time:

LA/LA," which funded the research, preservation, and exhibition project "*Recuerdos de un cine en español*: Latin American Cinema in Los Angeles, 1930–1960," these edited volumes augur well for more nuanced local and transnational understandings of Hollywood's Spanish-language films.[23] Assisted by much greater access via digital archives to film periodicals and other materials, we may be entering a period in which we come to better understand the complexities of the production, distribution, and reception of this misunderstood moment in film history. Or, not unlike various points in the history of Hollywood's Spanish-language film production, we may simply be at yet another false dawn.

3

"The Biggest Revelation of Hispanic Cinema"

José Mojica's Transnational Stardom

Working as a contributing writer and movies editor for the Lozano newspapers, Los Angeles' *La Opinión* and San Antonio's *La Prensa*, Gabriel Navarro was one of the United States' most important cultural critics of the 1920s and 1930s writing in Spanish. Not only through his criticism, but also through artistic work such as the serialized novel *La ciudad de irás y no volverás* (*The City of No Return*, 1926–27), numerous plays, and, especially, *revistas* (musical reviews), Navarro thought deeply about what it meant to exist between Mexico and the United States.[1] By the time his essay "Cinema from Here and There" appeared—on June 19, 1938, in *La Opinión* and one week later in *La Prensa*—Navarro's ideas would have been well known to readers.[2] Echoing arguments made earlier in those pages, some as early as the beginnings of Hollywood's Spanish-language film production nearly a decade earlier, Navarro laments "Hispanic dishes made in an American kitchen." Even though his writings were generally pessimistic and often critical of the emerging Mexican film industry, Navarro argues that the films produced in Mexico better connected with audiences, stating "*Sentimos en ellas a lo nuestro* [We feel or find ourselves in them]." Hollywood's Spanish-language films may have been technically superior, but would never really appeal to audiences if Hollywood studios continued to rely on foreign film workers, especially directors. Navarro argues, "But as long as they serve us with *salsa extranjera* [foreign sauce], they cannot have the same taste as *lo auténtico* [what is authentic]." Even Cecil B. DeMille, Ernst Lubitsch, and William Dieterle—"nor other, better [directors] to come, could achieve offering us *una verdadera película hispana* [a real Hispanic film] for the simple reason that they cannot, not even with the greatest effort, feel what we feel."

Navarro's resolute advocacy of Mexican cinema would lead to an equally spirited defense of Hollywood's Spanish-language production by Miguel de Zárraga, studio consultant, scriptwriter (and adapter), and one-time film journalist. Writing from Columbia's publicity department, and having recently completed work on Cantabria Films' *Verbena trágica* (Tragic Festival, dir. Charles Lamont, 1939), Zárraga contends in "Spanish Films Made in Hollywood" that "[i]n Hollywood, the supreme center of Cinema, there is everything for everyone, without having to resort to risky improvisations. And there is money—in dollars—to bring here at any moment the artists, writers, or musicians who may be wanted to appear."[3] Zárraga holds that while it may be true that Hollywood's big studios' Spanish-language films failed, fledgling U.S.-based independent production companies such as Cantabria promise to connect with audiences throughout the Spanish-speaking world with their new efforts. New production and distribution strategies, however, failed to sufficiently penetrate exhibition practices, something recalling the unequivocal epigraph to "Cinema from Here and There." In it, Frank Fouce—who, at the time, was almost certainly the most important single person in U.S. Spanish-language film exhibition as the owner of theaters such as Los Angeles' California, Eléctrico, Mason, and Roosevelt—avows, "None of the Hispanic films made in Hollywood—not excluding Gardel's and Mojica's—have ever given at the the box office what Mexican productions give. The performance of the best of those films has not been equal, or even half, of the best that have been shot in our country. That is the painful truth." Setting aside the productive confusion of "our country," attributed to the Hawai'i-territory born Fouce (whom the Spanish-language press called Francisco), validation of cultural politics is sought through consumption, through box-office returns. The proof, it would seem, lies in the spectators.

What is ultimately notable about the ensuing dialogue that unfolded over weeks within the pages of *La Opinión* and *La Prensa* is how "these debates also demonstrate the extent to which such boundaries were consistently challenged, particularly by the transnational activities of talent and studios."[4] In his original essay, Navarro tackles the question, "What is the reason for the imbalance between the cinema here and the cinema there?" Setting aside his answer, we should shift our attention to what the question signals by its demarcation of borders. We should ask ourselves, if only rhetorically, what happens if we are unable to (fully or partially) differentiate between here and there? What is made possible by not giving in to overdetermined categories of national cinema? What happens if we recognize that there is some truth to Zárraga's assertion that "[o]utside of our countries, in lands officially foreign, there are enormous nuclei of compatriots who continue to speak our language and continue feeling the same emotions as us. California, New Mexico, Arizona, Florida, Puerto Rico, the Philippines, Morocco, and so many other regions of the world are—spiritually—extensions of the Hispanic world"? What happens if we allow our perspectives of the cinemas from here and there be shaped by other means?

Even though audiences and critics had largely rejected the *films hispanos* by 1938, one of many reasons why Hollywood studios wholly abandoned the strategy the next year, local debates concerning them swirled not only in the United States, but also throughout Latin America and Spain. These debates, however, dissipated with time, so much so that their immediacy became lost by the time the first national film histories were written. Hollywood's Spanish-language movies seem to exist in film historiography as always here and there, but also neither here nor there. Because of their in-betweenness as films produced in the United States in Spanish by film workers from throughout the Spanish-speaking world (and beyond) for transnational audiences, these adaptations and original shorts and features have been largely ignored by film studies.[5] Due to the lack of serious work in Latin America, Spain, and the United States on Hollywood's Spanish-language films, we have yet to differentiate between what happened in one circumstance and what did not. They have yet to be fully placed within film history. Some of Hollywood's Spanish-language films were huge hits. Lisa Jarvinen notes, "Paramount, with films starring Carlos Gardel, and Fox Films, with musicals featuring the Mexican tenor José Mojica, produced box office hits—allowing Gardel and Mojica to gain substantial control of their contracts and projects. While Gardel and Mojica commanded higher salaries, they were closely followed in popularity by singer and actress Imperio Argentina, who starred in some of the biggest movies of the decade in the Spanish-speaking world."[6] Gardel, as one of Argentina's most important cultural icons, and Imperio

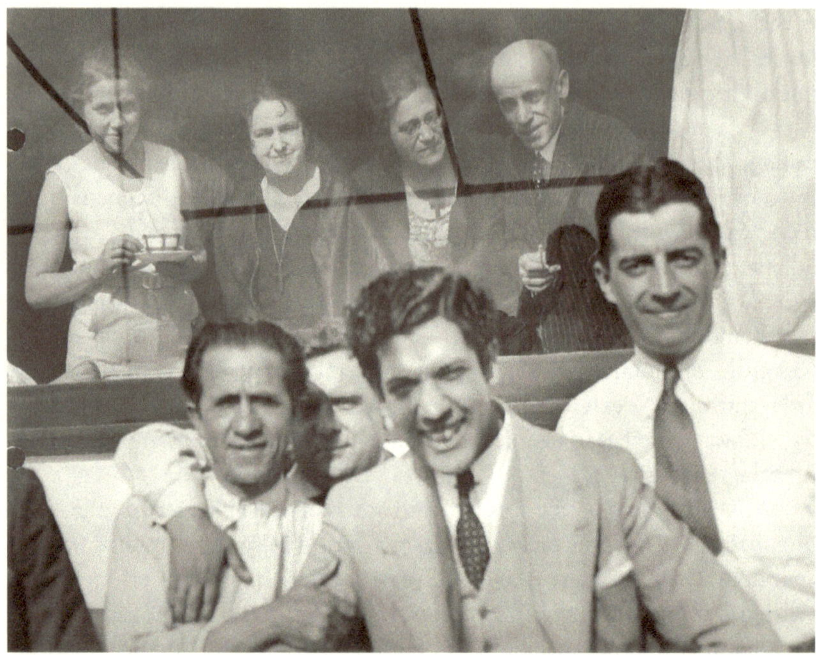

Figure 3.1. José Mojica, front center, undated. Others unidentified. From the core collection biography files of the Margaret Herrick Library, Academy of Motion Picture Arts and Sciences.

Argentina, due to her continued success in Spain into the 1940s, found their (sometimes uncomfortable) places within Argentine and Spanish film history. But, unlike Gardel and Argentina, as well as more famous stars who worked in English-language Hollywood cinema such as Lupe Vélez, Dolores del Río, and Ramón Novarro, José Mojica remains of the cinema of here and there.[7] Or, better yet, neither.

In this chapter, I approach José Mojica's transnational fame by examining key aspects of his bright, if fleeting, star. I focus primarily on the two films in which he starred that are currently available to cinephiles and scholars: *El rey de los gitanos* (*The King of the Gypsies*, dir. Frank Strayer, 1933) and *La cruz y la espada* (*The Cross and the Sword*, dir. Strayer, 1934). Along with *Un capitán de cosacos* (*The Capitan of Cossacks*, dir. John Reinhardt, 1934), whose sole known extant print requires preservation, they are the only films that remain of Mojica's short-lived, but hugely impactful career with Fox, which are (at least partially) representative of the ways in which the he was able to connect with audiences throughout the world, but especially in Latin America.[8] Considering these films as star vehicles "designed to exploit the popularity of a particular performer by accommodating their established 'type' and both reworking and advancing aspects of their previous work that had already proven popular with an audience, providing a delicate balance between novelty (originality) and familiarity (repetition)," I particularize how Mojica's films created market attention throughout Latin America.[9] Like other Hollywood stars, Mojica was the creation of the vertically integrated factory of dreams, but the processes and production lines through which his star was created were distinct from those of his compatriots del Río, Novarro, and Vélez.[10] He may have been a star there, but he did not work like one here.

By tracing the exhibition and reception of *El rey de los gitanos* and *La cruz y la espada*, I show how how spectators and critics reflected reworkings and advancements of Mojica's star image.[11] Already having been proven popular with audiences, he "personified the urbane, middle- and elite-class musical establishments. Mojica moved easily between both countries, and between Spanish- and English-speaking audiences in California and throughout the United States. He also crossed the borders between high art and popular culture."[12] His ability to cross borders easily, to be at once here and there and neither there nor here, made him a bankable asset whose star image was familiar, but sufficiently elastic to allow for originality. His commerciality resided in a star image "made out of media texts that can be grouped together as promotion, publicity, films and criticisms and commentaries," but which also consisted of Mojica's performances.[13] More specifically, I examine how Mojica's screen presence (acting, performing, singing, etc.) commercializes the diegeses of *El rey de los gitanos* and *La crùz y la espada* through inhabiting their cinematic spaces in novel, but familiar ways. Rendered on-screen within a particular historical context, these iterations of his persona were constructed cinematically by Mojica (as well as others) so as to appeal to audiences throughout the world. But, as a note published in one of the September 1933 issues of the Argentine trade publication *Imparcial Film*, reminds us, what is on-screen is never entirely unconnected from what is not: "Mojica . . . Mojica . . . Mojica . . . ! The reader can imagine who sings the name of the star of the films spoken in Spanish in the heart of Fox to himself is Enrique Gil, the kind sales manager, who I hear, at the precise moment of entering, is launching into a sermon to a client that Mojica is not only an ace of the screen, but also of the box office."[14]

From San Gabriel to Santa Monica

On the September 21, 1974, front page of *La Opinión*, a headline reads, "José Mojica Died in Peru."[15] A brief news wire article from UPI (United Press International), which contains details on his life as a Franciscan monk and death the day previous due to hepatitis complications, it notably begins, "The once famous star of Mexican cinema, Fray José Guadalupe Mojica, passed away." Unlike other major publications in the United States and Latin America such as *Excélsior* (Mexico City), *Folha de São Paulo*, *La Nación* (Buenos Aires), *The New York Times*, and *The Washington Post*, *La Opinión* did not run an obituary recalling Mojica's life, but rather reported the events unfolding in Peru as front page news.[16] By framing him as both "once famous," which he was, and "star of Mexican cinema," which he also was, *La Opinión* also distances Mojica from the career he once had as the brightest star of Hollywood studios' *films hispanos*. Mojica's star had dimmed so much that *La Opinión* fails to recall that he was once a regular feature of its own pages. This amnesia was, at least in part, a fabrication of the singing priest. A UPI piece that ran several days later in *La Opinión* describes, "It was here in a place of the countryside, called los Tunales, where Mojica wrote his work 'I, A Sinner,' which was taken to the screen and in which the priest narrated his first years of life and his successes in the opera, cinema and theater, as well as the principal motives that led him to renounce all his belongings and embrace Franciscan habits."[17] In his autobiography *I, A Sinner*—its English translation appeared in 1963, some four years after the original publication of *Yo pecador* and its film adaptation (dir. Alfonso Corona Blake, 1959)—Mojica continued a career-long effort to fashion our understanding of who he was, which, much like *La Opinión*'s coverage of his death, diminished the importance of Hollywood's Spanish-language films.

José Mojica's origins could easily have been a thing of the movies.[18] He was born on September 15, 1896, the illegitimate son of Virginia Mojica, a woman of means, and Dr. J. Jesús Chavarín Vázquez. In accounts of José's life, his father is a shadowy figure who remains unnamed: in some, he was a doctor who intended to marry Virginia before he died tragically in a car accident and, in others, he was the town priest.[19] It may be that, as noted in a 1931 *Cinearte* profile, his father died when José was six.[20] Or, conceivably, as Mojica recounts his mother's words in *I, A Sinner*, "Several years later he died in an accident. The horses that were pulling his carriage went wild, and he was smashed against the bridge of San Juan de Dios, in Guadalajara. May he rest in peace. Pray for him."[21] Due to the increasing precariousness of their situation, both personal and economic, Virginia and José moved to Mexico City in 1906. Encouraged by his mother, he studied at the Escuela Industrial José María Chávez, then the Escuela Nacional de Agricultura (National Agricultural School). With his studies at the prestigious Escuela Nacional

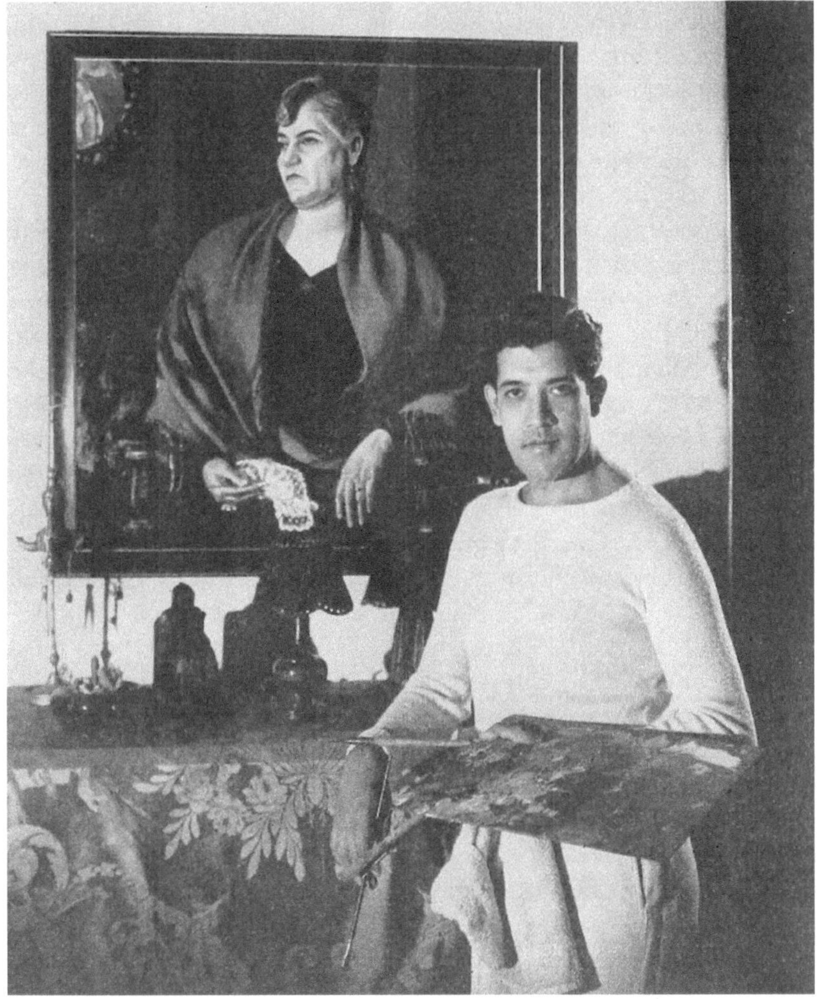

Figure 3.2. Mojica in front of a painting of his mother. *Cine-Mundial*, October 1934.

de Agricultura interrupted by the Mexican Revolution, Mojica entered the Conservatorio Nacional (National Conservatory) and the Academia de Artes Plásticas (Academy of Visual Arts) in 1915. Painting, an aspiration that would become a lifetime avocation, would be eclipsed by singing.[22]

Mojica "discovered a vocation for opera through exposure to performances given by resident and traveling opera troupes in the capital during the turbulent years of the Revolution," eventually, as John Koegel notes, becoming a student of José Pierson, who also trained Tito Guízar, Jorge Negrete, Alfonso Ortiz Tirado, and Pedro Vargas.[23] Under Pierson, Mojica was incorporated into the Compañía Impulsora de Ópera (Opera Promotion Company). Small parts led to lead roles, and, according to a 1922 report in the *San Diego Union*, his work in Mexico City caused him to be discovered in 1919 by Mary Garden, the "Sarah Bernhardt of opera" and, later, the "Impresaria Diva of the Chicago Opera Company."[24] Except, according to Mojica, this is not quite what happened. After returning back to Mexico from a failed attempt to make it big in New York, Mojica participated in a parade of artists at the Teatro Abreu in honor of Enrico Caruso (whom, he describes, he had seen perform *Rigoletto* in New York).[25] "Mokika," as Caruso would call him, joined the Italian superstar tenor on stage, playing roles such as Edmondo in *Manon Lescaut* (Giacomo Puccini, 1890–1893) and Harlequin in *Pagliacci* (Ruggero Leoncavallo, 1892).[26] From September 29 to November 17, 1919, Caruso gave twelve performances in Mexico City. Two months after Caruso left Mexico, Mojica received a telegram offering him a six-week contract with the Chicago Opera Company.[27] He would soon meet Mary Garden, and he would stay in the United States for years to come.

In its March 7, 1921, issue, published as Mojica's second season came to a close, the Mexico City daily *Excélsior* published Luis Lara Pardo's profile, "José Mojica, Legitimate Mexican Glory."[28] Three photographs accompany its text: the young tenor in a suit, sitting while looking into the distance; the performer in a period ensemble for *Andrea Chénier* (Umberto Giordano, 1896); and, finally, in costume as Harlequin in *Pagliacci*. Some details on the singer's life are included, but the focus of the piece is an evaluation of Mojica's talent. Lara Pardo places Mojica within a category of performers "who cannot by isolated from the scene." Though Lara Pardo does little to precisely locate Mojica's performance style, he emphasizes the centrality of acting to Mojica's work as an opera singer. "He has entered the lyric scene with this feverish enthusiasm, with this infinite yearning, with this intense devotion that is called a true artistic vocation." And, perhaps most notably, as Lara Pardo concludes in its final paragraph, "José Mojica, contrary to other artists of *nuestra tierra* (our land) does not hide his origin. Far from it, he proclaims it loudly." His *mexicanidad* was always central to his star image. *Excélsior* also later reported on Mojica's participation in the world premiere of Sergei Prokofiev's *El amor de las tres naranjas* (*The Love for Three Oranges*, 1921).[29] With some success in the United States, Mojica's renown continued to grow in Mexico, where he was even used to market the New Edison phonograph in 1922.[30] As he continued his performing career in the United States with the Chicago Opera Company, he began to gain greater attention.

Somewhat unsurprisingly, Mojica's star image also came to include stereotypes associated with Rudolph Valentino. The comparison, Mojica once said, "gives me bilious stomach cramps."[31] Deemed the "sheik of the opera," Washington, D.C.'s *Sunday Star* ran a profile of Mojica on April 12, 1925.[32] The profile itself, however, focuses on Mojica's current situation, as well as his past (including biographical details supporting Caruso's inadvertent influence in landing him the contract with Garden's company). A year later in her *Cleveland Plain Dealer* column "Main Street Meditations," Eleanor Clarage recounts an anecdote: "We said the other day that Jose [*sic*] Mojica, the Valentino of the Chicago opera company, was the best looking thing we had ever seen, and also the least temperamental."[33] Pettily, and borrowing from racist stereotypes of the hot-blooded Latin, she speaks of an incident in which Mojica was annoyed at hearing "now we are getting to hear and see the handsomest man in opera." Gossip, "the nutritive plankton of the star system" according to Edgar Morin, would be fed to Mojica's fans throughout his career.[34] His beauty was so striking that it would even be recalled decades later. In an unsigned note published in London's *Times* in 1960, a former super of the Chicago Civic Opera Company recalls a girl so stricken by a Valentinoesque photograph of Mojica in *Carmen* (Georges Bizet, 1875) that she would "sit gazing at it, murmuring when anyone came near, 'That man is dangerously beautiful. Dangerously beautiful.'"[35] Mojica had other interactions with the cinema as well, as he accompanied the Chicago Theatre Orchestra in "The Serenading Cavalier" (prefiguring, perhaps, some of his movie roles) in a screening of the film *Zander the Great* (dir. George W. Hill, 1925).[36] In the mid-1920s, his voice also reached other new forms of mass media. His records for Edison and Victor signal the figure that Mojica would cut in popular culture: he might eventually star in *cursi* (corny, or in bad taste) films in some sense, but he is always marked as being high class. In addition to his recording career, he also had contact with the radio.[37] In what was described as "one of the greatest hookups in the history of radio," his company's 1927 season was transmitted live by the National Broadcasting Company.[38]

It would not be long before the opportunity to perform in another form of media would present itself to Mojica. As Jarvinen relates:

> Sometime in 1928, he traveled to Los Angeles to film some screen tests at various studios, where in sang in both English and Spanish. Back in Chicago, he soon received offers from several studios, but only Fox sent someone in person who had been instructed to offer Mojica more than the other studios. He later wrote that he accepted a contract for forty weeks and nearly $80,000. It was actually somewhat less, but still a star salary by Hollywood standards.[39]

Reports of his contract began to emerge in mid-1929. In a piece including somewhat curious biographical information, *Hollywood Filmograph* notes "His looks have been compared to Valentino's and his voice to Caruso's."[40] A story in the *Morning Oregonian* sensationally adds, "While the monetary consideration involved was not made public, it is understood to exceed half a million dollars."[41] Part of a move by Hollywood studios, which were realizing the potential of vocal performances in shorts even though they "may have initially focused their attention on feature films with instrumental scores and intermittent speaking sections," singers were highly sought out, especially men.[42] Including Mojica in a group with Lawrence Tibbet, Elsa Alsen, and Tito Ruffo, *Picture Play* states, "The welcome sign is out to the operatic singers. In the beginning it looked as if the films didn't care anything about them, feeling that they were too highbrow."[43] However, according to the headline of later *Variety* article, "Opera More Concerned Over Losing Choruses Than 'Names' to Pictures."[44] Fox, MGM, and Paramount, "unlike Warners, were unable to unify the notion of film stardom with the signifiers of operatic quality, and so they promoted their singers' ethnicities instead of their operatic talent."[45] Because of this, Mojica would eventually bring the talents he learned on the stage to the cinema, but he would not do so as an opera singer.[46]

Mojica's crossover to the cinema also coincided with Hollywood studios' initial explorations into producing films in other languages, primarily French, German, Spanish, and Swedish, but also including,

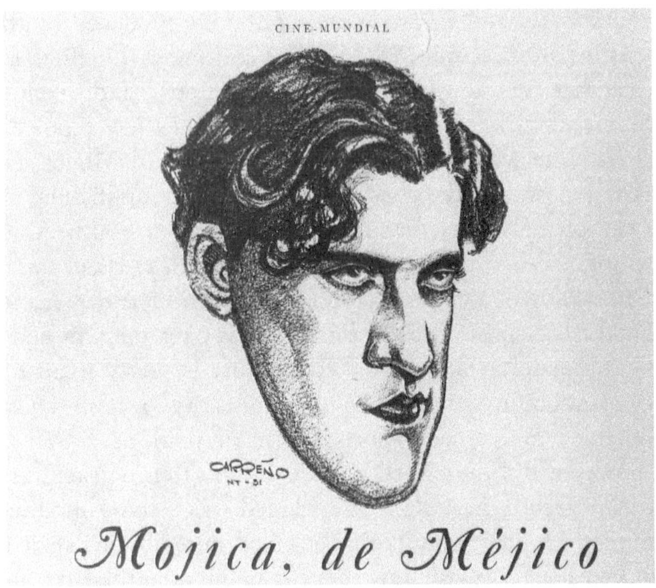

Figure 3.3. Caricature of Mojica by Alberto Carreño. *Cine-Mundial*, May 1931.

but not limited to, Czech, Italian, Japanese, and Portuguese. As Ginette Vincendeau notes, "As soon as the question of foreign versions came up in Hollywood, the Latin American Spanish-language market was clearly the most attractive, in terms both of audience and number of theatres. All studios immediately launched into Spanish versions, facilitated by the presence of Spanish-speaking personnel in Los Angeles."[47] It may be that Fox saw Mojica as a player in both English- and Spanish-language films, somewhat akin to other polyglot actors such as Maurice Chevalier, Greta Garbo, and Adolphe Menjou, or that they saw Dolores Del Río or Ramón Novarro in him, but by late 1929, publicity stills of the Fox Movietone artist Mojica began to appear in both English- and Spanish-language press.[48] In *The 1930 Film Daily Year Book of Motion Pictures*, Clayton Sheehan, Fox's General Foreign Manager, promotes "further[ing] the true internationalization of the motion picture industry."[49] In addition to technological innovations, Sheehan argues that Fox "will continue to devote its energies to making the best in sound pictures with an eye first for quality and suitability to the markets and taste of the whole world." Among the films mentioned is Mojica's first movie. Or, perhaps more appropriately, movies.

One Mad Kiss and *El precio de un beso* were produced by the same unit, consisting of directors Marcel Silver and James Tingling, a largely shared cast that was "a whole League of Nations," and, likely, mostly the same crew.[50] *One Mad Kiss* was a flop.[51] *Variety* reported, "Fox considers its 'One Mad Kiss,' starring Don Jose [*sic*] Mojica as a sour one. It now reposes on the shelf with a possibility of sticking there. A Spanish version of the picture is being released in South America."[52] It was reshot, at least in part, at the same time *El precio de un beso* was filmed. *One Mad Kiss* was released on July 13, 1930, and received harsh reviews in the U.S. press. *Motion Picture News* pans the plot and praises the music, ultimately concluding, "The picture is pretty weak from the box office standpoint, as it lacks selling points" and recommends that it be accompanied by "comedy shorts, if you must play it."[53] *El precio de un beso*, however, did quite well abroad. In an often repeated anecdote, shared with *Cinearte* in 1941 and included (with some modifications) in *I, A Sinner*, Mojica recounts that it failed miserably when it initially arrived in Barcelona.[54] It lasted two days at an important theater. Someone, however, had the idea to show it at a popular theater. It was a smash. As Mojica tells *Cinearte*, " '*Vox populi, vox dei*' . . . It is not the opinion of those who attend premieres who mark success."[55] Even though he came from a decidedly more highbrow medium, his films were produced to appeal to the masses.

His star image may have been originally shaped in the opera, but his entrance into the movies eventually made him subject of countless profiles and features in the popular press throughout the world.[56] Often centered around his *ranchito mexicano* in Santa Monica, and usually in the presence of his mother, these texts present the image of a man for whom fame means little beyond making possible a connection to others. In mid-1932, the Mexican writer and frequent contributor to Lozano's *La Opinión* and *La Prensa*, Hortensia Elizondo, interviewed Mojica at his home.[57] Elizondo had hoped to talk about his films and performing career, but doing so would have entailed Mojica focusing attention on himself. She writes:

> And Mojica, the idol of the masses today, the favorite of audiences who deliriously laud him and give formidable ovations like those at the Teatro California in Los Angeles when two powerful policemen had to "rescue him" from an enthusiastic crowd. Mojica, the star of the screen, does not know how to

> speak about himself and, in this *oropelesco* [glitzy] and *bluffista* [showy] Hollywood, Mojica forms a separate circle for his complete naturalness and unique modesty.

This indifference, this detachment from Hollywood as a machine of wealth and fame manifests itself in something else on which Elizondo centers: the immateriality with which Mojica treats his career. He gives Elizondo a record instead of playing it or, even, singing. He shies away from discussing his movies. She concludes the piece: "*Mamita* is the one who has told on previous occasion that José has three *películas hispanas* in the movie listings with Fox. It is that Mojica forgets about himself to be the hospitable and cordial host, and to make anyone who visits him into a friend. Kind, sincere, so courteous, and very nice."

Mojica's next five films—*Cuando el amor ríe* (When Love Laughs, dir. David Howard and William J. Scully, 1930), *Hay que casar al príncipe* (You Have to Marry the Prince, dir. Lewis Seiler, 1931), *La ley del harem* (Law of the Harem, dir. Seiler, 1931), *Mi último amor* (vers. *Their Mad Moment*, dir. Seiler, 1931), and *El caballero de la noche* (*Dick Turpin*, dir. Tingling, 1932)—were produced under quite different conditions.[58] "From 1930 to 1931, Fox made twenty-three films in Spanish: eighteen feature-length films and five short films. Of the eighteen features, fourteen were straight versions produced at approximating the same time as the English-language originals."[59] Of Mojica's five films, four were adapted from scripts used for English-language silent films in the 1920s, and one (*Mi último amor*) was a multilingual.[60] Much like the early incursions many of its competitors, Fox's adaptations into Spanish were largely unsuccessful, but, unlike other studios, Fox pivoted and approached its Spanish-language films using a different philosophy. Among the important changes Fox implemented was the formation of a production unit. Just as *One Mad Kiss* was to be released, *Motion Picture News* reports, "With its own staff of writers, directors and technicians, Fox's new Spanish department will commence production immediately. The unit will concentrate on all Spanish talkers, with John Stone, formerly in charge of silent and synchronized work, in control."[61] "By contrast, from 1932 to 1935, the studio made twenty-two Spanish features, of which only two were straight versions and the rest were originally productions for the Spanish market."[62] Mojica's next film, the original production *El rey de los gitanos*, would indicate to Fox the commercial possibilities made possible by properly exploiting its Spanish-speaking talent and, especially, its biggest star.

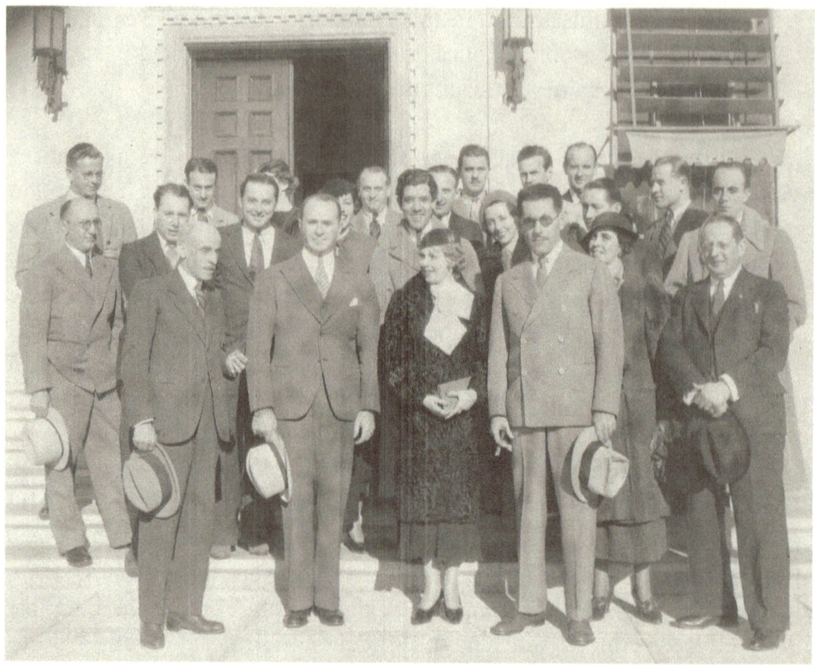

Figure 3.4. Fox Film Corp. Spanish-language department (ca. 1932). From the core collection subject files of the Margaret Herrick Library, Academy of Motion Picture Arts and Sciences.

El rey de los gitanos: Mojica and Fox Give it Good

El rey de los gitanos is one of six José Mojica films that were produced between mid-1932 and mid-1934. Filmed in Fox's studios in Hollywood, and overseen by Stone's Foreign Department, these films saw Mojica play a range of characters inhabiting exotic spaces, with the exception of *La cruz y la espada* and *Las fronteras del amor* (*The Love Flight*, dir. Strayer, 1934).[63] In a profile in its September 14, 1932, issue, Mojica tells the Brazilian film magazine *Cinearte*:

> I am very excited about this new contract. It has facilitated many things for me, and the stories will be chosen with more care and more discretion [*mais criterio e mais apuro*]. I will have songs, as all my films are musicals, stories where music and song are the predominant note. The musical part will all be

> choose with much forethought [*muito escrupulo*]. I have just recorded new records and I have them here. They are the first ones out, and in them I have Cuban, Mexican, and Spanish songs, essentially Latin.[64]

Recognizing the failures of previous efforts, if they could be called that, Fox adjusted how it approached its productions. In a February 1934 profile in *Movies*, John Stone described this strategy: "The market for our pictures was good, and I thought it could be better. That is, it seemed to me that if we tried to give as good in Spanish as we did in English, the South American and Spanish market could be built up."[65] Stone attributes this success to Mojica, who, in his earlier interview, understood how giving it good allowed him to better perform. Intentionally or not, Mojica also recognizes the commercial benefits of greater attention to the crafting of his films' diegeses, their storyworlds. Mojica's performances on set best served him if they were to harmonize with his renditions on stage, as well as in recording and broadcasting studios. He played the roles crafted for him, whether in a movie or a song, but Mojica also worked to fashion how the public understood him. Not only did he continue to tour extensively, but, as Koegel reminds us, "Besides his work as an opera singer and film star, Mojica was very active in the recording studio, where he recorded many Mexican and Latin American popular songs of the day for the Edison and Victor (later RCA Victor) companies, as well as a number of opera arias."[66] Mojica's films and his music meant to appeal to people throughout the world, to transnational audiences. Mojica uses *latinas* in *Cinearte*'s original Portuguese, but one wonders what adjective he would have used to describe his songs (*musicas*).[67] And what about his films, his adoring fans, his target audience?

Even though it may have gotten lost within the torrent of José Mojica vehicles, such that if it were not one of his two surviving films it might have been ever more forgotten than it is today, *El rey de los gitanos* is an important film if we are to better understand Mojica and Hollywood's Spanish-language films. We might not remember, for example, that the idea of a "Gypsy King" was a mainstream notion at the time, so prevalent as to be the subject of the song "El Rey Gitano," which had been recorded in Mexico.[68] We may also fail to recall that *El rey de los gitanos* also exploits common cinematic tropes of the early 1930s, the gypsy and the Hungarian, in no small part due to the success of Ernst Lubitsch's films.[69] Both cinematic tropes projected mirages of *mestizaje,* of miscegenation, but kept their excesses comfortably at a distance from the spectators. As Martin Shingler reminds us, "Drawing upon a diverse range of international talent and making films for numerous national audiences, Hollywood has tended to overlook national, cultural, regional and ethnic differences in favour of more generalised identities, chiefly (and crudely), American and non-American."[70] Because "nationality hardly mattered unless it was racially or ethnically marked," even in the *films hispanos, El rey de los gitanos* somewhat erases nationality (it takes place in an imagined country), but the marks of race and ethnicity may be faint, but are indelible.[71] Owing to a (partial) reconstruction of its exhibition and reception, we are able to see how spectators throughout the world reacted to this somewhat ordinary film in sometimes extraordinary ways. Similarly, by focusing our attention on *El rey de los gitanos*, we are able to make sense of a storyworld that, nearly ninety years after its creation, may seem curious. More specifically, I analyze how Mojica's exoticism is constructed through an abstract transnational identitary aesthetics expressed primarily in music and performance in *El rey de los gitanos* and, thus, seeks to appeal broadly to audiences in Latin America, Spain, and, potentially, beyond.

Worldwide exhibition of *El rey de los gitanos* was symptomatic of the uneven and often asynchronous circulation of film, especially in the 1930s. Even the big budget or prestige films with which it shared movie listings such as RKO's *King Kong* (dir. Merian Cooper and Ernest Schoedsack, 1933) or Warner Bros.' *Gold Diggers of 1933* (dir. Mervyn LeRoy, 1933) were irregularly distributed and exhibited in markets throughout the world. *El rey de los gitanos* was no different, and a partial reconstruction of its initial exhibition run hints at the complex, nonparallel ways in which local film cultures received and appropriated Mojica's star text. The film was first screened to much anticipation but little fanfare in Barcelona at the Kursaal on May 23, 1933.[72] As would be the case throughout the world, it would eventually move from first-run theaters to those in the *barrios,* running sporadically for months, if not longer. The gala premiere of *El rey de los gitanos*, which drew "great interest and enthusiasm in the public," took place in Los Angeles' Teatro Hidalgo on May 26.[73] The film was preceded by a prologue directed by Manuel Moreno. According to a note in *La Opinión*, "In said prologue, artists like Rodolfo Hoyos, Nelly Fernandez, Romualdo Tirado, Manuel Noriega, Pepet, Mena and other elements of recognized prestige take part. The musical numbers are very beautiful, and its little plot takes place in a gypsy camp for which set designer Amador Arca has painted special scenery."[74] Its next major premiere was down Argentine way on July 13 in Buenos Aires'

ESCENA DEL ESTRENO DE HOY EN LA PANTALLA DEL HIDALGO

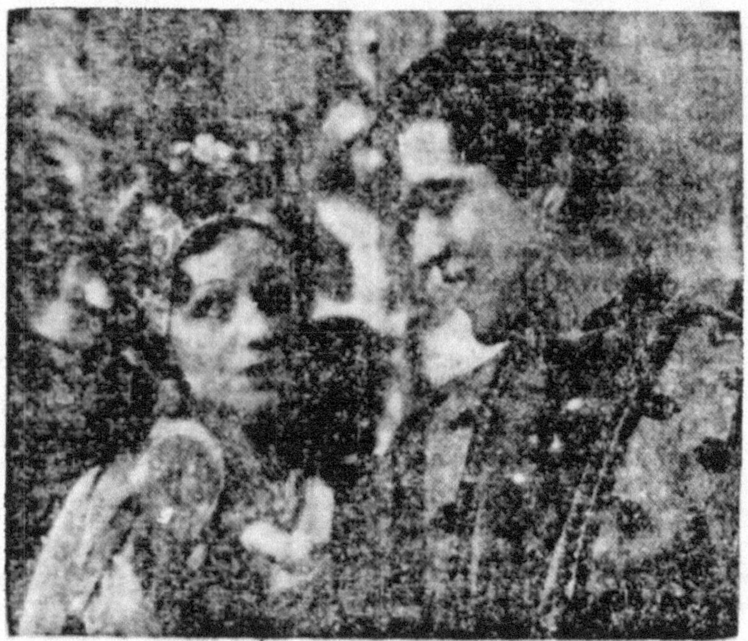

Sobre estas líneas publicamos la fotografía de una interesante escena de la película "El Rey de los Gitanos", la cual será estrenada esta noche en el teatro "Hidalgo" en función de gala y con un espléndido prólogo especial. En la escena aparecen José Mojica y Rosita Moreno, intérpretes principales de la obra a que nos referimos.

Figure 3.5. News of the premiere of *El rey de los gitanos*. *La Opinión*, May 26, 1933.

Cine Ambassador.[75] In a note, *Film* reports that after screening in the Ambassador for fifteen days, a substantial run at the time, *El rey de los gitanos* immediately moved on to the Hindu theater.[76] On July 21, it opened at the Ariel in Montevideo.

Several months later, *O rei dos ciganos* was released in Rio de Janeiro. After opening on October 2, it circulated over the next five months between most *carioca* theaters, including the Eldorado, Cinema Modelo, Cine Fluminese, Mascotte, Paris, Primor, Paris, Nacional, Haddock Lobo, Popular, Cinema Floresta, and Guarany.[77] It even inspired a work capitalizing on its success: *Mujica*, "a fantasy opera in the manner of the recent film 'O rei dos ciganos.'"[78] Beginning on October 7, *El rey de los gitanos* played in Madrid for the first time, spending thirteen days on-screen. It finally reached San Antonio, Texas, in December, where it showed at the Teatro Nacional from the nineteenth to the twenty-second.[79] Several weeks later (January 14–16, 1934), moviegoers in Brownsville had the opportunity to see it in the Dittman Theater.[80] *El rey de los gitanos* would not screen in Mexico until March 3, 1934. It premiered on screens at the the Teresa, Granat, Venecia, Parisiana, Rívoli movie theaters.[81] Originally scheduled to play in April for the city's vibrant Spanish-language film culture, the closure of the Flora in Brooklyn prevented its release in New York City.[82] *A Cigány Kilárly* would, however, make its way to screens in Hungary, first in Budapest and later in the interior.[83] *El rey de los gitanos* would take much longer to arrive in another important film market in Latin America, Peru. Also screened under its alternative title, *El zíngaro vagabundo*, it did not premiere at the Cine Excélsior in Lima until July 13, 1935.[84]

Fully reconstructing critical reception of a film is a quixotic task, but *El rey de los gitanos* generally was met with positive reviews in newspapers and film magazines. In brief reviews published in various counties, *El rey de los gitanos* was determined to be an entertaining film featuring a performer whose voice was the star. Mojica was photogenic, but his appeal was also phonogenic.[85] More terse than Barcelona's *La Vanguardia*'s assessment that "[t]he majority of the public—who in the movies looks for certain romanticism, certain idyllic atmosphere, who likes, above all, to admire the beauty of the heroine and the prowess of the gallant—will enjoy, without a doubt, admiring this latest José Mojica film presented by Fox," New York's *The Film Daily* determines it is a "[s]entimental combination of romance and comedy, together with some agreeable singing by Jose [*sic*] Mojica. Fine all-around cast and good production."[86] Spotlighting Mojica, as well as his singing, these reviews also illuminate the importance of affect in *El rey de los gitanos*. As a light romantic melodrama, *El rey de los gitanos* elicited emotional (even corporeal) reactions. It made spectators feel.

Perhaps most broadly indicative of how critics received *El rey de los gitanos* was its reception in Argentina. Like other anticipated releases, local reception of Mojica's most recent film was initially framed by reports from abroad. In *Imparcial Film*'s "News from Spain," for example, a correspondent speaks to its success in the Catalan capital: "We cannot mark it with extraordinary epithets, but we can say that it is an entertaining and decent film."[87] Much more muted than its review in *La Vanguardia*, this direct evaluation gives *porteño* audiences an idea of what to expect when it arrives in Buenos Aires' theaters months later. *Heraldo del Cinematografista* echoes these sentiments, explicitly or implicitly, in its review of *El rey de los gitanos*:

> This movie is very well done. There are interesting comic scenes and well rationed. Mojica's songs are good, and the photography presents considerable skill. The dialogue is agile and even when it is too *castizo* [born-and-bred, pure, traditional] in some places, it amuses the spectator. Good presentation, tight direction, and discreet propaganda give it value. It will draw interest, within its category, especially popular theaters. Rosita Moreno is fine, except when she sings. The copy shown at the theater of its premiere is a bit out of sync. Suitable for any section and day.[88]

Perhaps because it is one of the U.S.-produced *films hispanos*—their reception in Argentina was uneven, and by mid-1933 they would compete directly with talkies produced in Argentina—*Heraldo del Cinematografista* seems reticent in its praises of *El rey de los gitanos*. Other cultural politics also seem to be at play, as the magazine seems unwilling to give legitimacy to any Spanish-language cinema. In "On the Margin of the Premieres," a note appearing in the same July 19 issue as its review, it is argued, "*El rey de los gitanos*. Like all of the films spoken in Spanish, it did not draw interest *en primera línea* [first-run movie theaters]. It received good reviews. It was liked. It is not a film for theaters of the *primera línea*."[89] In 1933, some four years after sound film had arrived in Argentina, movie palaces playing much-anticipated first-run films were dominated by Hollywood, something that continues to be the case. Even though the film was profitable in Argentina, it was unable to break critics' and audiences' preconceptions, which, undoubtedly, were heavily influenced by (Anglophone) Hollywood's influence and advantage (cultural, but also industrial).[90]

In addition to its Argentine reception—warm, but not overly so—there are two additional lines of critical discourse regarding *El rey de los gitanos* that are important to explore. If the previous reviews give us a wide-angled shot, somewhat distorting their image of the film so as to provide broader coverage, one line of reception gives us a close-up of José Mojica. Mojica, in this line of thought, orients spectators as the film's brightest star. This tendency, which is expressed to various degrees in many reviews, is clear in Miguel de Zárraga's review of the film for *Cine-Mundial.* Given his proximity to Hollywood, not only geographically but professionally, Zárraga was drawn to Mojica's star in ways that his Argentina counterparts were not. This does not mean to say, however, that *porteños* would not have identified with Zárraga's assessment. In his review, he writes:

> José Mojica has returned to triumph on the sound screen and, just as we hurry up to consign him, with even more brilliance than in "El Caballero de la Noche." "El zíngaro vagabundo" is a delicious operetta with a lot of movement and inspired music that easily sticks to the ear. Rosita Moreno, very pretty—but nothing more than very pretty—does not upset the ensemble next to Mojica, who, as usual, gets all of the work's interest, filmed to showcase him exclusively. Romualdo Tirado, very funny. The others, without being out of place in the picture. Very clever *el libro* [the scenario] by José López Rubio and very suggestive Rosita's bathroom scene. What more could be asked? "El zíngaro vagabundo" will show once again that film musicals are the most attractive for our audiences. . . . Fox knows it, and this one barely shot, it announces to us "La melodía prohibida" with Mojica himself, seconded this time by Conchita Montenegro and Mona Maris. Like a good cognac, it will be worthy of the brand. 3 Stars.—Zárraga.[91]

Zárraga not only reminds us that *El rey de los gitanos* is another Mojica star vehicle, but also relates nearly every element of the film to the Mexican tenor. Clustered around Mojica, but much dimmer, other parts of the film (performers, script, etc.) exist in relation to Mojica. This attests to Mojica's increasing popularity, but it also speaks to the significance of his role as a contracted star at Fox. Functioning within the laws of the studio system of the early 1930s, Mojica was one of Fox's brands.

To maximize his commercial possibilities, John Stone and Fox sought out ways such as the development of film musicals to capitalize on his talents. Whatever surrounded Mojica existed to make best use of Fox's most important, and perhaps only, Spanish-language star.

Something made clear by its mass reproduction in the pages of newspapers and magazines is that the reception of *El rey de los gitanos* did not only occur within the walls of movie theaters. This is not to say that reviews did not comment on its intertextuality with other films—*Cinearte*'s review, for example, notes "An imaginary realm. A capricious princess. Caricature ministers. A passionate gypsy . . . this sounds like Lubitsch, right? But it is nothing more than a talkie with Don José Mojica"—but that other forms of popular culture were important in its reception.[92] Similarly, Mojica's stardom was not solely bound to the cinema. In *Correio da Manhã*, *carioca* moviegoers were reminded not only of Mojica's arrival on the screen via the stage (and, more specifically, the opera), but also of Rosita Moreno's recent visit to Rio de Janeiro.[93] The attention given to Moreno in the review, both in terms of focus and praise, attests to the importance of an active performing career for many early sound film stars. Touring, as well as appearing on the radio and recording records, served as one of the ways with which audiences interacted with stars. In the same review, *Correio da Manhã* also notes the importance of Mojica's primary musical collaborator in the film, Desider Josef (D. J.) Vecsei. Also connected to Rio de Janeiro, as he is identified as having lived there, Vecsei "knows how to admiringly compose melodies where all of the beauties of *latinidade* shine."[94] This conflation of gypsy exoticism with *latinidade* is central to the commercialization of the film's storyworld.

El rey de los gitanos takes place in a small, unnamed Eastern European kingdom. Recently returned to her country after studying abroad, the young princess María Luisa (Moreno) tires of life in the court, especially the visits of the Great Duke Alejandro (Julio Villarreal) whose frequency is only outmatched by their fastidiousness. María Luisa implores her maidservant Renée (Ada Lozano) to break the tedium, to break her out of her gilded cage. Night having fallen, they dress up as peasants and leave the castle to attend a local fair. Caught up in the festivities, María Luisa almost forgets her station when she is allured by the Tzingane melodies of Karol (Mojica), the so-called King of the Gypsies. His beautiful, passionate voice, singing "Canción de la buenaventura" ("Palm Reading Song"), draws María Luisa close as he ostensibly reads her fortune. So close, in fact, that a furtive kiss crosses lines not only of propriety, but of national security. Alejandro learns of their tender moment, and seeks to discredit his rival by telling the princess that Karol had stolen her necklace, which, in fact, had been discovered in her coach upon return to the castle. Alejandro's scheming leads to Karol's arrest, and several misunderstandings occur. Karol eventually kidnaps María Luisa, taking her back to his people's camp. They spend days enjoying their back-and-forth, love-hate flirtation. Alejandro leads a rescue effort that fails miserably. He is challenged to a duel by Karol. María Luisa fears Karol's imminent death, as Alejandro is a world-class shot, but the King of the Tzinganes cannot be beaten in the forest. Karol overtakes Alejandro, but has mercy on his rival. Karol then not only orders his caravan to move on, but tells María Luisa to return to the palace. He tells her that it has been like a dream, but he has woken up. Karol rides off with his people, singing "Cuando el amor te llama" ("When Love Calls You").

By providing the film's exotic music, Vecsei provides the soundtrack through which the film's emotional tones are most effectively conveyed. Born in 1882 in Budapest, Vecsei lived a peripatetic life as a concert pianist until he eventually settled in California. In the early 1930s, he attempted to make it in popular song in New York and Los Angeles.[95] On the edges of Hollywood, Vecsei contributed the songs "Anywhere With You," "Love, Bring My Love Back To Me," and "In a Gypsy's Heart," to the Mack Sennett film *Hypnotized* (1932) (whose working title, tellingly, was *Little Gypsy*).[96] *Hypnotized* led to work on two Spanish-language films for Fox: the original *El rey de los gitanos* and the multilingual *No dejes la puerta abierta* (vers. *Pleasure Cruise*, dir. Lewis Seiler, 1933).[97] Collaborating with L. Wolfe Gilbert, whose lyrics were adapted into Spanish by star Raúl Roulien and José López Rubio, he composed music for *No dejes la puerta abierta*'s four songs.[98] Similarly, Vecsei provided music and Gilbert lyrics (translated by Mojica and López Rubio) for *El rey de los gitanos*. These songs, however, relied less on popular music of the time and more on traditional musical fantasies in its songs "Cuando el amor llama," "Zíngaro vagabundo" ("Song of the Romany Band"), "Mansión sin amor" ("Without Love in a Palace of Dreams"), "Serenata bufa" ("Serenade"), "Canción del carnaval" ("Carnival Song"), and "Canción de la buenaventura." Vecsei recalls his past, not necessarily (though possibly) his life in Hungary but his classical training, in the songs' musical phrasings. "Canción del carnaval," in particular, recalls Maurice Ravel's *Tzigane: Rhapsodie de Concert pour Violon et Piano* (1924). Swirling violins give way to Karol's episodic storytelling of his amorous adventures, which, in turn, also gives way to the swirling chorus, "Baila, baila, baila, / la danza del amor / que el que no la baila, / se pierde lo mejor" ("Dance, dance, dance / the dance of love / he who does not dance / misses what is best"). Finally, the song's three verses give way to swirling dancing, increasingly frenzied by everyone's clapping, until the sole dancer left is a twirling María Luisa.

Just as Vecsei draws from his high-culture formation in the creation of a song in the film, which is decidedly low-culture, Mojica's performance in *El rey de los gitanos* is influenced by his work in the opera. He continues to be, as Lara Pardo noted a decade earlier, a performer "who cannot by isolated from the scene." In a *Cinelandia* feature published around the time of *El rey de los gitanos*' production, Joaquín de la Horia touches upon similar ideas that Mojica's on-screen personality was not limited to his voice, but rather as as a performer who brings himself into the scene.[99] De la Horia also quotes Mojica as revealing that

> I consider the singer to be a performer [*un intérprete*]. His figure, his mimicry, his emotionality—even in exchange for sacrificing a vocal effort or an irresistible fermata—everything must form part of his interpretative labor. I made detailed effort in that regard, and critics praised me, encouraging me. I must be frank. I never expected to drive an audience crazy with my voice, but to satisfy them with the whole of my work.

Mojica's self-fashioning is more complex than it might seem at first glance. In addition to the arduous task of attempting to express performance through his entire body—perhaps having realized earlier in his career the limits of his talents as an operatic singer or, perhaps, for some altogether different reason—Mojica also contours his public image as an actor dedicated to delivering the entirety of his work, perhaps even himself, to his roles. On-screen and in the pages of film periodicals, José Mojica becomes much more than his voice.

In *El rey de los gitanos*, this is manifested in different ways, including Mojica's noted ability to allow his co-stars to shine.[100] Mojica's support of the rest of the cast, especially Rosita Morena, cannot be untangled from his character's generous spirit. Karol is charismatic, gorgeous, but he is only king because he takes care of his people's way of life. Like (and as) Karol, Mojica provides *El rey de los gitanos* with its brightest light. The radiance of other aspects of the film are determined by Mojica's ability to inhabit the role of Karol in a way that appeals broadly, especially to an abstract transnational Hispanic identity. Mojica draws from his experience playing a range of exotic figures in the opera to level, to a degree, the film's orientalization of the Roma and Hispanics. By othering Karol and his people, the film distances the Roma from their courtly counterparts María Luisa and her subjects. Divided by race, as well as tradition, the two factions of *El rey de los gitanos* reflect binaries often reproduced in Latin America. Mojica is able to traverse identities and, consequently, appeal to wider audiences. Through the exoticization of both Karol and Mojica, which is expressed equally through its melodramatic plot and its songs, *El rey de los gitanos* was assembled by Fox's Foreign Department to be more culturally homogenous, but sufficiently heterogenous to better appeal to audiences throughout the Spanish-speaking world and, sometimes, beyond. After its initial run in theaters, *El rey de los gitanos* would continue to be shown throughout the world for several more years; eventually, its copies slowly degraded and audiences' memories faded. Presumed lost for some time, it was restored by the UCLA Film & Television Archive in 2017.[101]

La cruz y la espada, A (False) New Dawn of Hispanic Cinema

In the early 1930s, readers of *Cine-Mundial* caught up on Hollywood news and gossip in columns by Don Q.: *Centelleos* (*Sparkles*) and *Hollywood*.[102] Quick, undeveloped news items were shared in *Centelleos* such as: "Hollywood things: in Maurice Chevalier's contract appears a clause in which he is prohibited from speaking English without a French accent" and "Paulette Goddard has desisted from marrying Charles Chaplin. Or vice versa. The fact is that they are not getting married."[103] Much like its briefer counterpart, *Hollywood* touched upon the public and private matters of stars and industry insiders (and, sometimes, outsiders), but with greater attention to detail and observation.[104] Some examples include notes on the Hispanization of Liechtensteiner actress Medea de Movarry (or de Novara, as she would later become known), extras quitting their jobs on the set of Edward G. Robinson's *Two Seconds* (dir. Mervyn LeRoy, 1932), and the new It Girl, Mae West.[105] In both *Centelleos* and *Hollywood*, Don Q. would touch upon the Hollywood's *colonia hispana*, whose members existed within its very distinct realms, linguistically and industrially. Given the proximity not only to huge stars working in English such as Dolores del Río, Lupe Vélez, and Ramón Novarro, but also to less-well-known figures laboring in Spanish-language productions, it is not surprising that *Cine-Mundial* generally, and Don Q. more specifically, frequently commented upon the the evolving situation of the *colonia hispana.*

In a particularly important iteration of *Hollywood*, published in December 1933, Don Q. surveys the current state of Spanish-language film production.[106] In it, he argues for an upcoming new beginning that is not only cinematic, but also ontological. He begins:

> The big Hollywood film studios only made up their minds to produce films in Spanish—in order to not lose our markets—upon becoming convinced that they could not continue offering us those spoken in English. But everything they offered us, then, was no more than a series of colorless and insipid translations of American works, written by Americans and for Americans. . . . And, thus, the more-or-less Spanish-language film production with which Hollywood tried to saddle us necessarily had to fail.

Using these failures as a pretext, Don Q. argues, Hollywood studios began to export their films to Latin American markets "with the attachment of some simple explanatory signs!" Fox was the exception. Instead of investing in post-production techniques such as subtitling (or even dubbing) to repackage their films for consumption in the Spanish-speaking world, the studio "Began by substituting the primitive translations with clever adaptations" (such as *El rey de los gitanos*) and then alternated these with films written by Spanish playwright Gregorio Martínez Sierra. But something was lacking. He continues, "But all of this, being a lot, was still little. Original works expressly written for *el Cine Hispano* were needed. And they just began to be filmed!" The first of these new works was *La cruz y la espada.*[107]

Don Q. notes the team of film workers that assembled the film: Miguel de Zárraga, a frequent contributor to *Cine-Mundial* and correspondent to newspapers and magazines throughout Latin America and Spain, wrote both its scenario (*libro*) and dialogues; Paul Schofield and William DuBois adapted it to screen; Troy Sanders and Ernesto Lecuona composed music; and José Mojica plays the lead. These film workers came together, according to Don Q., to create something new.

> What is *La cruz y la espada*? A romantic Californian poem, about one of those historical Missions that made immortal the name of Fray Junípero Serra. Mojica incarnates one of those glorious Franciscan Fathers who, at the same time as the Cross, wielded the Sword. And we should not say anything more about this film, which initiates the production of *obras puramente hispanas, de hispanos y para los hispanos* [purely Hispanic works, by Hispanics and for Hispanics], in Hollywood studios.

As the product of Hispanic workers, *La cruz y la espada* initiated a new era in Hispanic cinema, in Don Q.'s perspective. By his logic, this era was not only cinematic, in that what was seen on screen was more representative of the cultural desires and anxieties of its audience, but also ontological. More direct inclusion of Hispanics in the production of *La cruz y la espada* made it a more Hispanic film, one that by extension would better appeal to spectators throughout the Spanish-speaking world.

La cruz y la espada's attempt to better appeal to Spanish-speaking audiences was a commercial strategy used by Fox and its Foreign Department.[108] Unlike other Hollywood studios, who had mostly abandoned making films in Spanish by 1933, Fox continued backing Mojica. In an interview published in the December 1933 issue of the Mexican film periodical *Filmográfico*, John Stone says, "The representatives of Fox have made many and frequent trips to Spanish-speaking countries with the sole purpose of understanding the tastes of the public, and keeping this very much in mind the films in Spanish are made with the same preparation as if they were a movie with Warner Baxton [*sic*] or Janet Gaynor."[109] Filmed between October and November 1933, *La cruz y la espada* premiered before the year was over.[110] After initially tracing its worldwide circulation, I reconstruct the ways in which critics reacted to *La cruz y la espada*. In no small part due to their proximity to the film's production—geographically, culturally, economically, and maybe even spiritually—the U.S.-based, Spanish-language press argued that the film heralded a new beginning. It was received more mutedly in venues distanced from Hollywood, and even in very specific and local ways. While Don Q. seems to minimize Mojica's centrality to *La cruz y la espada*, the film would not only be defined by his performance, but, in the end, would come to define who José Mojica—the person, as well as the star—would eventually become.

Similar to *El rey de los gitanos*, the exhibition of *La cruz y la espada* gestures toward broader patterns in Hollywood and world cinemas, but it also signaled a shift in the way in which Mojica and his film were marketed to local audiences. Moving from downtown Los Angeles' Teatro Hidalgo, an "immigrant- and Mexican-oriented entertainment [venue]" built in 1912, to Santa Barbara's Fox-Arlington Theater, a recently constructed exoticist Spanish Colonial movie palace where "The Spanish Feeling Predominates," the world premiere of *La cruz y la espada* on December 7, 1933, was a more highly anticipated event.[111] Held in conjunction with a fundraiser benefiting the restoration of the Misión de Santa Inés in Santa Barbara, and filling the movie palace "despite the high price of entry," the premiere of *La cruz y la espada* was a grand affair.[112] Beginning on February 1, 1934, it played at the Teatro Variedades in New York City.[113] Preceded by strong publicity in the Catalan press, *La cruz y la espada* debuted in Barcelona on February 26, 1934, in the Cataluña.[114] In Buenos Aires, it began its run at the Cine Renacimiento on March 14, 1934. In Rio de Janeiro, *A cruz e a espada* ran in theaters from March 27 into April. Initially run at the Alhambra as part of a special Holy Week celebration, it continued in the theater until the end of the next week due to its success.[115] It would also later screen at the Mascotte, Nacional, Ipanema, Haddock Lobo, often competing against another Mojica feature, *O capitão dos Cossacos.* As it played on screens in Argentina and Brazil, it also hit the Teatro Baquedano in Santiago de Chile.[116] It would have a similarly successful run in Mexico City, where it played at the Goya, Teresa, Odeón, Rialto, Monumental, Granat, Edén, Venecia, Parisiana, and Rívoli from May 3, 1934. One day later, it opened in Montevideo's Ariel. It played throughout the Southwest in cities such as Santa Fe, Albuquerque, Brownsville, Nuevo Laredo, El Paso, and Tuscon, as well as other cities in the United Sates such as San Francisco and Tampa.[117] Representative of the unevenness of film distribution and exhibition in Latin America, *La cruz y la espada*'s premiere at the Cine Excélsior on May 4, 1935, actually preceded the Peruvian release of *El rey de los gitanos* two months later.[118] Tracing *La cruz y la espada*'s asynchronous initial exhibition run gives us insight into the ways in which audiences (worldwide, but especially in Latin America) and critics received the film, as well as how his performances interacted with local understandings of José Mojica, the star.

Upon its premiere in Santa Barbara, U.S.-based film critics for the Spanish-language press were finally able to consecrate *La cruz y la espada* as the first real triumph of the *films hispanos*. Echoing the language used by Don Q. in *Cine-Mundial*, Gabriel Navarro wrote a piece published days after the premiere. Entitled "Are We Finally at the Beginning of

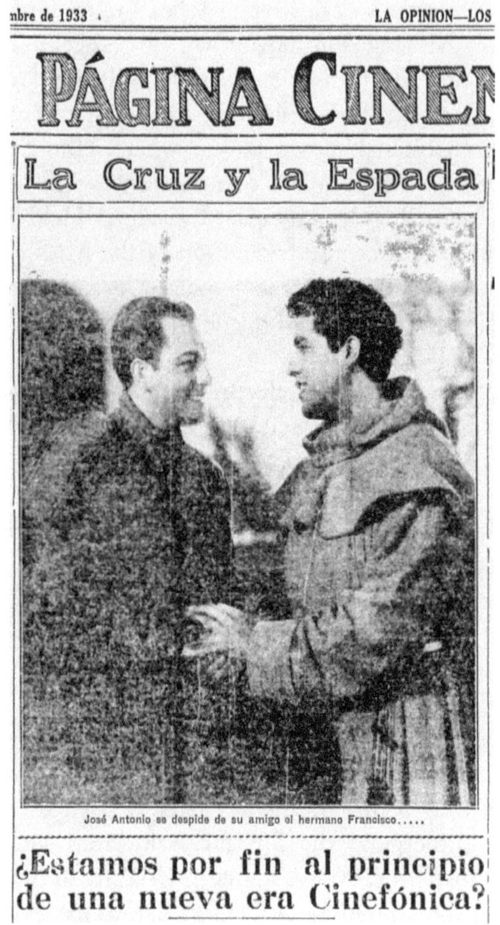

mbre de 1933 · LA OPINION—LOS

PÁGINA CINE

La Cruz y la Espada

José Antonio se despide de su amigo el hermano Francisco.....

¿Estamos por fin al principio de una nueva era Cinefónica?

Figure 3.6. Gabriel Navarro heralds *La cruz y la espada* as the beginning of a new era. *La Opinión*, December 10, 1933.

a New Era of Sound Film?" in *La Opinión* and, more mutedly, "The Movie 'La Cruz y la Espada,' in Spanish, Has Been a Big Hit" in *La Prensa*, Navarro explains that its premiere occurred "before two thousand enthusiastic people. That enthusiasm, by the way, had a plausible reason for being. We were attending the rebirth of *la película hispana*, or better yet, its true birth as a clearly Latin diversion."[119] Navarro says he will leave the critic's magnifying glass to the side, opting instead to see the film through the eyes of a spectator. Similarly, in his review for

Cine-Mundial, Francisco J. Ariza somewhat apologetically provides a metacritical description of film reviewing. He then continues (italics are mine): "But there are times, very few times, in which the task of opining turns out to be very simple because *in advance it is known, it is felt,* that the reviewed photodrama will be liked wherever it is exhibited. That is to say, there are cases that turn out to be impossible to make a mistake. 'La Cruz y la Espada' is one of them."[120] Ariza lavishes praise on the film, especially its protagonist: "Mojica has advanced as a film performer, has improved his enunciation and sings as he had never sung. His voice alone—and there are many other merits of his work here—would make this photodrama stand out over any of the music-talkies filmed in our language."[121] In a sense, Mojica is understood to have been allowed to be his best self. *La cruz y la espada* makes possible Mojica's continued actualization as a film star. Navarro recognizes this as well, but extends his praise to what allowed the filmmakers to realize the project: "The indisputable freedom that the producers seem to have left the director, *libretista* [librettist, composer], and performers, and the correctness of the argument and staging, are highly significant for *la industria hispana del Cinema* [the Hispanic cinema industry]."[122] He attributes this change to Fox's Foreign Department: "Its bosses have opened their eyes, from which the old blindfold of prejudice has fallen. They have left ours to feel like *hispanos,* to talk like *hispanos,* to live their own lives in front of the cameras. And this, we are sure, they will not regret."[123] Like Navarro, Ariza also looks back to the past, concluding, "The work realizes a dream that seemed impossible a few years ago: the creation of a cinema legitimately ours. In Hollywood no less!"

The heralded new *hispano* cinema was not apparent to all reviewers of *La cruz y la espada*. In many places, especially those displaced linguistically or geographically, reviews of the film were a continuation of the reception of Hollywood's Spanish-language films generally, and Mojica's films more specifically. Soon after Fox began widely distributing the film, Harry T. Smith wrote a review for the *New York Times*.[124] Smith, a longtime scribe who often "relied on categories of evaluation modeled on the Hollywood star system" in his reviews of non-English-language films, directed his attention to plot and performance.[125] Smith considers *La cruz y la espada* to be an "an entertaining, if somewhat melodramatic, film" and argues that "[e]ven those not familiar with the language of Cervantes can enjoy the numerous songs of all types in which Señor Mojica displays his virtuosity, and follow the romantic story in a general way."

The acting may be "in the spirit of the picture," as Smith concludes, but Mojica enables spectators to inhabit the film's universe, even if they do not speak Spanish. And, to recycle a theme in most reviews of Mojica's films, he does so through song. In Argentina, critics also responded to *La cruz y la espada* by focusing on Mojica and placing the film within their previously formed understanding of Hollywood's Spanish-language films, something especially clear in reviews in two periodicals directed to industry insiders.[126] *La Película* recognizes, to a degree, what the film tries to achieve, but cannot step outside of how it understood Spanish-language films by commenting, "We must regret, however, that the cinematic experience that it should have already acquired has yet be dispossessed of that theatrical affectation that so little favors the performers."*Heraldo del Cinematografista*'s review offers more about its technical specificity and its publicity, but it also attempts to define the film's audience: "Suitable, in cinemas working with an audience with a soft spot for productions in Spanish, for any section and day."[127] Signaling particular prejudices, held by *porteño* exhibitors and spectators (of different kinds) to varying degrees, *La Película* and *Heraldo del Cinematografista* qualify the possibilities of the film. The anticipated reception of *La cruz y la espada* limited the ways in which "The idol of Latin America, José Mojica, in the best performances of his artistic career," according to *La Película*'s suggestions, "For the Program," was received by critics in Argentina and beyond.

Entre a Cruz e a Espada premiered in Rio de Janeiro around the time it hit screens in Buenos Aires. Its promotion and exhibition, however, was vastly different. Even though some of its publicity materials mirror those of *O rei dos ciganos*, as well as other Mojica vehicles, *Entre a Cruz e a Espada*'s initial run in *carioca* theaters revealed idiosyncrasies of a local film culture too often forgotten in transnational accounts of exhibition.[128] Breaking from the previous week's fare—*Delirio de Hollywood* (*Going Hollywood*, dir. Raoul Walsh, 1933), *Sempre no meu coração* (*Ever in My Heart*, dir. Archie Mayo, 1933), *O rei vagabundo* (*The Vagabond King*, dir. Ludwig Berger, 1930), and *O Bamba da Zona* (*The Bowery*, dir. Raoul Walsh, 1933) played in Cinelândia's movie palaces—*Entre a Cruz e a Espada* was one of several religious films screened during Holy Week.[129] These films competed with other religiously themed entertainment options, including the theater spectacle *O martyr do calvário*, which ran with two separate casts in the Theatro Recreio and Theatro República.[130] *Entre a Cruz e a Espada*'s exhibition in Rio de Janeiro during Holy Week commercialized not only its diegesis, but also particular aspects of José

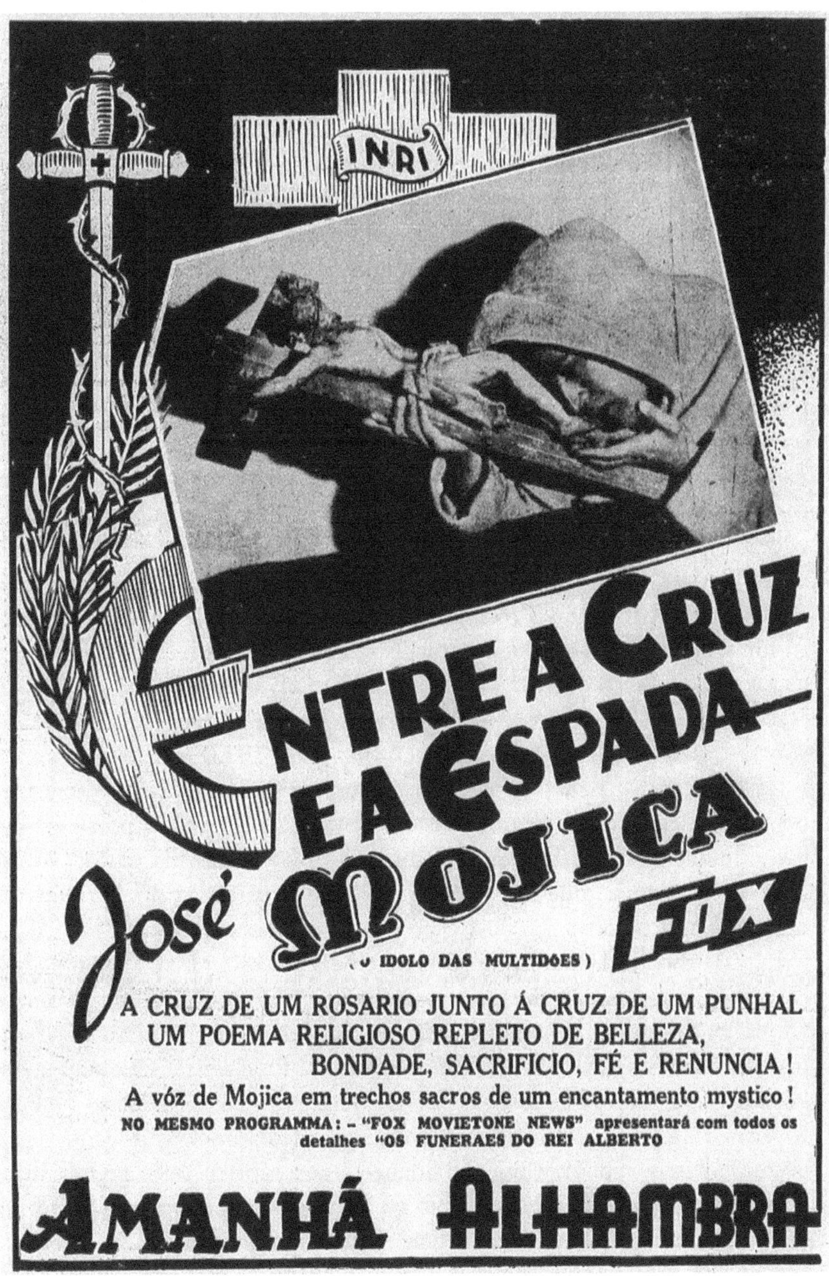

Figure 3.7. Advertisement in Rio de Janeiro for *La cruz y la espada*, *Correio da Manhã*, March 25, 1934.

Mojica's star image that were not always foregrounded in the publicity of his films. A *Correio da Manhã* piece anticipating its release baroquely argues, "This beautiful film (in the most perfect conception of the word), this mystical film, grandiose and, above all, of a clear realization of the ideology of Catholicism that its principal performer had as the supreme aspiration of his artistic career. Fervent Catholic, obedient servant of the commandments of God and of the Church, José Mojica, the Brazilian public's favorite star, receives communion and attends every Sunday the holy sacrifice of the Mass."[131] Mojica's well-known Catholicism is conflated into his role in *Entre a Cruz e a Espada*, and spectators are urged to watch a true believer on-screen. This appeal to a kind of religious identity politics worked—or, perhaps, *carioca* audiences continued to enjoy Mojica on-screen—as the film was a hit. In a later review, *Cineарte* notes that *Entre a Cruz e a Espada* is "[a] film of religious theme very appropriate for its launch during Holy Week. Also one of José Mojica's best works," which is also "[o]ne of the best *hablados* [talkies, in Spanish] presented to us to date, and it was a great success, staying for two weeks on the marquee."[132] After Holy Week ended, Cinelândia's movie palaces returned to films such as *Dancing Lady* (dir. Robert Z. Leonard, 1933), *Finanças do amor* (*The Big Executive*, dir. Erle C. Kenton, 1933), *A hora do cocktail* (*Cocktail Hour*, dir. Victor Schertzinger, 1933), and *Luzes da Broadway* (*Broadway Thru a Keyhole*, dir. Lowell Sherman, 1933).

La cruz y la espada takes place in sunny Alta California, where life passed as it always had until one day gold fever arrived. Upsetting the townspeople, as well as a small community of Franciscans who devoted their lives to preaching the Gospel, gold fever spread, bringing with it criminals and outlaws. *La cruz y la espada* centers on *Hermano* Francisco (Mojica), the well-liked young friar; José Antonio (Juan Torena), his best friend; and Carmela (Anita Campillo), a beautiful young woman whom both young men love. Although deeply committed to his best friend, Francisco develops secret feelings for Carmela after he alone saves her from a group of bandits led by the tellingly named Mestizo (Julián Rivero). Later, Francisco attends to a wounded miner. His good deed is immediately repaid when providence leads him to take shelter in a cave, where he discovers a valuable gold mine. Caught up in gold fever, Francisco transgresses decency when he attempts to seduce Carmela, but she spurns him. Francisco comes to his senses, and tells José Antonio about his discovery in hope that it will atone for his behavior. Meanwhile, whispers swirl around town. Told by a drunk of rumors of the kind that demand revenge, José Antonio seeks out Francisco to defend Carmela's honor. Francisco refuses to defend himself and receives a knife through the palm of his hand. José Antonio repents at the sight of his dear friend's blood. Francisco promises to sing in honor of the couple when José Antonio and Carmela are finally married.

The cultural and political context of *La cruz y la espada* is immediately defined in the film, not only through the direct monologue of its opening scene, but in increasingly more subtle ways throughout its first act. With the credits having rolled, and overlaying long picturesque shots of a Spanish mission (a pastiche of images taken at various missions in Southern California), the viewer is introduced to the world of Alta California by a heavily accented Peninsular voiceover.[133] The narrator states:

> To the heroic Franciscan Fathers, with no other weapon than the Cross, the civilization of California is owed. Captained by the glorious Fray Junípero Serra, they Christianized the Indians without enslaving or oppressing them. Each of the missions erected by them on the virgin soil [*el virgen terruño*] was a monument to Peace and Love, a hymn of stone to faith, to culture, to progress. Their bells seem to have been cast solely to ring out His Glory. The *hispano* spirit penetrated with immortal roots in this paradisiacal land, exalted by those same Fathers who, adapting themselves to the demands of colonization, alternated the religious habit with civilian clothing, challenging as simple men the most dangerous adventures, filled with sacrifices. In the shadow of one of these missions, still shrouded by the poetry of the dawn of California, developed—one hundred years ago!—this intimate spiritual tragedy of a Franciscan novice. The story begins like this [*El romance empieza así*]. . . .

Functioning as a frame within which the rest of tale plays out, as well as providing a clear idea of its ideological context, the monologue foreshadows some of what will happen in *La cruz y la espada*. In this *hispanista* fable, not only is California reinscribed within the Spanish empire, but colonialism is (erroneously, dangerously) reimagined to be benign. Its *hispanidad*, "a project designed to unite the Hispanic world through Spanish language and culture," may have been seen to be appealing to transnational audiences, but it also came into contact with local cultural anxieties. The sense of brotherhood afforded by *hispanismo* was one recourse to increasingly more prevalent experiences of cultural and racial othering by Anglos in the United States, which, at once, also represented a reactionary response that sublimated difference, especially regarding class and race, within its community.[134]

With the frame set, the first act presents how the bucolic, everyday life at the mission is interrupted by the discovery of gold.[135] The spiritual world of Francisco clashes with the material world of José Antonio. In a conversation at the mission, more melodramatic tension is introduced: José Antonio recounts to his friar friend about his difficulties winning the approval of Carmela's family, for financial and racial reasons. As later revealed by her Tía Mónica (Carmen Rodríguez), José Antonio is not only poor, but he is also a *vaquero* (i.e., not Spanish). Gold may provide José Antonio with the means to marry Carmela, but the prospect saddens Francisco. As he is departing, José Antonio asks Francisco why he is sad. Francisco replies, "It is that I am thinking of the future. It is that I am thinking of the day in which the fever that now attacks you all spreads throughout the world, when the world learns that there is gold in these mountains, and the peace and charm of this Arcadia disappears forever. I pray to the Lord I shall not live to see that day." Bookended by medium shots of the pair, Francisco's monologue is shot largely through a close-up that allows Mojica the opportunity to use his childlike features and vocal performance, especially through a resolute but forlorn cadence that expresses his fear of the social changes to come. Little does Francisco know that he too will be tempted.

Francisco's road to (near) perdition in search of earthly happiness unfolds through interactions in the film's second act, often in sequences culminating in song, but, revealingly, not always. Thought of diegetically as a kind of punctuation or, better yet, as signaling classical use of film sound as "privileged moments when narrative space and sound space work in lockstep," as Nilo Couret argues, songs perform a critical function in *La cruz y la espada*.[136] In the second act of *La cruz y la espada*, songs are employed to express the tenderness of a blossoming friendship, and perhaps more, but they also signify danger for Francisco.[137] Mojica gives voice to affective tension in the songs "Gratia plena" ("Full of Grace," one of Mojica's hits for RCA), "Jota número 3" ("Jota Number 3"), and "Carmen Carmela," but is later required to employ his talents in harmony with other formal elements in a key sequence in which Francisco is forced by a torrential downpour to take refuge in a cave. Rosario Vidal Bonifaz notes that the cave sequence recalls several of El Greco's paintings, as well as "Francisco de Zurburán, who captured the apostles and monks at the moment of being tempted by the devil."[138] Mojica's Francisco has little to do as he waits out the storm; he is provided with respite, with refuge, but he is exposed to an even greater peril, the danger of his own thoughts. Describing Francisco's temptation to acquiesce to worldly pleasures, Gabriel Navarro states, "This scene, surely, is one of the most beautiful and best achieved that we have seen in any movie, not only in Spanish, but also in English productions."[139] Through its use of superimposition and orchestral score, among other audiovisual formal techniques, the viewer is given entrance into Francisco's inner conflict, one whose tensions were previously expressed more indirectly. To the upper right of the frame, a wicked, alternative Francisco urges his meeker self, "Fool! Tormenting yourself like this. You are a man. Be a man! Look!" The two Franciscos here are differentiated not only by the way in which they are lit by the uncredited cinematographer, but also by how Mojica's subtle performance rises above the musical underscoring. Through his vocal performance, which often has slightly affected Peninsular tones, Mojica employs a deeper, darker voice that is (paradoxically) much more explicitly Spanish. Through his eyes, Mojica contrasts the forlorn novice with his depraved counterpart. This contrast ceases, at least temporarily, when Francisco looks to the cave's entrance.

Vanishing only to return, wicked Francisco tells his better self, "I still live.. Despite everything. Your longing for poverty, humility, and chastity." The camera lingers on Mojica's defeated, sunken Francisco in a melodramatic moment of overindulgence that is interrupted by even more diegetic excess: he discovers gold. Visually, his discovery is made explicit through the sparkle of a few nuggets; sonically, the scene is underscored by the use of dreamlike bells. Wicked Francisco returns just as good Francisco pulls the precious metal out of the cave's stream. Francisco's two selves are again contrasted through Mojica's delivering of its dialogue. Expressing innocent surprise, he first says, "*¡Virgen Santa!* The ground is full of gold nuggets." Almost whispering, as if it were a secret they alone could share, his base desire tempts him, "And everything can be yours. Do not hesitate anymore. This is your strength, your freedom. With this you can buy the whole world for you and her." Mojica's performative excesses go beyond realistic acting, especially in his final reaction to the allure of earthly pleasure, but they express a hope for happiness and pleasure in this life, one underscored by an orchestral sweep as the scene dissolves into an imagined nighttime scene in Carmela's bedroom. The sequence draws to a close as Francisco becomes a man possessed by his own romantic and sexual longing, communicated through a demonic smile and expressive lighting. Covering up his discovery, he runs down the mountain dementedly, but is eventually caught in a bush by his rosary. By the light of day, and in another wonderful demonstration of melodramatic excess, the cross reminds Francisco of his duty to his god and his friends.

La cruz y la espada ends with a wedding. In what initially seems like a tracking shot, the camera follows José Antonio and Carmela out of the church as the townspeople shower the couple in flowers. It then tilts up and sweeps camera left to the choir loft above, where it stops in a medium shot as Mojica sings, "Aleluya." What remains in frame is the simplicity of its mise-en-scène, especially in Francisco's humble monk's habit, as well as Mojica's vocal performance. Evoking the opera, his sweeping arm movements also recall the film's melodramatic denouement. In what is likely the film's most emblematic image, one that was used in publicity materials throughout Latin America (if not the world), the viewer necessarily recalls Francisco's bloodstained hand pierced by a large knife.[140] Removed by the censors in

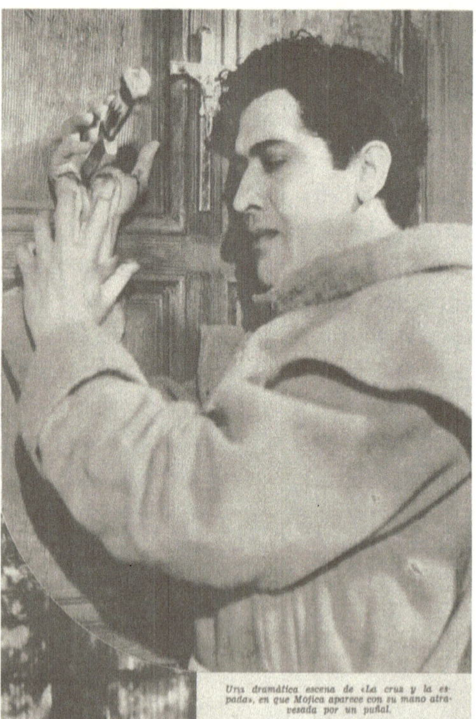

Figure 3.8. One of Mojica's most iconic scenes as a movie star. *Ecran*, February 13, 1934.

New York, and perhaps in other places as well, the piercing of Francisco's hand by José Antonio shows the film's viewers two sides of humanity: the depths to which we fall when we have lost faith and the strength with which we are endowed if we devote ourselves to serving God.[141] Visually excessive, a crucifix is framed by Francisco's face (oddly expressionless), arm (down which blood is rushing), and hand (through which the knife has entered the wall behind). Possessed, but this time by his Lord, Francisco's saintliness tells José Antonio that he was hurt "more with your doubt than with your knife," and, as she rushes in to thwart what she believes will be a violent scene, tells Carmela a little white lie (that "José Antonio has come to ask me to sing at your wedding"). By reuniting José Antonio with Carmela and, more importantly, Francisco with God, *La cruz y la espada* communicates a kind of reactionary Hispanism that looks to the past as what binds together its viewers. Rather than looking to the present or the future, temporalities with which Hollywood's Spanish-language films had found nearly impossible to deal, this imagined colonial past gives Fox a commercialized diegesis suitable to be marketed globally, but especially throughout the Spanish-speaking world.

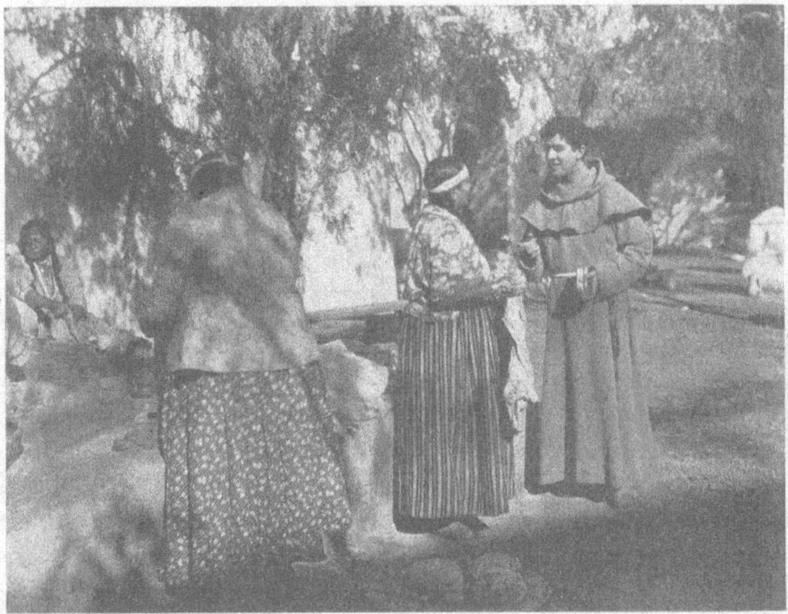

Figure 3.9. Mojica's new habit. *Cinelandia*, February 2, 1934.

Steps toward a New Habit

In the February 1934 issue of *Cinelandia*, a publicity still from *La cruz y la espada* shows its star, José Mojica, as a Franciscan friar, talking with an indigenous woman in traditional dress.[142] It reads, "The habit does not make the monk, even though José Mojica does his role very well in the film 'La cruz y la espada,' production in Spanish by Fox. In the cast Anita Campillo and Juan Torena are also found." By highlighting Mojica as the star of the film, the caption captures the convergence of his star image and screen presence in one film. Identified in relation to his costars, as well as the numerous technicians and other film workers who helped create the movie, Mojica's Francisco helps us to better understand the star's controlling force.[143] Like his role in *El rey de los gitanos*, another star vehicle, Mojica fashions meaning through his performance that not only later interacts with other aspects of his star image, but also relates back to previous ways in which it was understood. Through his own kind of authorship, exerted both on- and off-screen, Mojica helped to create his own star, as well as the (ultimately unrealized) possibilities of Hollywood stardom *en español*. In both *El rey de los gitanos* and *La cruz y la espada*, Mojica was employed to appeal to transnational audiences. In order to bring spectators from Latin America and beyond into cinemas, he had to embody characters who were of the cinema of here and there. That is to say, through engaging notions of in-betweenness such as the indeterminate spatiality of *El rey de los gitanos* or the redolent atemporality of *La cruz y la espada*, Mojica and Fox sought to sell his films to spectators from Los Angeles to Barcelona to Montevideo. For a brief time, he became a *monster sacré* (to borrow from Morin), but his image as *the* star of Hollywood's Spanish-language films eventually faded, his decline precipitated by numerous entangled factors (critical, industrial, historiographic, etc.), which included, in no small part, his own work to diminish the significance of his films for Fox. He died as the singing priest.

As its readers of *Cinelandia* would soon learn, it might have been that the habit ended up making the monk. By the end of 1934, Mojica's proposed retirement hit the pages of the magazine. It would take nearly a decade until Mojica finally joined the Franciscans, but it is one of the reasons that makes *La cruz y la espada* such an important film in his career. It was, also, a key film in the short, curious history of Hollywood's experimentation with Spanish-language films, as it promised to open opportunities for a cinematic and industrial project that had seemed abandoned.

Its promise, however, did not make the industry, even though it was a critical and commercial success. After *La cruz y la espada*, Mojica starred in two more features for Fox: *Un capitán de cosacos* and *Las fronteras del amor*. In an autobiographical turn, Mojica's Carlos Segovia in *Las fronteras del amor* is a famous tenor who gives up the entertainment industry to return to his roots in Jalisco. For years, in interviews Mojica intimated, if he did not declare outright, his intention to step out of the spotlight. In 1931, he told the San Francisco weekly *Hispano-América*, "My idea is to retire as young and as rich as possible," even though only two of his films had been released to that point.[144] In late 1932, he explained more to *Cinelandia*'s Joaquín de la Horia, "I will retire sooner than one might think. I will hide the actor to dedicate my activities, entirely, to the practice and teaching of this new art of musical performance that, I am sure, will not reach its development for many years."[145] News of Mojica's retirement swirled for years throughout Latin America, from initial reports in 1934 to his return to the screen in Mexico in Arcady Boytler's 1938 *El capitán aventurero* (*The Adventurous Capitan*). As late as mid-1940, it was reported by *Film Daily* that "John Stone has opened negotiations with Jose [*sic*] Mojica, the opera star, with the possibility of starring him in a series of musical films in both English and Spanish."[146] His return to Hollywood never materialized, but he would make two more films in Mexico before he took up the Franciscan habit: *La canción del milagro* (*The Miracle Song*, dir. Rolando Aguilar, 1940) and *Melodías de América* (*Melodies of America*, dir. Eduardo Morera, 1942). Mojica's dedication would eventually change, especially after the death of his mother in 1940, but his ambivalence toward his professional career continued.[147] As Fray José de Guadalupe Mojica, he appeared in three more films in his life, *El pórtico de la gloria* (Glory's Porch, dir. Rafael J. Salvia, 1953), *Yo pecador*, and *Seguiré tus pasos* (I Will Follow Your Steps, dirs. Alfredo B. Crevenna and Félix A. Ramírez, 1967).

4

Mexico City Dreams

The Emergence of Latin America's Most Important Film Industry

Alongside the March 30, 1932, premiere of *Santa*, Mexico's first sound film, a new movie magazine appeared, *Filmográfico*. If not a manifesto, its first article, "A Centerpiece," immediately defines its goals: "Moments of reigning commercial disorientation, transitory, are the least appropriate to launch into the market a publication of this nature, but shielded by good faith and the energy of our principles, we are confident in the era of prosperity that lies ahead."[1] Like countless other film periodicals published throughout the world at the time, *Filmográfico* hoped to promote the ambitions of local entrepreneurs and artists to establish the foundation of a national cinema industry. It continues, "Our magazine, modesty aside, comes to fill a gap in the current needs of this great city, more yet, of our entire Republic. We joined the young Cía. Nacional Productora de Películas, to drive the nacent film industry, which, in a not too distant day, will put us in a preferred place among Spanish-language producers." *Santa* may have been preceded by other fascinating experiments with sound-on-disc such as *El águila y el nopal* (The Eagle and the Cactus, dir. Miguel Contreras Torres, 1929) and *Filmográfico* was not, by any stretch, the sole Mexican film periodical, but both can be seen to have led to unprecedented professionalization and industrialization of the Mexican film industry. Foreigners are integral to the development of both, elements of stories projected on screen or published on the page, but they have almost always played secondary, if not tertiary, roles. It is not that foreigners are not present, but their storylines are often kept separate from the main plot, starring a Mexican *galán* or local director. The study of their subplots, however, helps us to better understand the emerging Mexican film industry.[2]

In the period from 1931 to 1936, Mexican cinema moved toward industrialization.[3] Sputtering initially—only three films were produced in 1931 and six in 1932—it was clear that there was a market for national cinema by 1933. The next three years saw greater production and consistency, seeing twenty-four films in 1934, twenty-three in 1935, and twenty-four again in 1936. Without an industrial framework, it was easy for filmmakers to continue making movies as they had before. "Strictly speaking, this era of Mexican cinema may well be seen as preindustrial. Sporadic producers abounded who hoped to achieve economic success with a single film and then invest what they earned in lower-risk businesses such as real estate."[4] It is not only that their mode of production continued to reflect that of the silent era, but also they were limited by other industrial factors, particularly, limited means of production and restricted financing. These years saw, however, attempts to construct the requisite industrial framework necessary to maintain continued production, such as the 1932 opening of Jorge Stahl's new studios, México Films. Though many of these fledgling production companies were not able to make more than a few films, they drew capital (economic, cultural, and social) into what was an emerging industry. They also employed many of the same people. The industry consolidated through efforts to structure the means of production: guilds such the Unión de Trabajadores de los Estudios Cinematográficos Mexicanos (UTECM, Union of Mexican Film Studio Workers) and the Asociación de Productores Mexicanos de Películas (APMP, Association of Mexican Film Producers) were established in 1934. While it could not be said then that Mexico yet had an industrial studio, it had many production companies who employed the same casts and crews. In 1935, however, this would change: CLASA (Cinematografía Latinoamericana, S.A.) established new studios. "The studios were far superior to those existing and were equipped with equipment comparable to those of Hollywood companies: for the first time in Mexico, they had Mitchell cameras, re-recording equipment [or sound synchronizing], developing machines based on the 'gamma curve,' back projection equipment, and an optical printer."[5] With CLASA, specifically, and other developing industries in other sectors, more generally, the mid to late 1930s would see direct and indirect governmental support. The next year, the Unión de Directores Cinematográficos de México (UDCM, Film Directors' Union of Mexico) was established.[6] Later that year, its president, Fernando de Fuentes, would direct the first blockbuster of Mexican cinema, *Allá en el Rancho Grande*. By the end of 1936, Mexican film had become industrialized.

Allá en el Rancho Grande is often considered to be the film that began the *Época de oro del cine mexicano*.[7] In many ways, however, it was less the beginning than the end of an era. In its transition to sound, Mexican cinema also became industrialized. Contributions of returning Mexicans and foreigners were integral. Referring to the versatile Alejandro Galindo, Francisco Peredo Castro writes, "Undoubtedly, experiences and learning in Hollywood were also fundamental in his subsequent development, in the same way that it was for all directors, actors, cinematographers, sound technicians, etc., who later were incorporated into the Mexican cinema of the 1930s and 1940s, despite their different nationalities."[8]

Galindo was one of many Mexicans who returned to their homeland to work in its developing film industry. Among those who came back were Guillermo Calles, Raúl de Anda, Alejandro Galindo, Roberto Gavaldón, Carlos Navarro, Andrea Palma, Ramón Pereda, the Rodríguez brothers, Raphael J. Sevilla, and Chano Urueta. From 1931 to 1936, a number of foreign workers were incorporated into the fledgling Mexican film industry, some more continually than others. To this day, these workers are overshadowed by Sergei Eisenstein and, to a lesser extent, his collaborators on the unrealized project *¡Qué viva México!*, Grigori Aleksandrov and cinematographer Eduard Tissé. These directors include John Auer, Arcady Boytler, Robert Curwood (née Ioan Balaş), Jorge M. Dada, David Kirkland, Boris Maicon, Antonio Moreno, Ramón Peón, Ramón Pereda, Robert Quigley, and Fred Zinnemann.[9] In addition to directing, hyphenates such as José Bohr, Juan Orol, and Eva Limiñana (Duquesa Olga) took on acting, producing, and scriptwriting. They were joined on the set by cinematographers Jack Draper, Ross Fisher, Alex Phillips, Arthur Martinelli, Paul Strand, and Alvyn Wyckoff, all of whom had experience in Hollywood, and other technicians such as editor Charles L. Kimball and sound engineer B. J. Kroger, who became mainstays in the Mexican film industry. The composer Max Urban scored many films, and Federico Ruiz a few. Influential producers Paul H. Bush and Jorge Pezet marked the industry, as did production manager Paul Castelain. In an industry that had yet to produce a star, foreign actors such as René Cardona, Clifford Carr, Alfredo del Diestro, Juan José Martínez Casado,

Medea de Novara, Carlos Villarías, and Julio Villarreal worked alongside their Mexican counterparts.[10] Many of these foreign film workers, such as Phillips, arrived as the Mexican film industry was beginning to get on its feet, while others, such as Kimball, arrived as it was taking its first sure steps. Some of them have been recognized as important contributors to Mexico's transition to sound, while others, like *anotador* (script supervisor) Pablo Caicedo Álvarez, are barely remembered. The contributions of many more, large and small, have been lost to oblivion.

Between 1937 and 1940, the Mexican film industry continued its consolidation. It saw production increase from thirty-eight films in 1937 to fifty-eight in 1938, then a decline from forty in 1939 to twenty-seven in 1940. Sustainable growth proved difficult, as modes of production had not become industrialized, particularly in terms of financing. Producers were still largely unwilling to take upon themselves greater risks, which led to smaller, but less ambitious films. "A cinema without 'stars' would rely its economic calculus too much on themes and genres, and hence the mass invasion of lands inaugurated by *Rancho Grande*."[11] Efforts were made in 1938 to import stars from Hollywood, especially in the star vehicles *La Zandunga* (dir. Fernando de Fuentes), featuring Lupe Vélez, and *El capitán aventurero* (dir. Boytler), with José Mojica, but Mexican cinema took some time finding stars that resonated with audiences. These issues, however, were products of a developing industry. In late 1938, Esperanza López of the magazine *Cine* related producer Alberto Monroy's ideas:

> The film industry in Mexico has developed faster than expected. The disorganization that is noted comes from the majority of producers working on credit. Oftentimes a movie is made in two, three, or more stages, depending on how the money made available is being spent. The day when Mexican investors convince themselves that the movie business is big business, and invest their money in it, this industry will be number one in Mexico.[12]

Amid other more direct forms of state involvement—most notably, the expropriation of the oil industry—there were moves to promote development of the film industry. In 1937, the creation of the Banco Refaccionario Cinematográfico (Film Credit Bank) was proposed, but efforts stalled (due, at least in part, to the complexities of oil nationalization).[13] In 1938, an exhibition quota was established by presidential decree. Despite this, producers continued to have difficulty distributing and exhibiting their films. Workers also continued to advance their interests: 1938 saw a strike and the creation of a directors' guild, limiting membership and access to directing, under the auspices of the UTECM. Even if the industry had yet to overcome some long-standing problems, which led to some pessimism regarding its future, *Cinema Reporter* deemed 1939 the "Golden Year of Mexican Cinema." Roberto Cantú Robert argues, "The delay suffered in the quantity of works filmed in 1939 should not surprise us if we attend to important factors that mediated and delayed, beneficially, even it seems like a paradox, the development of our producers."[14] These factors, these growing pains, could not obscure the fact that, by 1940, "In México, the cinema is already an industry."[15]

Industry insiders continued to advocate for the inclusion of foreign workers. In his fascinating overview *La industria cinematográfica de México* (1939), Alfonso Pulido Islas argues for "permission to enter the country, for a convenient period of time, for foreign technicians of the different branches of production, with the obligation of communicating their knowledge to national workers."[16] Also, transnational productions revealed new strategies for engaging audiences beyond Mexico's borders: *La justicia de Pancho Villa (El gaucho Múgica)* (Múgica the Gaucho or The Justice of Pancho Villa, dirs. Guz Águila and Calles), a peculiar film in which an Argentine gaucho travels to Mexico to fight in the Mexican Revolution; *María* (dir. Chano Urueta, 1938), an adaptation of Jorge Isaac's classic nineteenth-century novel; *Juan soldado* (*Soldier Juan*, dir. Louis Gasnier, 1938), which recalls late U.S. Spanish-language productions, as it was shot in both Tijuana and Hollywood; and *Miente y serás feliz* (*Fib And Be Happy*, dir. Sevilla, 1939), a film marked by notable Spanish presence.[17] In a period that saw the arrivals of stars Cantinflas and Fernando Soler, who were soon to be joined by Jorge Negrete, Arturo de Córdova, and Pedro Armendáriz, foreign actors such as Sofía Álvarez, Mapy Cortés, José Crespo, Vicente Padula, José Pidal, Manolita Saval, and Mercedes Soler began to make their mark on Mexican cinema.[18] Known as *la diosa de oro* (Golden Goddess), Chile-born Peruvian bullfighter Conchita Cintrón appeared in the documentary *Mujeres que torean* (Women Who Bullfight, dir. Ignacio Rangel, 1940) and the feature *Maravilla del toreo* (Queen Of The Arena, dir. Sevilla, 1942). Foreign directors also made their debuts in Mexican cinema: Alfredo del Diestro, Francisco Elías, Louis Gasnier, Quirico Michelena, Vicente Oroná, and William Rowland.[19] Earning their first credits (as well as checks) in Mexico were Arnaldo Malfatti

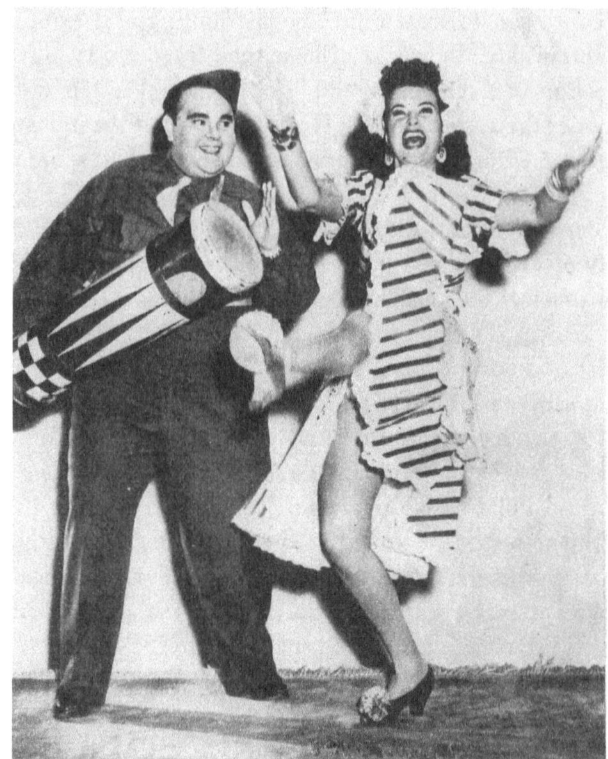

Figure 4.1. Mapy Cortés dancing with Cuban musician and choreographer Sergio Orta. *Cinema Reporter*, July 24, 1943.

and Nicolás de las Llanderas, Alberto Novión, and José López Rubio. Cinematographers Max Liszt, Fred Mandel, and Roland Price were hired, as was editor Mario González. The aural landscapes of films were entrusted to composers Enrique Bryon, Manuel Penella, and Hugo Riesenfeld and sound engineers Eduardo Fernández, Gerson Jawett, Howard Randall, and Douglas Winie. Having gained experience with Gregorio Martínez Sierra, Manuel Fontanals began a prolific career as a production designer in Mexico on *María*.

"Usually, there is talk of an *época de oro del cine mexicano* with more nostalgia than chronological precision. If that time existed, it was that of the years of World War II: 1941 to 1945."[20] García Riera's assessment is substantiated not only by the continued, sustainable growth of film production—thirty-eight films were produced in 1941, forty-seven in 1942, seventy-one in 1943, seventy-four in 1944, and eighty-two in 1945—but also in the premieres of classics of Mexican cinema such as *¡Ay, Jalisco, no te rajes!* (Oh Jalisco, Don't Back Down!, dir. Joselito Rodríguez, 1941), *El baisano Jalil* (*Citizen Jalil*, dir. Joaquín Pardavé, 1942), *Distinto amanecer* (*Another Dawn*, dir. Julio Bracho, 1943), *Flor silvestre* (dir. Emilio Fernández, 1943), *María Candelaria* (dir. Fernández, 1943), *Gran Hotel* (dir. Miguel M. Delgado, 1944), and *Campeón sin corona* (*The Uncrowned Champion*, dir. Galindo, 1945). In the midst of World War II, the Mexican film industry saw the creation in 1941 of important, well-organized production companies such as Filmex, Films Mundiales, and Posa Films.[21]

In 1942, the Asociación de Productores de Películas sought governmental assistance to bolster the industry, including the reinforcement of exhibition quotas for national cinema, imposition of tax abatements for exhibitors who showed Mexican movies, elimination of taxes on the importation of film production equipment (from raw film stock to laboratory apparatuses, none of which were manufactured in the country). More importantly, that year saw the establishment of the Banco Cinematográfico. "The creation of the Banco Cinematográfico was a solid indication of the importance in which the national film industry was held in high official circles. In an effort to centralize the sporadic activities of small, undercapitalized producers, the Banco in its first year extended credits of 5 million pesos to nine production companies."[22] More regular access to capital allowed for both greater productivity and more ambitious projects. 1943 would be "The Great Year," according to Emilio García Riera. Beyond important cinematic advances, especially in the quality and commerciality of its films, the Mexican film industry benefited both from its domestic situation as well as geopolitical factors. Unlike Argentina and Spain, whose film industries declined as they remained neutral in World War II, Mexico joined the Allies.[23]

From 1941 to 1943, foreign actors would become incorporated into the Mexican film industry, ranging from stars Rosario (Charito) Granados, Carmen Montejo, and María Antonieta Pons to character actors like Jorge Reyes (Silveyra) and Charles Rooner.[24] Even though there were fewer new foreign directors (José Díaz Morales, Norman Foster, Herbert Kline, and Dudley Murphy), cinematographers (John W. Boyle and Enrique Wallace), sound engineers (Adolfo de la Riva), and editors (Mario del

Río), many more new foreigners were brought into the writing room: David T. Bamberg, Alfonso Lapena, Antonio Monsell, Jaime Salvador, Budd Schulberg, and Eduardo Ugarte.[25] Similar to del Diestro and, later, Tito Davison, del Río and Salvador would eventually direct after working in other aspects of filmmaking. The sounds of Mexican cinema continued to integrate foreign rhythms, as Elías Breeskin, Antonio Díaz Conde, Rodolfo Halffter, Rafael Hernández, and Severo Muguerza Gil all appeared in films. These foreign workers worked on- and off-set not only on films with international appeal such as *La liga de las canciones* (*League of Songs*, dir. Chano Urueta, 1941), *Jesús de Nazareth* (dir. Díaz Morales, 1942), and *Cinco fueron escogidos* (Five Were Chosen, 1942), but also movies such as *Soy puro mexicano* (*100% Mexican*, dir. de Anda, 1942) and *María Candelaria*.

Seemingly impossible, the dreams described in the premiere issue of *Filmográfico* were eventually realized. By June 10, 1943, the day Foster's remake of *Santa* premiered at the Palacio theater, not only had *Cinema Reporter* (as *Filmográfico* came to be known in mid-1938) become the most important trade publication in the industry, but Mexico was home to the most dominant Spanish-language film industry in the world.[26] Always present, even as characters in a (figurative or literal) subplot, foreign workers were integral to the emergence of the Mexican film industry. Sometimes left in the shadows in Mexican film historiography, whose robustness precludes a full, detailed bibliographical review of the period, these film workers are an integral element of Mexican film history. Their stories unique and their contributions diverse, these foreigners helped Mexican cinema arrive at its *Época de oro*.

5

"The Best We Have in This Forsaken Place"

Cinematography and Collaboration in Alex Phillips's Films with Arcady Boytler and Fernando de Fuentes

In a series of articles published in *Revista de Revistas* in 1933, the film journalist Esteban V. Escalante explores the direction of the emerging Mexican film industry in dialogue with producers and directors. Setting aside a wide-angle look, he focuses on a specific issue in "Our Technicians and the Future of Mexican Cinema," writing, "Today we are going to change topics. That is to say, we will continue to talk about national cinema, but under another aspect: that of cinematographers."[1] By framing the article more narrowly, and through interviewing Julio Lamadrid, a single affected cameraman, Escalante is able to attend to how the transition to sound fundamentally reorganized the labor market and why this is problematic for the Mexican film industry and its workers. He writes:

> Many pessimists blindly believe that in Mexico there are no cameramen and that we must always be under the yoke of foreigners because ours are more than inept. To those pessimists we must tell them that our silent cinema never had strange [i.e., foreign] operators and if they presently shine due to the absence of locals, it is because the advent of spoken cinema took them [i.e., locals] unprepared, like those [previously] in Hollywood.

Mexico, Escalante argues, was forced to endure the negative effects on cinematography of Hollywood's transition to sound, so why, he wonders, should the local film industry not allow its own technicians a similar period? This transitional period, too, is occurring in Mexico, and will not end, according to Escalante, until the country's cinematographers are allowed to gain experience. He continues, "A phalanx of young people is being trained and those of the 'old guard' only wait for their opportunity to prove that they have not gotten dusty and handle the crank as they did in the age of silent cinema." Somewhat subverting his point—new cameras were not cranked by their operators—Escalante nonetheless draws attention to the lack of opportunities for Mexican cameramen. Their work was increasingly being given to foreign cinematographers, especially those imported from Hollywood, which included Jack Draper, Ross Fisher, Paul Strand, and, most notably, Alex Phillips.

Between his first credit in Mexico—the country's first sound film, *Santa* (dir. Antonio Moreno, 1932)—and his final—Arturo Ripstein's *El castillo de la pureza* (*The Castle of Purity*, 1972)—Alex Phillips (né Alexander Pelepiock) worked on more than two hundred projects in the country. Similar to other foreign film technicians of the early sound period, which not only included cinematographers but also Mexican workers who had previously plied their trade in Hollywood such as the Rodríguez brothers, Raphael J. Sevilla, and Chano Urueta, the Canadian-born, partially Russian-raised Phillips sought out newly emerging professional opportunities in Mexico. Eventually overshadowed by Gabriel Figueroa, his one-time assistant (and, perhaps, one of Escalante's "phalanx of young people"), to whom he introduced Gregg Toland and whose significant work has received considerable critical attention—to the point that he has achieved almost mythical status in Mexico—Phillips worked with noted directors such as José Bohr, Luis Buñuel, Emilio Fernández, Alberto Gout, Juan Orol, Ramón Peón, and Orson Welles, as well as many others. Despite this, Phillips's cinematography remains largely unstudied.

What follows is not a badly needed history of Mexican cinematography of the 1930s and early 1940s in the vein of Patrick Keating's scholarship, but rather a humbler attempt to better understand often invisible work whose authorship is often impossible to ascertain.[2] "[F]rom the earliest days of cinema directors and cinematographers have worked together as creative partners," as Christopher Beach argues, representing forces of art and technology.[3] "As a general paradigm, the cinematographer is responsible for discovering, introducing, and improving new visual

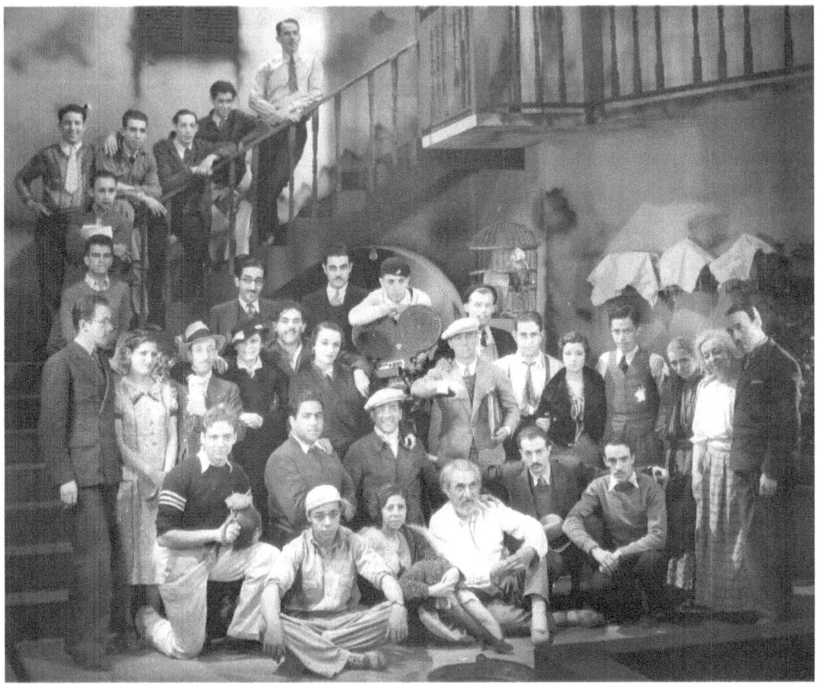

Figure 5.1. The cast and crew of *La mujer del puerto*, perhaps Alex Phillips's most well-known film. Courtesy of Mil Nubes-Foto.

technologies that the director can then apply in the creation of cinematic art. However, the functions of the cinematographer and director are by no means mutually exclusive, nor are they rigidly fixed."[4] The dynamics of Phillips's collaborations with his directors are impossible to discern, particularly at a historical remove, but there is something intrinsic to his craft of cinematography that inscribes Phillips's place within film criticism and, later, history. In the 1930s and early 1940s, as I show in this chapter, Phillips was often tasked with lighting his films so that their cinematography would be unseen (or, at the very least, unrealized) by spectators. He was to render his work invisible. Along with the craft of many other foreign workers, especially technicians, Phillips's invisibility became a pervasive tendency in Mexican film criticism and history, but it also is illustrative of the cultural nationalism of the emerging film industry. If *mexicanidad* differentiated Mexican films from Hollywood imports dominating the local market, some even produced in Spanish, then technicians such as

Phillips were required to remain inconspicuous. Present, but out of the spotlight, Phillips serves the story of Mexican cinema.

In order to understand Phillips's impact on Mexican cinema, I examine two interlocking aspects of his work as a cinematographer in the early sound period, focusing on his films' positions within the emerging Mexican film industry and his labor, especially in the crafting of lighting strategies. Through studying his collaborations with two of the most important directors of the 1930s and early 1940s, Arcady Boytler and Fernando de Fuentes, I argue that Phillips's films reveal tendencies that were present—and in tension—throughout the early sound period: the use of lighting strategies and visual technologies to serve specific generic conventions that had been established primarily (but not exclusively) in Hollywood, as well as his own, personal style, developed within narrative and professional constraints. These particular collaborations are suggestive as well of how Mexican cinema dealt with cultural (trans)nationalism. I detail Phillips's style (or, really, styles) within the framework of these collaborations, and also within specific limitations of the role of the cinematographer in the emerging Mexican film industry. Through closely examining his work on films directed by Boytler and Phillips, as well as (partially) reconstructing his place in the industry by studying contemporaneous articles in film magazines and other periodicals, I aim to shed light on Phillips's tone-setting work both on-screen (through the implementation of visual technologies) and off (as a foreign-born technician). I propose that, through his work on set and on-screen, as well as reception of both, Phillips's professional relationships can be seen as indicative of broader trends in Mexican cinema of the 1930s and early 1940s. Though somewhat analogous to the careers of other foreign workers in emerging national film industries in Latin America—not only the aforementioned technicians in Mexico, but others such as the cinematographer John Alton, who shot numerous films in Argentina before returning to Hollywood—Phillips's trajectory gives us insight into distinctive labor particularities found within the development of national cinema in Mexico as it moved into its so-called *Época de oro* or Golden Age.

Fairy Tales and Realities of a Life in the Movies

Like so many who work in the film industry, Alex Phillips's life exists as a historiographical tapestry stitched over the course of decades by reporting, gossip, reputation, and, later, oral testimony, but it also survives in historical loose threads, some already lost to oblivion and others so scattered as to be difficult to piece together. In Mexican film historiography, Alexander Pelepiock was born on January 11, 1900, in Ontario, Canada. In his childhood, he returned with his immigrant parents to Russia, where he was schooled. "Because of his disagreement with the Tsarist government's treatment at that time of the people, from a very young age he constantly asked his family to allow him to return to Canada to live with his uncles; until he succeeded."[5] He returned alone, later enlisting in the army at the tender age of fifteen. The course of Alex's life would irrevocably change in the Great War. With his fellow volunteers, Alex fought on the Western Front in France and Belgium. His family in Russia would disappear, victims either of a German attack or Revolutionary forces. He also underwent two experiences that proved significant for his future: he joined the Canadian Official Photography and he met Hollywood star Mary Pickford, who became his regiment's *madrina*. In the fable of Alex Phillips's life, she was more than a patron or a sponsor, two possible translations of the term; rather, Pickford took on a more magical role: fairy godmother. She first offered to aid him if by chance he were to move to California. Later, her offer was reiterated in England, where Pelepiock laid in convalescence for several months after being gravely wounded in battle. His tale has him returning to Canada in 1919.

What remains in the historical record suggests a different story. For example, in the Canadian Personnel Records of World War I, a boy goes to war and struggles with his experience as he grows into manhood. In Calgary on October 19, 1915, the day after his eighteenth birthday (the age at which he could enlist), Alexa Pelepiuk (an alternative transliteration of his Russian surname) filled out a personal information form (attestation paper) in order to join what was then called the Canadian Over-Seas Expeditionary Force.[6] He was issued regimental number 447720. According to the document, Pelepiuk was born on October 18, 1897, in Ottawa. He initially listed his next of kin as Nicholas Pelepiuk, but crossed out the name and replaced it with Katrina Leipull Pelepiuk of Podolskoi Kaminetz, Kiev, Russia. His trade? Laborer. Some six months later, he sailed with the Fifty-sixth Battalion from Hailfax, upon the S.S. *Baltic*. Private Pelepink (as numerous documents list him) transferred to the Fifteenth Battalion. A year after he enlisted, after fighting for five months on the front, Pelepink was wounded in his right leg. Admitted initially to the First Australian

General Hospital in Rouen, he was later transferred to England, to the Second Western General Hospital in Manchester, where he was treated both for the gunshot wound and for psychogenic paralysis. He also spent time in other hospitals, such as the Canadian Military Hospital in Eastbourne, Sussex. He departed from Liverpool, sailing back to Canada under special authority on the S.S. *Missanabie* on October 18, 1917.[7] In Canada, he was treated at the Ogden and Manitoba Military Hospitals for hysteria caused by the "strain of trench warfare." On May 2, 1919, Pelepiuk left the service, discharged for medical unfitness. According to his discharge certificate—a copy of which, curiously, is briefly shown in *La magia entre la luz y la sombra* (dir. Ernesto Medina, 1998) with a single addition to the original: "Phillips"—young Alex was nineteen. In his short form, a document drafted upon discharge, Alex's proposed residence after discharge was Long Beach, California, USA.[8] These historical details serve not to undermine Phillips's military record, much less his character, but rather to remind us that the cinema is a place of myth and legend, created by storytellers who (self-)fashion tales for consumption on screen and in the pages of movie magazines. Facts are sometime unsuitable.

A new chapter of Alex Phillips's life would soon begin. "He arrived in Hollywood with another name and the dream of being an actor," as Claudia Negrete describes Phillips's move to California.[9] Much historical research remains to be done, but the fable told in Mexican film historiography has it that Phillips moved to Hollywood to seek out Mary Pickford, with the hope of obtaining a job. In a 1975 interview, he told María Alba Fulguiera,

> We talked and [Mary] asked me what I wanted to be. I replied, actor. She said, "No, I recommend that you look for something where you can work constantly, because an actor needs income to sustain himself while he reaches his point." Then, she paid me twenty-five dollars, just like the *galanes* (leading men), for acting in one of her latest films, and she provided me with salary until I got a job. She gave me recommendations for Griffith, for Christy Comedies. In different studios: Fox and Paramount. I went everywhere without being able to be placed, as everyone had been hired for five or ten years. My only chance was as a film extra.[10]

Eventually, Phillips jumped at the chance to work for an independent production company run by fellow Canadians, the brothers Al and Charles

Christie. At Christie Film Company, Phillips replaced an assistant cameraman, having served Canadian Official Photography in the war. "The producer was amazed by my ability to carry two cameras at once. For me, it was very easy, since in the trenches it was custom to carry the dead. That is much harder than two cameras."[11] Alec Phillips (as he was sometimes credited) worked on many films for Christie, including silent shorts *See My Lawyer* (dir. Al Christie, 1921) *Choose Your Weapons* (dir. Christie, 1922), *Away We Go* (dir. Archie Mayo, 1924), *Madame Behave* (dir. Scott Sidney, 1925), *Up in Mabel's Room* (dir. E. Mason Hopper, 1926), *Meet the Folks* (dir. Christie, 1927); short race films *Music Hath Harms* (dir. Walter Graham), *Oft in the Silly Night* (dir. Arvid Gillstrom, 1929), *The Framing of the Shrew* (dir. Gillstrom, 1929); and talkie *Divorce Made Easy* (dirs. Neal Burns and Walter Graham, 1929). With the arrival of sound in the cinema, the Christies bought Metropolitan Studio and invested in its expansion and conversion to sound. The timing was unpropitious, however, as the collapse of the stock market would eventually lead to the departure of independent producers and, later, the company's acquisition by Educational Pictures in 1931.

By that time, Phillips had long since departed. Sometime earlier in this tale, perhaps in the mid-twenties, Phillips began his education as a cinematographer. It reflects some of the ways in which the complex fashioning and promotion of individual film workers (actors, cinematographers, directors, etc.), shaped by a wide range of people (often including the workers themselves), mirrored the (self-)promoting and (self-)fashioning characteristic of national cinemas, especially during the early sound period. Having tired of his bosses' use of cinematographic strategies typical of silent comedies (such as the bright, flat lighting, which allows the viewer to easily follow gags and which maintains a generally positive mood), Phillips began a kind of apprenticeship under Al Christie, learning what it meant to produce a film. He bought a camera and began his education by watching films. "The moment when production [at Christie's] stopped, I went with Samuel Goldwyn and worked with the best Hollywood photographers at the time: George Barnes, [Arthur] Edeson, and [Arthur Charles] Miller, the photographer of John Ford. I really liked that time because I already had to do artistic things."[12] He almost certainly met other cinematographers and technicians as well, including Gregg Toland, to whom he famously sent Gabriel Figueroa. "At the same time that he ventures into cinematography, Alex Phillips sets up a still photography studio that is gaining popularity in the light of the great stars."[13] Moonlighting would eventually push Phillips out of studio work. In an oft-repeated anecdote, an assistant of Toland's who was sent to fetch (the hours tardy) Phillips forced his way into Phillips's apartment by breaking a window.[14] Such was Phillips's exhaustion that the assistant had to physically extract him from his bed. On the set, the production manager presented Phillips with a three-film suspension and a choice: continue to work as a film cameraman or dedicate himself to portraiture. His work at his studio was a formative experience that he would apply later as a cinematographer, particularly in framing and lighting his female stars in early Mexican sound cinema. "Those who came to Hollywood and wanted a portrait were sent to me because I was an expert in taking pictures to sell to producers."[15] He shot some of Hollywood's brightest stars—Gloria Swanson is said to have given Phillips a sports car for his work—and socialized with even more of them, including some of the Mexican *colonia*. Carmen Guerrero reached out to a suspended Phillips, telling him that Rafael Ángel Frías and Gustavo Sáenz de Sicilia (investors in Compañía Nacional Productora de Películas) were seeking a cinematographer to shoot what would become *Santa*, Mexico's first talkie. So, Phillips contacted another friend, who told him, "Go so you can get away from all of these *sinvergüenzas* [scoundrels], so they will let you sleep. Go to Mexico. You will enjoy, do not stop yourself from going!"[16] That friend was Emilio Fernández.

"A Great Photographer Arrived Yesterday in Mexico," read the headline of an article about Phillips published in the November 8, 1931, issue of *El Universal*.[17] Its subtitle: "He Has Done All of the Films in Which Gloria Swanson Works." It is fitting that the story contains exaggeration (if not fabrication), opinion, and, well, some facts. Phillips, in this sense, is almost metonymic for Mexican national cinema. The *El Universal* note begins by reiterating that Alec [*sic*] Phillips has worked on all of Swanson's films, and states that he had spent the previous year working as one of Paramount's chief photographers and had been named one of the twenty best cinematographers in the U.S. film industry by *Film Daily Yearbook*.[18] Traveling from Los Angeles to Mexico City by car, the portraitist Phillips was taken in by the country's landscapes:

> "Mexico," he affirmed, "is surely one of the most beautiful countries in the world from the point of view of cinematography. I cannot understand how this privileged country has not been exploited in the movies and I am perfectly sure that immediately after the first talkie films here are made, a real

> avalanche of producers will flood the country, even trying to exhaust its inexhaustible natural resources. Mexico, for some inexplicable reason, is not yet a global film emporium. . . . But it will be!"

Recalling the ideas of other cinematographers who worked in Latin America, such as John Alton, Phillips sees himself as a technician capable of helping unlock Mexico's industrial potential.[19] But, tellingly, Phillips argues that the commercial possibilities of Mexican national cinema are predicated upon what it already possesses: natural beauty. Awaiting director Antonio Moreno's arrival, Phillips will begin preproduction work on "the first production spoken in Spanish that will be filmed in Mexico," *Santa*. Contracted for six months, Phillips would eventually live in the country for the next forty-six years.

More than *La mujer del puerto*: Phillips's Collaborations with Arcady Boytler

Some six weeks after the publication of "Our Technicians and the Future of Mexican Cinema," *Revista de Revistas* published Escalante's feature "Arcady Boytler, a Director of Importance."[20] A continuation of his exploration of the current state of the local film industry, Escalante begins, "For a long while I followed in the footsteps of the Russian director Arcady Boytler because I knew in advance that he, as a foreigner, could tell me many things inherent to national cinema that others have not told me."[21] Shadowing Boytler during the filming of *La mujer del puerto*, a film whose critical and commercial success continues to mark our understanding of *el gallo ruso* (the Russian Rooster, as he was known), Escalante allowed Boytler to define his own relationship with Mexico. Boytler states, "Your Mexico is beautiful, friend Escalante. In this privileged land, wherever you may turn your eyes, you will find a painting, a painting worthy of the most demanding of masters. Look at the moon: does it not seem softer and more luminous than that which shines in other countries?" Exuding excess, at least in comparison to Phillips's similar observation, Boytler continues, gushing that "Mexico is the land of color!" It even surpasses the wonders of the rest of the world, which he, ever the cosmopolitan, had experienced firsthand.[22] The interview, however, is imbued with a dual exoticism: Boytler's Mexico is shadowed by his Russia. Escalante provides space for Boytler's performative Russianness, which not only conflates the director with Sergei Eisenstein, but by extension also places Boytler as part of the Russian avant-gardes (cultural but also political) impacting Mexico at the time. Boytler claims his life's dream is to "[t]raverse the Mexican Republic from Sonora to the Yucatan to make a film just like Eisenstein did," even though, ultimately, his films were decidedly more conventional, more commercial.[23]

Among Boytler's somewhat eccentric ruminations, in which he seems to relish playing the role of the unconventional artist, Escalante draws out the director's opinions on cinematography in early Mexican sound films. Returning to the conversation from a melancholy aside about the comings and goings of ships, Boytler tells Escalante, "You ask me what is my opinion about Mexican national cinema? Well, ok: I see a great future. Each film that is released will be a big push. And each ordinary film, too, because it is a step forward that makes us recognize the defects that we involuntarily made." Beating Escalante to the punch, Boytler addresses recent criticisms regarding photography, revealing his understanding of the contemporary division of labor in industrialized film. Boytler places blame on directors, stating that "due to a lack of experience, they neglect composition and they leave everything to he who willingly picks up the lens. The director does not have to be a photographer, but he must be a composer of angles." Escalante, however, insists, and asks Boytler if the director believes Mexican cameramen to be inept. Boytler equivocates, answering:

> "No! *¡Qué barbaridad!* I had my eye on Ezequiel Carrasco for *La mujer del puerto*, but it happens that domestic cinematographers, out of misunderstood embarrassment, do not want to go to the studios to learn what they do not know. In Russia, for example, those interested in the film industry migrate to other countries to learn, and later return with their new wealth of knowledge. That is why Russian cinema is surpassing itself every day and each new production that is released is less flawed."[24]

Initially hesitant to criticize, perhaps intuiting that shouldering the blame as a director would be better received by the local film press than expressing a foreign director's negative assessment of local labor, Boytler nevertheless gestures toward difficulties facing filmmakers in the transition to sound. Mexican cinematographers would soon overcome these difficulties through both cultural and institutional transformations, as emerging talents soon received greater support at home, and some also sought out training abroad, but until then, foreigners would dominate lighting on set. Of Boytler's eight sound features, only three were shot by Mexican cinematographers: the Cantinflas films *Así es mi tierra* (*This Is My Country*, 1937) and *Águila o sol* (*Eagle or Sun*, 1937), with Víctor Herrera, and the director's last, *Amor prohibido* (*Forbidden Love*, 1945), with Carrasco. The rest were all filmed by Alex Phillips.[25]

Working together on *Mano a mano* (*Hand to Hand*, 1932), *La mujer del puerto, El tesoro de Pancho Villa* (*The Treasure of Pancho Villa*, 1935), *Celos* (*Jealousy*, 1936), and *El capitán aventurero* (*The Adventurous Capitan*, 1939), Phillips helped Boytler shape the films' distinctive visual styles, most notably (for critics) in *La mujer del puerto* and, to a lesser degree, *Celos*, while also attending to genre conventions through the use of specific lighting strategies. In my analyses of these films, I both broadly discuss lighting strategies serving the films' distinct diegeses and use close formal analysis of key sequences. Through this zooming in and out, I argue that Phillips formed a unique relationship with Boytler by confronting the narrative demands of each film while he also employed techniques that were prevalent in his collaborations with other directors going as far back as projects with Al Christie (in silent comedies such as the 1925 *Madame Behave* and talkie race films such as 1929's *The Framing of the Shrew*) and as recently as contemporaneous work on movies like *El tigre de Yautepec* (The Tiger of Yautepec, dir. Fernando de Fuentes, 1933) and *Juarez y Maximiliano* (dirs. Miguel Contreras Torres and Raphael J. Sevilla, 1933). If the influence of Hollywood training on Mexican filmmakers in the 1930s has been well established in film history, Mexican film historiography—understandably so, given the difficulties of studying the period, particularly in the pre-digital age—has not sufficiently attended to the formal contributions of workers like Alex Phillips.

Phillips's work with Arcady Boytler on five features spanning seven years—malleable, even formative years for the Mexican film industry—is usually tethered to *La mujer del puerto*. Although understandable, given its commercial and, subsequently, critical success (all too frequently connecting Boytler to Eisenstein, exploiting the coincidence of their shared nationality at the expense of much more immediate influences), it is, well, also somewhat paradoxical.[26] Like Phillips's, Boytler's cinematic roots originated in comedy, and was generically rhizomatic in his filmmaking. Like Víctor

Herrera, Phillips had much liberty in his collaborations with Boytler.[27] Throughout his work with Boytler, Phillips used lighting strategies he first learned in Hollywood that provided the right mood for the story.[28] This freedom, however, came within particular limitations imposed by his role as cinematographer in the Mexican film industry in the early sound period: in particular, adherence to the director's technical script (which usually, however, had been prepared by a technical director) detailing the type of shot and its angle within each scene. With his work already framed by José Benavides in *El tesoro de Pancho Villa* and Benavides and Roberto Gavaldón in *Celos*, Phillips crafted the films' individual visual styles with light and shadow.

In many ways, *Mano a mano* is representative of Phillips's collaborations with Boytler. Produced by José Alcayde's short-lived company México Nuevo Studio and filmed partly in the studio (at the Compañía Nacional Productora de Películas) and partly on location (in the Valley of Mexico), the short feature (*mediometraje*) premiered on December 10, 1932, as a part of a program with *La edad de amar* (*The Age for Love*, dir. Frank Lloyd, 1931) at the "Cines del Primer Circuito" ("First Circuit Movie Theaters"): the Granat, Odeón, and Monumental.[29] Much like Boytler's later films, *Mano a mano* is a popular movie to which (at times tenuous) artistic labels were attached in its anticipated reception, which were subsequently perpetuated after its release. Several months before its premiere, a *Filmográfico* article contends, "Our producers not only have cared about making films for 'grown-ups,' who go to movie theaters dedicated to the seventh art in search of psychological themes, intense dramas of passion, morbid emotions that we mortals so like. . . . For this time, 'short people' as well as their progenitors will like the recent filmed work *Mano a mano*."[30] Its broad appeal would also be framed within nationalistic terms, something visually evident through stereotypically Mexican publicity stills in the subsequent piece in *Filmográfico*, "*Mano a mano* . . . We Plan on Meeting."[31] Similar lines of criticism continued into its post-release reception. Several days after its premiere, *Exélsior* reports, "the Mexican public, which embraces movies made in Mexico with true enthusiasm, has literally filled on Saturday and Sunday the theaters exhibiting 'Mano a mano,' demonstrating a marked evolution of the once prevailing criteria of seeing with indifference what is ours."[32] Similarly, a program distributed at its rerelease at the Cine Goya on February 16, 1933, tellingly describes the film as a "sensational artistic event" that "makes the soul of *la Raza* vibrate with intense emotion. It is not a cinematic rehearsal, it is not a *pinino* [the first steps of a child]. It is something defined that brings to light the advances of Mexico in the Seventh Art."[33] Emphasizing *Mano a mano*'s artistic merits and contributions to national culture, the film's reception seems to intentionally minimize its entertainment value.

Mano a mano is a melodrama that explores moral corruption and the redemptive nature of love.[34] Having lost everything in a game of cards, Manuel (René Cardona) attempts to use his sister Anita (Carmen Guerrero) to get to the fortune of his purported friend Armando (Miguel Ángel Ferriz). The three return to Armando's unattended ranch, which had become threatened by bandits. Using ranch festivities (a *charreada,* a bullfight, and some cockfighting) as their opportunity to take leave, Manuel and Anita escape, only to struggle without water. Manuel is found by the bandits, and Anita by Armando. The malevolent forces band together and attack the hacienda. Armando is injured, but the bandits are run off or, like Manuel, killed. With her innocence established, Anita and Armando enjoy a happy ending, punctuated by the film's musical performance, Los trovadores Tamaulipecos' *canciones rancheras* "Mano a mano" ("Hand to Hand") and "Siempre me dices que sí" ("You Always Tell Me Yes").[35]

Phillips's work on *Mano a mano* suggests two ways in which he would impact cinematography in Mexico. His experience in Hollywood is clear in the exterior work on *Mano a mano.* Recalling Boytler's and Phillips's observations of a "land of color" with "inexhaustible natural resources," *Mano a mano*'s exteriors were one of the film's attractions. Not only are the action sequences on horseback shot extremely adeptly, even artistically at times (particularly those in which Phillips employs framing strategies quite common in his early sound period films), but also these beautiful landscapes prefigure one of the hallmarks of Mexican cinematography, which is too often ascribed to another cinematographer, to another collaboration. "In his work for [Emilio] Fernández, [Gabriel] Figueroa had constructed a new national identity by associating the Mexican people with the grandeur of the Mexican landscape."[36] Long left in the shadow of Figueroa, especially his work in the 1940s with Fernández, Phillips (and Boytler) prefigured the ways in which the landscapes of Mexico would come to be used in national cinema. This important aspect of Phillips's work was eventually recognized by contemporaneous criticism. For example, an anticipatory article in *El Exhibidor* states, "A film of *charros,* horses, and gunshots in the style of the famous cowboy films with which some North American producers have obtained abundant revenue, has just been filmed in this capital. Photography in the care of

Alex Phillips, who managed this time to capture very beautiful landscapes and effects that will greatly please the public."[37]

Equally important to the emerging Mexican film industry was how Phillips photographed its female stars. In an exchange early in the film in which Anita and Manuel, arguing, are overheard by Armando, Guerrero has been left by herself. Continuing the sequence's lighting treatment, which had shot the glamorous, if morally suspect, siblings in a similar way, Anita is lit relatively flatly, with a glowing backlight. Following a shot that panned and then dollied so as to direct the spectator to the conflicted love interest, this shot at once depicts Guerrero's beauty and Anita's interior thoughts. Though often shot from strange angles by Boytler, Carmen Guerrero's close-ups in *Mano a mano* hint at how Phillips's experience with portrait photography and *foto fijas* (stills) would impact how actresses were to be filmed from the early sound period well into the *Época de oro*.

La mujer del puerto, the second film on which Alex Phillips collaborated with Arcady Boytler, is commonly considered one of the masterpieces of the early sound period in Mexican cinema. It is almost certainly the film for which both director and cinematographer are best known. *La mujer del puerto*'s eventual place within Mexican film historiography was foreshadowed by the reports about the film that appreared during its production, which began in México Films' studios in November 1933. It was a film so anticipated by critics that it would have seemed almost impossible to think that it would not be a success. A *Filmográfico* feature, "Arcady Boytler Director of 'La mujer del puerto,'" gestures toward this anticipation.[38] Written by Roberto Cantú Robert (under the pseudonym of Denegri), perhaps the most influential Mexican film journalist of the 1930s, it primarily focuses on Boytler's "strong spirit, modeled in the crucible of life." His "refined artistic taste," visually emphasized in a photograph with Eisenstein, and cosmopolitan experiences are suggestive, but so is his work on *Mano a mano*, "a movie that currently is among those that has given the most money to its producers." "Boytler is an author and a poet," whose most recent work, *Joyas de México* (Gems of Mexico), was produced by Warner Bros and "is exhibited quite successfully abroad."[39] If *La mujer del puerto* is now regarded as one of the early classics of Mexican art cinema, it also promised to be a hit at the box office. And it was.

Perhaps the most suggestive review of *La mujer del puerto* was published in the February 1934 issue of *Filmográfico*. "A Mexican Film Establishes a School," begins bombastically, "Faint will be the praise made

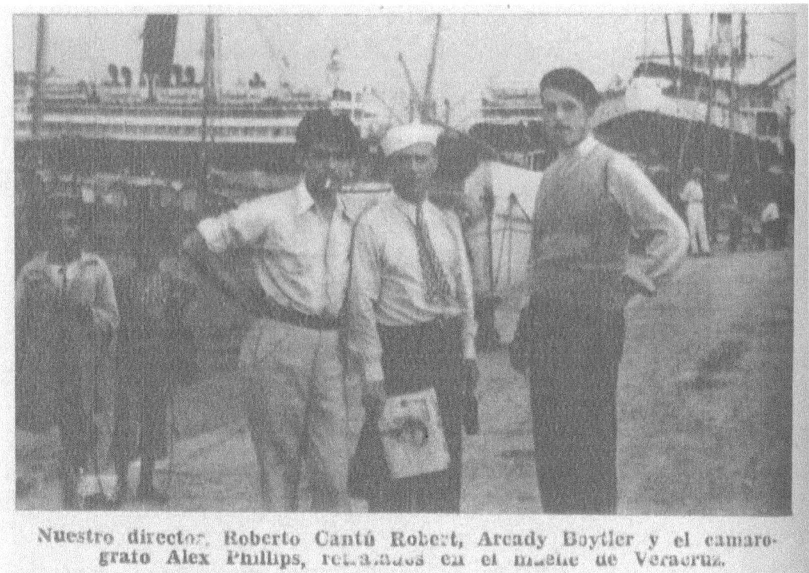

Figure 5.2. Boytler and Phillips talk with film journalist Roberto Cantú Robert on the set of *La mujer del puerto*. *Filmográfico*, December 1933.

in these columns of the first film produced by Eurindia Films, 'THE WOMAN OF THE PORT.'"[40] In the next paragraph it continues, "In this film, many reasons come together to make it not only the best film produced in Mexico, but we dare to say that those produced by foreign companies that can overcome it are counted, well, with fingers." The review focuses its attention on the film's stars: Andrea Palma, subject of a profile in the previous issue of the magazine, and Domingo Soler, "one of the most prominent members of the Soler dynasty."[41] Following the largely binary interests of film criticism in Mexico at the time, the review shifts from stars to director, contending, "The plot is of a dramatic tension of which filmmaker Boytler's directorial talent knows how to take advantage and he gives it enormous production value, something unusual in most of the films produced to today in Mexico." In its praise of the film, the review demonstrates a productive tension:

> It is, without a doubt, the best Mexican film produced in our studios with the distinctive feature that neither *charros* nor bandits appear in it, making our beauties shine without having

> to turn to such exploited matters in its plot. "La mujer del Puerto" is an international film, which, as it takes place in the port of Veracruz, could well have been recorded in Shanghai or in Conchinchina.

It is an achievement of national cinema, but one that eschews national stereotypes. It calls for a kind of nationalist cosmopolitanism that, to that time, had yet to appear in Mexican cinema.

La mujer del puerto, in some ways, was received so positively because it allowed critics to envision new possibilities for Mexican cinema. In "'La Mujer del Puerto' is an Excellent Mexican Film," *Mundo cinematográfico* (one of *Filmográfico*'s principal competitors) centers on Palma and her emergent star ("the first actress of national cinema").[42] In its report of a private screening in the *sala del teatro* Regis, about which many reports were written, *Mundo cinematográfico* shows its desire not only to have an industry that produces good films, but also one that produces stars. In *El Universal*, the film is described as "an effort that deserves to be rewarded with the audience's benevolent applause."[43] More tellingly, it is reported

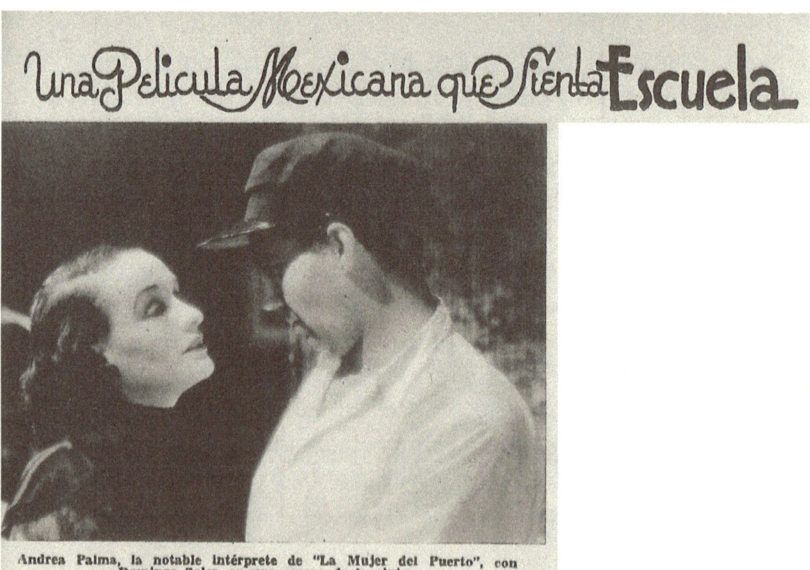

Figure 5.3. *La mujer del puerto* makes possible a new school of Mexican cinema. *Filmográfico*, February 1934.

that Servando de la Garza, the production manager of Eurindia Films, took the print of *La mujer del puerto* from the private screening to Cuernavaca so that it could be shown to President Abelardo L. Rodríguez and to the *Jefe Máximo,* General Plutarco Elías Calles, Mexico's de facto ruler. It was a film that drew power closer. This is not to say that all reviews of *La mujer del puerto* were positive. In March 1934, *Filmográfico* published another review in which Adolfo Fernández Bustamante argues, "Of course, it is a film that has two aspects: one that was developed during the first phase where the action is slow, monotonous, and that of the second part, full of drama, intense, sober."[44] He harshly criticizes its first part, whose three sequences are long and boring. "With a little more exacting scissors, it would have become a great film. All films, even foreign ones, have defects, and that's why, even if they have them, it does not reduce their value." He does, however, come to the conclusion that "[i]t is one of the films that can be shown abroad without diminishing our prestige."

Critical enthusiasm for *La mujer del puerto* continued beyond its initial run in theaters in Mexico City. Looking back on 1934 for *Filmográfico*, Esteban V. Escalante placed it among the six best pictures of the year, along with *La sangre manda* (*The Call of the Blood*, dir. Bohr, 1933), *El compadre Mendoza* (dir. de Fuentes, 1933), *Corazón bandolero* (*Bandit's Heart*, dir. Sevilla, 1934), *Dos monjes* (*Two Monks*, dir. Juan Bustillo Oro, 1934), and *Cruz Diablo.*[45] He concludes, "Of the seven photodramas mentioned, we put 'La Mujer del Puerto' in first place because of its beautiful and touching plot, its direction, its photography, its sound, its acting, and its staging." This critical enthusiasm, alive and well today, also extended beyond the mid-1930s. In 1942, for example, *Cinema Reporter* noted, "It seems a lie but a Mexican movie filmed in 34 still fills the theaters; we refer to 'La Mujer del Puerto.'"[46]

Drawing not only from Guy de Maupassant's short story "Le port" but also Leo Tolstoy's "Natasha," *La mujer del puerto* uses screenwriter Guz Águila's literary inspirations to craft a serious psychological drama. Initially set in Córdoba, a small city in the interior in the state of Veracruz, the film centers on Rosario (Andrea Palma). Rosario is seduced by her beau Victorio (Francisco Zárraga). While she is caring for her ill father Antonio (Fabio Acevedo), Victorio kisses another woman at the local carnival. The doctor visits Antonio and prescribes medicine they cannot afford. With no one else to turn to, Rosario visits her father's boss Don Basilio (Antonio Polo), who tries to take advantage of her. Victorio's betrayal is later discovered and leads to Antonio's death. Rosario, meanwhile, visits the

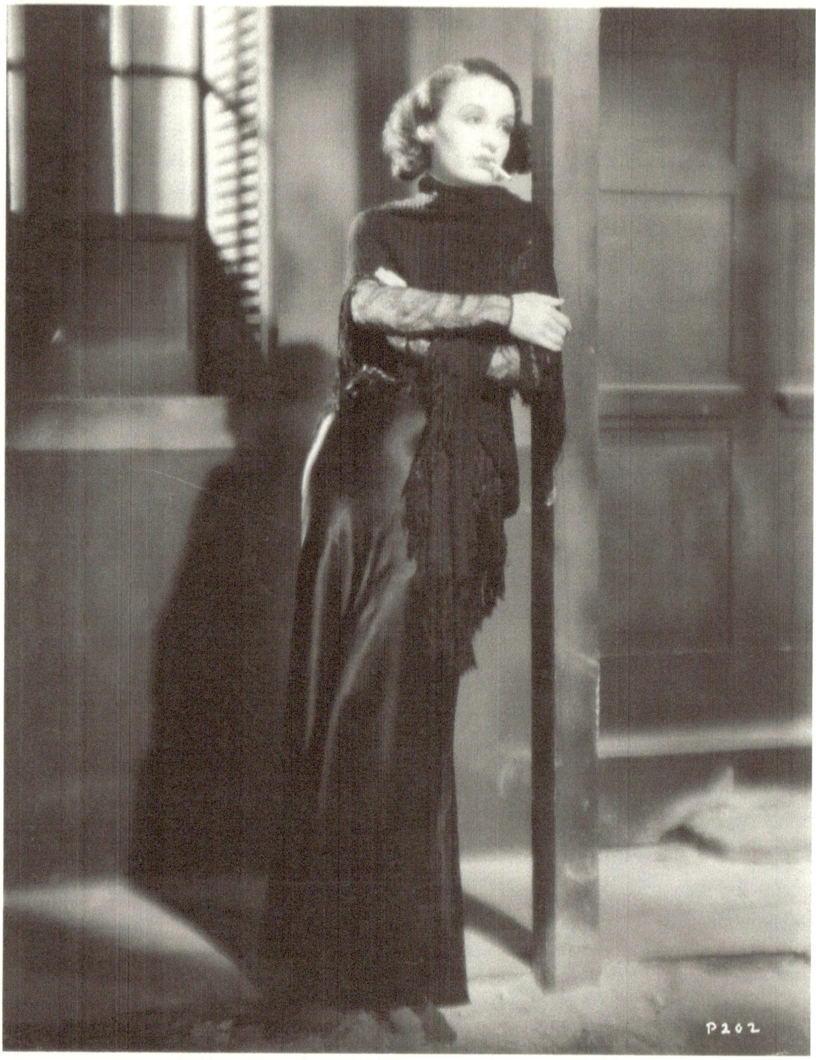

Figure 5.4. One of the most iconic images of Mexican cinema: Rosario (Andrea Palma) smoking a cigarette on the street in *La mujer del puerto*. Courtesy of Mil Nubes-Foto.

pharmacy; the pharmacist takes pity on her and gives her the medicine. She arrives home, only to find her father's body lying at the foot of the stairs as gossipy neighbors look on voyeuristically. No one accompanies her in the funeral procession. Walking behind a horse-drawn hearse, Rosario macabrely encounters carnival revelers. Hysterically, she implores them to stop. Eventually, they all lugubriously join her. She goes alone, however, to the cemetery, where she is met by Basilio. *La mujer del puerto* dissolves to the *Tegucigalpa*, a ship flying under the Honduran flag. Sailors discuss home, but one—Alberto (Domingo Soler)—concludes, "Us sailors don't have a home, though." Finally, they dock in Veracruz. Joining up with people from around the world, as well as a few prostitutes, the sailors head to the Salón Nicanor. The dead streets soon become the living night, as dancing, music, revelry, alcohol, and sex are in the air inside the dive. The sequence dissolves to the port, soon superimposed by an image of the *femme fatale* Rosario smoking a cigarette. Soon thereafter, Lina Boytler sings "Vendo placer" ("I Sell Pleasure") from a window to a superimposed montage of Rosario's experiences as a prostitute since she was forced into sex work. Alberto's attention is immediately drawn to her. Eventually, Rosario evocatively ascends the stairs, directing her gaze

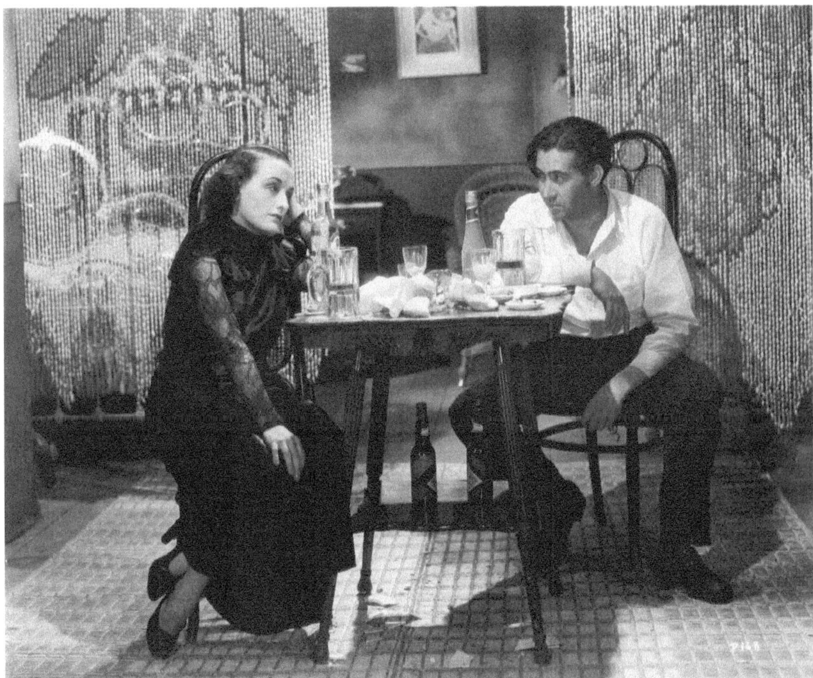

Figure 5.5. Rosario (Andrea Palma) and Alberto (Domingo Soler) before they become conscious of their misfortune in *La mujer del puerto*. Courtesy of the Colección Filmoteca UNAM, Filmoteca de la Universidad Nacional Autónoma de México.

toward Alberto. He follows. Night becomes day, and the two talk evasively. Still drunk, they come to realize that they are siblings. They embrace each other, horrified of their incestuous night of passion. Overcome, Rosario leaves Salón Nicanor and runs in fits and starts to the wharf, then to the pier. She steps out onto its rocks, where she is consumed by the ocean's waves. Alberto arrives in time to find nothing more than a shred of her clothing. He falls to his knees, crying.

In "Of National Cinema," his review of Mexican films released in 1934, Esteban V. Escalante writes, "best photography, Alex Phillips." Of the six films put forth as the best of the year, Phillips shot all but two (*El compadre Mendoza* was photographed by Ross Fisher and *Dos monjes* by Agustín Jiménez, in his first credit).[47] Phillips's work on *La sangre manda*, *Corazón bandolero*, and *Cruz Diablo* was notable, but his painting with light and shadow on *La mujer del puerto* almost certainly helped him earn this accolade.[48] In pieces such as Antonio Acevedo V.'s "La mujer del puerto," the film's aesthetic and cinematographic triumphs were frequently ascribed to Boytler, who, in Acevedo's essay is compared to Eastern European creative geniuses (Pudovkin, Sagan, von Sternberg, and, of course, Eisenstein).[49] He concludes, "Eurindia Films has opened a school. Arcady Boytler is the teacher." Among other who deserve praise, he notes, "Phillips for his colossal cinematographic work." Acevedo's intervention opened a line of criticism that has continued within Mexican film historiography. *La mujer del puerto* and, more generally, Boytler's filmography are placed within the context of art films, especially European, as opposed to commercial Hollywood movies. De la Vega, for example, gestures toward avant-garde movements of the 1920s such as "the so-called French impressionist school," the Soviet school, and New Objectivity, as well as D. W. Griffith's "North American classicism."[50] He continues, "The amalgam worked very well and, in fact, *La mujer del puerto*, came to signify as well Boytler's declared homage to cinematic avant-gardes emerging from countries that had formed part of his long pilgrimage through Europe and America."

The diegetic unevenness of *La mujer del puerto* is easy to overlook because of the film's cinematography. In its close-ups, Phillips's work as a still photographer is particularly apparent. Some forty years after shooting the film, Andrea Palma recalled, "For *La mujer del puerto* they decided to hire Alex Phillips, who was considered *todo un señor* (quite a man) in Hollywood. He was a specialist in close ups. I noticed it immediately, because when I saw the tests, I wondered, 'From where did that man extract beauty I do not have?' And he said, 'The skull. The skull is worth millions.' He was fascinated by my face. It was a great advantage!"[51] Phillips's expressive, glamorous lighting of Palma is visible throughout the film. Its opening sequence, which culminates in the two lovers lying together in the grass, is particularly poetic. With out of focus grass slightly obscuring the frame, Phillips uses a back light to draw attention to Rosario's elegant hair. This sequence draws to a close with Rosario and Victorio lost to darkness as Phillips and Boytler focus on the skies behind the young lovers returning to town. Similar to Phillips's work in other films, here we see the skies that are so well known in classical Mexican cinema. The innocence of their moment in the grass contrasts deeply with her lighting in the second half of the film. The use of effect lighting, a street lamp in particular, helps visually to express the changes Rosario has experienced since her fall from grace.

Boytler emphasizes the importance of the collaborative process in another *Filmográfico* feature. Even though his *La mujer del puerto* contract stipulated "'THE DIRECTOR' will have absolute authority in the artistic part of the film," Boytler entrusted his technicians with great responsibility.[52] In "Boytler, the Great Director" he observes, "In any way, this film has afforded me the opportunity to become known and I think, modesty aside, that my work in 'La Mujer del Puerto' would have meant nothing were it not for the collaboration of elements that the producers put at my disposal."[53] Interventions on the film's cinematography tend to perpetuate the idea that Boytler is a visionary auteur, much like his compatriot Eisenstein, while forcing Phillips into the shadow as a technical craft worker if, in fact, he is discussed at all. Authorship of the moving image is ascribed to the director, which is to say, the cinematographer's work is subsumed into the figure of the *auteur* by these critics. Emerging out of this film criticism of the early 1930s, these discussions continue into contemporary scholarship as understandings passed down to the next generation. Phillips's work painting with light on *La mujer del puerto* fades into the background, obscured to the extent that it is rendered almost imperceptible. Boytler, however, brings these film workers into the center of the frame. Responding to an unprinted question, he continues, "Yes, that is also true, but we directors must count on the fifty percent of the work that must be developed and interpreted by the many elements related to the production of a film." Perhaps betraying a lack of modesty as he downplays the roles other workers and collaborators play in making a film, Boytler acknowledges others' key contributions on a movie such as *La mujer del puerto*. "[T]he Russian with a Mexican soul," as he is described, argues that "elements identified with the seventh art" should be well remunerated, as the development of national cinema depends on producers providing adequate investment in their films rather than looking to make easy money on bad movies. In early 1934, this would seem to suggest that additional foreign labor was required in the short term, until technicians were adequately trained, tempted by pay. Boytler concludes the interview by divulging that he would make two films in 1934 with budgets exceeding one hundred thousand pesos. (To that time, only *Santa* had exceeded that figure, by twenty five thousand pesos; the budget of *Mano a mano* was seventeen thousand pesos.)[54] Neither film would be made.

Premiering on July 4, 1935, in the Cine Principal, Boytler's next film (and his next collaboration with Phillips) was not *El primo Basilio* (Cousin Basilio) as had been expected, but rather *El tesoro de Pancho Villa*.[55] Nearly forgotten today, despite attracting heavy interest from periodicals such as *Revista de Revistas* and being a fascinating film in its own right, *El primo Basilio* aspires to be a serious psychological drama adapted from foreign literature (in this case, Portuguese author José Maria de Eça de Queirós's 1878 novel *O Primo Basílio*). Eurindia Films, however, was unable to secure contracts with the production team and, consequently, developed the film with Carlos de Nájera as director and Gabriel Figueroa and Alvin Wyckoff as cinematographers (who were ultimately unable to recreate the commercial success of *La mujer del puerto*).[56] Roberto Cantú Robert reported, "Arcady Boytler tell us, categorically, that his separation from 'Eurindia Films' is a fact. Thus, 'El primo Basilio' will be directed by Carlos Nájera. He tells us that he is putting the final touches on 'Celos,' a work he hopes to soon direct. The company that will finance it is not yet known."[57] Rumors swirled around a potential agreement, and Boytler and Phillips would soon begin working with a new producer, Felipe Mier.[58] *Celos*, however, would have to wait.

El tesoro de Pancho Villa is a genre film meant to appeal to a broad audience.[59] Filmed quickly at (and later processed by) México-Films, Jorge Stahl's studios and laboratory, and on location in the Coapa hacienda, which today is a heavily urbanized area of Mexico City, it little resembled its antecedent. Perhaps a response to *Viva Villa!* (dirs. Jack Conway, Howard Hawks, and William Wellman, 1934), *El tesoro de Pancho Villa* is a Western of sorts that revolves around treasure buried by the *villista* División del Norte after a defeat.[60] Before fleeing to the United States, Chemo

(Antonio Frausto) is the sole survivor of a gun battle and as a result is the only person who knows the precise location in which the treasure is buried. Barely surviving his border crossing, he begins working for the *gringo* rancher Smith (A. M. Williams) whose beautiful daughter Mary (Victoria Blanco) comes to constitute (for a time, at least) one angle of a love triangle with the ignoble foreman, Jeff (Carlos Cabello), who comes to challenge Chemo for the treasure. Later, Mary's eventual—and, within the logic of the film, more correct—partner appears: Mexican rancher Arturo (Raúl de Anda). The film received generally positive reviews from critics, but seems to have had only a fleeting impact on audiences.[61] In a particularly interesting review published in *Revista de Revistas*, Escalante (writing under the pseudonym Hugo del Mar) argues that *El tesoro de Pancho Villa* "is far from what [Boytler] did in the unforgettable film *La mujer del puerto*, not because we have observed it to be weak [*floja*], but because the plot, gunshots and horse chases, does not have the emotivity and realism of that production of Eurindia Films."[62] *El tesoro de Pancho Villa* might not be weak, but del Mar makes its lightness into a point of critical contention; it is not a heavy, serious, artistic film, but one guided by entertainment, by commercial interests.

With melodramatic twists and turns, action and romance, *El tesoro de Pancho Villa*'s genre-bending makes it visually complex. A review notes that "[t]he photography is admirable and we are convinced that at the moment Alex Phillips is the best cinematographer we have."[63] By employing shifting and often high-contrast lighting styles that better serve different kinds of scenes tied to specific genres, Phillips seeks the right mood for the story, interpreting and expressing the film's diegesis with light. Phillips's photography in the film incorporates different kinds of low-key lighting strategies often used in disparate genres. In so doing, Phillips adheres to lighting conventions established in Hollywood in the 1920s that would continue into the 1930s (and beyond). There are moments, however, when *El tesoro de Pancho Villa*'s expressive lighting is more reflective of a particular genre.[64] In these instances, Phillips uses light to tell a particular aspect of the film's story. Take, for instance, a romantic scene between Chemo and Mary on the plains in the second act. Recalling a *noche americana* (day for night) scene from *La mujer del puerto*, as well as frames from *La última canción* and *Juarez y Maximiliano*, and maybe even anticipating *Doña Bárbara* (dir. de Fuentes, 1943), this scene depicts the protagonist's unrequited love, allowing spectators to see how Chemo feels. Of the ways in which Phillips does this, perhaps what is most notable are the skies. The sequence's high contrasts silhouette Chemo and Mary, especially in full and medium shots, thus allowing the spectators to experience one of Mexico's "inexhaustible natural resources," the skies for which Gabriel Figueroa would eventually become famous.

Celos's final shot is a close-up, using expressive lighting to communicate visually a woman destroyed. By expressive I do not mean to refer back to German expressionism, but rather to point toward the 1935 essay "Creating Moods with Light," in which Victor Milner argues, "The Cinematographer should train himself to think directly in terms of lighting. . . . [T]he really important thing is to be able to form such a clear mental picture of the light-treatment of a scene that the lighting itself expresses the scene's mood, tempo and character as clearly as do dialog and action."[65] Perhaps not the film's most memorable shot, it nonetheless is representative of how lighting strategies employed throughout the film shed light on its characters' psychological states.[66] With the notable exception of melodramatic, almost proto-*noirish* night scenes, several nearly social-realist close-ups of patients at the psychiatric hospital, and soft-style pictorialist close-ups, moderate contrast, which Negrete, curiously, deems as naturalistic and de la Vega ambiguously describes as expressionist, is utilized throughout the film.[67] *Celos* depicts the slow descent into insanity of Dr. Armando Torrescano (Fernando Soler). Consumed by jealousy over his wife Irene (Vilma Vidal), whom he saves after her failed suicide attempt, and her nonromantic relationships, not only with his protégé Federico (Arturo de Córdova) but also with his loyal assistant Sebastián (Emilio Fernández), the doctor eventually hangs himself.

Production notes regarding *Celos* were widely published. Emerging first as Boytler, Phillips, and their team were noted as moving on from Eurindia Films, and even before reports of their filming *El tesoro de Pancho Villa* for Felipe Mier's new production company, *Celos* drew the attention of local journalists.[68] It is possible that this increased attention arose from Boytler's return to filming more artistic movies in the fashion of *La mujer del puerto*, something about which the director spoke in an interview with Escalante. A similar piece published in *Filmográfico* states:

> From the lands of Lenin came to us, a long time ago, Arcady Boytler, a man of great artistic temperament, as he left displayed in the direction of "La mujer del puerto." Boytler, in his thirst for emotions, reaches lands few of us understand and takes advantage of the beauties that he encounters on his steps to

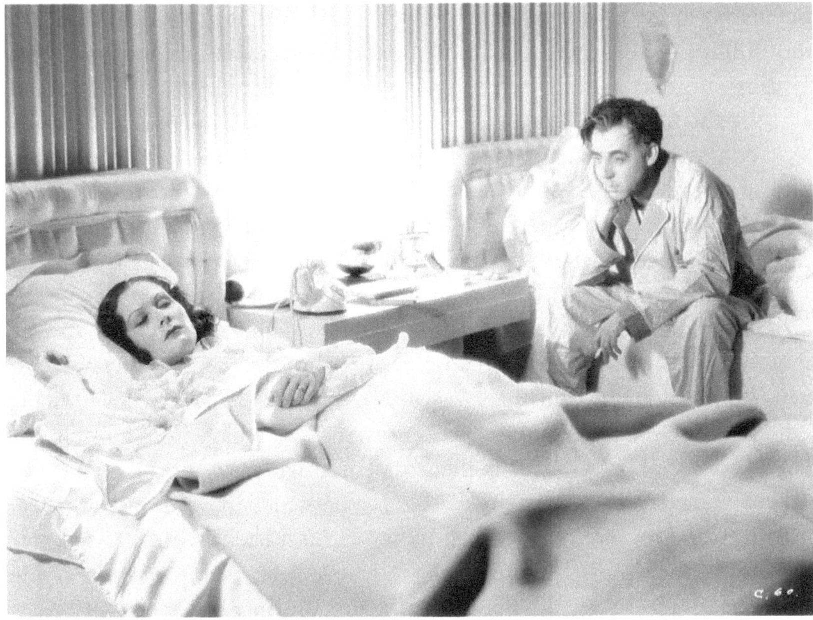

Figure 5.6. Phillips' suggestive lighting in *Celos*. Courtesy of Mil Nubes-Foto.

> model and present them, always always, in a pleasant, soulful [*sentimental*], and lasting way. This man has the ability of quick understanding. Always timely and ironic in his word. Soon he will direct "CELOS," a work owing to his imagination.[69]

Unlike his previous genre film, which, curiously, is generally more in line with Boytler's other works than *La mujer del puerto*, *Celos* was seen by some as a return to the director's authentic interests. That said, the increased attention in the press also may have been due to increased attention paid to publicity by the fledgling production company.[70] Most reports on the film centered on the film's actors, especially Vilma Vidal (brought from Spain by Boytler), but also Soler, Fernández, and newcomer de Córdova. Like many other of Boytler's films, it was filmed primarily in the Estudios México Films (with key exterior locations shot in places such as Toluca, in the case of the psychiatric hospital).[71] The review in *Revista de Revistas* argues, "For its rhythm of beauty and art, for the emotion that emerges from its scenes and the purity of technique with which it is made, *Celos* is a film that marks a flattering success in the process of building national cinematography." The film adds to Boytler's success in *La mujer del puerto*, and Phillips's photography is deemed to be "impeccable and uniform, with lighting in good taste and very praiseworthy quality."[72]

In the film's final sequence, Federico and Sebastián are accompanied by a doctor to visit Armando in the psychiatric hospital. Moving from natural lighting in the first scene, whose slight shadows on the left lead the viewer into the room, we see the simple image of a man. Hanging. Particularly in contrast with the rest of the film, which is visually striking, the use of light and shadow on an unadorned wall is moving. Using the latticing employed as a visual motif throughout the film—although not, notably, that of the gate into the room—the shot disorients the viewer *just enough* by overlaying the shadows of a grid and a lifeless body. Quickly cutting to the men's reactions at seeing Armando, which functions almost like a serial shot, the viewer is then presented with the horror they experience. Staged proscenium style, slightly darkened by a few additional steps into the room, and muddled by the natural backlighting, the viewer is presented with all three reactions. Cutting back to the room and the men's reactions—here, Boytler (as both director and editor) and Phillips use montage and cinematography in harmony—the portrait of Federico changes as he turns away (and into the light, allowing de Córdova's eyes to communicate his character's emotions), while Sebastian's remains fixed (profile lit by what is ostensibly natural light, and shadows beyond). The light of the mental hospital is replaced by the darkness of what is likely the Torrescano home. Similarly flat, without visual texture, the camera closes in on a grieving Irene, who is now lit in the foreground with high contrast so as to isolate her hand, brooch, and face. The film ends with a signature Phillips portrait, a close-up of a grieving widow that is at once somber and glamorous. It is less low-key than one might have imagined, but with low fill and little (if any) backlighting, Irene's face is lit camera right with the key. Recalling Milner's understanding of expressiveness, Phillips's cinematography clearly conveys the scene's drama and emotion to the viewer without the assistance of sound.

Boytler reunited with Phillips on *El capitán aventurero* after working with Herrera on the Cantinflas vehicles *Así es mi tierra* and *Águila o sol*. A prestige film with big box office aspirations, *El capitán aventurero* marked José Mojica's debut in Mexican cinema. Perhaps the brightest star of Hollywood's Spanish-language productions, Mojica brought charisma, gravity, talent, and screen presence not only as a singer (as a classically trained operatic tenor) but also as an actor. Reverberating on radio, records, and stage, his performances on-screen helped him become a bankable star throughout the region, able to open up other Latin American markets. Mojica was supported by other important figures: "the production company Cinematográfica Internacional, managed by Pedro Maus and Felipe Mier, formed around the cinéaste [i.e., Boytler] *un equipo de lujo* [an epic team] that included the famous essayist and poet Salvador Novo, the muralist Roberto Montenegro (who also had became friends with Eistenstein during the filming of *¡Qué viva México!*, and Alex Phillips, Manuel Castro Padilla, and José Rodríguez Granada."[73] News regarding the film began appearing in mid-1938 in film periodicals, including somewhat odd notes such as "Felipe Mier Provided a Meal," in which the producer is reported to have brought together figures such as screenwriter Novo, script supervisor Montenegro, and some of the other talents who collaborated on the film to discuss the name of the then-titled *Don Gil de Alcalá*.[74] Filmed between October 3 and November 26, 1938, on locations in Morelos and in the studios of México-Films and costing between four hundred and six hundred thousand pesos (then a record), *El capitán aventurero* was highly anticipated, as noted by *Cinema Reporter*: "1939 offers us two big hits: 'Don Gil de Alcalá' y la 'Casa del Ogro.'"[75]

El capitán aventurero was met with a positive critical reception, especially by *Cinema Reporter*.[76] Writing for the periodical, Manuel Horta describes its February 24 opening night at the Teatro Alameda thusly: "'El capitán aventurero' screened in an 'intimate' premiere for TWO THOUSAND PEOPLE, has before and above all a positive artistic dignity. It is the most inspiring film that has been pulled off in Mexico. Impeccable and of the best taste are film's sets, propriety, elegance, dazzling touches."[77] Set in the Viceroyalty of New Spain of the mid-eighteenth century, the film's diegesis is constructed so as to both showcase its talent and broadly appeal to audiences in Mexico and beyond. The film begins with the Spanish captain Don Gil de Alcalá (Mojica) and his loyal companion, the sergeant Carrasquilla (Carlos Orellana), coming upon the song of lovely young woman. Carmina (Manolita Saval), the goddaughter and ward of the *corregidor* Don Martín de Alhucenas (Eduardo Arozamena) and his wife Catalina (Sara García), laments her upcoming arranged marriage to Don Diego de Bustamante y Escalona (Alberto Martí). After coming again fortuitously upon information, Gil and Carrasquilla are able to thwart bandits' attempt to attack the stagecoach transporting Martín and Diego. Sensing the threat posed by Gil, whose good looks and charm have attracted Carmina's affection, Diego arranges for his lover, the marchioness Leonor de Cáceres y Acevedo (Margarita Mora), to seduce Gil. At a party arranged by the grateful *corregidor*, Gil and Carrasquilla are arrested due to Diego's subterfuge. Leonor, however, helps the pair flee. Eventually, Gil is apprehended at Leonor's. Threatened by the possibility of exile into indigenous lands, Gil is saved by Carrasquilla and a young boy. Gil encounters Diego and kills his rival in a sword duel. Again imprisoned, Gil is eventually freed by truth: not only was Diego the bandits' boss, but Gil is Martín's *hijo natural* (a child born out of wedlock). Freed from obstacles, Gil marries Carmina. All's well that ends well.

Phillips's cinematography in *El capitán aventurero* is often unobtrusive, almost invisible, only adopting higher contrast and stronger shadows in melodramatic scenes. This is to say that he employs genre/scene conventions typical of a costume drama like *El capitán aventurero*, which aims to allow spectators to enjoy imagined memories of the colo-

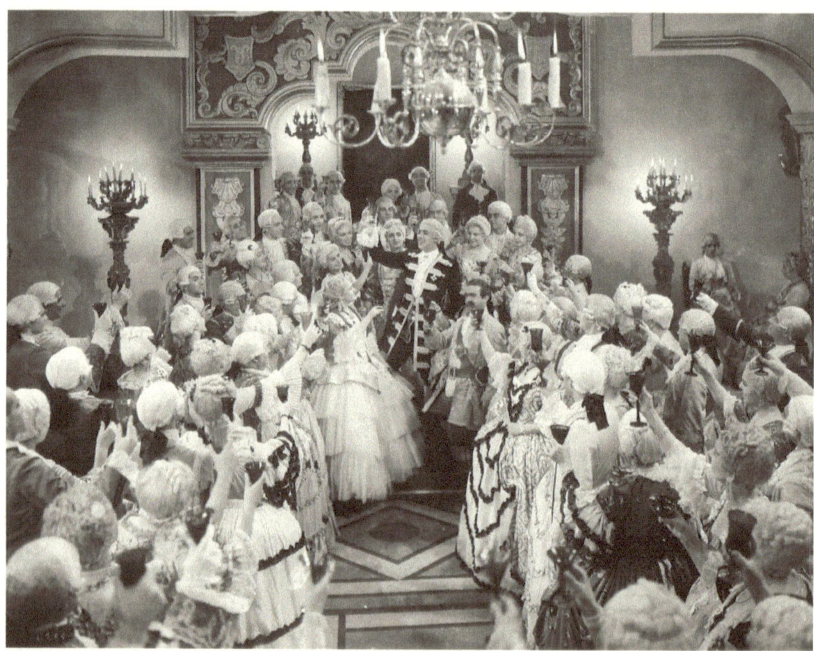

Figure 5.7. Phillips's lighting in *El capitán aventurero* directed attention to the historical melodrama's mise-en-scène and its star, José Mojica. Courtesy of Mil Nubes-Foto.

nial court, catalyzing praise for those, such as Montenegro, working on its mise-en-scène.[78] The little scholarly analysis written on the *El capitán aventurero*'s cinematography does the film scant justice. De la Vega notes that "[t]he commercial and artistic ambitions of the film became evident from its first shots: long shots and full shots that reproduce, in obvious Eisensteinian style, the 'majestic' landscapes of the Valley of Cuernavaca. From that moment, the uninterrupted display of sets, choreographies, costumes, and Phillips' photographic wonders hope to synthesize the sumptuous atmosphere of a whole era: luxury for luxury itself."[79] Recalling rather worn comparisons to Eisenstein, which do little to take into account Phillips's important work with landscapes, de la Vega directs attention toward lighting strategies used to spotlight period drama. Negrete focuses more closely, noting the film's use of high-key lighting and contrasting it with *La mujer del puerto*, arguing "there darkness and shadows prevail, here the brightness of day."[80] Brightness also pierces the night, as *El capitán aventurero*'s courtly interiors are generally luminous, shot flatly with high-key lighting flooding its spaces. Phillips's lighting is almost invisible, making other aspects of the film more immediately conspicuous, especially those generic conventions of costume drama.

There are several exceptions in the film, however, when its story dictates the use of low-key lighting. One example happens early, when a lascivious Carrasquilla takes advantage (somewhat willingly, as underscored by playful strings) of a servant he calls *luciérnaga* (firefly), only to be interrupted by five bandits who enter the stable to plot the stagecoach attack. The high contrast of low-key lighting is used to imply what might be done in the shadows and imbue the scene with romance, fleetingly, and drama. Conspiring in a circle, the bandits' faces betray their treachery. Later in the film, low-key lighting is used to a much different effect, albeit one that also serves the story. In it, Mojica's Gil serenades Carmina with the habanera "Todas las mañanitas" ("Every Little Morning"). Cutting initially between Gil outside and Carmina inside, the sequence appeals to different constructions of glamour.

El capitán aventurero did well, but did not prove to be the box office smash anticipated by both its producers and the specialized press.[81] A few days before the film's premiere, *Pantallas y Escenarios*, a magazine published in Guadalajara, wrote, "Soon, we will have on our cinemas' screens the most expensive film that national cinema has made [six hundred thousand pesos]. . . . With this cast, the producers dreamt not of what they will have to lose because they saw in the singer a guarantee for their interests, as it must be in dealing with an original theme and a stupendous cast, as well as the lavishness and propriety with which the work has been put together."[82] It is this propriety, this adherence to convention, that marks Phillips's collaborations with Boytler. In many ways, *El capitán aventurero* is representative their work together on *Mano a mano*, *La mujer del puerto*, *El tesoro de Pancho Villa*, and *Celos*. In each of these films, Boytler and Phillips sought visual styling that furthered the films' plots. Often, but not always, lighting in these films was less reminiscent of the ostensible expressionism of European (especially Russian) avant-gardes and more the commercialism of Hollywood. Or, perhaps better yet, we should recall what Boytler told *Filmográfico* in a 1933 survey of key figures of national cinema: "I believe that not all films should be too vernacular so that they are accepted and understood in other Spanish-speaking countries. . . . I have a lot of faith in Mexican cinema. Here, I feel like I am in my home."[83] Though perhaps overshadowed by their most enduring, their most visible success, *La mujer del puerto*, Phillips and Boytler's films demonstrated flexibility and range.

A Forgotten Collaborator: Phillips and Fernando de Fuentes

The week after the publication of "Our Technicians and the Future of Mexican Cinema," which probes the marginalization of local cameramen after the arrival of sound film technologies, *Revista de Revistas* published a similarly named piece by Esteban V. Escalante in which he discussed the emerging national film industry with Fernando de Fuentes.[84] Closely tied to his Revolution Trilogy of *El prisionero 13* (*Prisoner 13*, 1933), *El compadre Mendoza*, and *Vámonos con Pancho Villa* (*Let's Go with Pancho Villa*, 1935), de Fuentes's eventual consecration was also inextricably linked to the transnational blockbuster *Allá en el Rancho Grande* (*Out on the Big Ranch*, 1936), which not only established the *comedia ranchera*, one of the dominant genres of classical Mexican cinema, but also Mexican national cinema itself, as García Riera, Castro Ricalde and Irwin, and others argue. For Escalante, the cineaste is emblematic of the possibilities of Mexican cinema: "Fernando de Fuentes, in the directorial field, is a clear product of our film industry. Without ever having been to Hollywood, he was initiated into cinematic technique with no more preparation than his intuition and his culture."[85] Working for Paramount's distribution agency in Mexico City, de Fuentes was credited with inventing *los títulos superpuestos* ("superimposed titles") that made U.S. productions more accessible to local audiences and being "a kind of messiah savior for foreign films."[86] Fernando de Fuentes was not only a national filmmaker who made movies for local audiences, but, effectively, he made the movies Mexican.

In the interview, Escalante surveys de Fuentes's opinions on key issues concerning the national film industry, especially in production and distribution. Drawing attention to the effects of undercapitalization of the film industry, which "with a little help by our government and the confidence of capital, in very little time could become one of our country's most important export industries," de Fuentes holds that filmmakers are doing the best they can with limited resources.[87] Cutting corners (fewer, imperfect takes, inadequate laboratories, etc.) adversely affects the Mexican film industry's ability to make films that meet the standards set by Hollywood. Eschewing Escalante's overt nationalism, conspicuous throughout but especially so in a question concerning perceived inept photography in recent films, de Fuentes pragmatically argues for a Mexican film industry controlled, eventually, by Mexicans. In a follow-up, of sorts, Escalante directly asks, "What do you believe to be the cause behind Mexican cameramen not being used by our producers?" De Fuentes's response is telling of an industry in transition. Initially blaming local cameramen for their own lack of opportunity, and empathizing with producers' risk aversion, de Fuentes nonetheless continues, "I am sure that the day when any of them shows a producer a developed reel or two (interiors or illuminated, naturally), he will be hired immediately. Everyone wants our film industry to be totally in the hands of Mexicans." Cinematography on his films, however, would remain in the hands of foreigners, at least partially, until 1936's *Allá en el Rancho Grande.*

By the time shooting of *El tigre de Yautepec* had begun in Morelos in September 1933, Alex Phillips had already shot five features in Mexico and de Fuentes had directed three films. Even though they had previously worked on John Auer's *Una vida por otra* (*One Life for Another*, 1932), de Fuentes's only cinematographer to that point was Ross Fisher. *Filmográfico* reports that "[t]he direction of 'El tigre de Yautepec' has been entrusted to Fernando de Fuentes, recognized as the 'ace' of our directors," and "Photography is under the charge of Alex Phillips," who, according to another piece, is "*lo mejorcito que tenemos por estos andurriales* [the best we have in this forsaken place]."[88] Like *Filmográfico*, which claims that "[e]verything makes us hope that 'El tigre de Yautepec' will come to

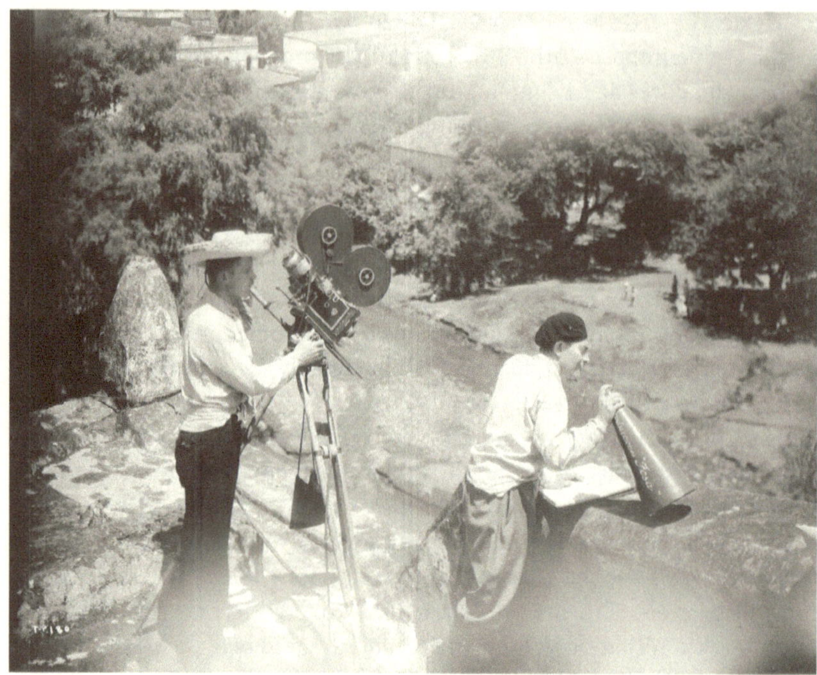

Figure 5.8. Alex Phillips filming with Fernando de Fuentes directing *El tigre de Yautepec*. Published in *Revista de Revistas*, the photograph was taken by Gabriel Figueroa. Courtesy of the Colección Filmoteca UNAM, Filmoteca de la Universidad Nacional Autónoma de México.

mark a new stage of orientation and success in the national industry," de Fuentes expects the film to be his greatest success, claiming that it "combines all the elements and factors that I would have liked to gather in a film such as: intense drama, action, romance, constant interest, and a wonderful Mexican color." *El tigre de Yautepec* takes place in the the mid-nineteenth century and pivots on the life of Pepito. Travelling with his well-to-do father, Pepito is kidnapped by a band of outlaws, *Los chacales* (The Jackals). Twenty years later, *Los plateados* (The Silver Ones), now terrorize the area, led by the fearsome El Tigre (Pepe Ortiz), also known as Julio. Julio falls in love with Dolores (Lupita Gallardo). His maternal figure (Consuelo Segarra), the suggestively named La Comancha, is eventually instrumental when she informs Pepito's mother Doña Lupita (Adria Delhort) that El Tigre is, in fact, Pepito. Doña Lupita and her daughter Dolores (Luis/El Tigre/Pepito's sister) attempt to save him from execution, but, mirroring his experience playing as a child, El Tigre takes the bullet. The film ends with superimpositions: Doña Lupita holding Pepito's body as Dolores wraps her arm around her mother, while drummers play and a church bell rings.

In anticipation of its November 22, 1933, premiere in the Cine Régis, *El tigre de Yautepec*'s production company, Producciones FESA (Films Exchange, S. A.), organized a private screening attended by *Revista de revista*'s Escalante. In an extended review of the film tellingly titled "Una orientación mexicanista en nuestra cinematografía" ("A Mexican[ist] Direction in Our Cinema"), Escalante argues that it opens up new possibilities for Mexican cinema, as it is based in "Mexicanism inspired by the beautiful legends of our past, so rich in episodes worthy of being brought to the silver screen."[89] And it is this imagined past, not the film, to which Escalante directs his attention, as he recounts the legend on which the film is based (accompanied by six publicity stills). Similar to

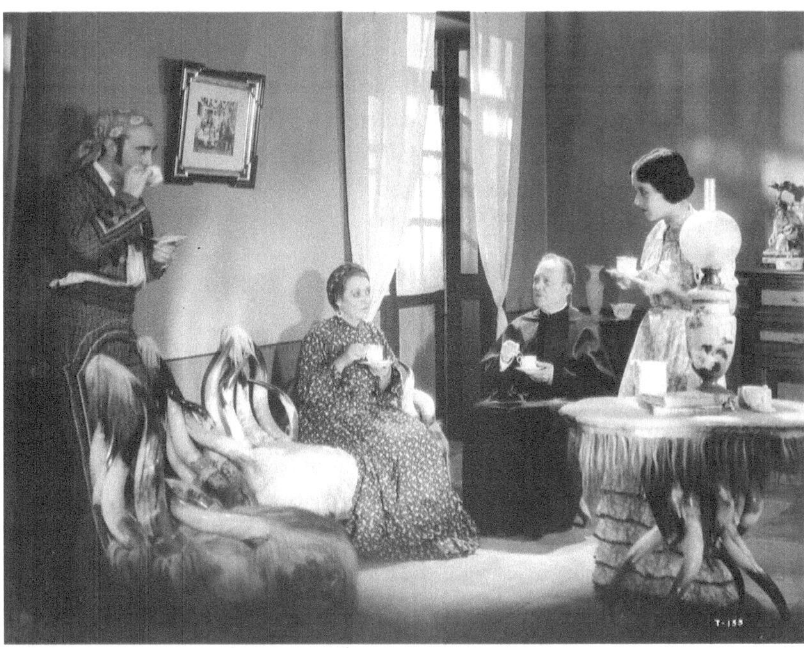

Figure 5.9. Contrastive lighting is used selectively in *El tigre de Yautepec*, especially interiors. Promotional photograph courtesy of Mil Nubes-Foto.

Escalante, Alejandro Campos Bravo argues for the promise shown by *El tigre de Yautepec*, "a period production of high cost."[90] It is not that Campos Bravo only argues that Mexican cinema will soon compete more fiercely in the domestic market, but also that "[i]t is essential that those who hold the tambourine in hand look a bit beyond their noses and think that, indeed, Mexican films can become in short time a first-rate product in the Spanish-speaking film market and, perhaps, even of others where other languages dominate." Following Campos Bravo's logic, *El tigre de Yautepec* is a film imbued with local color, but one that appeals to a kind of more widely shared nineteenth-century, postcolonial heritage.

In her review of *El tigre de Yautepec*, which appeared in *Ilustrado*, Luz Alba (a pseudonym used by Cube Bonifant in her film criticism) asserts that "[t]he national films made until today present a feature: they have the same virtues and suffer from the same deficiencies."[91] In great contrast with Escalante, who in his series had criticized the poor photography of recent films, Alba argues, "In effect, what they almost always possess is excellent photography, which means to say that in the production of our cinema the photographers are the most competent characters; and what they generally lack is good acting, especially when it comes to individual effort." She continues, "'El tigre de Yautepec' does not escape the first rule. Its photography is, at times, a succession of beautiful watercolors and, considered together, of the cleanest that has been done." Unlike many other critics, especially those of *Revista de Revistas* and *Filmográfico*, Alba does not praise de Fuentes, choosing instead to not even directly mention the director's name.

In her analysis of *El tigre de Yautepec*, Negrete touches upon three notable aspects of its cinematography: its framing, especially its use of high- and low-angle shots, uncommon in previous de Fuentes films (perhaps due to the immobility of the cameras used at the time); its camera movement, dominated by "pans, brief tilts, tracking shots with which some long takes are made up"; and its use of superimposition and the shot-reverse shot, which she claims was "a narrative element that was not yet of regular use in national cinematic discourse."[92] While she strays from what Phillips controlled on *El tigre de Yautepec*—as editor of his own films, de Fuentes would almost certainly have assembled the latter aspects—Phillips contributed to making them possible. This is particularly the case in abstracting and geometrizing framing strategies. Phillips's influence in *El tigre de Yautepec* is especially evident in his use idiosyncratic glamor lighting with Lupita Gallardo. Betraying his work not only in Hollywood in the 1920s but also as a still photographer, Phillips's use of backlighting and diffusion to blur the edges of Gallardo's Dolores contrasts with Ross Fisher's work on Carmen Guerrero's *tocaya* (homonym) in de Fuentes's *El compadre Mendoza*.[93] Unlike Fisher, who infrequently lights his Dolores differently than other characters, Phillips takes pains to employ the visual style of portraiture to soften his.[94] In a sequence midway through the film, Dolores and Julio discuss their love before he must depart. Even though Phillips may have been tempted to shoot Gallardo and Ortiz similarly—out of consideration of time or, perhaps, deference to a different lighting paradigm—Gallardo's Dolores is much more pictorial. Not only does Phillips employ glamour lighting in the foreground, especially through the use of a strong side-light on Gallardo, but he utilizes the heavy contrast of light and shadow (ostensibly the latticing of a gate, even though the lighting used in the medium long shots would make this impossible) to make the shot more visually complex. Ortiz is given neither. More in line with figure-lighting conventions of the late silent era than those emerging in Hollywood in the early 1930s that would come to mark classical cinema, Phillips adds depth to Dolores's characterization by using light to express her thoughts, her moods, her interiority.

In the year between the production of *El tigre de Yautepec* and *Cruz Diablo*, the next film on which Phillips collaborated with de Fuentes, the cinematographer would work on at least seven films—organized by production schedules, they are *Enemigos* (*Enemies*, dir. Urueta, 1933),[95] *La mujer del puerto*, *La sangre manda*, *Chucho el roto* (*Chucho, The Dandy*, dir. Gabriel Soria, 1934), *¿Quién mató a Eva?* (*Who Killed Eva?*, dir. Bohr, 1934), *Corazón bandolero*, and *Mujeres sin alma* (also known as *Venganza suprema*) (*Soulless Women*, dirs. Peón and Juan Orol)—and the director two [*El compadre Mendoza* and *El fantasma del convento* (*The Phantom of the Convent*, 1934)], both with Ross Fisher). Despite their very distinct paths throughout most of 1933 and 1934, the year in which each aforementioned film was released, *Cruz Diablo* marks a continuation of *El tigre de Yautepec*'s commercial, diegetic, and stylistic strategies. In it, the masked swashbuckler Cruz Diablo robs from the rich and gives to the poor. To aid the imprisoned Capitán Carlos (Juan José Martínez Casado), Cruz Diablo and Chacho (Vicente Oroná) impede the villainous Diego Barrera (Ramón Pereda), who passes for Count Luna, from marrying off his daughter Marcela (Lupita Gallardo) to an elderly nobleman. However, Carlos and Marcela love one another. Diego's plot is foiled, and Cruz

Diablo's true identity is revealed. Tragedy begets felicity, as a death allows Carlos and Marcela a happy ending.

Not unlike other big budget films, news of *Cruz Diablo*'s development was detailed in the film press from script to prerelease private screening.[96] Often focusing on production costs, especially of its elaborate sets, these updates finally reported Phillips's involvement after shooting had already begun.[97] In this sense, a *Jueves del Excélsior* column by Roberto Cantú Robert is illustrative, but it is also illuminating.[98] The caption of a still from the film reads: "The luxury and ostentatiousness of the sets lend a sumptuous frame to this scene from the film 'Cruz Diablo,' the most expensive film that has been made in Mexico, [produced] by Impulsora Cinematográfica, S.A. under the correct direction of Fernando de Fuentes." In the column, Cantú reports that representatives from Paramount were stunned by the film, concluding, "We never imagined that in Mexico they would be able to produce a film of the magnitude and importance of 'Cruz Diablo.'" In addition to triangulating anticipation for the film through Hollywood's praise, the column also reveals an important detail of its production: "As for the technical personnel, Mr. Paul H. Bush, general manager of Impulsora Cinematográfica, took good care in selecting those who, due to their previous merits, have earned highly favorable comments from the press and the public in general." Bush provided the emerging Mexican film industry with different forms of capital. In his work he employed cultural capital in the hopes of converting his knowhow into economic capital for himself and his backers.

With the support of excellent publicity, most notably a series of pieces published in *El Universal* exploiting the sometimes sensational stories about historical figures connected to its legend and a contest sponsored by its distribution company, *Cruz Diablo* was a commercial and critical success.[99] This success, as Alfonso de Icaza notes, was a result of greater investment. He writes, "*Cruz Diablo* is, of all of our films, one of the best assembled and of those that most abounds in skillful acting. So with care, with seriousness, with preparation, and with . . . money, is how you can arrive to making an enduring work."[100] In reviews such as Bertha Elena Castañeda's in *El Universal*, which implored, "Reader, if you have a coat on these cold nights, I congratulate you, and if you do not, get yourself to the movies and enjoy yourself with 'Cruz Diablo,'" we see generally positive critical response which is matched by reports of its box office success.[101] In a note appearing a week after its premiere, which highlights the difficulties facing Mexican productions in relation to the distribution and exhibition sectors, *El Universal* observes, "It had been hoped that 'Cruz Diablo' would last another week, but the need to exhibit the French film 'La batalla' [*La bataille*, dirs. Nicolas Farkas and Viktor Tourjansky, 1933] starting on Thursday prevented the Mexican from continuing on the program, even though the public had cried out for it."[102] Similar to Fernando Rondón's review in *Ilustrado*, which calls attention to the film's set and proximity to Hollywood genre films, Luz Alba argues that, "It is true that *Cruz Diablo* reminds us of Douglas Fairbanks in *La marca del Zorro* [*The Mark of Zorro*, dir. Fred Niblo, 1920], of the burial mound where Lupita Gallardo lies and in the event of her fictional death there are outside reminiscences of *Romeo y Julieta*."[103] Generally a critic of de Fuentes's nationalism, Alba does not see these influences as negative, continuing, "But even if the director has been inspired by others, something that even celebrities do, the truth is that he was able to the film a lightness of development, an ease of expression, a balance,

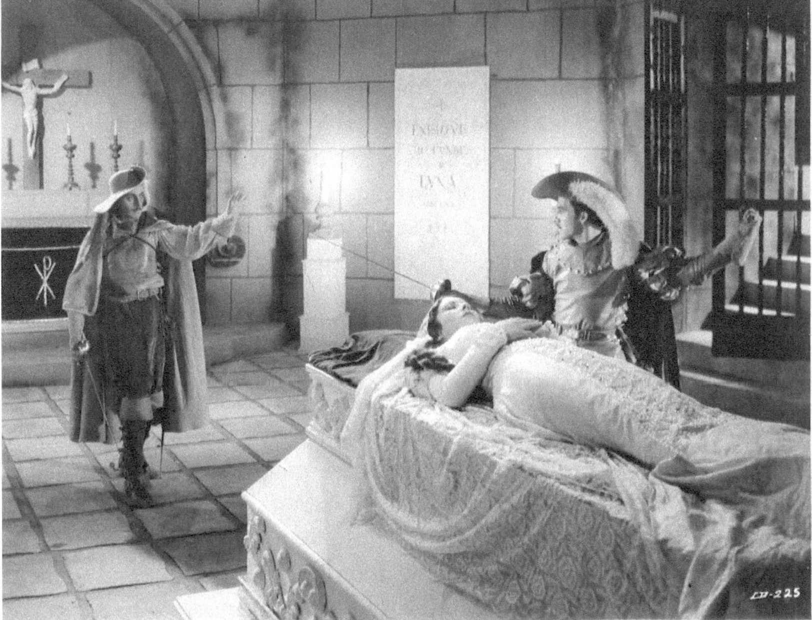

CRUZ DIABLO

Figure 5.10. Promotional still showing Phillips's highly adaptive and expressive lighting in *Cruz Diablo*. Courtesy of Mil Nubes-Foto.

which are not common in national production. From the point of view, then, of Mexican cinema, *Cruz Diablo* is a work that stands out without difficulty and an effort that is worth encouraging." It was de Fuentes's most discreet and measured film to that point for Alba.

Cruz Diablo, among the six best films of the year, was one of the films for which Alex Phillips was named best cinematographer of 1934 by *Filmográfico*'s Esteban V. Escalante.[104] In the film, distinct lighting strategies are used in service of the development of the film's story(world). An integral aspect of its lighting, especially compared to other films in the early transition to sound in Mexican cinema, is Jorge Fernández's more competent set design. Perhaps referring to Rondón's review, in which he writes, "The sets reproduce, with fidelity that Hollywood would want for itself, the sombre and severe elegance of the colonial chambers and halls," García Riera observes that its sets "have been constructed with skill and knowing that they were not to be occupied, but photographed."[105] With cinematic proportions in mind, Phillips's work on interiors in the film works to both highlight the mise-en-scène and express the melodrama and mystery of its narrative. This is clear, for example, in the lighting of the Conde de Luna's sepulcher. In one of the sequences in which it is a setting, *Cruz Diablo*'s denouement, the eponymous hero's double identity is revealed: Nostromus (Julián Soler), the real Conde de Luna, and Chacho, his son. Phillips uses bright lighting to bring out the intricacies of the set, while employing more expressive, at times low-key, figure lighting. Chacho eventually carries his father out of the sepulcher, and sits him down on a chair in the house. As Nostromus lies dying, the background is given texture through fill, while Phillips uses top-lighting to convey the scene's emotion, particularly on Oroná's Chacho. In *Cruz Diablo*, Phillips balances the storytelling needs of the historical drama.

In a column in *El Universal*, Fidel Solis asserts that "[n]ational cinema—a friend tells us—represents in our midst the crystallization of private industry: dispersed, with scores that sometimes have been failures and others half-triumphs. They still need many things, of course, for the effective values to join, to group together, to make a single work as a whole."[106] These two films represented promising steps toward a more cinematically accomplished film industry. Solis continues, arguing that the industry would rise as soon as investors found names that were guarantees of success: "It is only necessary that the elements that have now stood out, directors, photographers and artists, come together so that the capitalist may find them as the basis of his company." A commercially and critically acclaimed national cinema was possible, according to Solis, only if film labor acquired sufficient cultural capital to attract greater economic capital. As *Cruz Diablo* seemed to demonstrate, it took money to make money.[107] Mexican cinema's stars had yet to fully come out, but with successes like this film de Fuentes started to attract people to the cinema.

It would be another year until Phillips was reunited with de Fuentes. Moving away from the genres for which he had become largely known, the revolution and historical dramas, de Fuentes's *La familia Dressel* is contemporary family melodrama.[108] Revolving around the gravitational force of a German immigrant family's matriarch, Frau Dressell (Rosita Arriaga), the film's characters negotiate their new places in an increasingly modern Mexico City. Her oldest son, Federico (Jorge Vélez), seeks the opportunity to grow the family's business through advertising on the radio. Her youngest, Rodolfo (Julián Soler), prefers easy nightlife to hard work. While at the radio station, Federico runs into a childhood classmate gone but not forgotten—the singer Magdalena (Consuelo Frank). The two reconnect, fall in love, and marry. Collapsed into Frau Dressell's traditionalism, for whom little exists beyond the family's hardware store and their small circle of German friends, Magdalena reencounters an old flame, the now-famous singer Gonzalo (Ramón Armengod). Working their way out of convoluted misunderstandings, Federico and Magdalena are reconciled, and join a recently married Rodolfo (to a German immigrant, no less!) outside the hardware store, newly renamed "Dressell y sucesores."

La familia Dressel's release in mid-1935—it premiered on July 31 in the Regis—is a nexus of ways in which developing sectors of the Mexican film industry connected. Competing against structures already in place, and often supported by Hollywood either directly or indirectly, these sectors are suggestive of a much more heterogeneous film industry. It may be that de Fuentes and others would have liked their film industry to be in the hands of Mexicans, but foreigners continued to be ubiquitous. Following *Cruz Diablo*, *La familia Dressel* is Impulsora Cinematográfica's second film. Earlier notes on the production company generally focused on Paul Bush, but with *La familia Dressel* more was written about Impulsora Cinematográfica's president, Gerardo Hanson. "[T]he intelligent Argentine promotor," as Miguel de Zárraga described him, Hanson helped drive greater industrialization, leading to "the first time a company shoots two films simultaneously in the history of our cinema."[109] Produced by a foreigner, the film would also reach its audience in Mexico through the work of another foreigner, the Peruvian

Juan Pezet. Unlike *María Elena*, which was distributed by Columbia, *La familia Dressel* was distributed by Distribuidora Mexicana de Películas, S.A., along with *Hoy comienza la vida* (*Life Begins Today*, dirs. Phillips and Juan José Segura, 1935) and *La isla maldita* (*The Cursed Island*, dir. Boris Maicon, 1934). Pezet, who had earlier produced de Fuentes's *El tigre de Yautepec*, had since become the fledging company's manager.[110] *Mundo cinematográfico* noted that the company "has brilliantly inaugurated its activities with the presentation of 'La familia Dressel,'" which allowed Impulsora Cinematográfica's excellent production to become "the greatest triumph obtained so far by any national film."[111]

In *La familia Dressel*, Alex Phillips also continues to negotiate a somewhat different place within the Mexican film industry. Phillips's work on the film is co credited with another cinematographer, Ross Fisher. This is not to say that he was not experienced collaborating with others in Hollywood—he had, of course, learned the trade through working with others like Anton Nagy, Gus Peterson, and Edgar Lyons on Al Christie silent shorts and features such as *Choose Your Weapons* (1922) and *Madame Behave* (1925) and race films such as *The Framing of the Shrew* (1929)—and Mexico—in his three and a half years in Mexico, he had already teamed up with cameramen and still photographers Agustín Delgado, Agustín Jiménez, and Gabriel Figueroa, who worked as *ayudantes* and on *foto fijas* and would become cinematographers—but rather the Mexican film industry followed Hollywood's model in leaving the specialized work of cinematography in the hands of a single worker. Collaborative efforts were atypical, but not without precedent. Phillips, for example, had already joined up with others on two Miguel Contreras Torres films: Phillips and Fisher shot Contreras Torres's *fotodrama histórico Juárez y Maximiliano* with Ezequiel Carrasco, Arthur Martinelli, and Manuel Gómez Urquiza, and he teamed with Gabriel Figueroa on *Tribu* (1934).[112] Such collaborative work among equals was relatively uncommon not only in Mexico's fledgling film industry, but also in Hollywood and other more established European industries. Phillips and Fisher, whose work on the film seems impossible to disentangle, were attributed throughout, appearing together in *La familia Dressel*'s preproduction news, promotional materials, and, of course, the film itself.

In the *Anuario 1938* (*1938 Yearbook*) of *El Cine Gráfico*, Alfonso Patiño Gómez recalls, "Fernando de Fuentes made the first Mexican film that could be shown with pride in any part of the world. The first film that brought together positively notable performance and technique in its perfect finish. Its premiere was a success of significance . . . it was not a box office success."[113] *La familia Dressel*'s reception after its initial release mirrored Patiño Gomez's in that it was generally very positive, but somewhat superficial. Arriving during a lull in the 1935 film season, something that Linder notes in "Films of the Month" while complaining about "the momentary failure of American production companies (*casas americanas*)," it was even deemed by Roberto Cantú Robert as the best film of the year.[114] In his review of Mexico's 1935 films, Cantú Robert writes, "Criticism, both spontaneous and that paid by the word [*la de a 'tanto la línea'*], gave the film warm praise, and the public, which began to abandon the theaters in which a national film was announced, has had to be revived in the face of the sincerity of this film, which in the studios of Universal Pictures caused a fuss and not a few highly favorable comments for our industry."[115] This was not entirely the case, however, as Luz Alba argues, "Despite the enthusiasm with which this film has been received by film writers—something that, moreover, happens with every national production, barring the exceptional case that makes some achievement—the new product of the Mexican industry far from deserves a tenth of even the unconscious praise to which it is paid."[116] Alba's assessment of the film evinces the increasing tension felt by film critics of the time, who felt themselves stretched between the forces of their own cultural patriotism and the unsteady growth and industrialization of national cinema.

In the film's contemporaneous reviews, Phillips and Fisher's work on *La familia Dressel* receives imprecise, but unequivocal praise. In the English Section of *Mundo cinematográfico*, C. L. Ellis writes, "The production is easily comparable with American productions of a like type," and, "The photography is excellent throughout."[117] Its review in *Excélsior* adds that it possesses "a magnificent photography [that] gathers details of gesture with strict attention to detail, and exteriorizes for us profiles of souls, which complete the splendid sight of the figures."[118] De Icaza is briefer, "photography, impeccable," and, similarly, Cantú Robert lists it among the film's strengths, arguing that it has it all.[119] More detailed formal analysis of *La familia Dressel* is difficult to achieve today, as the most accessible print of the film, held by the Cineteca Nacional de México, is tinted blue due to an error in its transference. Negrete speculates that Phillips shot its interiors, given their careful lighting and the use of *flou*, the blurring of soft-lighting so often used in the still photography of the day and in late silent cinema, in close-ups of female characters.[120]

Low-contrast, high-key lighting was used throughout, but Phillips and Fisher also implemented more melodramatic low-key lighting when its story necessitated, visually communicating its contrasts.

In the transitional years of 1935 and 1936, Fernando de Fuentes pivoted away from the modes of the Revolution Trilogy toward more broadly commercial cinema. He worked with teams of cinematographers on *Vámonos con Pancho Villa* (1935), *La familia Dressel*, and *Las mujeres mandan* (1936) throughout this period. In addition to contracting Phillips to team up with Fisher on one film, de Fuentes experimented on the other two with the new team of Jack Draper and Gabriel Figueroa. He even employed five cameramen (Agustín P. Delgado, Draper, Álvaro González, Figueroa, and Phillips) on the now presumed lost state-commissioned short documentary *Desfile deportivo o Desfile atlético del 20 de noviembre de 1936 conmemorando el XXVI aniversario de la iniciación de la Revolución Mexicana* (Sports Parade or Athletic Parade of November 20, 1936 Commemorating the XXVI Anniversary of the Beginning of the Mexican Revolution). His next feature, *Allá en el Rancho Grande*, would break with this pattern, as he collaborated with the rising star of Mexican cinematography, Figueroa, who would shoot eight of the director's next nine features. *La Zandunga* was the exception.[121]

Shot by Alex Phillips, *La Zandunga* heralded the arrival of one of Mexico's most famous movie stars into its increasingly competitive (and profitable) film industry, Lupe Vélez.[122] Like other performers, most notably Dolores del Río, Ramón Novarro, and José Mojica, by the time Vélez returned to her homeland, her star shone a little less brightly than it once had, clouded by the passing "enormous vogue of things Mexican," the increasing homogenization of Hollywood after it transitioned to sound, and a rising wave in the United States of anti-Mexican white supremacy. Heralding dark changes in the film industry, they were left unseen in Roberto Cantú Robert's account of a night out on the town with Vélez. In "How Mexican Artists Live in Mexico," an image-laden feature that also included interviews with Rosita Moreno, Lupita Tovar, Dolores del Río, and Movita Castañeda, Cantú asks Vélez some telling questions between drinks in some of Hollywood's hottest nightclubs.[123] "Why do you not film here anymore?" "Man, they do not pay what I ask," to which Cantú somewhat curiously concludes that Vélez is the only artist beyond the reach of Hollywood producers. Employing a well-worn publicity tactic, Vélez concludes the night by telling Cantú, "You cannot imagine the desire I have to go to Mexico. Price does not matter to me there. There, the public matters." "When?" "Soon, you will see. We will see if it happens." Some six months later, *La Zandunga* went into production.

La Zandunga is regional film with international aspirations. Legendary producer Pedro A. Calderón's Films Selectos hoped to convert Vélez's transnational star into success throughout the Spanish-speaking world. S. L. de Ortigosa Jr.'s review of the film notes, "The performance of our biggest star, Lupe Vélez, whose name full of glory is known and appreciated throughout the world, was more than a guarantee for the thousands of fans who beat all the opening ticket records of national films the night of its premiere at the cine Alameda [on March 8, 1938], they expected to see a great movie. And we can assure you that they have not been disappointed."[124] Lupe Vélez was not, however, the only important investment in assuring the *La Zandunga*'s success. The film, unsurprisingly, received a huge amount of publicity before its premiere.[125] In *El Universal*, A writes:

> Very few national film productions have had sensational advertising and none has been announced in a such a dramatic and spectacular fashion as *La Zandunga*, months before it was released.
>
> So when it was finally presented, enormous expectations reigned among the audience. Ten days it has been exhibited, and people have overflowed in torrents to see it. The day of the premiere there were knocks at the doors of the theater. Thousands of people crowded around on sidewalks, in corridors, in the movie theater, and the lines to acquire tickets were huge. That atmosphere and that liveliness were the product of publicity.
>
> The reaction of the public has been diverse. For most people, the film is very beautiful, which is true; for others, not so much, an opinion based on their liking of Lupe Vélez, or in that they wanted to see another type of narrative. . . .
>
> The plot offers as spectacle customs and traditions of one of the most picturesque regions of the country: Oaxaca and Tehuantepec. The plot of the story is incidental.[126]

Just as the film's success at the box office was nearly predetermined by the capital invested in its promotion, friction caused by tensions between *La Zandunga*'s commercial aspirations and its reception by critics and the public was unpreventable. This was the case not only because it marked Vélez's first sound film in Mexico, but because it was the emerging Mexican film industry's first opportunity to produce a film with one of its Hollywood stars. Tito Guízar may have already returned to the country to headline in de Fuentes's *Allá en el Rancho Grande*, but it would take more time before stars José Mojica, Ramón Novarro, and Dolores del Río came home.[127]

La Zandunga is a romantic comedy of sorts with melodramatic moments. On the Isthmus of Tehuantepec, which marks the shortest distance between the Gulf of Mexico and the Pacific Ocean, Lupe (Vélez) is courted by three men: a *jarocho* sailor, Juancho (Arturo de Córdova); the *tehauno* Ramón Miranda (Rafael Falcón); and an older man, Atanasio (Rafael Icardo).[128] Lupe loves Juancho, but he is forced to set sail. Atanasio attempts to exploit his financial control of Don Eulogio (Manuel Noriega) to gain possession of Lupe, but Ramón obstructs his maneuvers and defends her. After Atanasio and Ramón are jailed by the town's mayor, Don Catarion (Joaquín Pardavé), and in the absence of news from Juancho, Lupe promises to marry Ramón. The sailor returns, however, and the gracious but heartbroken Ramón lets her return to her true love. The film ends as Lupe and Juancho happily arrive at the *zandunga*. As more fully described by Ortigosa, and alluded to by *El Universal's* A, the film is chiefly distinguished by Lupe Vélez and *costumbrismo*. The local color is distinctly Mexican, of course, but it is also exotic, bringing onto the screen one of the most picturesque regions of the country. In a savage review in *Ilustrado*, Luz Alba harshly critiques this *costumbrismo*: "*La Zandunga*, which must occupy number fifty in the series of *films costumbristas*, has come to change the attire of the *comparsas* [extras] and the music a bit, but in no way the content of the representation. Yesterday they were *charros de revista* [musical-review *charros*] and now they are *tehuanas de revista* [musical-review *tehuanas*]."[129]

In an effort to replicate the unprecedented success of *Allá en el Rancho Grande*, in 1937 producers looked for new ways to integrate popular culture into films such as *Las cuatro milpas* (*The Four Corn Stalks*, dir. Ramón Pereda, 1937), *Amapola del camino* (*Poppy of the Fields*, dir. Bustillo Oro, 1937), *Bajo el cielo de México* (*Under Mexican Skies*, dir. de Fuentes, 1937), *Ojos tapatíos* (*Tapatío Eyes* or Eyes of Jalisco, dir. Maicon, 1937), *Huapango* (dir. Bustillo Oro, 1937), and, of course, *Allá en el Rancho Chico* (*There on the Small Ranch*, dir. René Cardona, 1937). It is no surprise that García Riera's chapter on that year is entitled, "More than Twenty Ranchos Grandes."

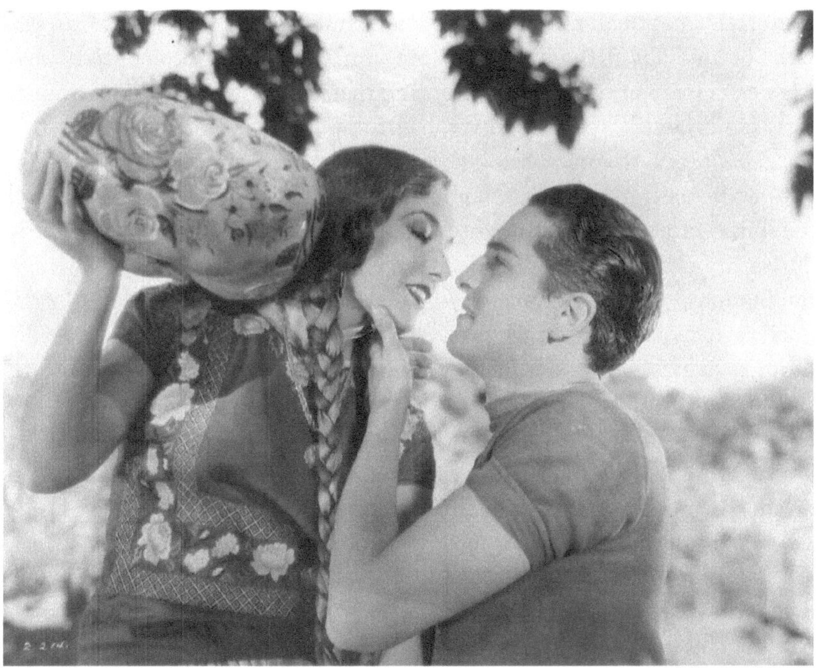

Figure 5.11. Lupe Vélez's Lupe about to be kissed by Arturo de Córdova's Juancho in *La Zandunga*. Even though it is a *foto fija*, the bright, high-key lighting is typical of the film. Courtesy of Mil Nubes-Foto.

Alex Phillips's work on *La Zandunga* also seeks to call attention to Lupe Vélez and its *costumbrismo*. Unlike some of Phillips's other work with de Fuentes, *La Zandunga* is bright, allowing the viewer to focus her attention on its exotic setting, its mise-en-scène, especially its costume design, and, most importantly, its star. In so doing, of course, *La Zandunga* whitens the indigenous regional type so as to make the *tehuana* more commercial, more compatible with national patriarchal norms.[130] In many ways, the film does not quite work due to this brightness; it never is able to fully coincide with the darker undertones of its diegesis. De Fuentes and Phillips are unable to unlock the quandary regarding how to tell this particular story in the bright sun of Tehuantepec. In a review that praises the film's photography, particularly its beautiful landscapes and irreproachable photography of Lupe Vélez, Xavier Villaurrutia works through an idea: "After the exhibition of *La Zandunga*, it is thought that, technically, national cinema has advanced many steps gracefully. Can the same be said about the content of the film? I think, on the contrary, that Mexican cinema finds itself, concerning that which is not technique, in its early childhood."[131] Signaled by Villaurrutia, Alba, and many other critics, *La Zandunga*'s strained dialogue and slow pacing limited its resonance with audiences. Alba, however, notes that Phillips' figure-lighting allowed the film's actors to express themselves unhindered by dialogue, particularly during its otherwise lagging denouement. She writes that "Nowhere is the inappropriateness of this way of making films so noticeable as in the final part, which by exception is very brisk because the camera visually captures expressions underlined by dialogue, instead of doing the opposite, according to our cinema's habit."[132] Even though in some ways Phillips used lighting strategies more closely connected to late-silent cinema, Alba praises him: "If the advances we have made in photography and sound extended to other branches of the film tree, our cinema would sometime emerge from adolescence to become a formal art."

Phillips and de Fuentes would not work together again until 1943, five and a half years after *La Zandunga*.[133] "Promoted internationally to be a major blockbuster," *Doña Bárbara* is illustrative of the increasing transnationalism of the Mexican film industry.[134] It was initially reported that de Fuentes was to follow up his 1942 film *Así se quiere en Jalisco* (*That's the Way They Love in Jalisco*) with *La trepadora* (*The Climber*), but news began to emerge about a different project: an adaptation with Venezuelan author Gallegos of his critically (by some) and popularly acclaimed novel *Doña Bárbara*.[135] As preproduction news swirled around the film, usually involving its authors (literary and cinematic) and stars (literary and cinematic) in pieces that revealed, for example, that "María Elena Márques has been designated by Rómulo Gallegos and Fernando de Fuentes the role of Marisela, daughter of the protagonist, in 'Doña Bárbara,'" so too were notes about Alex Phillips's helming of Miguel Contreras Torres's historical biopic *El padre Morelos* (*Father Morelos*, 1942) and, later, the largely forgotten Jorge Negrete period adventure *El jorobado (Enrique de Lagardere)* (The Hunchback [Enrique de Lagardere], dir. Jaime Salvador, 1943).[136] Despite careful and exhaustive coverage in the pages of *Cinema Reporter*, Alex Phillips's participation in *Doña Bárbara* would not be mentioned until filming began in mid-March 1943.[137] Shot in CLASA's studios in Tlalpan and on location in Veracruz, *Doña Bárbara*'s production was extended several times, lasting through the end of April, as "Fernando de Fuentes, its director, like the actors . . . like all the technical personnel, have enthusiastically taken this prolongation, as everyone has an interest in the success of the film."[138]

Doña Bárbara's reception after its much-anticipated release—so eagerly anticipated, in fact, that the *Cinema Reporter* article "'Doña Bárbara': It is a barbarity . . . ," which begins, "that it has not yet been taken to the screen"—could not live up to its expectations.[139] With several delays pushing its premiere in the cine Palacio back to September 16, 1943, excitement for the film built to such an extent that it was written that "[t]his expectation obeys the fact that it is a cinematic version of the most popular and read novel of Latin America and the comments of praise that have been lavished upon this film" by those who attended private screenings, leading to the conclusion that "[s]ome *cronistas* have already formulated their judgment, assuring that 'Doña Bárbara' is unquestionably the film that will win the award for best production of 1943."[140] Even more hyperbolic was *Cinema Reporter*'s description of its *avant première* in the Palacio: "Let us explain the presence of diplomats in the premiere. It was about introducing them to a colleague: CLASA Films and Fernando de Fuentes' film, who as a special ambassador, will go to the south of *América* to unify our peoples."[141] Its success, repeatedly detailed in the film press even beyond its five-week run in Palacio, would not be enough to satisfy everyone.[142]

In many ways, a brief *Cinema Reporter* column foreshadowed its reception, especially in its first sentence: "Not few are the very favorable comments that have been picked up as a result of the private exhibition of this great film for the large group of journalists and other people connected with filmic activities, because, truthfully, 'Doña Bárbara' is a film that will convince even the most skeptical [people] and a few other enemies, if they still exist, of national cinema."[143] By 1943, national cinema in Mexico had very little, if anything, yet to prove, and this comment seems to strike even its author as somewhat anachronistic.[144] Coupled with vague praise, the note *signals Doña Bárbara*'s later critical reception. Its initial review in *Cinema Reporter* states: "Good, very good. For us Mexicans, Rómulo Gallegos' stupendous novel has been very admirably captured for the cinema. Will they think the same in Venezuela? If this happens, we will have no qualms in declaring that 'Doña Bárbara' is one of the best national films. It has it all."[145] In a follow-up review appearing a week later, it concedes that the film may be a little too long, a common complaint about Mexican films (in the Argentine press, for example), but it concludes with similarly broad platitudes, "'Doña Bárbara' has it all and is, artistically and technically, a film that honors national cinema."[146] In *El Redondel*, a weekly specializing in bullfighting that also covered the movies, Alfonso de Icaza writes, "Welcome to the new national film, *Doña Bárbara*, called to give national cinema more and more prestige in all Spanish-speaking countries."[147] A similar line of thought is found in a piece written by María Álvarez de Burgos, first published in the Caracas daily *La Esfera* and later reprinted in *El Universal*:

> I am certain that this film is one of the most anticipated and discussed, and that it immediately attracts the curiosity of all audiences, for being the first real and effective step toward the appreciation of plots with customs, landscapes, feelings of an America that the heart does not really recognize in spite of being united by so many things that cross borders and make us familiar, we could say that in *Doña Bárbara* two aspects are realized, the artistic and the human, magnificently united in their admirable result.[148]

Doña Bárbara was expected to be much more than simply a box office success. It was to be, as de Icaza writes in the *Cinema Reporter* piece "Our Cinema and the Hispanic World," an affirmation of the Mexican film industry's ability to produce films for the Spanish-speaking world. He argues that "'Doña Bárbara,' film, is as Venezuelan as 'Doña Bárbara,' novel. And just as we made a great Venezuelan movie, we can make an Argentine, a Peruvian, or a Guatemalan one."[149]

Doña Bárbara begins as the Caracas lawyer Santos Luzardo (Julián Soler) arrives at Venezuela's vast *llanos*. He soon discovers that Altamira, his family's land, has come to be controlled by Doña Bárbara (María Félix). His cousin Lorenzo Barquer (Andrés Soler) is a drunk, at the mercy of his disease and Doña Bárbara, with whom he has a daughter, Marisela (María Elena Márques). Lorenzo's condition has worsened such that he is tempted into selling Marisela to the lecherous foreigner Don Guillermo (Charles Rooner) for whisky. Santos, however, impedes this, taking Lorenzo and Marisela to live with him. Eventually a love triangle forms. Doña Bárbara falls in love with Santos, who stands up to her. Santos is also loved by Marisela, who stands up to her evil mother. Tempted back to drink by Don Guillermo, Lorenzo dies. Doña Bárbara fails to put an end to a situation spiraling out of control, gives up her curses, and disappears. Santos and Marisela are left to enjoy their love and happiness.

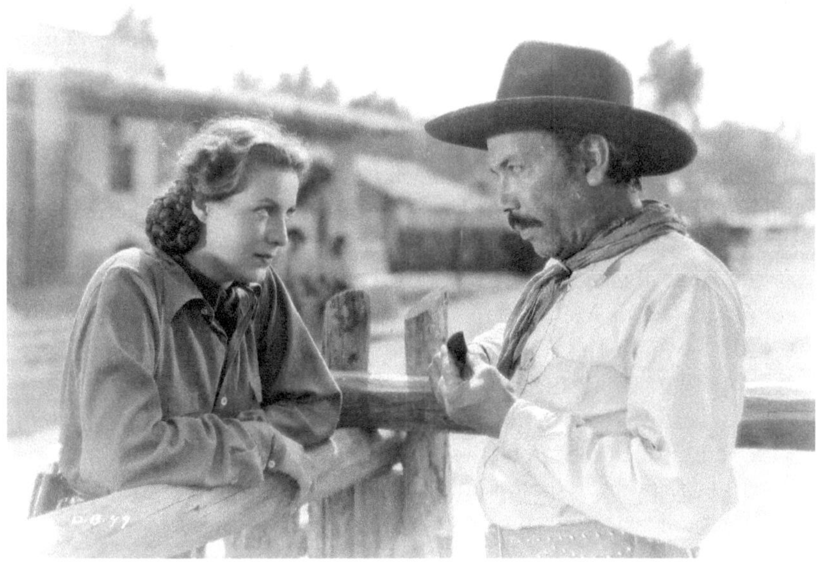

Figure 5.12. Doña Bárbara (María Félix) discusses machinations with Melquiades (Miguel Inclán). Courtesy of Mil Nubes-Foto.

Much like de Fuentes's direction, Phillips's work on *Doña Bárbara* fails to fully adapt Gallegos' novel to the screen. The dramatic contrasts demanded by the representation of the Venezuelan *llanos* fall a little flat, especially in comparison to Figueroa's cinematography at the time. Phillips's lighting of characters such as Santos and Marisela often seem dated, as he uses many of the same strategies he had been using since the early 1930s. Somewhat isolated from the rest of the film, Phillips's lighting of María Félix's Doña Bárbara is at times some of the best work of his career. He often uses softer lighting to barely illuminate her striking face. But, perhaps more notably, he also uses more contemporary contrastive lighting to visually express the danger Doña Bárbara represents. Again, Phillips uses soft, almost flat lighting on her face, but this time in contrast with the shadows on the walls in the background.

Even with its popular and critical acclaim—it was not only named best film of the year in an open poll carried out by the influential columnist Lumiére for the magazine *Hoy*, but took in best picture of 1943 in the Unión de Periodistas Cinematográficos de México's awards, as well as individual prizes for María Elena Márques (best supporting actress) and Agustín Isunza (best supporting actor)—there was an emerging sense that *Doña Bárbara* did not quite match the heights of other important films released that year.[150] It may have been a critical and, more importantly, commercial success, but cinematically it was overshadowed by other films in 1943, ones that would come to be much more influential as the Mexican film industry continued to shape its own classical cinema. In the December 4, 1943, issue of *Cinema Reporter*, the young screenwriter Edmundo Báez notes in the article, "Julio Bracho vs. El Indio Fernández":

> *Distinto amanecer* [*Another Dawn*] and *Flor silvestre* [*Wild Flower*]: two Mexican films of two different Mexicos. Julio Bracho and Emilio Fernández: two film directors of two opposing, antagonistic Mexicos. Is it possible to say which, artistically, is the better of these two Mexicos and these two Mexicans? Surely not. They do not have the least point of contact, they do not admit the most minimal comparison. They are two opposing worlds. They are the two poles from which the authentic personality of this country is being born.[151]

The present progressive of *Distinto amanecer* and *Flor silvestre* were indicative of new directions in Mexican cinema, ones that diverged from the present perfect or preterite of the other two films listed in *Cinema Reporter*'s list of top films of 1943: *Doña Bárbara* and the remake of *Santa* (dir. Norman Foster). In the list, we see senses of place rooted in the nineteenth century competing with emergent understandings in both cosmopolitanism (*Doña Bárbara*/*Distinto amanecer*) and *mexicanidad* (*Santa*/*Flor silvestre*). Báez's piece contrasts Bracho's urbanity with Fernández's organic, almost primitive *mexicanidad*, but he ignores Foster and de Fuentes when he concludes, "What would the national cinema do without the thought and emotion of Bracho and Fernández? What would Mexico do without the sentiment and the action of men like Julio Bracho and Emilio Fernández? Without these two factors, this great nation in progress would not be creating itself, would not be being born." It may be unsurprising that Bracho would end up winning best director, having eclipsed a director now known for his Revolution Trilogy, but it is even less so that Gabriel Figueroa took home the award for best cinematography for his work on both *Distinto amanecer* and *Flor silvestre*.[152]

Two Collaborations among Many

Presented in alphabetical order, it is nonetheless somewhat poetic that portraits of Arcady Boytler and Fernando de Fuentes appear facing one another in *La primera guía cinematográfica mexicana para el año de 1934* by Santini Publicista (Miguel Santini Ávila).[153] Visually contrasting, Agustín Jiménez's traditional portrait of de Fuentes clashes with Boytler's expressionist cosmopolitanism (perhaps taken by Phillips). In juxtaposition, Boytler's and de Fuentes's significance to the emerging national film industry are especially clear. Each meant something, something particular, to what Mexican cinema was at the time and what it hoped to become. Three and a half decades later, this contrast led Emilio García Riera to consider 1932 to be the year of "New Directors: Boytler and de Fuentes" in the first edition of his monumental film history *Historia documental del cine mexicano*. (Later, tellingly, the chapter was retitled "Six Minor Films.")[154] Boytler and de Fuentes—who, in the words of García Riera, "would make the most interesting national films of the following years"—were in many ways emblematic of Mexican cinema as its industry emerged after the arrival of sound.[155] In their own ways, both were uniquely Mexican: Boytler, the creative Russian who like Eisenstein came understand the cinema in Mexico, and de Fuentes, the native genius who had never even been to Hollywood. Though they would have diverging futures in the 1940s—Boytler shot a single film, *Amor prohibido* (*Forbidden Love*, 1944), while de Fuentes directed more than ten more, never returning to the heights of his work in the 1930s—their films in the early sound period promised those in industry and those in movies theaters that much was to come of Mexican cinema. These promises, however, were made in collaboration with foreign film workers, such as Alex Phillips, whose efforts are often forgotten, ignored, or overlooked. If *mexicanidad* was a marketing strategy differentiating the productions of the national film industry from those of foreign competitors, it was commercially advantageous to render invisible foreign technicians such as Phillips. We can see some of the magic between light and shadow (to riff on the title of Ernesto Medina's documentary on Phillips) through studying his collaborations with Boytler and de Fuentes. This magic is also seen between reports published in periodicals, often casting light on Phillips's labor, and his films, themselves casting shadows on Phillips's work as it aimed to become invisible to better serve story. Phillips's cinematography on Boytler's and de Fuentes's films from 1932 to 1943 show some of the ways in which he implemented lighting strategies serving generic conventions. In these films, we see how Phillips's styles adapt according to his collaborator. Boytler and de Fuentes, however, were but two of many directors with whom the prolific Alex Phillips worked in the early sound period.

6

"But only one, Juan Orol, is fundamentally different from the rest"

Orolian Melodrama and *cursilería* in the 1930s

Tilting up green waters, the camera reaches a canoe floating just off the rocky banks of one of the Lago de Chapultepec's islands. With the Casa del Lago in the background, a young woman and an old man are enjoying a sunny day. The couple is immediately identifiable in *El mundo fantástico de Juan Orol* (*The Fantastic World of Juan Orol*, dir. Sebastián del Amo, 2012) as Juan Orol (Roberto Sosa) and his wife Dinorah Judith (Fernanda Romero). The scene cuts to the man, whose striped blazer, creme shirt with large collar, and maroon cravat complete a look set by oversized brown glasses and white hair. He angrily crumples up the magazine he has been reading, throwing it down into the canoe.[1] In a counter-shot, the beautiful young woman's flipped-out ends gesture toward the white parasol she is holding. Contrasting, but at the same time complementing the old man's appearance, she wears a red dress, glamorous oversized sunglasses, large hoop earrings, and merlot red lipstick. She asks him, "What's going on, Juanito?"[2] Just before the scene cuts back, he begins to answer, "Those damn critics. They have never let me be!" In another counter-shot, the woman calms him, reminding Juan, "Aren't you going to be honored by The General Film Organization. Come on, cheer up, man." In the final shot in the canoe, he replies, "You are right, darling. At least I'll have the chance to say hello to good old friends." As he kisses her hand, the scene cuts back to the establishing shot and rises above the waters of the Lago de Chapultepec via a crane shot. The scene ends with a bird's eye shot, whose tenderness is underscored by orchestral strings, but not before a moment of levity when Juan asks, "Should I paddle, or will you?" Dinorah replies, "*Ay*, Juan." An iris out takes the viewer back to the film's initial diegetic space, "México D.F. ✦ 1982."

Having finally completed the tale that began *El mundo fantástico de Juan Orol*, Juan says, "And . . . Here we are. Right, chief." Juan finds his interlocutor, the movie usher (Rodrigo Corea), sound asleep. The eponymous protagonist's alter ego, Johnnie Carmenta (also played by Roberto Sosa, but in black and white), reappears and tells Juan, "What matters is not where you begin, but where you finish." Juan might have been born in Spain, but he died a key figure in Mexican cinema. His movies may have been panned throughout his career, but his lifetime achievements were celebrated by cultural institutions. Briefly, Juan and Johnnie discuss achievement and legacy. There, at the Ciclo Orol, Johnnie tells Juan goodbye, "We've had fun. It's been a pleasure, my friend." *El mundo fantástico de Juan Orol* culminates not in a touching scene in which a shattered Juan (in the background with Dinorah) and Johnnie (alone in the foreground) mourn the burning of the Cineteca Nacional, but in the final touches of Sebastián del Amo's recreation of Orolian cinema.[3] The film's credits nostalgically reproduce the visual sensibilities of Orol's

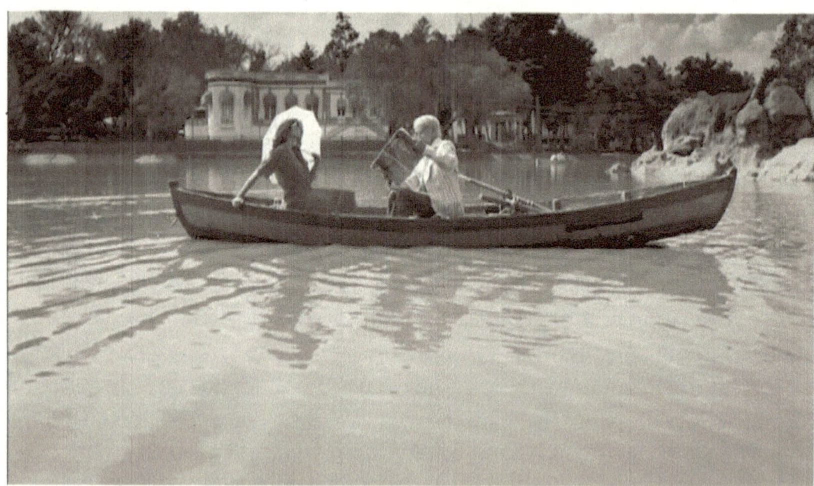

Figure 6.1. Juan Orol (Roberto Sosa) and his wife Dinorah Judith (Fernanda Romero) on the Lago de Chapultepec in *El mundo fantástico de Juan Orol* (dir. Sebastián del Amo, 2012).

lobby cards, particularly those of the 1950s and 1960s. They are, in a sense, the logical conclusion of *El mundo fantástico de Juan Orol*'s wistful nostalgia for a lost, unironic cinema. Neither Juan (the character) nor del Amo quite comes to terms with Orol's legacy, even though he was fêted during his lifetime by institutions such as the Dirección General de Cinematografía de la Secretaria de Gobernación, the city of Madrid, and the Filmoteca de la Universidad Nacional Autónoma de México.[4] As Juan tells the usher as he is about to begin his tale, "Life is so ironic. When they called me *el Rey del Churro* (the King of the B's) theaters were sold out. Now, that I have some recognition, no one shows up."[5] By projecting Orol's deep, late life melancholy, if not depression, del Amo overemphasizes Johnnie's assessment of Juan's career. Where Orol finishes is all that matters.

Juan Orol's films have garnered little scholarly interest, even in Mexico. If Orol was never left alone by critics of his films, his cinema never received much attention at all, much less the attention it deserves in Mexican film historiography. "Regardless of his cult status . . . and of his commercial success, Orol's work is usually absent from readings of the period, perhaps because of the questionable quality of his work and the loss of many of his negatives in the Cineteca Nacional fire of 1982."[6] Even though most of his filmography has since been recovered, unlike much of the Cineteca Nacional's cultural heritage lost that day, Orol's films continue to suffer from the negative cultural value associated with their *cursilería* (cheesiness or vulgarity). They are bad movies, so-called *churros*, as they would come to be known. Writing in 1968—the same year in which Orol's *Contrabandistas del Caribe* (*Smugglers of the Caribbean*, 1966) and *Antesala de la silla eléctrica* (*Waiting Room for the Electric Chair*, 1966) were released in Mexico—Jorge Ayala Blanco argues in his foundational book *La aventura del cine mexicano*, "The fame of overlooked humorist, of involuntary surrealist that Juan Orol enjoys is totally unjustified.The movies of the 'genius of cretinism' are totally devoid of cinematic values. They are tedious, and bad to the point of depression. His editing and production errors could perhaps be his only, insufficient and nonexclusive skills."[7] Emilio García Riera is not much less acerbic in his criticism of Orol's films throughout his monumental *Historia documental del cine mexicano*, and infrequently references the director in his other works.[8] Not unlike Ayala Blanco or García Riera, film historians writing outside of Mexico in the 1980s and 1990s such as Joanne Hershfield, Carl J. Mora, Paulo Antonio Paranaguá, and Charles Ramírez Berg reference Orol tangentially, if at all. Giving some continuity to García Riera's work, but recognizing that "[t]he passage of time makes us change our perspective," film historian Eduardo de la Vega wrote *El cine de Juan Orol* and, later, *Juan Orol*, the only books on the director.[9] A "mini-book-homage" and an assemblage of criticism, documents, history, periodical sources, and research, these books are only now starting to be supplemented by more thorough scholarship.[10] This work recalls something film historian Aurelio de los Reyes wrote:

> [T]hose who want to approach the mentality of the majority sector of the population must begin, necessarily, by analyzing box office successes, which may not be the best films from the point of view of quality, but perhaps the most the most anodyne story lines and the films with the greatest narrative and technical defects (Juan Orol is the most obvious case).[11]

Recent scholarship by Ignacio M. Sánchez Prado, Maricruz Castro Ricalde and Robert McKee Irwin, Francisco Peredo Castro, and Rosario Vidal Bonifaz, for example, take Orol's place within Mexican cinema more seriously, but have yet to do so more substantially (as their primary interests lie elsewhere).[12]

Signaling a shift in scholarship on Orol, which initially focused on films he made as *el Rey del Churro* (that have since become cult classics), more contemporary treatments of Orolian cinema have begun to explore how his work in the 1930s contributed to Mexican cinema. Of these pieces, Ana M. López's essay "Before Exploitation: Three Men of the Cinema in Mexico" is perhaps the most significant.[13] Alongside fellow foreign directors José Bohr and Ramón Peón, López places Orol as a precursor to what would later become exploitation cinema. Contending that exploitation as such could not really be produced due to industrial factors until the late 1940s or 1950s, López explains, "However, what emerged earlier, especially in the effervescent experimental period after the arrival of sound were multiple alternative cinematic practices that, attempting to find the 'magic' formulas for box-office success and audience satisfaction, laid the groundwork for both the mainstream 'national' cinema and future exploitation practices."[14] Drawing from López's insights, this chapter explores the contributions Juan Orol's films of the 1930s to the emergence of what would later become the *Época de oro* of Mexican cinema. Even though he was "a 'one man orchestra' in the films that he made," I examine his work as the director of *Madre querida* (*Beloved Mother*, 1935), *El calvario de una esposa* (A Wife's Agony, 1936), *Honrarás a tus padres* (Honor Thy Parents, 1936), *El derecho y el deber* (*Law and Duty*, 1937), and *Eterna mártir* (*Eternal Martyr*, 1937).[15]

It may be tempting to interpret Orol's work through the lens of theory and scholarship on melodrama, touching upon reference points such as Peter Brooks, Hermann Herlinghaus, Ana M. López, Carlos Monsiváis, and Silvia Oroz, but to do so would to miss the opportunity to explore how Orol theorizes melodrama cinematically in his Mexican movies of the 1930s.[16] In these films, content and form are employed to express a distinctly Orolian melodramatic understanding of the cinema. Undistracted by the inconspicuousness, if not the invisibility, of film form, the viewer pays close attention to the narratives' twists and turns through the Orolian melodramatic universe. Within this universe, distinct Manichaean forces play out in relation to ever-distancing, but still controlling, patriarchy. To simply characterize Orol's diegeses as convoluted would be to willfully disregard melodrama's nonclassical narrative mechanics in which the *cursilería* of excess enables access into the characters' world, especially emotionally. They allow the viewer to feel the moral forces at play, to experience firsthand good and evil, even though (or perhaps because) they are in bad taste. By closely reading these films, particularly their plots, we come to better understand the ways in which Orolian melodrama channeled (and commercialized) cultural anxieties of mid-1930s Mexico, especially regarding gender. Later, more broadly and perhaps more subtly adopted by the emerging Mexican film industry, Orolian melodrama was highly influential cinematically in addition to being popular with audiences. Eventually marginalized by critics, as well as elements within the emerging Mexican film industry, Orol left for Cuba in 1938, only to return in 1941. Even though *El mundo fantástico de Juan Orol*'s Johnnie Carmenta would disagree, I aim to show that where you finish matters, but so does where you begin.

Realities (and Fictions) of a Life Eventually Told in the Movies

The life of Juan Orol may have eventually been told somewhat fantastically in the cinema, but his real life story was no less interesting nor, it would seem, less full of artistic license or fiction. In *El fantástico mundo de Juan*

Orol, Juan begins to relate his life's tale by saying, "I have always liked to say that everything began in Ferrol." In the provincial city of Ferrol, one of Galicia's largest at the time, Juan Orol was said to have been born on August 4, 1896. Settled for centuries, long before it would be renamed *El Ferrol del Caudillo* in reference to Francisco Franco (who was born there four years earlier than the director), Ferrol was a community whose port connected it to places far beyond Galicia. "The case is that Orol was the only son of a Spanish naval commander and of a woman also born in El Ferrol, whose names the filmmaker prefers to keep anonymous. Orol retains very vague memories of his childhood in El Ferrol."[17] He would live there until he was seven or eight, at which time serious family issues compelled his mother to send her son to Cuba to live with rich relatives. Except, it seems, that was not the case. In fact, Juan Orol was born on July 30, 1893, in Santiso, a small village in central Galicia.[18] Baptized Juan García García, he was the illegitimate son of Ramona García and Juan Orol Maseda (his officially "unknown father"). He was raised by his maternal grandparents. In 1905, he was sent from Ferrol to Havana as he "[g]ot in the way of the plans of his mother, a lady of the evening (*una mujer de la vida alegre*) known as *A Bufa* (The Fool)." However intermittently, he would have some contact with his Spanish family throughout his life.[19] In Cuba, he was welcomed by Carmen Fondevila, a Galician émigré from Lalín. Restless, as he would be to the end of his days, Orol embarked on what would be one of many trips back and forth between Cuba and Mexico.

Arriving in Veracruz sometime early (1910/11) in the Mexican Revolution, Orol would not stay there long. Suffering from hunger, he visited the Cuban consulate, which returned him to his first adopted country. In a 1975 interview, Orol recounted the (fantastic) tale of his twenties and early thirties:

> There, I got into the matter of automobiles. I was in a garage and learned a lot about mechanics. Car races came, and I went to one race all the way in Indianapolis. But I did not make the grade because you had to average a certain number of miles: one hundred and eighteen per hour. I remained on one hundred and seventeen-something, and they ordered me to keep training, but I got bored, and I went to Havana. I said, "I do not want any more cars. No races. Nothing." I returned to Mexico. I was already about nineteen or twenty

> years old. As I knew a bit of mechanics I began working in this specialty, but then I reconsidered: "No, mechanics is not for me. I want to live by something else." And I became a bullfighter, after having been a baseball pitcher in Cuba. I was determined to be a bullfighter in Mexico. Why? Because, as I was a very uneven pitcher, I got so nervous that I gave up lots of bases per pitch and I said to myself, "No. Either I am a big star [*figura grande*] or nothing." Man (or woman, I also think) should know what he is good at. Back in Mexico, I raced a car at the track in La Condesa, and remembering Indianapolis, I told myself, "I'm not continuing this." And I dedicated myself to bullfighting because I have to live from the crowd. I fought for about seven years.[20]

In this story, Orol omits a spell as a boxer, as well as performances on stage. Orol also affirms that he worked as an undercover police officer for General Roberto Cruz (circa 1925). Orol remained with Cruz until the assassination of Álvaro Obregón in 1928. Few of these claims have been verified.[21]

Orol's tale is a raconteur's blend of fact and fiction, but his personal life in the mid-1920s was also of the movies (albeit of a different genre). On January 24, 1924, Juan Orol García and Amparo Moreno were married in Mexico City.[22] (Orol's profession is listed as mechanic on the marriage certificate.) It is said that Amparo, whose family appears to have been quite large, was one of the sisters of Consuelo Moreno, who was to star in several of Orol's films in the 1930s.[23] A little over a year later, on June 25, 1925, the newlyweds welcomed their son Arnoldo into the world.[24] Orol would use later use names of both mother and son in *Honrarás a tus padres* and *Los misterios del hampa* (*Mysteries of the Underworld*, 1944). On February 18, 1931, Amparo Moreno died of a "puerperal infection-acute lobar pneumonia" at the age of thirty, according to records.[25] Her cause of death suggests she had recently given birth. Orol, famously loquacious, does not seem to have ever discussed her death on record. Later, sometime in the 1950s, tragedy would strike again, as Arnoldo died in an accident.

Orol eventually transitioned from a cinematic life to a life in the cinema. But first, he spent a formative period working in the radio. Sometime in 1929 or 1930, he began working at XEO Radio Nacional.[26] Orol worked as an artistic director for the affiliate of the Partido Nacional Revolucionario (National Revolutionary Party), the precursor of the Partido Revolucionario Institucional (PRI; Institutional Revolutionary Party). He remembered, "They said I was a big fighter and that I got very good advertising. There, well, I networked in such a way that I entered the cinema while still on the radio; I developed programs."[27] After a convoluted set of twists and turns, Orol reinvested capital gained from the sale of property to create a production company to develop a script by Quirico Michelena. Aspa Films' *Sagrario* (dir. Ramón Peón, 1933) was a huge hit. According to *La primera guía cinematográfica mexicana para el año 1934*, by Santini Publicista (Miguel Santini Ávila), *Sagrario*'s box-office earnings (90,000 pesos) in Mexico to that time far exceeded the cost of its production (32,000 pesos).[28] Aspa Films' second production, *Mujeres sin alma* (also known as *Venganza suprema)* (*Soulless Women*), was to follow the formula that made *Sagrario* a success, but Orol fought with Peón, eventually taking over the film.[29] Unlike Peón, who by that time had been directing since 1920's *Realidad* (Reality), Orol lacked experience, but he made up for it in belief in his own Orolian cinematic universe.

Of (Neither) Mothers and Wives: *Madre querida* and *El calvario de una esposa*

Aspa Films' next two projects represent an important rupture for Orol's production company. Orol's assumption of the role of director—in addition to actor, producer, and scriptwriter—gave him greater creative control than he had ever enjoyed when working with Peón on *Sagrario* and *Mujeres sin alma*, but it also forced distinct modes of production that ran counter to the new direction of the emerging national film industry. By taking the path of Miguel Zacarías, Miguel Contreras Torres, and José Bohr instead of that of Jorge Pezet, Felipe Mier, and Jesús Grovas, Orol could no longer act as a conductor for his subsequent films.[30] The *hombre orchestra* assembled a kind of production unit around Peón, which was succeeded by greater turnover in personnel between projects, with the notable exception of some actors (Consuelo Moreno, René Cardona, and, of course, Orol), ubiquitous composer Max Urban, and editor José Marino. But by picking up another instrument, Orol was able to perform to his own tune.

Consequently, the way in which melodrama was enacted by his films' female characters changed. The scandalous, modern women of *Sagrario* and, especially, *Mujeres sin alma* were replaced by the self-abnegating and suffering figures of more traditional mothers, wives, and mothers and wives-to-be. *Madre querida* and *El calvario de una esposa*, his first feature films, are the first full displays of Orolian cinema.[31] To twist López's words a bit, "Dripping in melodramatic excess, the film[s] required few stylistic flourishes beyond [their] already excessive narrative[s]."[32] What *Madre querida* and *El calvario de una esposa* lack in diegetic development or formal unity, they far surpass in making audiences feel. Their plots, based on Julián Cisneros Tamayo's novel *Huérfanos del destino* (Destiny's Orphans) and Orol's own unpublished novel *La cantante del Waikiki* (The Waikiki Singer), are convoluted melodramas that emotionally connected with audiences in the mid-1930s.[33] That said, even though the films' melodramatic plots were considered by critics (then and now) to be female-oriented, their male-centered plots call into question how we should understand Orolian melodrama.

Madre querida premiered on Mother's Day (May 10), 1935, in Mexico City. Created in Mexico by *Excélsior* some thirteen years earlier, Mother's Day had become a popular holiday by 1935.[34] Unlike event movies as we now understand them—or even Hollywood releases at the time that were so anticipated that they were sensations worldwide, such as *City Lights* (dir. Charlie Chaplin, 1931), *The Merry Widow* (dir. Ernst Lubitsch, 1934), and *Mutiny on the Bounty* (dir. Frank Lloyd, 1935)—Orol's *Madre querida* was produced to take full advantage of the local celebration of the holiday. Initially reported by *El Nacional* as scheduled to open to "the eleven cinemas of the prestigious First Circuit: Goya, Teresa, Ordenó, Rialto, Monumental, Granat, Eden, Venecia, América, Roma, and the Rívoli," Orol's first feature hit the ground running at the Mundial, Alarcón, Alcázar, Lux, Royal, Majestic, and Capitolio theaters.[35] In an oft-repeated but uncorroborated anecdote related in *El fántastico mundo de Juan Orol*, Orol "handed out handkerchiefs as viewers bought their tickets, promising a complete refund if they were not used during the screening."[36] Usually in brief notes, sometimes referring to alternate titles *Honra del destino* (Destiny's Honor) or *Huérfanos del destino* (Destiny's Orphans), *Madre querida*'s production was covered by publications such as *Jueves de Excélsior* and *Revista de Revistas*.[37] In view of the commercial, if not critical, success of Aspa's earlier productions *Sagrario* and *Mujeres sin alma*, Orol's first feature was anticipated by Mexico City's newspapers, entertainment magazines, and film periodicals. In the *El Nacional* article announcing *Madre querida*'s premiere, it is noted that "[t]here is a real interest among capital audiences to go to this magnificent movie in which

Juan Orol, who achieves the most perfect continuity exhibited in any film, triumphs as a director."[38] Quite obviously over the top, as was much (if not most) of the reporting on early films of the emerging national film industry in Mexico, the article nonetheless signals the anticipation that awaited this event film.

In his review for *El Redondel*, Alfonso de Icaza calls attention not only to its Mother's Day premiere, but also its well-crafted use of genre. He writes, "The opening of this new national film could not have been more opportune, provided its being dedicated to mothers. It was exhibited for the first time on the day in Mexico in which the purest of earthly loves is venerated."[39] Its built-in audience surely assisted *Madre querida* commercially, and perhaps even critically. In surpassing José Bohr's *Tu hijo* (*Thy Son*, 1934)—the earliest example of the "cult of motherhood" films in Mexico in the sound era—*Madre querida* more effectively appeals to well-established narratives and their tropes, especially those appearing in print media (from serialized novels in periodicals to cheap editions of paperbacks) and *radionovelas*. De Icaza argues that "[b]eing the film itself a 'classic' melodrama, it has interesting parts and one could have benefitted from its plot, at least for the taste of certain audiences." Writing several weeks later in *Revista de Revistas*, Hugo del Mar (Esteban V. Escalante) substantiated de Icaza's intuition: "Against everything that was expected, the premiere of *Madre querida* or *Huérfanos del destino* in the capital's second circuit was a resounding artistic and financial success."[40] Even though his directing met with some disapproval ("Orol's direction has its deficiencies, excusable in an individual such as Juan who for the first time takes charge of the megaphone"), Orol was praised by del Mar in a different role. By arguing that "Juan Orol and Don Gabriel Flores, associate producers of this film, must feel very satisfied, as they gave a very sensitive and well-acted film to our public," del Mar attributes a kind of authorship to the producers for packaging *Madre querida*'s diegesis. In so doing, del Mar also erases Orol's role as director in forming Orolian melodrama. Other writers, including the author(s) of two notes in *El Cine Gráfico*, adopted a similar critical line, one of which still dominates writing on *Madre querida*.[41] Orol's direction was bad, *cursi*, or incompetent, but his films sold.

Madre querida begins not with its characters, but with Juan Orol's didactic, interpretive introduction. Much like the film's plot itself, the introductory sequence instructs the viewer how to feel about what is ostensibly, but perhaps not practically, the subject of the film: mothers. The credits having concluded, *Madre querida* fades to black and then back in to a seated Orol. The camera tilts slightly up as Orol stands. The staging of the introductory sequence is quite simple: in a nondescript room, Orol is dressed in a suit. With a thick Spanish accent, Orol declaims:

> I have the pleasure of dedicating this film to all the *madrecitas* [little mothers] of the world and, at the same time, paying a sincere and just homage to all of them. I dedicate this film to them because by being mothers they have suffered and because in them, as in a divine crucible, goodness and sacrifice have united. Their hands are sowing hands of ideals that go through the world cultivating hearts, hands that have been purified by the force of so much blessing. After God, they are on Earth the supreme artifices that wisely and sweetly mould the souls of men until making the miracle of finding a life, a heart, a conscience, to the warmth of their hearts. Men must forget quarrels and petty ambitions because the mother is the only means to make men more human as in every man there is an aftertaste of sweetness, no matter how bitter the heart is, when the sacred memory of his mother endures. And remembering this being who is pure goodness, we feel with the poet when he says: "Mother, I was scented by your breast / as a drop of water is scented by the flower."[42] Mothers from all over the world: this cinematic episode serves to fan the sacred flame of the red lamps of our hearts, our affection, admiration, and respect, because they are on Earth—Oh, mothers!—symbol of love, peace, and *confraternidad universal* [universal brotherhood/fellowship].

As he preaches about "Their hands are sowing hands," Orol dissolves into six static shots of monumental images of sculptures representing motherhood. The sequence dissolves back to Orol, this time in a close-up, as he proclaims "our affection, our admiration." In *Madre querida*'s introductory sequence, we hear social, but also intermedial and intertextual, reverberations. We can hear voices of political discourse, but this sequence also resounds with the tones of serial fiction and the radio. It also echoes newsreels (especially when his speech becomes a voiceover), as well as the practice of expository introductions to films in the movie theater.[43] Wherever these reverberations might be coming from, Orol's introductory exegesis gives the viewer an ideological and moral framework through which to understand its storyworld. Perhaps not intentionally, Orol also intimates that the theme of *Madre querida* is not really the mother, but rather the ways that her children come to be affected by her.

After Orol's introduction fades to black, *Madre querida* opens at a schoolyard in Mexico City. On the eve of Mother's Day, a group of boys discuss grand plans for gifts. Just outside the circle, Juanito (Antonio Liceaga) tells his friend Luisito (Carlos Domínguez) that he does not have anything to give his mother to celebrate her special day. Luisito confesses that he does not have a mother, and insists on giving his friend fifty cents. After some hijinks, bordering on bullying, all the schoolboys gather in an assembly and sing "Mornings upon waking / *Mamita mía* / Will give me a kiss." Almost like a political rally, the school's director says, "Tell me, who is the being to whom do you most owe gratitude?" to which the boys reply, "Our mothers! Our mothers!" Dissolving to a well-appointed home, Manuel (Alberto Martí) tells his uncle (Miguel Wilmer) his story of ill-fated love. Before marrying Margarita, who has since passed away, Manuel fell in love in his native Cuba. Flashing back, Manuel's love, Adela (Luisa María Morales), sings a melancholy tune that ends, "Today the moon asked / Why do you cry so alone / In my garden." Sent to Mexico to attend to his disapproving father's affairs, and unable to find her when he returned, Manuel lost contact with his beloved Adela. He did, however, learn that Adela began to perform on the radio, which led to a contract in Baja California. Hoping to find her there, Manuel was told that Adela had been fired for protecting herself from a lecherous rich man. Manuel tells his uncle, "If I come to find her, I could still be happy." Juanito, meanwhile, does not have the three pesos to buy Mother's Day flowers, so he steals some from a garden. He is caught, but a kind man helps him collect more. Juanito eventually returns home after working at a gas station, and his mother, who is none other than Adela, serves him dinner. Meanwhile, Luisito and Manuel, his father, listen to the radio; XEB's announcer reminds children that tomorrow is a special day.

On Mother's Day—May 10, 1933—the boys sing "Las mañanitas" for Adela, fight in the schoolyard, make up in detention, and return to Juanito's, where Luisito meets Adela. Some time later, the boys set off fireworks so spectacular that they cause a large fire. They run off, but are caught by a policeman who takes away Juanito, even though Luisito lit them. Sent to reform school, Juanito learns that his mother is ill.

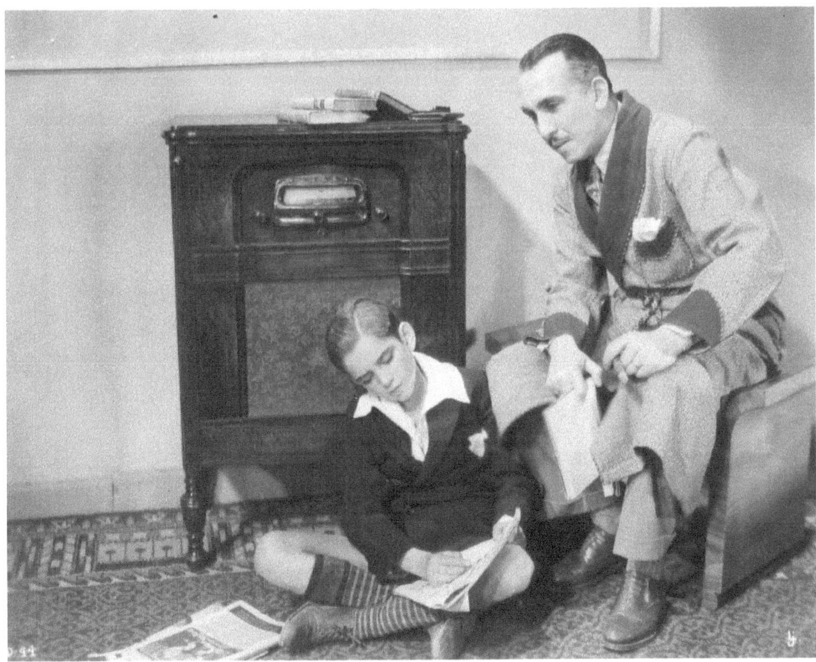

Figure 6.2. Father and son gather around the radio in *Madre querida*, listening to an announcement reminding children tomorrow is Mother's Day. Courtesy of the Colección Filmoteca UNAM, Filmoteca de la Universidad Nacional Autónoma de México.

Wracked by guilt, Luisito confesses everything to his father. Manuel takes it upon himself to right the situation, so he visits Juanito's mother. He immediately recognizes his long-lost love. Before her life slips away, Adela reveals that Juanito is their son. As his mother lays dying, Juanito escapes from the reform school. Destroyed, Juanito lives on the streets. Manuel looks for the boy, even running into him one day, but does not recognize him. Father and son are reunited as they both lay flowers at Adela's grave. Juanito returns to his father's home, where the boy is then bedridden with illness. He learns that his best friend is, in fact, his brother, and his street urchin friend returns to sing, crooning "In my life I will be / always a beggar / a beggar of love that implores." The boys leave Juanito to rest. A gravely ill Juanito is later visited in his dreams by his mother, superimposed on his beside until she is replaced by Manuel, who holds the boy's hand. Juanito says, "Father, what a beautiful dream I have

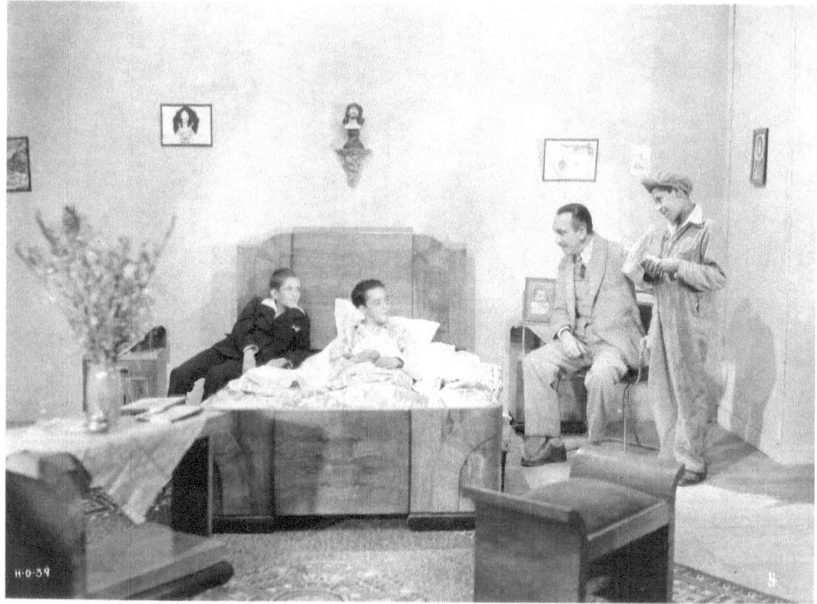

Figure 6.3. Surrounded by male loved ones, Juanito (Antonio Liceaga) heals from the loss of his mother in *Madre querida*. Courtesy of Mil Nubes-Foto.

had." *Madre querida* ends on May 10, 1934, where the boys gather again in the schoolyard and sing "In my journey, beloved mother, / I should put a monument / You, who gave me honor for life / In my journey, Sacred Woman."

With the foregrounding of *Madre querida*'s melodramatic narrative excesses, little was required of other cinematic elements, which were left in the background. Like that of other directors in the early sound period in Mexico and beyond, Orolian melodrama in the 1930s is enmeshed within works from other mediums of cultural production. Intermedial and intertextual connections with literary texts, especially serialized novels; theater, especially popular dramas; and radio, especially *radionovelas*, give depth to *Madre querida*'s storyworld of excess, everydayness, Manichean tensions between good and evil, and emotion. Of these connections, both de la Vega and López highlight the radio's impact. López argues, "Perhaps the key to understanding the film's success is to unravel its relationship to radio. *Madre querida* actually begins as an illustrated radio

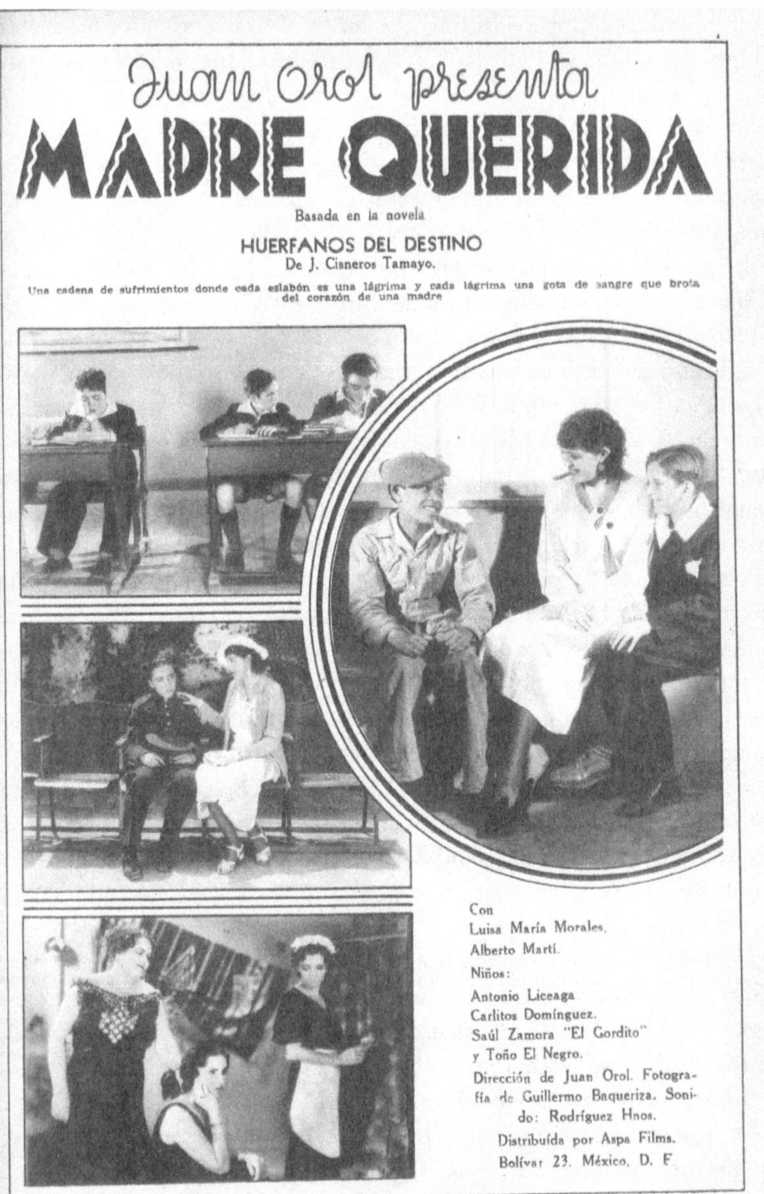

Figure 6.4. Advertisement for *Madre querida*. *Filmográfico*, May 1935.

program and, building radio into the narrative itself, sustains a constant radiophonic vision and affect."[44] Its place within the radiophonic imaginary is important, undoubtedly, but López underestimates how such an illustrated radio program might have been experienced as part of a larger program in the cinema, which may or may not have included nonfilmic entertainment, and, more importantly, Orol's intuitive filmmaking style. It may have been the first time Orol took charge of the megaphone, but Orol was not quite the inept director he would later be made out to be. In *Madre querida*, he adopted an unobtrusive visual style that allows the viewer to remain focused on its plot.

Madre querida's serpentine twists and turns would themselves be excessive if they were not to force the viewer into feeling over and over and over again. A May 1935 advertisement in *Filmográfico* demonstrates this not through images, as its four stills do little to express the film's diegesis, but through words. *Madre querida* is "a chain of suffering where each link is a tear and each tear a drop of blood that flows from the mother's heart."[45] The chain of suffering in the film, which connects its characters, originates from the mother, but, ultimately, is not the mother's. Left in the background in *Madre querida* is the figure of Luisa María Morales's Adela, whose self-suffering is experienced in the context of the foregrounded stories of father, Manuel, and son, Juanito. Their narrative chain of suffering is linked through Adela's self-sacrifice in the film. So while *Madre querida* may be an homage to all of the *madrecitas* of the world, it is a film whose narrative connects two androcentric plot lines: Juanito and Luisito, two friends who would become brothers, and Manuel and Juanito, a father who would again learn to love a son. As Orol suggests in *Madre querida*'s introduction, these relationships are made possible through Adela's self-abnegation, pain, hardship, and blood. Departing from the harsher representations of women of *Sagrario* and *Mujeres sin alma*, Orol uses a softened, but largely absent, mother in *Madre querida* to shape a more broadly appealing storyworld, one that had to be ready for Mother's Day.

El calvario de una esposa opened in Mexico City on September 5, 1936, simultaneously in seven unpretentious theaters: the Mundial, Roxy, Hipódromo, Alarcón, Parisiana, Capitolio, and San Juan de Letrán. It would take some time for Orol to exploit the success of *Madre querida*; his second feature film as director would take nearly a year to move out of development. Some context: "Reorganized and relying on government support, entrepreneurs in the sector of film production focused on making sequels throughout 1936 to successful films of the previous year."[46] Among a series of movies including Bohr's *Así es la mujer* (That's Women), Juan Bustillo Oro's *Malditas sean las mujeres* (*The Wicked Woman*), Fernando de Fuentes's *Las mujeres mandan* (Women Command), Roberto O'Quigley's *Cielito lindo* (*Dear Little Heaven*), and Miguel Zacarías's *El baúl macabro* (*The Ghastly Trunk*), *El calvario de una esposa* came to influence the kinds of stories Mexican cinema told. "And, with that, the generic bases are established on which the incipient business of cinema in Mexico will be developed."[47] In comparison to Bohr's or de Fuentes's films, however, Orol's next picture received little attention in the press during preproduction and production.[48] Filmed in the Estudios México-Films in mid-1936, it would take some time to reach theaters in the capital. In his column "Cases and Things of National Cinema," published in the August 1936 issue of *Filmográfico*, Esteban V. Escalante, curiously, reports "Juan Orol García will premiere his film 'El Calvario de una Esposa' in the course of the present month, a film that has already been released in the interior of the country and about which we cannot say anything because we have not seen it. And yet, we have the best recommendations."[49] We cannot say anything, of course, regarding Escalante's intentions, but it would seem that he was ridiculing the acritical, simplistic reception often afforded to films such as *El calvario de una esposa* in the press in articles that often were little more than extensions of the promotional materials provided by production companies. Take, for example, Fidel Solís's piece in *Ilustrado*.[50] He argues, "Juan Orol has made especially in Mexico the emotional film that comes—because of its plot—to vividly interest the spirit of the public." Solís does not revert to the formulas typical of such criticism, but his review does little to explore the meaning of Orolian melodrama or its impact on Mexican film culture of the day.

Mexican film criticism of the early sound period, however, was not without its more critical voices. In her review of the film for *Ilustrado*, Luz Alba (Cube Bonifant) excoriated *El calvario de una esposa*.[51] Known for her direct, impartial, and mature reviews, Alba was once called, "Mexico's most popular film critic [*cronista cinematográfica*]."[52] Alba's review begins: "A person who attended the premiere of this film, in one of the theaters where it was first shown, made the following suggestion, which has the sense of a synthetic judgment about it: 'it would had been appreciated had they called it *El calvario de un espectador* [*A Spectator's Agony*].'" Pouring more scorn on the film by playing with *calvario* (agony), Alba introduces a line of ironic critical reception of Orol's films that continues to be prevalent. She continues:

> As *filmófilos* with good memories will remember, national cinema [*la producción nacional*] is of an insurmountable mastery in the genre. It is difficult for there to be cinemas in the world where the fiction of death, the performance of pain, crying, and sadness become like ours, with such ineffable conviction, to the general delight of spectators. While greater truculence passes through the screen, the more distress that is emphasized and the characters' sorrow is deeper, the more fun spectators have, and the more they laugh. Well, in this sense, Mr. Orol's film is the masterpiece of national cinema.

Alba describes an often-overlooked characteristic of the reception of melodrama in early Mexican sound cinema. By catching sight of multiple audiences, but unable (or unwilling) to fully accept certain viewing practices, Alba notes how Orol's *El calvario de una esposa* is agonizingly melodramatic, but also agonizingly funny. Its excesses are channeled through the body in different ways by different spectators. Alba, ultimately, rejects unironic viewing, attributing it to bad taste. She concludes, "From what has been said, one might have guessed that the essential characteristic of this *aborto fílmico* to which we are referring with much sentiment: it is *la cursilería*." The bad taste to which Alba refers is inextricably enmeshed within her perspectives regarding class and gender.

El calvario de una esposa's critical reception opened up a new way of understanding Orolian cinema, but what little was published in *Filmográfico* about the movie reminds us of Orol's place within the Mexican film industry. Running opposite "Crónicas del mes" ("Chronicles of the Month"), the review section in which *El calvario de una esposa* never appeared, Escalante notes in a later iteration of "Cases and Things of National Cinema" that "[d]espite being terribly badly done, and artistically it is a disaster, Juan Orol's 'El Calvario de una Esposa' has made money by the handful."[53] In the column's next note, Escalante reports on Orol's next film, *Allá en los trópics* (Over in the Tropics, which would become *Honrarás a tus padres*), writing, "Juan Orol García, who knows a potato [i.e., nothing] as a director, has instead the gift of activity." More or less an afterthought—these two notes appear four pages into the column—and an object of ridicule, Orol existed on the margins of the emerging Mexican film industry.

Much like *Madre querida*, *El calvario de una esposa* begins with an instructive introductory sequence that foregrounds the film's moral lesson. In it, Orol defines how the viewer is to feel about the film's center: wives.

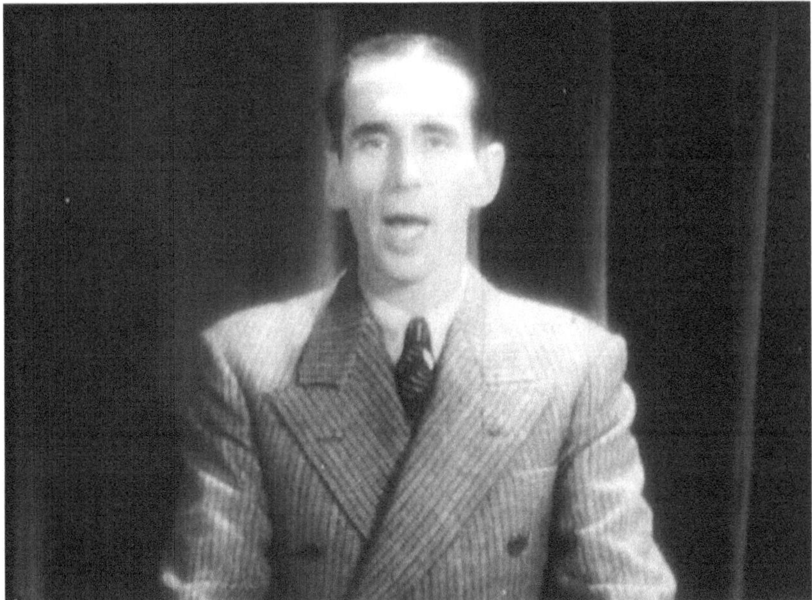

Figure 6.5. Juan Orol's edifying introduction to *El calvario de una esposa.*

Using *Madre querida* as both an expository and formal model, *El calvario de una esposa* opens with Orol (after its credits conclude). Dressed in a patterned suit, which gives some texture to the medium shot's simple composition, Orol is centered in the frame and gets extra light from above on his hair. Occupying the role of authority, during which a staged montage cuts in juxtaposing shots of an irresponsable father and husband drinking, a doting mother caring for her two daughters, an office worker engaging in inappropriate sexual activity with his secretary, and a wife carefully attending to her husband's wardrobe, Orol delivers a lecture that is less like an illustrated radio program and more like an educational film. In a much longer introduction, Orol states:

> Ladies and gentlemen, I feel honored to have filmed this movie, as it signifies a just and honorable tribute to *la mujer esposa* [the woman wife]; to that woman, symbol of abnegation and loyalty; to that suffering woman, companion to man in pain, who knows how to encourage him when his body and spirit begins to decline.

> I am sorry to have a role in this film that may provoke your antipathy. But that does not matter as long as it is for the benefit of all self-sacrificing and good wives.
>
> If we take a journey through all aspects of social status, we can see a humble man without awareness of his responsibility as a husband and as a family father. He leaves behind in the dishonorable cantina the salary that cost him so much effort to earn and that should resolve the problems that there in his poor home afflict his wife and small children who cry, exhausted by so many privations, while the selfless wife, the mother of her children, in an endless delay, awaits the arrival of a man who does not know how to encourage her.
>
> There exists cold in things and the soul, sadness in the little ones, because they have not known of the joys of children's games. Hunger has knocked on this door, to this home that the suffering wife wants to defend at the cost of her life. Only a piece of cold bread, and bitter as pain, which is divided up in equal parts, as the pain of an unjust and cruel abandonment is shared out in their souls.
>
> But not only the humble man is weak and makes victims of his loved ones by his weakness; also the man of the middle class, the employee who can live a little more comfortably, as well as the one who enjoys a great social position forgets that *una mujer amante* [a loving woman] and good wife awaits him and loves him, offering him loyalty, trusting, careful, *hacendosa* [house-proud], and honest, and always alert of how much he can favor or upset her. She takes care of his appearance. She desires that the man she loves so much appears in the street, in the office, everywhere, as quite the gentleman. And affectionately she moves the brush in his hands shaking the dust of those garments that she so loves because they are his. Of that man who does not know how to return her affection and loyalty. And she continues to naively wait. Therefore, for her, for *la mujer esposa*, my sincere homage, my admiration, and my best wishes that everyday she will be better understood and esteemed for the enormous moral value that the wife represents in society.

Ending with a slightly off-center medium shot, which features Orol's profile, *El calvario de una esposa*'s introduction reflects political and social discourse on women's roles in the family and society, while also signaling narrative excesses to come.[54] Women of all social classes bear the consequences of men's self-centered and ill-advised actions. They feel the effects of what their husbands cause. They are, again, almost tangential to Orol's broadside, which voices the moral mandates of postrevolutionary Mexico. The camera again static, Orol pivots at the end to declaim his final line. This functions to highlight the importance of his ideological and moral framework. It also returns his gaze to the camera, which, as Orol admittedly plays an antagonistic character, anticipates the viewer's ambivalent relationship with the man who seems to be the film's protagonist. It may portray the wife's agony, but *El calvario de una esposa* is largely the husband's film.

With Orol's introduction fading to black as he bows, *El calvario de una esposa* begins in a fractured home. A dolly shot approaches Irene Morel (Consuelo Frank), who encourages her young son to go to bed, and assures him that his father will buy his medicine. Some time later, her husband returns, only to coldheartedly abandon his family. Drawing away, another dolly shot introduces us to a more comfortable home in which a well-dressed woman sits and her boy, of a similar age, plays bullfighter. They wait, however, for a different reason; soon Pepe Luis (Orol) returns in his *traje de luces* to his wife, Inés (Consuelo Moreno), and son, Pepito (Ícaro Cisneros), only to promise not to again enter the bullring.[55] *El calvario de una esposa* also introduces Pepe's friends, his Spanish *banderillero* Paco (Saúl Zamora) and his unsavory Cuban friend Sebastián (René Cardona). Paco warns Pepe of Sebastián's bad influence, with little luck as Sebastián, who has just arrived, attempts to flirt with Inés. The three talk for a bit, and Sebastián invites his friend out to the Waikiki at eleven o'clock. Pepe assures Sebastián that along with the bulls, "no more cabarets, no more revelry." Putting up as much of a fight as he had earlier, it would seem, Pepe acquiesces. The friends drink as they enjoy the entertainment: Irene performs a rumba with Raulito (Saúl Zamora), her chubby boy partner; Raulito then performs the José Bohr foxtrot "Tu boquita" ("Your Little Mouth") [which had previously appeared in his 1934 film *¿Quién mató a Eva?* (*Who Killed Eva?*)]; and, finally, Irene sings, "Mi canción de amor es lo que te vengo a cantar" ("My love song is what I come to sing to you"). Pepe dances with Irene. After a drink, the two leave a drunken Sebastián at the club. Dissolving to Irene's bedroom, Pepe promises to see her again. Meanwhile, Inés puts Pepito to bed as she waits up for Pepe.

Inés and Pepito's suffering increases as Pepe dedicates more time and money to the easy life, showering Irene with gifts and lending (ostensibly) Sebastián cash. An honorable man, Paco visits Inés and listens to her troubles. Pepe eventually runs out of money. Irene avoids him, and Inés is having trouble making ends meet at home. Reforming, perhaps, Pepe gets a job as a radio announcer at XEFO; ever the same, Sebastián shamelessly attempts to take advantage of the situation, telling Inés he cannot ignore their recent poverty, which was caused by another woman, and trying to seduce her. On the first day at XEFO, Pepe walks off the job after being tasked with introducing Irene (sponsored, no less, by El Toreo, a bullfighting enterprise). They barely look at one another. At the bar, Pepe gets drunk listening to her sing on the radio. Meanwhile, in a dolly shot that recalls the one that started the film, Inés talks to Pepito about their poverty. Pepito, whose torn-apart shoes "are still good," tells her he cannot wait to grow up to provide for his mother. Pepe returns home drunk. Later, Paco returns to talk with Inés, leaving some money with her as he leaves. As soon as Inés gives Pepe the money, Sebastián knocks on the door. Pepe accepts Sebastián's offer to return to the bullring and requests the second *corrida*. Transitioning via an effect (an iris in that is out of place) to her apartment, Irene sings the last few words of a melancholy song. Evading three suitors, she retires to her room, where she tells her friend that she can no longer tolerate her so-called friends. In a long sequence, Pepe returns to the bullring. He has some trouble, initially, but eventually triumphs. At home, Pepe talks about changing the family's residence, while Inés asks him to change his friends. As with Paco, Pepe refuses to admit his friend's negative influence.

Sebastián arrives, and Inés reveals the truth of their situation. In interesting shot/counter-shot close-ups, Pepe approaches his friend with a knife in his hand. Sebastián draws a gun. The scene cuts to Inés, then to Pepito entering the room. After Sebastián's first shot, Pepito steps in front of his father and takes the second bullet, dropping to the ground. Pepe then throws the knife into Sebastián's chest, mortally wounding him. Improbably, *El calvario de una esposa* returns to Irene, who is discussing her situation with a friend and listening to the radio, which informs listeners of what had happened at Pepe's house. Irene discusses Pepe's situation with the judge, who assures her that he will go free. Returning home, Pepito lies on his death bed and asks his mother, as a last wish, to forgive his father. Just as Pepito dies, Irene arrives and apologizes for her role in the degeneration of Inés's family. In solidarity, Inés forgives Irene.

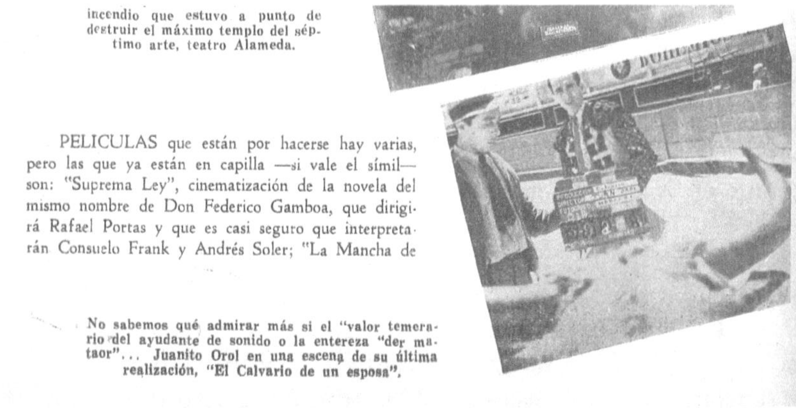

incendio que estuvo a punto de destruir el máximo templo del séptimo arte, teatro Alameda.

PELICULAS que están por hacerse hay varias, pero las que ya están en capilla —si vale el símil— son: "Suprema Ley", cinematización de la novela del mismo nombre de Don Federico Gamboa, que dirigirá Rafael Portas y que es casi seguro que interpretarán Consuelo Frank y Andrés Soler; "La Mancha de

No sabemos qué admirar más si el "valor temerario del ayudante de sonido o la entereza "der matador"... Juanito Orol en una escena de su última realización, "El Calvario de un esposa".

Figure 6.6. Orol preparing to bullfight on the set of *El calvario de una esposa*. *Filmógrafico*, November 1936.

Divesting herself of her ill-gotten gains, Irene gives money to Raulito (who must continue to work to support his grandmother) and the church. Resigned, Pepe attempts to give Inés everything he has recently earned, but she does not accept it, absolving him as Pepito had wished. The two abandon the city for their old hacienda. Placed into the countryside by a flamenco song, Pepe and Inés join the town's parishioners on their way to the church so that they can pray for the soul of their son.

A moral (and commercial) sequel to *Madre querida*, *El calvario de una esposa* adds to Orol's first film's agonizingly melodramatic excesses, extending its story and prolonging its characters' suffering. Its self-reflexivity also recalls *Sagrario* and *Mujeres sin alma*. Even though its representation of women is not tainted by the misogyny of the Peón films, *El calvario de una esposa* recalls the Orolian morality of *Sagrario*. Take, for example, words spoken by the secondary character Concha (Consuelo Moreno) to her friend Elena (Adriana Lamar), who is suffering her husband's absence. In a short conversation at the beginning of the film, Concha declares, "What could happen to him? He is probably out there looking at someone he likes. All men are cut from the same cloth!" and "What a fool you are! They all start out the same. By blaming drinks and friends. Look, I do not like getting into the intimacies of marriages, but . . ."[56] These recurring motifs are reflected in its promotion, which also evokes *Madre querida*. More clearly showing a wife's agony visually, as a publicity still shows Inés putting Pepito to bed, it states, "Madam, if your husband has been losing the respect and affection every man owes to the partner in the home, take him to see EL CALVARIO DE UNA ESPOSA." "Moral! Educational! Sentimental!," it is "A film for the public, and of those the public wants!"[57] In this July 1936 advertisement in *Filmográfico*, the fusion of storyworld and commercial strategy is clear. From "The director of 'Madre Querida,'" audiences are presented with "The first homage to wives."

El calvario de una esposa is structured, narratively and emotionally, by its male characters. Not only does Pepe and Sebastián's destructive relationship undergird its diegesis, but Pepito's drawn-out death gives the film its dramatic weight. Like *Madre querida*, its melodramatic narrative excesses are supported by few stylistic embellishments, but *El calvario de una esposa* is not entirely without formal technique. In the prolonged bullfighting scene, Orol uses a novel shot from the perspective of the bull showing Pepe's technique to break up long shots of the crowd and (often poorly framed) medium shots of the spectacle. Two other confrontations—Pepe/

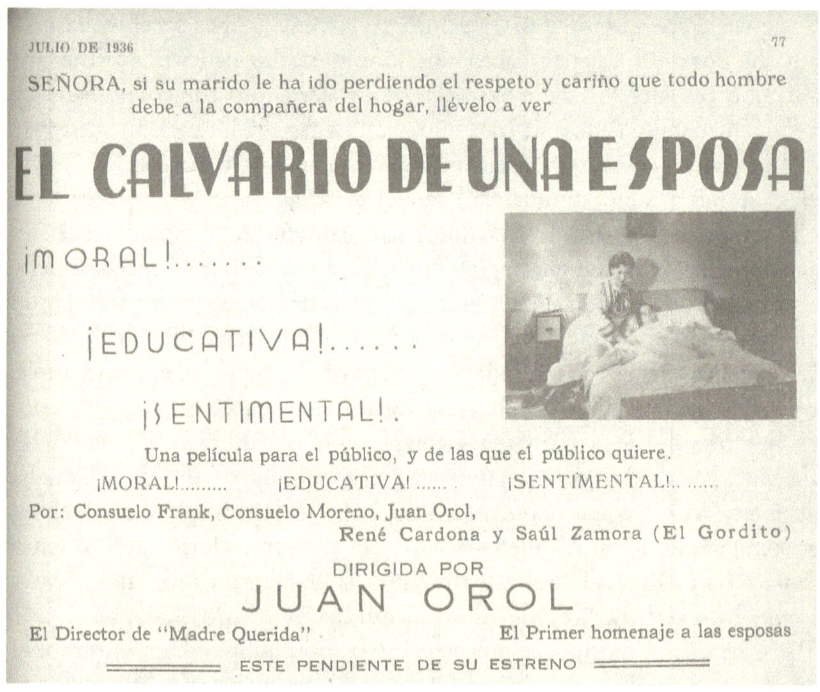

Figure 6.7. Advertisement for *El calvario de una esposa*. *Filmográfico*, July 1936.

Sebastián and Inés/Irene—show Orol's ability to frame action in such a way that emotions are heightened. Whether it is the shot/counter-shot of the two friends in the *plano americano* (medium-long shot), lit dramatically and more flatly to allow the viewer to both feel and see what is to come, or the proscenium-style staging of a conversation between women that creates solidarity through the careful expressive lighting of their close-ups, Orol uses formal strategies to diegetically round out *El calvario de una esposa*. These moments, however, are secondary to narrative events such as Pepito's death, which are often more stylistically direct. The film's final sequence, for example, is restrained in its representation of Pepe and Inés joining the procession toward church. It focuses attention on the ending of *El calvario de una esposa*: suffering forever after.

Daughters Verging on the Limit: *Honrarás a tus padres*

"There exists enormous interest among the public to recognize previous successes: 'Madre Querida' and 'El Calvario de una Esposa,' which constituted the artistic and box-office draw of the years that were exhibited, being 'Honorarás a tus padres' more touching (*emotiva*) and the one that goes directly to a woman's heart," reads a note published January 31, 1937, in *El Nacional*.[58] More commercially successful than critically so, *Madre querida* and *El calvario de una esposa* were dedicated by Orol to mothers and wives. *Honrarás a tus padres* is closely tied to another female figure, the daughter, but drops the abstract worship of her (perhaps causing the omission of an introduction). Based on Orol's unpublished novel *Allá en los trópicos*, it changes the successful formula of his previous two films, but does not stray too far diegetically, commercially, or affectively.[59] Like all of Aspa Films' productions (with the notable exception of the company's last, *Eterna mártir*), *Honrarás a tus padres* was filmed in Jorge Stahl's Estudios México-Films. Its production, which was lightly covered by the national press, began in August 1936. *Honrarás a tus padres* debuted on February 5, 1937, in the so-called *doble primer circuito,* which was comprised of the Edén, Rialto, América, Goya, Granat, Odeón, Monumental, Venecia, Teresa, Roma, and Rívoli.

Honrarás a tus padres was met by mixed critical reception. Fully reconstructing critics' reactions to the film is an impossibility, of course, but two important lines of thought can be discerned. In one, Esteban V. Escalante and Alfonso de Icaza note Orol's capacity to connect with audiences. In another, Luz Alba and Hortensia Elizondo admonish the *cursilería,* the bad taste, of Orolian melodrama. In his review in *El Redondel,* de Icaza recognizes the director's talent: "Juan Orol is, perhaps, of all our directors in the cinema, he who best has understood his role. He never satisfies the critics, but always moves the public, if not the upper-classes, the numerous masses."[60] De Icaza's review of the film is rather ambivalent, as he indicates incongruencies such as, "The action occurs in Cuba, but because it was made here, and with our elements, it lacks atmosphere," and noting (betraying racism, classism, or a combination of both) that María Luisa Zea "does not have the type of an aristocrat." De Icaza sets these observations aside, however, as he notes that "we left the cinema, and we realized that the great majority of the female spectators are crying." Escalante arrives at a similar conclusion in a note buried within "Cases and Things of National Cinema." He states, "We saw in a private screening 'Honorarás a tus padres,' by Juan Orol García, and even though the film, technically, is badly made, it has to its credit a plot that by itself reaches the heart."[61] With rather more flourish than his counterpart, de Icaza situates the audiences' affective reaction in the film's drawn out, melodramatic denouement: "That '*Mamacita linda,* for everyone you have died, except for me,' said by the little girl on her mother's grave moved the female sex to tears. May the theaters where this film is shown fill as those that ran the others by the same Juan Orol filled! *¡Vox populi, vox Dei!*"

In reviews published within days of each other in *Ilustrado*—published by *El Universal* and one of Mexico's most important weekly magazines—and *La Opinión* and *La Prensa*—published by Ignacio E. Lozano and two of the most important Spanish-language papers in the United States—Luz Alba and Hortensia Elizondo disparage *Honrarás a tus padres' cursilería.*[62] Alba writes, "Rarely does the public give greater showing of *incultura* [lack of education] than when watching Juan Orol's films." Elizondo, for her part, focuses her criticism: "But what matters most in the commentary we are making of 'Honrarás a tus Padres' comes from the selection of plot. Juan Orol cannot separate from *la cursilería* and *el mal gusto* [bad taste] in choosing the themes and titles that head them."[63] The themes and titles of Orol's films are incongruous, and Elizondo derides their capitalization of the family ("Now only a title dedicated to siblings is missing so that the domestic set could be completed"). She continues, "If in his plots and titles, Orol suffers from bad taste, in its dialogues, verges on the limit." Mocking the same lines Lolita delivers as her mother lies dying that are so praised by de Icaza, but paying special attention to "¿Vive aún?" ("Is she still alive?"), Elizondo criticizes the film's artificiality.[64] Alba, much like in her review of *El calvario de una esposa*, notes that spectators do not always react as they are supposed to: instead of crying with the film's characters at a grave, they laugh. Alba also jeers Orol's Cavalcanti in the fancy dress party scene: "Valentino was a plucked rooster next to this peacock!" Alba concludes her review sardonically, arguing that "[t]he only regrettable thing about all this, however, is that the only one who takes his productions seriously is Orol." Much like the rest of the review, which contextualizes *Honorarás a tus padres* not only within the national film industry, but also within Orol's own production, Elizondo is a little less caustic, concluding, "So it will be seen that in 'Honrarás a tus Padres' we have but one more film. Or, rather, another rehearsal of many that are needed to produce something worthwhile." Or, as Johnnie Carmenta says in *El mundo fantástico de Juan Orol*, "What matters is not where you begin, but where you finish."

Honrarás a tus padres opens to a young woman watering plants in window boxes and singing, her beautiful voice filling the surrounding forest. Dissolving to a much less idyllic, industrial scene, Don Fernando (Manuel Noriega) attends to his sugar mill's affairs. Returning to the hacienda, the young woman's voice provides a soundtrack for two men preparing for the day. One of them, Lieutenant Juan Cavalcanti (Orol), opens his window and looks out to the main house. Juan compliments Amparo's (Victoria Blanco) voice, while Don Fernando tells a man, who later will be presented as Rolando de Villanueva, the Count of los Pinares (René Cardona), that it is better to store sugar this year than sell. Cavalcanti and Amparo discuss her father's health. He promises to visit them later. The rural guard goes out into the forest to search for bandits led by El Zambo; meanwhile, Amparo visits Rolando, who promises to ask (as soon as sugar harvesting ends) for her hand in marriage and, thus, quiet her worries about their social differences. Soon thereafter, Amparo and her father discuss her future, albeit in different ways. She would like to travel to Havana to go to the beach, thus allowing Rolando an opportunity to talk with her father. Don Fernando tells her that he would like her to choose who she will marry, although he has his own preference: Cavalcanti. Coincidentally, or perhaps not, Calvacanti arrives at that moment, interrupting the conversation. Dissolving away briefly, only to return to the hacienda, Rolando and another woman, Doña Elvira de Montero (María Luisa Zea), talk about marriage. Just as Rolando reveals his (feigned) feelings for another woman, Amparo asks Calvancanti to sacrifice his love for her. Against his feelings, he agrees to tell Don Fernando that he is not interested in marrying Amparo. Rolando, of course, does not speak with Don Fernando, telling Amparo instead that he would love to get married, but social convention prevents it.[65] Unable to suffer further humiliation, Amparo writes her father a letter, asking him for his forgiveness for besmirching his name and informing him that she is leaving with "the fruit of her dishonor." Don Fernando confronts Rolando, who has the rural guard called. Before he removes the angry father, Calvacanti tells Rolando that his ignoble behavior is beneath his station. Elsewhere, Amparo seeks absolution through hard work, as she cares for her daughter.

Some time later, Rolando throws a fancy dress party in honor of Elvira. Calvacanti, who has searched for Amparo as he had promised her father before his death, plans to crash the party so that he may enlighten Elvira about Rolando's misbehavior. In an extended sequence, Calvacanti (ostensibly dressed as a gaucho) dances (ostensibly the tango) with Elvira (ostensibly dressed as an Andalusian gypsy), eventually taking advantage of the opportunity to reveal the truth of Rolando's character. In a scene reminiscent of *Madre querida*, Amparo tries singing at a cabaret only to be subject to lecherous men. Drawn into the establishment by her song, Calvacanti barely misses her, catching instead her friend's rumba. Conversing with an old woman (whom Calvacanti visits later), Amparo resolves to discuss her desperate situation with Rolando. She returns to his home with Lolita (Lucha María Ávila), begging her former lover to recognize his daughter. Refusing his obligation, and ignoring his daughter, he cynically offers them money. Calvacanti again arrives just in time, telling the Count that it was he who tipped off Elvira. Enraged, Roland pulls out a gun, but Calvacanti shoots him first. Amparo later tells the judge that both mother and daughter approached as Rolando lay dying. Amparo lovingly caresses her lover's head, and soon thereafter he briefly wakes, begging Amparo and Lolita for forgiveness. Calvacanti is condemned to death for premeditated murder. With Elvira in tow, Amparo travels to visit the Minister of War in a last ditch attempt to save Calvacanti. Amparo's testimony exonerates him, but the last storm has destroyed all telegraph and telephone communication. Racing against time, Amparo returns by train, then by horse through a terrible storm. Just as five members of the rural guard draw their weapons, Amparo arrives to stop the execution. Preventing one death, but causing another, Amparo's valiant efforts are rewarded with a double lung infection. Knowing her daughter will be taken care of, Amparo dies. Just after Calvacanti draws the blanket over her eyes, Lolita enters the room and asks if her mother is still sleeping. Unable to tell the girl anything, Calvacanti and the old woman watch as Lolita climbs onto her now dead mother. Lolita discovers the truth, and embraces the man who is now her father. Calvacanti and Lolita visit Amparo's grave. Lolita tells her, "*Mamacita*, you have died for everyone, except me, because I will always hold you here in my heart." Calvacanti and Lolita slowly leave the cemetery.

In their conversation at Rolando's fancy dress party, Elvira inadvertently defines Orolian poetics to Calvacanti. Expressing her gratitude to the gaucho for divulging information about Rolando's true self, she says, "Truth and good feelings are not seen, they are felt." The experience of truth, as well as the good, is felt in *Honrarás a tus padres* not only through the melodramatic excess of its narrative, but also the way in which those excesses are constructed in editing. Working with longtime collaborator José Marino, who worked on all of the Aspa Films productions except *Sagrario*, Orol uses editing effectively (although, perhaps, not intentionally) to elicit the viewer's affective response in two ways. Throughout *Honorarás a tus padres*, Orol fully implements a novel strategy with which he had experimented in previous films. In emotionally charged conversations, Orol uses an estranging technique of displacing characters in medium/close-up shots. In Amparo and Calvacanti's conversation after the Lieutenant shoots the Count in self-defense, Orol cuts from the careful lighting of medium shots of the two characters to close-ups of Calvacanti and Amparo. Not always existing within diegetic space, although in this situation lighting and mise-en-scène disorient, these sequences place the viewer within the characters' affective worlds. Seemingly the product of a bad director, this technique nonetheless is effective in focusing on the feeling of truth. This feeling of truth is also experienced in another displacement, this time temporal. In her flashback to the shooting, Amparo remembers events slightly differently than they were originally presented in the film. In contrast with the original scene, Amparo's recollection shows Rolando's prolonged fall into a chair, the setting of the important moment in which Rolando takes responsibility for his actions and apologizes. Presented in the film as a simple flashback, yet another narrative excess, the viewer does not immediately see the differences between the scenes, but certainly feels, likely for the first time, the death of the immoral Count.

Without Fault in an Unjust World: *El derecho y el deber* and *Eterna mártir*

Juan Orol's last films in Mexico in the 1930s, as well as the final projects of his production company Aspa Films, were *El derecho y el deber* and *Eterna mártir*.[66] These movies responded to increasing competition in the Mexican film industry in two distinct manners. Shot in 1937, the year of "More than Twenty *Ranchos Grandes*," according to García Riera, *El derecho y el deber* is one of a number of films that aimed to replicate the success of Fernando de Fuentes's blockbuster *Allá en el Rancho Grande*. Unlike *La Zandunga* (dir. de Fuentes), *Huapango* (dir. Bustillo Oro), *Allá en el Rancho Chico* (*There on the Small Ranch*, dir. René Cardona), among other productions of that year, *El derecho y el deber* leaned toward what was fashionable at the time, but did so in a way that was distinctively Orolian. What might have been a simple retread became something quite different. *Eterna mártir*, on the other hand, eschewed trends within the Mexican film industry in favor of recreating what made Orol successful in the first place: an homage to a suffering mother who is eternally self-abnegating for the betterment of the men in her life. *El derecho y el deber* and *Eterna mártir*, which might have existed in tension given the internal and external forces pulling at them, complement each other in such a way that they form the culmination of Orolian melodrama in the 1930s. Informing his later films, the diegeses of *El derecho y el deber* and *Eterna mártir* create an unjust world in which the central characters are without any fault. Suffering the consequences of things that lie far beyond them, these characters are forced to deal with their situations as best as they possibly can. Like Orol's films that preceded them, both *El derecho y el deber* and *Eterna mártir* rely heavily on narratives dripping in melodrama excess. The surfeit of emotion elicited by these narratives is supported by often inconspicuous formal strategies.

Foreshadowing delays that would become common later in Orol's career, *El derecho y el deber* went into production in February 1937 in México-Films' studios and would wait until the next year for its release. Similar to his previous films, it opened widely on the "doble primer circuito" of the Goya, Teresa, Odeón, Rialto, Granat, Monumental, Edén, Venecia, América, Roma, and Rívoli theaters on February 5, 1938. Not only did distribution issues slow down the film's arrival in theaters, but they also severely limited its impact on audiences, as well as critics. Orol's next film, and Aspa Films' last, went into production soon after *El derecho y el deber*. In a review published in *El Universal*, which puts into question the film's release date, the film's plot is connected to its marketing:

> This film is advertised by taking advantage of the phrase that has become indispensable in national "slang" as a description of goodness, and the ads read: "Watch this film . . . it's like a rifle." Orol has put into *El derecho y el deber* everything audiences can ask for in its amusement. Drama, romanticism, love problems, humor. In musical matters, it has everything: *jarabes, zandungas, huapangos, jaranas,* and *ranchera* songs.[67]

In March 1937, *Eterna mártir* was shot in the Estudios de la Nacional Productora. With a separate distribution agreement, *Eterna mártir* opened before *El derecho y el deber* on October 28, 1937.[68] A note in *El Universal* anticipated its release:

> Tomorrow the premiere of a new national film will take place in the Palacio theater. *Eterna mártir*, the most recent production by Juan Orol, the director who has most succeeded in drawing the interest of all Spanish-speaking audiences for the realism with which he brings to the screen issues of real life. His hits such as *Madre querida* and *El calvario de una esposa* place him within those directors who most know how to reach the masses and, for that reason, *Eterna mártir*'s triumph is assured in advance.[69]

Indifferent to, or (willfully) ignorant of, criticism leveled against his films, this short, hyperbolic piece in *El Universal* defines Orol's place within the national film industry. He is a director who reaches everyday people by projecting (sensational, but) everyday issues onto the screen. The meaning of its triumph, however, is left undefined. Is it artistic? Is it emotional? Is it narrative? Is it commercial?

If solely placed in the context of broader industry trends in Mexican cinema at the time, *El derecho y el deber*'s critical reception may have been predefined, as García Riera's was when he posited in 1969, "For [Orol] there is no place in *Rancho Grande*, and this would determine his distancing from national cinema for various years."[70] Separated by some thirty years from *El derecho y el deber*, and likely writing from his memory and notes on the film, García Riera misunderstands Orol's place within the Mexican film industry and, perhaps, did little to understand the meaning of his films. Alfonso de Icaza, however, followed Orol's filmmaking career throughout the 1930s in his column in *El Redondel.* Though perhaps a bit too forgiving of the director's shortcomings and too quick to praise, de Icaza's criticism is central to how Orol is understood today. Particularly important is his review of *El derecho y el deber*, which was published on January 30, 1938:

> One of the most difficult things in life is achieving a true personality.
>
> Among our film directors there are good ones, no doubt, but only one, Juan Orol, is fundamentally different from the rest. This is very easy to confirm. We can watch movies directed by so-and-so or by whatshisname, and if we are not told who directed it, we would never guess. Why? Because they do not have a special stamp, emanating from the personality of the director.
>
> With Orol's, the opposite happens.
>
> Without prior notice, without any warning, observant spectators would realize after a few scenes who had directed it all.
>
> That is the secret of the success of the films directed by Juan Orol. They are different from the others.
>
> *El derecho y el deber*, soon to premiere in one of our principal theaters, is not the exception to the rule, but rather its confirmation. It is a typical film of Orol's that will come to consecrate him as a universal film director.[71]

In his review of the film, de Icaza differentiates Orol and his films from others.[72] By designating Orol to be what we may anachronistically label an auteur, de Icaza gives Orol his own special place within Mexican cinema. It may have been that this special place—isolated from adequate capital to comfortably make his films (largely due to disadvantageous distribution deals)—led to his imminent move to Cuba to film *Siboney*, but de Icaza observes that even within twenty *Ranchos Grandes*, *El derecho y el deber* stands out as Orol's.

El derecho y el deber gets underway as Chucho (Orol), a revolutionary colonel, finally returns home. He tells his men, "Five years without seeing my son. . . . What a surprise for my poor wife! This is how I left

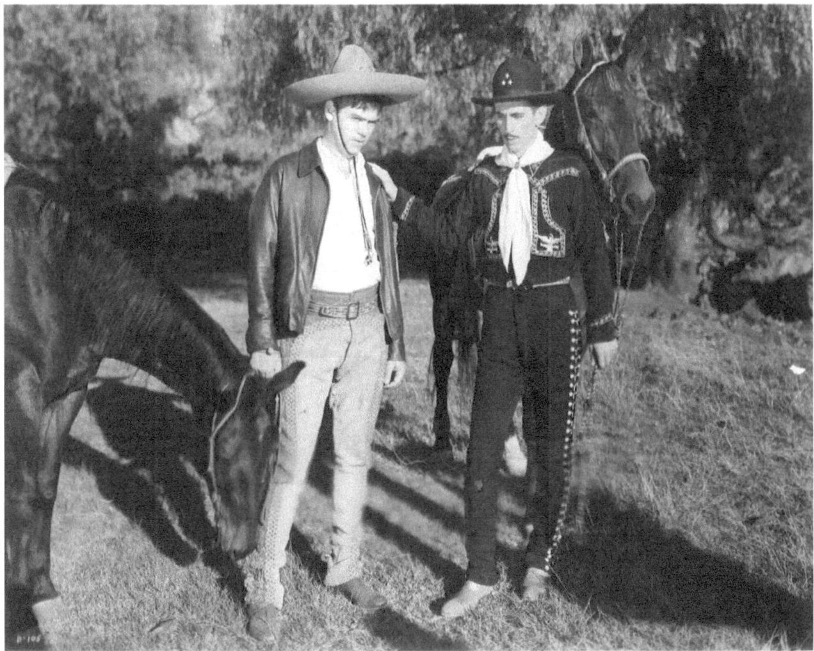

Figure 6.8. Promotional photograph from *El derecho y el deber* showing Chucho (Juan Orol) and Pancho (Leopoldo Ortín), his trusted righthand man. Courtesy of Mil Nubes-Foto.

him [showing a photograph of a baby] when they took me from home. Precisely today he turns six. Soon I will be with them." His men take leave. Chucho begins to lead his horse down to the hacienda. Several characters are fleetingly introduced as Chucho continues his homecoming. Eventually he runs into Pancho (Leopoldo Ortín), his old ranch hand, who, rather than excitedly greeting his *patrón,* has great difficulty in explaining his sullen mood. He begins to recount the tale, and the scene fades to black. Fading back in, Chucho tells Pancho that everything that has happened was caused by fate and that they are not at fault. Chucho will return to the mountain, but asks Pancho to let him know when he can visit his son without anyone knowing. Once he has seen his son, Chucho thinks he will return north to rejoin his forces. He asks Pancho to keep silent about his return. Some of the ranch hands recall Chucho's disappearance, which occurred not only on his son's birthday but also on the *Día de la Raza* (Columbus Day), a day of celebration at the ranch.

Miguel (José Eduardo Pérez), one of the men, recalls how he was heading to the United States, but Chucho and his wife made him feel at home. The men head off to the annual party.

Raconteurs and gossips stay on the margins of the revelry, which heats up with a *jarabe* (a mariachi song form). Quite a few couples head to the dance floor to enjoy "Jarabe tapatío" with their partners. More than reminiscent of the scene in *Allá en el Rancho Grande*, a man challenges Don Juan (René Cardona) by song, using *coplas*. With little subtlety, the song intimates that Juan has seduced Chucho's wife. An ally replies and defends Juan's intentions. Juan adds his own *coplas*. Imploring everyone to return to the party, two children dance to another *jarabe*. More song and dance follow, and later Juan joins Chuchito (Ernesto Fuentes R.) for bedtime prayer. Cutting outside, knowing that his wife is now with another, a melancholy Chucho listens to a man's song.[73] Shifting first to a subplot, Pancho's strained relationship with Chencha (Amelia Wilhelmy),

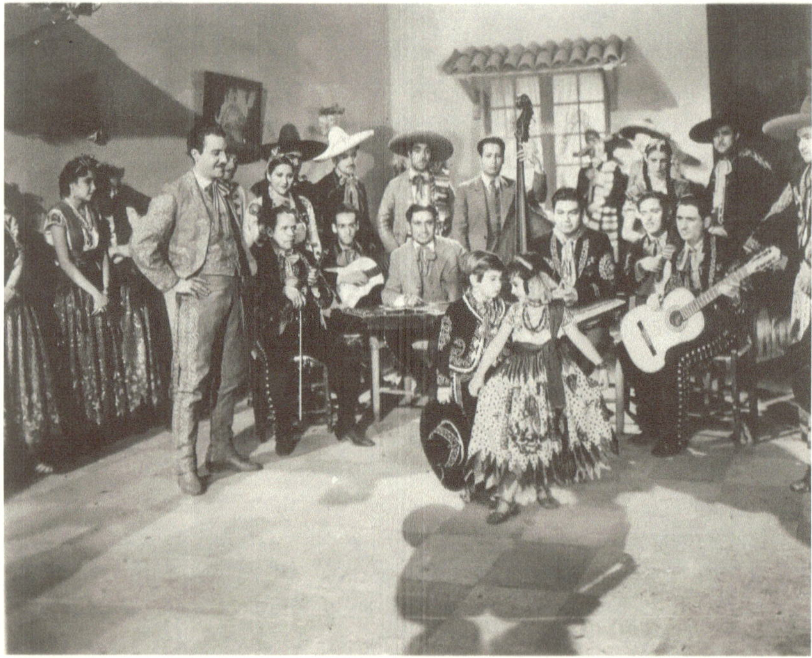

Figure 6.9. Even though Orol draws from *Allá en el Rancho Grande* in sequences such as this, *El derecho y el deber* is a distinctly Orolian melodrama. Courtesy of the Colección Filmoteca UNAM, Filmoteca de la Universidad Nacional Autónoma de México.

then to Pancho encountering Juan and Chuchito, Pancho then heads out to talk with Chucho. Learning that his wife still thinks of him, Chucho states, "Morally, neither one of them is at fault." Unable to wait any longer, Chucho enters his home through the window to kiss his son. Chuchito awakes, telling his mother he has seen a man, a ghost. In a moment of comic relief, Pancho and Chenchita quarrel and flirt, flirt and quarrel.[74] Later, as Juan discusses Chuchito's health with a doctor, Padre Agustín (Joaquín Coss) arrives at the ranch. Juan and Padre Agustín talk about Chucho's reported ghost. Soon thereafter, Chucho returns to talk with Juan about their situation. Chucho's wife, Amalia (Consuelo Moreno), only seen fleetingly to this point, sees him and faints. Exchanging words, Chucho tells Juan that if he had wanted, he would have already killed Juan, but that they will see each other in Morelia, Michoacán's state capital. The priest discusses the complex matter of the love triangle with Amalia and Juan.

Some time later, Chucho, Pancho, Amalia, Juan, Chuchito, and his half-brother travel to Morelia to attend a hearing to resolve their impossible situation. The facts of the case are laid out by Chucho, who describes how he was torn from the ranch and later fought alongside Pancho Villa; Juan, who unintentionally usurped his once dear friend due to the unfortunate circumstances of war; Amalia, who encounters her circumstances at a total loss; Padre Agustín, who asks, "And when both sides are right?"; and, finally, Juan's lawyer (Gustavo Lechuga), whose verbal contortions do little but show the depths of the moral ambiguity in which they find themselves. The judge, recalling the legal maxim "*primero en tiempo, primero en derecho*" (*Prior in tempore, potior in iure* or "First in time, greater in right"), sides with Chucho. Everyone is unhappy, especially Juan who holds his crying toddler son. Chucho tells his former friend, now his rival:

> Your place is this; the one who leaves is me. I told you I would claim my rights; now I just need to do my duty, as promised. And I did not do it before because you did not want to give me the reason. Mr. Judge; I beg of you that when I leave here, you open this envelope and read its contents, and thank you very much. Amalia, I advise you to take good care of the children and, from time to time, talk to Chuchito about me. Goodbye, Amalia. Juan, take good care of Amalia, who deserves it. And you, may you be very happy. Goodbye, father. Until we meet again. . . . Goodbye, Pancho.

He kisses Chuchito on the head, then leaves the room. Seconds later, a gunshot is heard outside the court. Chucho has committed suicide, escaping his tormented fate and resolving his family's situation. Juan begs for forgiveness, and asks Amalia and Chuchito to hold Chucho as he lays dying. Amalia also asks for forgiveness. Padre Agustín asks for piety, and the judge reads Chucho's letter, which details the division of his assets. Padre Agustín draws the film to a close, concluding, "Así interpretan en la sierra el derecho y el deber" ("That is how law and duty are interpreted in the mountains").

And with that Orolian melodramatic turn in the denouement, what initially might have seemed to be yet another *Allá en el Rancho Grande* ripoff becomes something quite different. Chucho's court case and his subsequent suicide in *El derecho y el deber* is the narrative culmination of Orol's exploration of an unjust world in which no one is truly culpable, at least no one is immediately so. Within the film's narrative, however, there are other aspects that show that Orol is working with a very different reality than "the imaginary bucolic past where macho pride and true love always prevailed," as Ana M. López describes de Fuentes's film.[75] Set on a ranch to which modernity has yet to arrive—something emphasized when Pancho is nearly hit by a car crossing the street in Morelia—*El derecho y el deber* makes references to real-world problems of real-world people. Miguel, for example, mentions his migration north. The legitimacy and parentage of Pancho and Chencha's children is openly discussed. As in *Honrarás a tus padre*, Orol seems unwilling to be overly nostalgic for bucolic countryside life. This awareness is also cinematic. The appearance of Pancho Villa, for example, may seem like a melodramatic excess, but in it there is a wink acknowledging his cinematic presence in both silent movies and talkies such as de Fuentes's trilogy. Earlier in the film, there is an exchange that directly alludes to the scene in *Allá en el Rancho Grande* in which José Francisco (Tito Guízar) and Martín (Lorenzo Barceleta) trade *coplas*. After an associate replied to a man that challenged Juan's legitimacy, Juan speaks for himself. He tells everyone at the party, "A moment guys. Before things go any further, I would like to tell you something, even by song, as is customary in many of our movies," before adding his own *coplas*. The festivities quickly resume, but the difference between the two films linger. *El derecho y el deber* uses film form selectively to heighten the film's emotional textures, but, generally, Orol implements strategies to make them invisible to its storytelling.

Eterna mártir may not be the apotheosis of the director's Aspa Films productions, but it is likely the film that best encompasses Orolian melodrama of the 1930s. By the time of its release, however, Orol seems to have exhausted the goodwill of critics. Even though he would later laud Orol as a kind of proto-auteur, Alfonso de Icaza was less forbearing in his assessment of *Eterna mártir* in his review of the film.[76] Ironically, as *El derecho y el deber* awaited release, de Icaza begins:

> In the midst of the streak of *mariachismo* from which our production is suffering, Juan Orol offers us something different. Different by being deprived of *huapangos* and wardrobe *charrería,* but the same as what Orol has done before. His films have the merit of being inspired by a noble and irreproachable moral and, therefore, possess the the virtue of reaching the heart of the *gross public,* who attends the cinema without the slightest analytical spirit.[77]

De Icaza contextualizes *Eterna mártir* within Mexican cinema, as well as within Orol's own filmography. Attentive to the connection Orol's films have made with spectators due to their "bombastic sentimentality" and themes evoking "those big, melodramatic novels of the beginning of the century that touched our childhood," de Icaza criticizes its technical elements and the overabundance of dialogue. This indulgence, he argues, "makes it possible to understand with eyes close by only listening. Notwithstanding what has been said, we believe that this film will be enjoyed in the cinemas of the circuit." De Icaza was much more generous than Carlos del Paso, who reviewed the film for the popular magazine *Sucesos para todos.* Giving the film a rating of 10 percent, which lands it in the category of *mala* (bad), del Paso harshly criticizes Orol and the film's actors. He writes, "Despite the enormous will with which Consuelo Moreno and Martinez Casado carried out their roles, it was impossible to obtain even fifteen minutes of the suffering spectator's attention. I do not know how they had the patience to watch this movie until the end." Echoing de Icaza's review of *Eterna mártir*, as well as Luz Alba's pieces on earlier Orol films, del Paso continues by bewailing, "Slow, of an exasperating slowness. With pretensions of dramatic comedy, it was on the verge of causing the disarticulation of my jaws slackened by frequent and prolonged yawns. Orol, the director, unfortunately conflates the cinematic art with the theatrical, giving us kilometric dialogues full of redundancy and repetitions." In addition to taking issue with the verbocentrism of *Eterna mártir*, del Paso also picks up on a critical line that continues to inform reception of Orol: his casual attitude toward framing ("The photographic technique is awful: frequently protagonists leave the frame that encompasses the objective of the camera"). In the end, as del Paso concludes, "Its authors and performers reveal the inexperience of a beginner lacking direction." In Orol's fifth feature as director, it would seem that certain lessons might never be learned.

Returning to the conceit of his earlier films centering on suffering and self-sacrificing wives and mothers, Orol begins with an interpretative introduction. Staged even more simply than *Madre querida* or *El calvario de una esposa*, the introduction to *Eterna mártir* presents Orol standing over an open book. Wearing a white tuxedo and a black tie, Orol gives his speech:

> Dear audience: once again, as in the series of films that I have made, I want to present to you another shred [*jirón*] ripped from real life to the screen, to graphically show you all one of the many tragedies of the home and where, in most cases, the protagonist is the eternal martyr. And who may be the eternal martyr of a home? I do not think it is necessary to tell you because we all know that it cannot be anyone other than a mother or a wife, given that they are the only ones capable of sacrificing everything, both for their children and for their husband. And neither of them have known how to appreciate in its generality this enormous sacrifice that only a loving mother or a self-sacrificing wife are capable of suffering. That is why I ask my fellow men, with all due respect, for a little more consideration and affection for the ones for she who gave them being and for the others for she who gave them her love with no other ambition than to be the faithful companion of their days. Thank you very much for your attention.

Offering little to nothing visually—Orol is static, the books are left unused, and only two, slightly different angles are used in its three shots—the introduction does not function didactically, but rather lightly scolds the audience for not sufficiently appreciating their mothers and wives. Less intermedial and more intertextual, particularly with his own films, the introduction to *Eterna mártir* provides an ideological and moral framework for the film, but does so with much less conviction than *Madre querida* or *El calvario de una esposa*.

Following the familiar fade to black that marks the end of Orol's introduction, *Eterna mártir* opens to Griselda (Consuelo Moreno) preparing to leave work, bidding adieu to her boss Don Gabriel (Ricardo Avendano). Returning home to the soundtrack of a song that begins, "I am a student dreamer, dreamer / bohemian without money and without love, without love / because I have to be a lawyer, engineer, doctor," thus defining the three performers Pedro, Alfredo, and Víctor (played by local radio stars Chucho Monje, Wello Rivas, and Roberto Soto Mejía), Griselda belts out "Sleep, little by little" as she rocks a crib. Griselda's knitting is interrupted by a knock at the door. Susana (Mercedes Moreno), Griselda's estranged sister, has come to visit. Through their conversation, details about Griselda's situation emerge. She has had a son with Fernando (Juan José Martínez Casado), a medical student who will soon receive his degree. As soon as he becomes a doctor, Fernando and Griselda will marry. Lamentably, despite their families' comfortable stations, especially Fernando's, the baby has suffered because of their destitution. Griselda relates her situation: she and her partner share a job as a cashier at a wholesaler (she works in the morning and Fernando in the afternoon), their combined salary is one hundred fifty pesos a month; they are fortunate to live among other students, who help each other out; and Fernando recently received from an uncle three thousand pesos, which has helped immensely. Fernando returns home as Susana departs. The couple discusses Susana's visit, holding each others' hands tenderly, then Griselda mentions that Don Gabriel asked to talk with Fernando. Fernando, slightly distressed, tells his partner he is heading out to talk to their boss. While he is absent, Griselda helps out her bohemian neighbors, particularly Pedro, who has fallen in love with Paulina (the Spanish actress Mary Carrillo). Throughout the rest of the film, Pedro and Paulina's relationship acts as a comic counterweight to the heaviness of Fernando and Griselda's.

Soon thereafter, a dejected Fernando returns home and begins to tell his partner something important but is interrupted by a knock on the door. Jaime (Manuel Noriega), Fernando's family's most trusted domestic worker, induces desperation in the soon-to-be doctor. Jaime has come from Sonora to tell them that Fernando's mother has been unable to weaken his hardhearted father, and has been unable to obtain the money he requested.

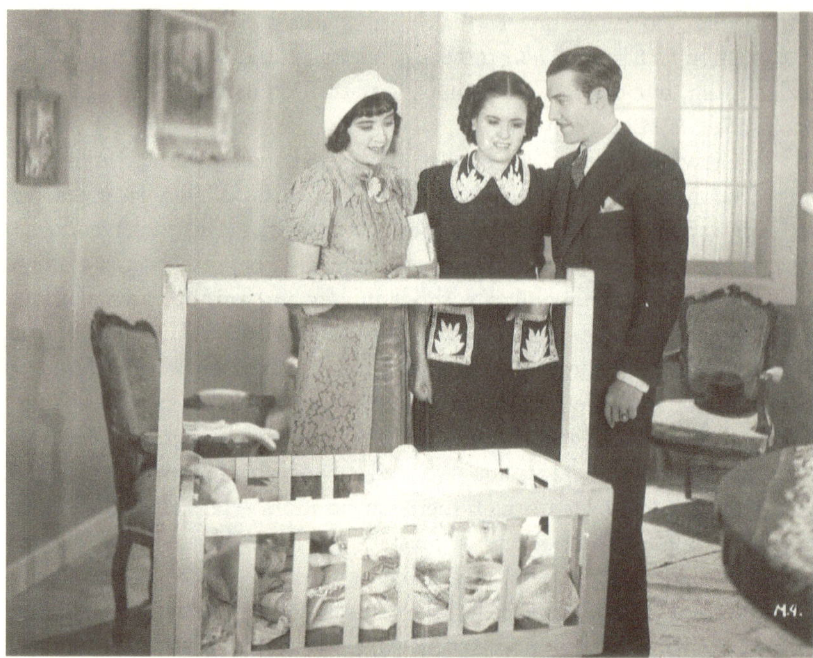

Figure 6.10. Susana (Mercedes Moreno), Griselda (Consuelo Moreno), and Fernando (Juan José Martínez Casado) gather around the crib in *Eterna mártir*. Courtesy of the Colección Filmoteca UNAM, Filmoteca de la Universidad Nacional Autónoma de México.

Fernando, enraged, tells Jaime to tell his parents that he hates them and orders, "Get out of here! Leave here soon!" Griselda gently reproaches her husband, then asks Jaime for forgiveness. Jaime retires, and Griselda begs her husband to tell her what has happened. He admits that soon Don Gabriel will report him for theft. After the baby's doctor warned them that their son would perish if he were not to receive better care, Fernando took the three thousand pesos from their workplace and hoped to replace it with money from his mother. Now, with his family's indifference, he must suffer the consequences. Griselda convinces her husband to allow her to take care of the situation. Yet another door knock intervenes, this time more urgent, as it is Don Gabriel. Griselda accepts responsibility, saying that Fernando knew nothing of the theft. After their boss leaves, Griselda tells Fernando that she took the blame, knowing that it is the best for their son. In the living room, she leaves Fernando—crumpled over, destroyed—and goes into the bedroom to bid farewell to her son. Drawing out her pain, she then says goodbye to Fernando, imploring him to take good care of their son. Betraying false optimism, or perhaps his social class, Fernando tells her that they will find an answer to their desperate situation. After visiting Griselda in jail, he visits his father and implores him to use his connections to help. Fernando's father provides a solution, but one that causes prolonged separation. Two old women arrive and tell Griselda that instead of staying in jail, she will serve her time (five years) in the Convento de las Hermanas de María.

Flashing forward some five years to a party, and in expository conversation with Alfredo and Víctor, Fernando explains that finally having given up hope of finding Griselda (and "perhaps more out of necessity than out of liking") he has decided to marry Alcira (Adria Delhort). Sometime later, Pedro and Fernando talk about women and love. Pedro describes Paulina's jealousy, while Fernando recalls his despair at being unable to find Griselda and his desire to provide his son with a mother. Alfredo and Víctor also appear. Víctor tells his friends that a woman had recently visited him. "Griselda?" Fernando asks. Indeed, Víctor says, and she is outside. Fernando asks his friends to step out; a melancholy Griselda and an anxious Fernando catch up, filling in what few holes of their story remain. Griselda sought Fernando out after being released empty-handed to the street, but she arrived in Sonora just after his wedding. She comes not to recriminate, having had time to wring out her heart after learning of Fernando's marriage, but to get her son. The star-crossed lovers converse about what that would mean until Alcira interrupts with their son. Carlitos (uncredited) has cut his hand. Fernando implores the boy to be consoled by the visiting woman. Alcira takes the child away. Unwilling to uproot the boy from his happy situation, Griselda tells Fernando she cannot take him. Fernando tells her, "Griselda, your self-sacrifice is divine." Griselda tells Fernando that she has been offered a job as a companion to a recently married wealthy woman who will soon depart for Europe. (She is later shown on a ship taking care of a baby.) Fernando again proposes to find another solution, but Griselda must take leave so that Carlitos may preserve and venerate the memory of his mother.

Flashing forward fourteen more years, Carlitos (Antonio Liceaga) finds himself in a similar situation to his father so long ago. About to become a doctor, he has fallen in love. Unlike his father, however, Carlitos's love has found support. The gravity of the situation leads the three to share their feelings for each other, as well as Jaime and Griselda. Again adding levity, Pedro and Paulina provide an emotional respite (continued in a comical phone call taken by Jaime). Moments later, Jaime answers the door. A veiled woman enters and asks to be attended by the son of Doctor Molina. Griselda tells Jaime that her long suffering will soon lead her to death. Jaime brings Carlitos into the office. Mother and son grow closer through sharing their emotions: her agony and pain that has brought her to death's door and his joy at being at the threshold of love (and, by extension, family). His felicity, however, recalls the pain of his mother. Fernando enters and identifies the woman as Griselda. After what happened is briefly explained, Griselda dies.

The denouement of *Eterna mártir* draws together not only the film's narrative threads, leaving a more complete diegesis that anticipates the later classical cinema of the *Época de oro*, but it also weaves together tendencies of Orolian melodrama of the 1930s that would linger on within

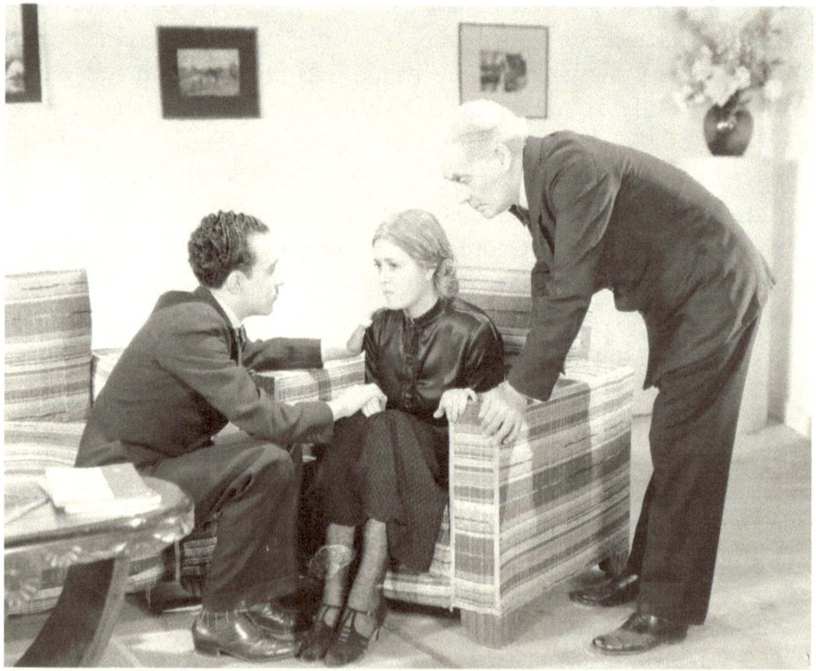

Figure 6.11. As Jaime (Manuel Noriega) stands, Griselda (Consuelo Moreno) shares a moment with her unknowing son, Carlitos (Antonio Liceaga). Soon, their truth emerges. Courtesy of Mil Nubes-Foto.

the director's later works. Implied initially by the young doctor's leaning toward his patient, Griselda and Carlitos grow closer throughout the sequence as they gravitate toward each other emotionally. Orol tightens his framing, eventually using medium shots in which mother and son occupy the screen equally. This allows the viewer to better inhabit the conversation. So, when she asks to kiss him in her name, and Carlitos says, "Yes, kiss me like you were my mother," the viewer is able to see the son's head in his mother's hands as she tenderly kisses his forehead. The lighting is so flat it is effectively invisible, rendering the emotional tones of the scene even more visible. With more contrastive lighting, Fernando enters. The scene cuts back to Griselda, whose face is highlighted (largely due to the characters' dark clothing). Fernando betrays the situation, uttering, "Griselda." Returning to earlier framing of the scene, the family is finally reunited. Orol uses expressive lighting in a close-up of Carlitos as he realizes that the woman is, in fact, his mother. The viewer feels a wide range of diegetic textures: Carlitos's conflicted emotions, his youth (especially through his thin but growing mustache), his understanding of his mother's impending death. In a medium shot showing the three characters (father and son standing, as mother, overcome with emotion, sits, holding father's hand), Fernando admits, "She is . . . she is your mother, my son." Cutting between medium shots and close-ups, the emotion of the scene builds. Pacifying their son, overcome with emotion, Griselda explains their situation, largely through a medium shot in which Carlitos again leans toward his mother. This allows the viewer to focus attention on her words: "Your father and I loved each other like you love your girlfriend. We were poor. You got sick. So, blinded by the terror of losing you, I committed a big crime. I took money that did not belong to me." Cutting to a close-up of Fernando, he replies, "No, that is not true. Your mother is a saint." Without fully clarifying the situation, Fernando allows Griselda to describe their collective misfortune. In a medium shot, Griselda attempts to leave, but faints as soon as she rises into the hands of the man who was to be her husband and the son she was to raise. They lay her down, and a counter-shot shows her last words as the men of her life flank her. She dies. Cut to its more dimly lit counter-shot that gives the young man more key-lighting on his face, Carlitos implores her, "Mother, mother of mine! Do not leave me just as I have met you." In what is perhaps the most expressive lighting in the entire film, Fernando looks on to Carlitos embracing his mother, the love of Fernando's life. He says the film's last words, "Son, your mother was a saint. Keep her always in your memory and in your heart." *Eterna mártir*—as well as Orol's time making films in Mexico in the 1930s—fades to black.

Bad Movies and New Beginnings

On April 18, 1937, San Antonio's *La Prensa* published Campos Ponce's "Boycott against Bad Films," a report from Mexico City.[78] Using Juan Orol's legal issues as a pretext—in typical Orolian fashion, he got into a convoluted dispute about the negatives of *Madre querida* during which he was jailed for two days, accused of (self-)theft—"Cameramen, painters, etc., and other filmworkers launched the initiative to stage a boycott against bad films that, like those of Juan Orol, smear the reputation of the country because of their poor quality." The report notes that the issue was also discussed by the powerful Unión de Directores y Productores Cinematográficos. A customs barrier was proposed to impede the exportation of Mexican films that were deemed to not be first category. It was argued that such films damaged the reputation of the Mexican film industry. Even though there was broad support for such a measure, several members, including Guz Águila and Fernando de Fuentes (the writer and director of *Allá en el Rancho Grande*), spoke out against it. These members declared that it would negatively affect film workers; not only would many technicians, actors, etc. lose work on which they depend, but it would not allow any kind of improvement either by those directors considered to be bad or new figures trying to break into the industry. Águila went on record, proposing that "we always need films that we consider to be bad, but that serve to satisfy the tastes of the gross public [*público grueso*]. Besides, that kind of film also has its market, that of Central America."

Juan Orol made bad movies for bad audiences. In *Madre querida*, *El calvario de una esposa*, *Honrarás a tus padres*, *El derecho y el deber*, and *Eterna mártir*, story is emphasized in such a way that its *cursilería* and the convolutions and excesses of plot come to be more important than film form and content. Of mothers, wives, and daughters, these films project onto the screen cultural anxieties, particularly concerning women's roles in modern society. This strategy, of course, was both cinematic and commercial, as it sought to sensationalize and exploit the everyday experiences of a specific audience. Characters (and spectators, too) suffer the consequences of their subjugation by patriarchal forces, usually personified

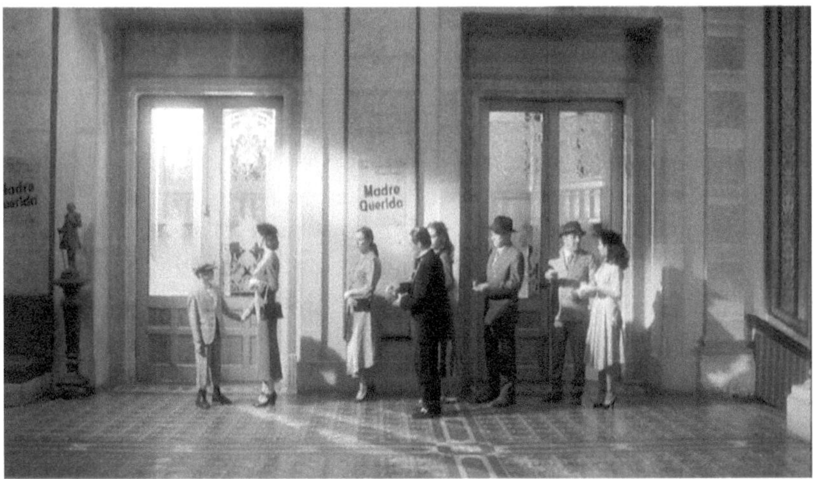

Figure 6.12. Juan Orol (Roberto Sosa) passes out handkerchiefs at *Madre querida*'s premiere, in *El mundo fantástico de Juan Orol* (dir. Sebastián del Amo, 2012).

by an evil man. Orolian melodrama is socially rooted in these films, but its Manichaeism almost becomes a quality of being in *El derecho y el deber*. Existence itself is unjust. Expressed in the denouement, but also at times in an opening edifying sequence, these lessons may provide a moral frame, but Orolian melodrama foregrounds nonclassical narrative mechanics. By closely reading these films, we can come to understand how Orol provides a cinematic theory of melodrama in which one plot twist too many seems an impossibility. In no small part due to *cursilería* and excess, Orol's Mexican films of the 1930s were popular with spectators, particularly when the films had broader access to distribution networks, but they also helped to shape how melodrama was expressed in Mexican cinema of the early *Época de oro*. Which is to say, Juan Orol taught Mexican cinema to feel in new ways.

In the mid- to late 1930s, the increasing consolidation of the Mexican film industry (as well as other factors, including governmental assistance and the support of U.S. distribution companies) led to the marginalization of figures such as Orol. In "News from Mexican Studios," an earlier *La Prensa* dispatch from Mexico City, it was reported that José Bohr was leaving Mexico permanently.[79] "In cinematographic circles, the natural confusion produced by such news reigns, since Bohr has produced several films and it is believed that he has not done the business that he had dreamed, giving rise to harboring doubts about whether the same thing will happen with all films that come out of our studios [*talleres*]." Representative of the incertitude regarding the state of the Mexican film industry before the success of *Allá en el Rancho Grande*, the report also notes that "[t]he desertion of elements working in national cinema continues. Following Bohr, Ramón Peón and Juan Orol are leaving. These two gentlemen are setting off to their native country: Cuba." Increasingly marginalized by the Mexican film industry, and unable to find adequate distribution to reinvest in future productions, Orol would eventually go to Cuba to film *Siboney*, but it would take him until 1938. If de Fuentes's film was the blockbuster that finally made possible the industrialization of Mexican cinema, culminating in a period later branded the *Época de Oro*, perhaps (at that time, at least) there really was no place on *Rancho Grande* for Juan Orol.

7

In the Studios of Buenos Aires

The Rise and Fall of Argentina's Film Industry

Just as two fledgling studios had begun work in Buenos Aires on what would become the country's first sound films, Augusto Álvarez's long running trade journal *Film* ran the story "Argentine Cinema Must Be Encouraged by a Rational System."[1] Headlining its front page, it begins by noting, "The Argentine Republic lacks various industries. There is no country in the world that can gather all industrial production within its borders and, less so, that is capable of hosting, equally flourished, all the arts." It later continues, "The Argentine Republic lacks a modern industry, which is art at the same time: *la cinematografía*." Its development is "long and arduous, and it is sown, sadly, with contrasts that could discourage some," but *Film* laments that it is being carried out "in the worst way that can be done: with enthusiasm and without method." Relating the film industry to modern shipbuilding, the piece argues for the central role of technicians (especially, but not limited to, directors), in the development of Argentine national cinema. "In conclusion, *la cinematografía nacional* [national film industry] should be encouraged. But the only method is rational and logical. Bringing a good teacher, a good director who, with two or three subordinate technicians, shows us what film production is." Even though different paths were taken in Argentina Sono Film's *Tango!* and Lumiton's *Los tres berretines*, film production in Argentine would would increasingly become more rational, more systematic, more industrial throughout the 1930s and 1940s.[2] The "institutional model," as Claudio España calls it, would become the industry standard, but emerged in two important moments: 1933–38, the early sound film era, and 1939–1943, the early classical period, sometimes called the *edad de oro* (golden age).[3] Promoted in *Film* more implicitly than explicitly, the integration of foreign film workers would be crucial for the emergence of a national film industry in Argentina.

Sparked initially by two studios, Argentina Sono Film and Lumiton, as España notes, "The industrial growth of Argentine cinema accompanied the process of widespread industrialization that happened in the country."[4] Industrialization was initially slow but picked up throughout the 1930s. The first years of the early sound period saw the production of relatively few domestic films. In both 1933 and 1934, six films were released. Initially lacking an industrial framework, earlier production models continued. A cycle of sporadic production, uneven distribution, and inconsistent exhibition made it difficult to establish a reliable local market for domestic movies. This, however, began to change in the next two years, as it became clearer that a market for national cinema existed. 1935 saw the premieres of fourteen films, more than the previous two years combined, while seventeen were produced in 1936. As a few studios implemented modern, industrialized modes of production, it became clear that other sectors of the Argentine film industry were in need of investment. Writing in late 1935 for *Sintonía* as its Hollywood correspondent, Carlos Borcosque notes, "I understand that in Buenos Aires there are already several studios that operate regularly, producing film after film, many of them organized by independent organizations. They may be splendid, good, regular, and bad. But what is done with them when they are finished? Who organizes their sale, their distribution?"[5] The piece's headline is even more succinct: "You do not only have to know how to make good movies. You need to know how to distribute them." The Argentine film industry continued its exponential progress in 1937 and 1938: thirty, then forty-one movies were produced. This expansion was facilitated by improvements in other sectors of the film industry: with greater control of film distribution (and more assured exhibition), more money could be reinvested back into production. Asymmetrically, as not all production companies grew in the same ways, the Argentine film industry began to produce films on a commercial scale. It would never beat Hollywood, but Argentine national cinema had come to distinguish itself from its foreign competitors at the box office.

Among the foreign film workers employed by the emerging national film industry in Argentina were a host of actors. Often, but not always, occupying secondary roles that complemented Argentine stars who were just beginning to shine, these foreign actors belonged to three groups: foreign-born Argentines, Uruguayans, and those whose careers brought them to Buenos Aires from further afield. From diverse backgrounds, and playing a wide range of roles, Argentines born abroad such as Enrique Chaico, Pedro Laxalt, Mecha López, Nury Montsé, Pablo Palitos, José Olarra, and Enrique Serrano all made their mark on national cinema, frequently in secondary roles.[6] Similarly, they collaborated on set and on-screen with a number of Uruguayan actors, including, but not limited to, Carlos Enríquez, Gloria Ferrandiz, Santiago Gómez Cou, Domingo Sapelli, and Luisa Vehil.[7] Joining them were foreign actors whose paths to Argentina were guided by professional, personal, and geopolitical factors. Sometimes working together on films such as Edmundo Guibourg's 1938 film adaptation of Federico García Lorca's play *Bodas de sangre* (*Blood Wedding*), and at other times integrated into a largely Argentine cast (e.g., most of Miguel Gómez Bao's or Enrique Muiño's filmography), these foreign actors made important contributions to national cinema.[8] In many ways 1938 was a turning point, as foreigners were increasingly contracted to act in Argentine films. Though usually only briefly, foreign stars such as Blanca de Castejón, Mapy Cortés, and Rosita Moreno were also incorporated into national cinema. Other actors such as Severo Fernández and Gloria Guzmán would make longer lasting impressions.[9]

In addition to on-screen artists and talent, there were a number of foreigners who plied their trades off-screen as well. Foreign-born producers Ángel Mentasti and Adolfo Z. Wilson helped build the Argentine film industry's institutional model. Despite *Film*'s exhortations, relatively few directors were contracted by the Argentine film industry in the early sound period. With a few exceptions, especially the Spaniards Luis Bayón Herrea and Antonio Momplet, those foreigners who directed in this period, such as Tito Davison and Ernesto Vilches, were largely unsuccessful.[10] However, foreign-born directors such as Luis César Amadori, Daniel Tinayre, and Mario Soffici highly impacted Argentine cinema for decades.[11] Joining these directors were screenwriters such as Enrique Amorim, Carlos Arniches, and Antonio Botta, who often took on other kinds of film work.[12] On set, production designer Hans Jacoby and important make-up artist Bruno Boval gave visual texture to the films on which they worked. Working closely with these directors and technicians were perhaps the largest and most important group of foreign film workers plying their trade in Argentina in the early sound period: cinematographers. In addition to John Alton were José María Beltrán, Gumer Barreiros, Francis Boeniger, Gerhard Huttula, Adam Jacko, Paul Perry, Bob Roberts, Adolf Schlasy, José Suárez, and Pablo Tabernero. Alfredo Murúa and Fernando Murúa were among the few foreign sound technicians who were credited during the period. Foreign musicians, however, abounded, from popular performers such as Francisco Canaro and Mario Maurano to composers who scored films, such as George Andreani, Hans Diernhammer, Alejandro Gutiérrez del Barrio, and José Vázquez Vigo.[13] Editing films in the early sound period were foreigners Victoria Durán, Lazlo Kish, and Emilio Murúa.[14] Some of these foreign workers arrived just as the film industry was beginning to emerge, while others arrived as it was being realized. They brought with them their expertise, artistic and technical, to shape Argentine national cinema, but later arrivals were also expected to adapt. Or, as a mid-1938 *Radiolandia* headline reads: "'I do not come to direct imported product,' says Borcosque, 'I will be a national collaborator.'"[15]

The rapid growth and expansion of the Argentine film industry in the early sound period leveled off in the subsequent five years, which saw greater investment in its infrastructure. By the late 1930s, the Argentine film industry functioned under an institutional model in which film studios produced films for local and foreign audiences. Majors Argentina Sono Film and Lumiton were joined by new studios such as SIDE (Sociedad Impresora de Discos Electrofónicos), EFA (Establecimientos Filmadores Argentinos), and Estudios San Miguel, as well as fleeting independents such as Baires Film and Cinematografía Terra. In the early classical period, a number of films were produced by an increasing number of studios: fifty-nine in 1939, forty-nine in 1940, forty-seven in 1941, and fifty-six in 1942. With thirty-six movies in 1943, the Argentine film industry entered a three-year decline, largely as a consequence of the country's neutrality in World War II. It was not until 1950 that production levels would match those of 1942. Beyond improving the artistic and technical quality of film production, as well as its consistency, Argentine cinema saw strengthening in national, regional, and international distribution. In his 1944 study of the film industry, Juan Carlos Garate reviews the impact of Argentine films in distinct foreign markets. He notes:

> Before commenting upon the characteristics of each of these markets, it is necessary to recognize and emphasize that there was a time—the years 1938, 1939, and 1940—in which the

> possibility of Argentine films being exhibited in most of countries of the world appeared in sight. Films were sent to Sweden, Germany, England, Romania, Italy, and Spain, in Europe; to Morocco and Cape Colony [South Africa], in Africa; and to Japan, in Asia. Of course, on many occasions it was nothing more than simple trials and that the economic possibilities of exploiting these markets did not become tangible. Unfortunately, the war threw all of these projects into disarray.[16]

Even though "It's not all roses," according to a late-1938 *Radiolandia* piece on the weak *carioca* reception of a popular Argentine film, the film industry's distribution networks became increasingly strong.[17] The increased profitability of commercial cinema drew other sectors of the Argentine film industry into production, as "[s]ome of these local proponents of European cinema, once the industrialization of the Argentine screen had initiated, joined up as producers."[18] The consolidation of the Argentine film industry also saw a greater demand for workers: from 569 in 1938 to 990 in 1943.[19] Many of those workers would come from abroad.

With increasingly transnational aspirations, the Argentine film industry continued to integrate foreigners into its casts and crews. Relatively few foreign actors may have been contracted in the early sound period, but the late 1930s and early 1940s saw the implementation of new casting strategies. Foreign-born Argentines such as Golde Flami, Maurice Jouvet, Delfy de Ortega, and Berta Singerman and Uruguayans such as Carlos Casaravilla and Domingo Márquez worked for the first time in Buenos Aires' studios, but Argentine cinema also incorporated a diverse group of Latin American actors such as Cuba's Bola de Nieve (Ignacio Jacinto Villa Fernández) and Chile's Raúl del Valle.[20] Among these Latin Americans were high-profile Mexican singers Tito Guízar, José Mojica, and Pedro Vargas.[21] Vargas performed a single song, "Ay, Caramba," in the Niní Marshall vehicle *Candida millonaria* (*Candida's Millions*, dir. Bayón Herrera, 1941). Guízar and Mojica, who had both previously acted in Hollywood and Mexico, each starred in a single feature: *De México llegó el amor* (*Love Came from Mexico*, dir. Richard Harlan, 1940) and *Melodías de América* (*Melodies of America*, dir. Eduardo Morera, 1942), respectively. In very different kinds of roles, actors from the United States (Gloria Grey and June Marlowe) and Europe (Vicky Astori, Hedy Crilla, Aline Marney) also received their first credits. Of the foreign actors working in Argentina from 1939 to 1943, the largest group was from Spain. Reeling from effects of the Civil War—socially, politically, economically, cinematically, etc.—Spanish actors such as Susana Canales, Ramón J. Garay, Francisco López Silva, and Conchita Montenegro made their mark, often in supporting roles or as character actors, although many others left little impression upon Argentine cinema.[22]

If the early sound period saw the integration of few directors and many cinematographers, the next five years saw the opposite. Cineastes with diverse experiences abroad took the director's chair in Argentina for the first time: some had worked in Hollywood on Spanish-language films (Carlos Borcosque, Richard Harlan, John Reinhardt, and Raúl Roulién), in Joinville on analogous projects (Adelqui Migliar [Miller]), in European cinemas (Catrano Catrani, Pierre Chenal, and Jacques Constant), and in Spain (Ricardo Urgoiti, Lorenzo Serrano, and, most importantly, Benito Perojo). And some, such as Antonio Cunill Cabanellas, Hans Jacoby (Juan Jacoby Renard), Gregorio Martínez Sierra, Henri Martinent, Luis Mottura, and Jacques Rémy, had no experience directing before helming their first films in Argentina. Collaborating with them on set were foreign cinematographers Paul P. Perry, Humberto Peruzzi, and Fluvio Testi. They shot the work of production designers Gori Muñoz and Ralph Pappier and make-up artist Narciso Ibáñez Menta. In many different ways, these workers adapted to screen the work of foreign screenwriters such as Alejandro Casona and Salvador Valverde Calvo, as well as a screenplay by famous Chilean writer María Luisa Bombal.[23] Whether on a single film, like Agustín Lara, or many, like Juan (Hans) Ehlert, Alejandro Gutiérrez del Barrio, and Paul Misraki, foreign composers also made important contributions to the Argentine film industry at the time.[24] Eventually, editors such as José Cañizares and Kurt Land would assemble films. Structuring their work was producer Henri Martinet, as well as a host of other technicians such as Rubén W. Cavalloti, Tito Davison, Leo Fleider, and Jack Hall.[25]

On the afternoon of February 15, 1943, Argentina Sono Film's studios in the Buenos Aires neighborhood of San Isidro caught fire. Burning well into the night, the fire consumed much of the studio's facilities, but, importantly, not the "many thousands of meters of film stock that the Mentasti had bought at a time when it began to run short to unforeseeable limits."[26] Covered well beyond Argentina—*Cinema Reporter* in Mexico and *Motion Picture Daily* in the United States, among many others, reported on it as well—the fire was a setback that Argentina Sono Film would not fully overcome for years.[27] "The reconstruction was prompt in terms of immediate needs. The studio's definitive structure with five sets, including the sound [stage], was finished shortly before 1950."[28] The fire, of course, proved to be inconsequential in comparison to the world's burning during World War II. Caught between the warring powers, Argentina remained neutral, which damaged the film industry, just as its primary regional competitor, Mexico, enjoyed the benefits of a closer relationship with Hollywood and the United States.[29] Because of this, "1944 marked a *turning point* in the history of Argentine film," argues Domingo Di Núbila in his foundational *Historia del cine argentino*.[30] While film critics and historians may take issue with harsh assessments such as "because later there tended to be fewer rather than more good films, artistic staff to reduce instead of grow, the economy to contract instead of expand, restlessness and innovative spirit to occupy an increasingly narrow space in the presence of mercenary calculation, and intelligence to lose ground to mediocrity," it nonetheless represents a pivotal year for the Argentine film industry. Having emerged since the arrival of sound film technologies, it now faced its first real crisis.

8

"The Primary Champion of National Film"

Ángel Mentasti and the Invention of Argentina Sono Film

In late 1931, *Heraldo del Cinematografista* ran a series of interviews with prominent members of the industry guild Sociedad Cinematográfica Argentina de Exhibidores (Argentine Society of Film Exhibitors).[1] Edited by Chas de Cruz, the biweekly periodical poses four questions to eight businessmen and, in so doing, provides readers with a cross-section of perspectives regarding the state of key aspects of national film culture.[2] What changes are fashionable in the film business? What is your opinion of the *films en español* and dubbed movies? Do you believe actors' draw is an indispensable factor [at the box office]? What is your opinion of American, European, and national cinema? Sounding out Pablo Coll, Domingo Di Fiore and Sebastián Martínez, Joaquín Lautaret and Pablo Cavallo, Clemente Lococo, Humberto Cairo, and Francisco Borranzas, the series gives us insight into the state of what was at the time undoubtedly the largest sector of the Argentine film industry. It also suggests, somewhat curiously, that even the most important exhibitors in Buenos Aires were unprepared for the impending emergence of Argentine national sound film production.

Regarding current trends in exhibition in Buenos Aires, the guild members all agree on the perceived excess of movie theaters, particularly the surplus of first-run venues. Humberto Cairo, whose legacy includes *Nobleza gaucha* (*Gaucho Nobility*, dirs. Humberto Cairo, Ernesto Gunche, and Eduardo Martínez de la Pera, 1915) but extends well beyond that foundational silent film, argues that "[i]n Brazil, not long ago, in the face of the overproduction, the government, with excellent judgment, threw many tons of the product into the sea. Something similar should happen here."[3] Most recognize the benefits of exclusive agreements with U.S. distributors, particularly to their own businesses, and convey some trepidation regarding a return to the previous, rotational system. The exhibitors reject two strategies used by producers: multilinguals and dubbing. Di Fiore and Martínez specifically reference MGM's *Min and Bill* (dir. George W. Hill, 1930) and its Spanish-language iteration *Fruta amarga* (dirs. Arthur Gregor and José López Rubio, 1931).[4] Even though an article in *Revista del Exhibidor* expresses some hope that *Fruta amarga* would become even more successful than its original version due to greater linguistic accessibility, both Coll and Di Fiore and Martínez assert that it cannot outdo *Min and Bill* despite its quality.[5] Spectators in Buenos Aires, the exhibitors contend, do not accept dubbing. Even though it allows actors like Marie Dressler and Wallace Beery, the stars of *Min and Bill*, to stay on screen, *porteño* film culture still finds dubbing too artificial and linguistically problematic. Most of the exhibitors also acknowledge the importance of film stars, although both Coll and Lautaret and Cavallo note that some films such as Universal's *Simiente* (*Seed*, dir. John M. Stahl, 1931) become hits without well-known actors.[6] Unlike Borranzas, who says that they are a "*sine qua non* for a film to triumph," Cairo takes an almost quasi-auteurist approach, proposing that films should be marketed based on their director.[7] Considering Hollywood's market dominance in Argentina at the time, it should come as no surprise that the local exhibitors note its importance. Even with the success of films like *El ángel azul* (*Der blaue Engel*, dir. Josef von Sternberg, 1930), which Cairo claims to be the "the best sound film made to date, the only original sound film," European films are seen to possess various afflictions, ranging from technical deficiencies to poor local distribution and little local commercial appeal (e.g., lack of established stars and slow pacing).[8]

Of the exhibitors, Borrazas is the most bullish about the future of Argentine cinema.[9] Borrazas has faith in the definitive strengthening of the national film industry, especially if proper resources are dedicated to increasing production quality through technical elements such as the construction of film studios and if more reasonable distribution demands are established. Di Fiore and Martínez are also optimistic about the future of national cinema, but believe that only "bit by bit national cinema could conquer the market" with modest films.[10] Using quite similar language,

Cairo concurs, and also warns that national films should not be marketed as super-productions as it sets up an unrealistic horizon of expectations.[11] For his part, Pablo Coll strongly disagrees.[12] He argues:

> I do not believe in national cinema. The lack of technical elements, and more so the lack of directors, form two insuperable issues at the moment. An occasional hit means little when talking of the bases of an industry. The only way would be to be to rely on huge resources and bring competent directors. It is painful to say it, inasmuch as our directors have a lot of enthusiasm, but it is the truth.

Noting that exhibitors would benefit greatly from a national film industry, Lococo nevertheless sees little immediate future, as producers are "'too green' to be taken into consideration."[13] Lautaret and Cavallo are even more categorical, saying, "We absolutely do not believe in national cinema, at least at the moment."[14] That moment would not last for long.

Within a year of the interviews in *Heraldo del Cinematografista*, Argentina Sono Film had nearly wrapped shooting *Tango!*, the first Argentine feature film to use optical sound film technologies. Emerging out of the short-lived distribution company Cosmos Film, the production company was a partnership between director Luis Moglia Barth and producer Ángel Mentasti. Over the next five years, as Moglia Barth continued to shoot movies, Mentasti would guide Argentina Sono Film from precariousness to precocity, shaping a company that moved beyond the unsustainable model of Argentine silent film production to become an industrial, vertically integrated motion picture company that controlled the distribution rights of eight feature films assembled by production units within its own studios. In the words of Carmelo Santiago, a long-time industry insider, "It became a company in which the films, before being produced, were already sold. Such was the credit he had acquired within the industry that after *Tango!* and *Dancing* he announced a film and businessmen bought. That is how he financed the next."[15] Argentina Sono Film quickly established itself as much more than an innovative newcomer: it became the dominant presence in the emerging Argentine film industry, as well as one of the most important entities in Latin American commercial cinema. After Mentasti's death in mid-1937, *Revista del Exhibidor* observed, "The success of the aforementioned company and the superiority it exercised upon other local producers was the work of

Don Ángel Mentasti and, therefore, his name will occupy a prominent place in the history of Argentine cinema."[16] By tracing the reception in *porteño* film periodicals of Mentasti's work in distinct moments in the development of the Argentine film industry, most especially those geared toward important sectors in the film industry such as exhibitors, I examine how the Italian immigrant took matters into his own hands, not only by structuring organizational strategies that would lead to the long-term success of Argentina Sono Film as a film studio and distribution company, but also by shaping what we have come to understand as Argentine national cinema. Unsurprisingly, especially given the commercial model according to which its films were made, Argentine film historiography has tended to focus its attention on directors and stars. Rooted in criticism contemporaneous to these films' releases, and later extended by early historians such as Domingo Di Núbila, this approach fails to sufficiently account for the importance of figures such as Ángel Mentasti who indelibly marked (the idea of) national cinema. Mentasti

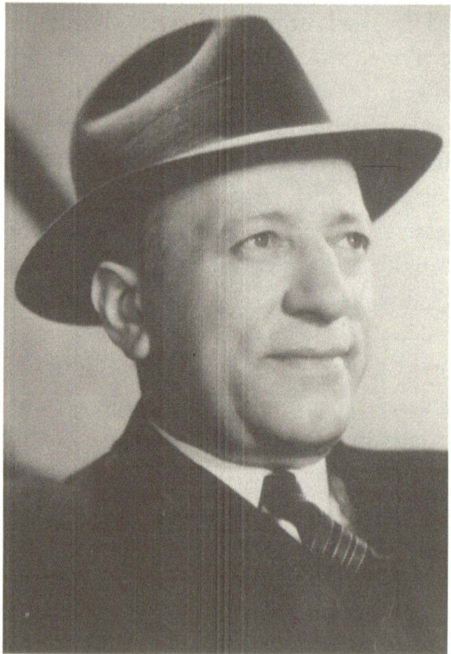

Figure 8.1. Portrait of Ángel Mentasti. Courtesy of the Museo del Cine Pablo Ducrós Hicken.

established modes of production that were replicated by other aspiring film studios, which had lasting effects on the film industry in Argentina and throughout Latin America. In so doing, he codified the processes, from preproduction to exhibition, by which his films' diegeses were commercialized as movies that appealed to broad popular audiences in Argentina and abroad.

From the Fields of Lombardy to the Cinemas of Buenos Aires

Unlike many other foreigners associated with emerging sound film industries in Latin America, although certainly not all, Ángel Mentasti's emigration in the late nineteenth century preceded his involvement in the movie business.[17] Along with some 1,221,883 Italians who immigrated in the period between 1890 and 1910, constituting nearly 51 percent of all arrivals, the young Mentasti sought to *fare l'America* or *hacer la América* in Argentina.[18] Whether in Italian or River Plate Spanish, as Samuel L. Baily has shown, making it in America implied the development of individual short- and/or long-term economic strategies negotiated within the structures of the new environment.[19] In Mentasti's case, tracing his participation in the labor market helps us to understand his adaptability to uncertainty when it came to the emergence of his own film studio, specifically, and the Argentine film industry more broadly.

He was born Angelo Battista Mentasti on May 24, 1877, to farmworkers Angelo Giuseppe and Virginia de Carli in the small northern Italian city of Varese, located just northwest of Milan in Lombardy.[20] There, on August 11, 1898, he married Virginia Forzinetti, who would later give birth in Argentina to their four children: José Atilio, Atilio José, Ángel Luis, and María Angela.[21] Mentasti's improbable rise to "founder and *alma pater* of Argentina Sono Film and the most enthusiastic cheerleader that Argentine cinema has had," who "knew how to predict time, advancing in ten years the progress of the industry," as he was described in obituaries published after his death on June 24, 1937, was shaped by his work in other lines of business.[22] It is through the ingenuity of an entrepreneur with a deep understanding of the most important sectors of the Argentine film industry—distribution and exhibition—that Mentasti was able to form modes of production that would eventually make Argentina Sono Film a commercially viable entity.[23]

In an interview published in the September 30, 1932, issue of *Imparcial Film*—in which he, notably, does not mention his move into film production or the creation of Argentina Sono Film—Mentasti details a personal history in the business of film distribution that diverges from accounts given by Di Núbila and Claudio España.[24] In Bahía Blanca, a port city in the Province of Buenos Aires, he accumulated some wealth by running the local branch of the moving company "La Confianza," among other business endeavors.[25] Riffing on the opening sentence of *Don Quijote*, Mentasti says that "a person whose name I wish not to remember at the moment" convinced him to facilitate a guarantee of some eighty thousand pesos for the distribution of films. Having lost nearly everything in the failed effort, Mentasti glosses over a period in which he moved to La Plata, another coastal city in the Province of Buenos Aires, then to Mendoza to work in the wine business.[26] There, he met Alejandro Gómez and, later, other distributors like Eugenio Cetrán and José Nebot. At Gómez's request, Mentasti acquired the rights to *La falena* (dir. Carmine Gallone, 1916), a title owned by the distributor Cinematográfica Sud Americana. Its success was followed by a failure—*La historia de los 13* (*La storia dei tredici*, dir. Gallone, 1917)—that Mentasti attributes to spectators' taste shifting away from Italian films to *cow-boys americanos* (U.S. Westerns). Later, he returned to Buenos Aires and, in 1916, began to work for the North American Film Service as a film distributor in the Province of Buenos Aires. Over the next decade, Mentasti would slide in and out of film distribution, as well as work in a range of other endeavors: running a boarding house, managing a theater company (both production and artists' tours), and, newly, operating a wine distributorship in the Province of Buenos Aires.[27] In his several fits and starts in the film industry, including a harrowing journey into the province during the *Semana Trágica*, Mentasti took positions in the distribution companies Programa Americana, Germania Film, and Reich Film.[28] Mentasti eventually took over as chief of programming for Pathé-Natan in 1932, and was joined by his longtime associate Luis Moglia Barth, who was hired as chief of publicity.[29] Soon thereafter, they joined Domingo A. (Dominico Américo) Tucci in the new distribution company, Cosmos Film.

Established in mid-1932, Cosmos Film joined a host of other distribution companies in marketing the rights of foreign sound films.[30] Expanding on a brief note in the previous issue, *Revista del Exhibidor* published an article titled "Cosmos Film Anticipates Interesting Material," on July 20, 1932.[31] The article details the new distributor's plans for *Los falsificadores de Londres* (*Sherlock Holmes' Fatal Hour.* dir. Leslie S. Hiscott, 1931) and *El rosario* (*The Rosary*, dir. Guy Newall, 1931), as well as two 1930 films directed by Hiscott that never screened in Argentina, *La casa de la flecha* (*The House of the Arrow*) and *El misterio de Villa Rosa* (*Mystery at the Villa Rose*).[32] *Los falsificadores de Londres* is announced as premiering in July.[33] After some success at the Cine Real (where it premiered on August 11, 1932), it ran at the Metropol Theater in Buenos Aires. In the same note, it is indicated that the film's Uruguayan rights had been sold to Demetrio del Cerro.[34] After its initial success, Cosmos Film was reported to be preparing October releases for *El rosario*, *Mme. Guillotine* (*Madame Guillotine*, dir. Reginald Fogwell, 1931), and *El correo de Lyon* (*The Lyons Mail*, dir. Arthur Maude, 1931).[35] Soon after Mentasti's interview with *Imparcial Film*, in which he stated that he was now Cosmos Film's operations manager, it was announced that Moglia Barth had assumed the position of chief of publicity for the distributor.[36] Cosmos Film was subsequently referenced as the distributor of the impending release of the national film *Tango!*.[37]

By October 1932, news surrounding the production of *Tango!* began appearing in film periodicals. In the October 30 issues of *Imparcial Film* and *Revista del Exhibidor*, readers learned of the founding of a new studio, Argentina Sono Film.[38] The front page piece in *Imparcial Film* informs readers that "the noted company has the necessary technical means and resources to carry out with efficacy the intentions that motivate it."[39] The note in *Revista del Exhibidor* affirms the same, and similarly lists those involved with the film's production (actors, director, musicians, and scriptwriters), details the production studio's plan for a second film, *Milonga*, and states that Argentina Sono Film "resolves to realize ten productions for next season, all directed by Mister L. Moglia Barth. Filming is done by the system of recording sound on film, having given excellent results in performed tests."[40] Neither article, however, mentions a fundamental figure, not only in the making of *Tango!* but in the emergence of a national film industry in Argentina: Ángel Mentasti. The producer, for the time being, is left in the shadows.

Toward a New Mode of Production: Argentina Sono Film's First Steps, 1933–1934

Argentina Sono Film's initial film production was somewhat improvised. Lacking an industrial model on which to base its transition to sound,

Argentine filmmakers of the early sound period experimented with cinematic and commercial strategies to connect their movies with not only domestic spectators but also, to a lesser extent, those in foreign markets. In its first two years, in which its sustainability and future were anything but assured, Argentina Sono Film first experimented with capitalizing on the popularity of musicians performing on stage and the radio, then moved toward showcasing the comedic talents of Argentina's first movie star, Luis Sandrini. Rather than being insufficiently cinematic, as early critics such as Domingo Di Núbila (often considered to be the founder of Argentine film studies) charged, Argentina Sono Film's first three films—*Tango!*, *Dancing*, and *Riachuelo*—are indicative of the firm's relationship with the two strongest sectors of the Argentine film industry, distribution and exhibition. They reflect shifting demand from exhibitors toward national films that more closely evince Argentine film culture's intimate understanding of Hollywood and European cinemas. Especially in comedies (to borrow from Nilo Couret), they begin to reveal Argentine cinema's mock classicism.[41] Because Mentasti was responsible for the commercialization of his company's films through his work as a producer, including the shaping of their diegeses, I trace the ways in which Argentina Sono Film publicized these films throughout production to draw the interest of exhibitors and, later, how the studio developed distribution strategies that allowed for expanded production.

In addition to publicizing Argentina Sono Film's founding, initial articles published in trade publications also establish a pattern of sporadic, but consistent production updates about its ambitious program. Informative but also performative, these updates functioned not only as signals to local exhibitors of the studio's ambitions, which, at the time, were unprecedented in Argentina, but also acted as a kind of guarantee that more local material would follow. Soon after a very general note was published in *Heraldo del Cinematografista*: "Under the direction of Sr. Moglia Barth, Cosmos Film has begun the filming of a sound film of local matters," an article in *Revista del Exhibidor* reported, "We'll now say that shooting of its first film, 'Tango,' is about to be finished, and that filming will immediately begin on its second that, as we have put forward, will be titled 'Milonga.'"[42] Unreported, interestingly enough, is that these films were made possible through Mentasti's and Moglia Barth's successful efforts to secure additional funding, which came from previously formed relationships within the film industry: Julián Ramos, who had promised Moglia Barth financing for the creation of a film company, and Carlos Favre, a friend of Mentasti's who had been a partner in Julio Joly's distribution company.[43] That aside, the initial oscillation between production and preproduction news not only signaled Argentina Sono Film's ambition to become the country's first industrial studio, but also underlay its efforts to regularly produce films for local exhibitors to show to local audiences.[44] It was, effectively, an attempt to publicize its industrial aspirations.

Despite his centrality to Argentina Sono Film—so deeply entrenched that its telegraph address became MENTASTI—the producer had relatively little media presence, especially in comparison with his studio's actors and directors.[45] Even though the stars behind or in front of the camera drove discourse around Argentina Sono Film's productions, Mentasti would occasionally give interviews hyping the possibilities of national cinema. In an interview with *Imparcial Film* on January 20, 1933, regarding the upcoming premiere of *Tango!*, Mentasti called attention to the economic potential of a commercial film made with the latest technologies.[46] After a short introduction, the interview states, "Once caught up to speed on reason that led us to interview him, he told us point blank without giving us time to formulate a question: '"Tango" will be our first big hit. Don't doubt it.'" He begins by underscoring the importance of its technical achievements. Unsatisfied in their attempts to complete the film "according to our desire of doing something of merit," he describes the move to Cinematografía Valle's studios, where, he states, "*amigo cronista,* I have found a real organization and a perfect technical setup." Of particular import, argues Mentasti, is the De Forest apparatus. Calling attention to the film's forty thousand peso budget, Mentasti states that "we have not spared any effort to give our national cinema a production that contributes to increasingly strengthen its possibilities, and on this matter we are calm."

By touching upon two fundamental commercial aspects—technical execution and capital investment—Mentasti signals ways in which the storyworld of *Tango!* is itself always commercialized. This is made clearer in his subsequent description of the film's diegesis. Mentasti states:

> Contrary to what some may assume, "Tango" has a plot; a plot distinctly *criollo,* and it is made according to the unique preferences of our public. For this reason, we selected artists among the favorites of the *porteño* public, and as for the musical part it is constituted by those orchestras whose name alone is by

> itself a powerful appeal . . . Filiberto, Maffia, Fresodo, Donato, Ponzio . . . each name perfection. Among the performers are Alberto Gómez, Tita Merello, Pepe Arias, Azucena Maizani, Libertad Lamarque, Mercedes Simone, Alicia Vignoli, Meneca Tailahade, Luis Sandrini, and others, but overall, and I stress this, "Tango" has a good plot.[47]

The lack of specificity regarding the film's plot would seem to belie Mentasti's insistence that it is more than a series of musical performances; however, through his enumeration of renowned orchestras and famous players, Mentasti emphasizes that the film's diegesis is enmeshed within tango culture, itself a source of commercial viability, a proven commodity. Despite this, or perhaps because of it, critics (including myself) have misprized *Tango!*'s plot, disparaging it, lavishing it with abstract praise, or minimizing it.[48] In *Tango!*, a love triangle develops, threatening to draw Tita (Tita Merello) away from her true love, Alberto (Alberto Gómez). Tempted by malevolent *compadrito* Malandra (Juan Sarcione), whom Alberto nearly kills, thus sending him to prison, Tita is left alone to lament the errors of her ways. After his release, Alberto is guided by his self-absorbed manager Bonito (Pepe Arias), who encourages Alberto to leave friends like Berretín (Luis Sandrini) and seek his fortune as a tango singer in Paris. Growing closer to the wealthy Elena (Libertad Lamarque), Alberto forms another love triangle. Upon returning to Buenos Aires, Berretín divulges Tita's situation to Alberto, and the singer decides to abandon international mass media stardom in favor of returning to his authentic roots: his *barrio* and his true love, Tita. As if speaking to the audience, he states, "There is nothing like my *barrio*, from here I will leave never again" and, a little later, reiterates to Tita, "You yourself are the tango. Our *barrio*, our friends. Only in the *suburbios* of Buenos Aires do tangos have soul."

By citing the names of of renowned orchestras and famous entertainers—both Maizani and Simone perform songs that are kinds of diegetic asides–Mentasti foretells the commercial promise of *Tango!* through indexing their bankability.[49] The interview concludes with a similar look toward the future: Mentasti shares a possible date for the film's premiere ("possibly the first few days of March"); teasers about Argentina Sono Film's next production, as well as "our plan to release various national movies of quality next season"; and his beliefs regarding the future of national cinema. Responding to the assertion, "It would appear that you are a resolute supporter of national productions," Mentasti argues that a long-lasting Argentine national film industry will be made possible through a foundation built on the production of quality movies. In the interview's final sentence, Mentasti states that "'Tango' is our trial by fire, we are thoroughly convinced we will come out thoroughly successful."

Often overshadowed by an emphasis on promoting the potential of the Argentine national film industry in the domestic market, especially in Buenos Aires, Argentina Sono Film was attuned from its inception to the importance of foreign film markets. If the production company acted as a distributor of foreign films such as *Sherlock Holmes' Fatal Hour*, it also understood its own productions as readily exportable commercial goods. In his interview with *Imparcial Film*, Mentasti is asked whether the film will be of interest to other film audiences. Even though its plot is distinctly *criollo* and performed by a laundry list of important figures in *porteño* tango culture, Mentasti indicates that he believes that *Tango!* will sell abroad. He substantiates this assertion, per a parenthetical remark in the article, through his actions: "(That said, Mentasti searches his *escritorio* and he displays various telegrams and letter in which pieces of information and other details about 'Tango' are requested)."[50] Soon after the interview, and anticipating the film's premiere, *Imparcial Film* published further notes reporting that rights had been sold to distribute *Tango!* abroad in Chile and Spain, as well as in important cities in the provinces such as Rosario, Santa Fe, and San Juan.[51] It serves as a demonstration of the extent of the fragmentation of film distribution in the early sound period, in which production companies such as Argentina Sono Film negotiated individual deals with exhibitors in different markets, both domestically and internationally, for fixed sums, thus limiting production companies' ability to profit from big hits. These rights deals also underlined the importance of narrative salability, thus, the always commercial nature of the diegesis. National and, increasingly, international distribution became of interest to film trade publications directed to exhibitors. Following the premiere of *Tango!*, *Revista del Exhibidor* and, later, *Film* reported on deals that Argentina Sono Film signed with distributors in Rosario, Santa Fe, Chile, Peru, Bolivia, and Uruguay.[52] These updates cut two ways, signaling both *Tango!*'s success and the future commercial possibilities of national cinema.

In anticipation of its spectacular premiere on April 27, 1933, *Tango!* received plenty of publicity in Argentine film periodicals. Along with a detailed summary of its plot, which was published in *Imparcial Film*, Argentina Sono Film drew further attention to its premiere by simul-

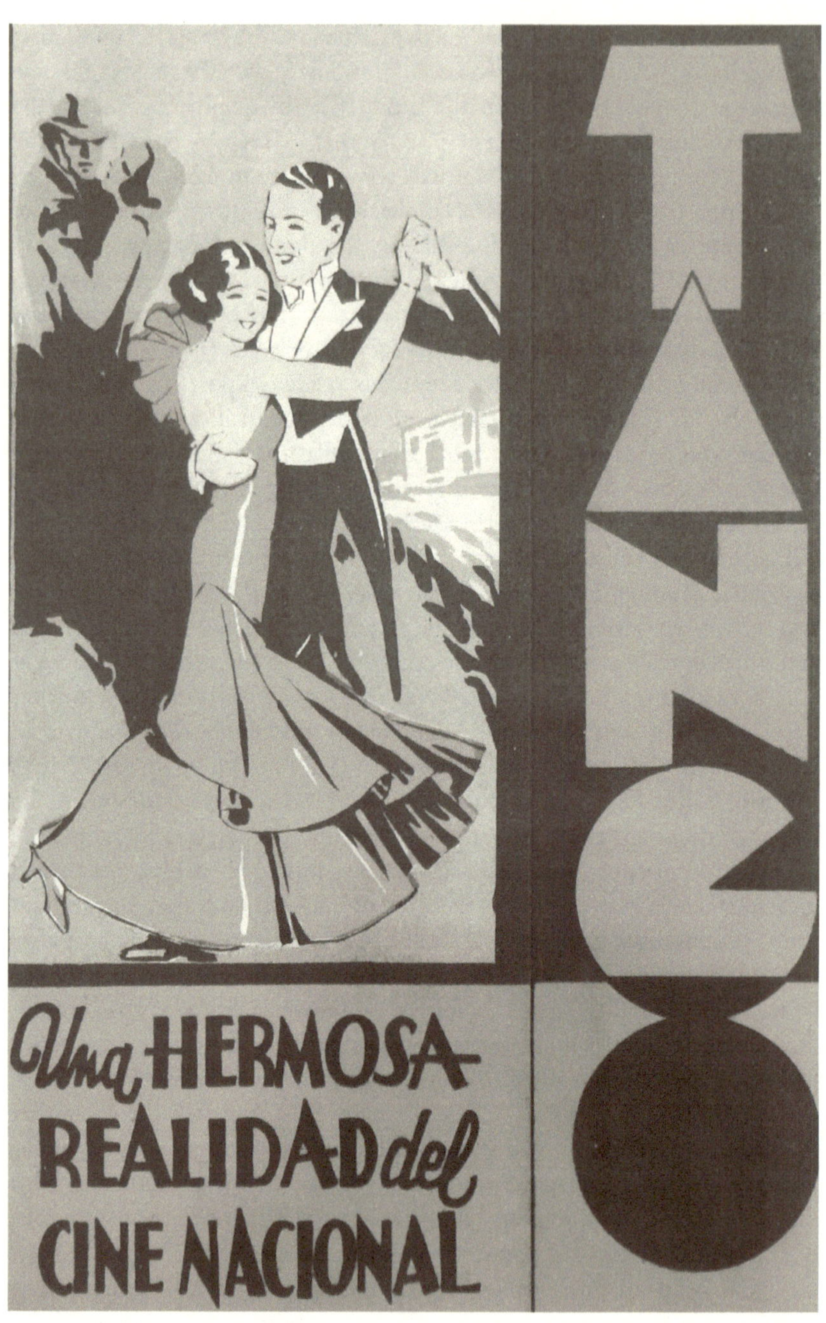

Figure 8.2. Advertisement insert for *Tango!*. *Imparcial Film*, February 5, 1933.

taneously screening the film in a number of important film venues.[53] Though its principal premiere was staged at the Cine Real in Buenos Aires, Mentasti had resolved to bring the film to audiences throughout the country as soon as possible. *Imparcial Film* reports, "Thus, in consideration of it, Mr. Ángel Mentasti, member of the firm, resolved to release 'Tango' simultaneously in the capital and important points of the interior."[54] Furthermore, the simultaneous release of the film on April 27 in Buenos Aires, Rosario, Santa Fe, La Plata, Mendoza, Córdoba, and San Juan was linked to its exhibition in fifty other theaters, from the periphery of Buenos Aires to the provinces.[55] In addition to exploiting the growing anticipation of the film, this exhibition strategy also mitigated the risk of negative word of mouth. By making such a big initial impact, Argentina Sono Film both turned the premiere of *Tango!* into a historic event for local film culture and insulated the company from risk. The spectacle of its simultaneous release in so many theaters was inextricably enmeshed within Argentina Sono Film's initial distribution and exhibition strategies; through the creation of an event, the film itself was somewhat minimized in favor of the novelty of a cinema that was national and nationwide. An unsustainable strategy, it nonetheless enabled Mentasti to continue the film studio's development of new productions.

Headlining a program at the Cine Real that included *La cita* (*One Way Passage*, dir. Tay Garnett, 1932) starring Kay Francis, William Powell, and Aline MacMahon, as well as a "Comic Section and Sound Variety Acts" comprised of *Paramount Sound News N. 59-33* (1933), *La pesadilla de Mickey* (*Mickey's Nightmare*, dir. Burt Gillett, 1932), "*Paramount Gráfico N.19*, and *Fiesta alegre* (*Mickey's Beach Party*, dir. Burt Gillett, 1931), *Tango!* is entangled within *porteño* popular culture.[56] In addition to situating its most famous stars Azucena Maizani ("The one and indisputable queen of tango") and Mercedes Simone ("One of its most emotive cultivators") within tango culture, the program distributed that night associates other performers in *Tango!* such as Libertad Lamarque ("top vedette of the Teatro Maipo") and Luis Sandrini ("the revelation of Muiño-Alipi's season in the Teatro Buenos Aires") with their recent work in specific theaters, while Alberto Gómez ("singer for Victor") is connected to the multinational record label. In the handbill, further links are established with local popular culture both through the listing of the orchestras and dance troupes that appear in the film and the tango songs that are performed. The program was a logical extension of Mentasti's, and Argentina Sono Film's, promotional strategy for *Tango!*.[57] It also was representative of the inextricable ways in which *porteño* film culture was enmeshed with the global film industry, especially Hollywood. Not only did it include several shorts and a feature from the United States, but the program also notably states that the the premiere of *Tango!* was, "Courtesy of PARAMOUNT FILMS who, having exclusivity in this cinema, makes an exception because it is a National production." Even though it inarguably marked one of the most important events in the history of Argentine national cinema, its *argentinidad* is often overemphasized by its decontextualization from its always transnational horizons.

In the days following the premiere of *Tango!*, a series of reviews were published in *porteño* film periodicals. These reviews not only provide insight into critical reaction to the film, often expressly for local film exhibitors, but also into Argentina Sono Film's capacity to create a commercial product representative of its marketing and publicity. In this sense, they establish a horizon of expectations for the film's success, even though critical acclaim does not necessarily yield commercial profit, and extend an alternative horizon for expectations already formed by the press. The reviews did both. *Film*, for example, argues, "For the exhibitor: It is difficult that the amount of value that is presented in this totally Argentine film—by its performers, its direction, and its plot—will converge again. For the program: each scene of 'Tango' has great local color, an extraordinary *sabor a 'cosa nuestra'* ['our thing' taste] that immediately distinguishes it from other films of Argentine themes, but made abroad."[58] (Perhaps this is why *Tango!* was a huge hit in Rosario—it sold out for four consecutive days—even though Carlos Gardel's Paramount-produced feature *Melodía de arrabal* [dir. Louis Gasnier, 1933] is reported to have flopped).[59] This is not to say, however, that the film was met by universal acclaim. Mirroring Domingo Di Núbila's later assessment, a touchstone of its critical and academic reception, *Heraldo del Cinematografista* concludes that "[i]t lacks plot consistency, which had been a pretext to reunite in a single film an exceptional number of Argentine singers and composers of great prestige in the country." Unlike these points, which Mentasti and Argentina Sono Film had anticipated, some technical deficiencies are also criticized, something also noted in reviews in *Imparcial Film* and *La Prensa*.[60] The review in *La Prensa* concludes, "Other defects: titles; twisted, inefficient phraseology; the abuse of close-up scenes, not at all beneficial; and sometimes deficient sound recording." While performances by Alberto Gómez and Pepe Arias were panned, others' were praised, especially Libertad Lamarque's and Luis Sandrini's.[61] Its musical performances lauded and its filmmaking disparaged, *Tango!* was seen as a sure hit with popular audiences, especially if sufficient attention was given to promoting its numerous stars, as argued in *Heraldo del Cinematografista* and *Revista del Exhibidor*.[62] Reviews mirroring similar language and reception were published in the newspapers *Crítica*, *La Prensa*, *La Nación*, *Noticias Gráficas*, *El Mundo*, *El Diario*, *Última Hora*, and *La Razón*, and were used in advertisements promoting the film.[63] In fact, the insert published in *Imparcial Film*, whose footer reads "Each Argentine Soul is an Argentine Movie," lists its impressive programming in some 131 specific theaters, as well as "Forty More Theaters in Suburban Towns and Fifty in Cities and Towns in the Interior."[64] In one of the somewhat freely edited reviews in these ads, "What I Saw Last Night. In 'Tango' They Give Us an Abundance of Tangos," *El Mundo*'s film critic Néstor (Miguel Paulino Tato) writes, "Tango, tango, and even more tango! . . . Here in a few words is the most comprehensive summary of this film. Which is its biggest praise, moreover, if kept in mind the deep rootedness with which this type of music has come to penetrate the *alma popular* [the popular soul]."[65] Far from a criticism, Néstor sees this appeal as the film's strength. He finishes the piece by writing, "For what has been said, 'Tango' is, more than a movie, a kind of little cage in which the most celebrated larks and swallows of autochthonous song sing, among which have snuck in, as is natural, a few sparrows. But the truth is that it gives pleasure to hear them sing."

Subsequent to the premiere on May 19 of Lumiton's *Los tres berretines* (The Three Whims, dir. Equipo Lumiton, 1933), various film periodicals began to publish pieces championing the possibilities of national cinema. In the editorial "Well Understood Patriotism in National Production," *Imparcial Film* argues that mere patriotism is not sufficient to oblige writers to exalt Argentine productions or exhibitors to show these films. That said, in the case of applause-worthy productions such as *Nobleza gaucha*, *Hasta después de muerta* (*Until After Her Death*, dirs. Martínez de la Pera, Gunche, and Florencio Parravicini, 1916), *Tango!*, and *Los tres berretines*, "It is fair to reward the efforts of editors that are patriotic presenting worthwhile productions, enhancing our industry and our guild's name."[66] That said, an earlier piece by Athos argues that "it would be an error to expect that from the beginning [Argentina Sono Film and Lumiton] would realize extraordinary works: it is enough that they are modest, and with that there will be more than enough to assess how much can be hoped from both production companies for the future of our autochthonous cinema."[67] Managing expectations became important for the emerging national film industry. On one hand, Argentina Sono Film and other studios tempered expectations, so that audiences would not disparage their films as being inadequately cinematic or spectacular. On the other, they publicized their ambitious production plans, implicitly insisting upon the long-term viability and sustainability of their business model in terms of both the quantity and the quality of their features. They needed it both ways.

Discourse surrounding the kind of support Argentines should provide the national film industry continued in various forms and permutations throughout the 1930s and 1940s (as it does well into the twenty-first century), but it was coupled with a unique situation in the early sound period: an almost unsustainable demand from an overabundance of movie theaters whose exhibitors needed content. With headlines like "Alarming Statistic. Argentina is the Country that Has the Most Movie Theaters in Relation to its Number of Inhabitants," a panic about the surfeit of screens in the country was reported on for years by *porteño* film periodicals, particularly those with connections to the exhibitor's guild.[68] Anxiety for exhibitors yielded opportunity for producers and distributors, which presented Argentina Sono Film with various possibilities in situating itself within the marketplace. Unable to produce films on a sufficiently industrial scale, despite overly ambitious (and surely unrealistic) promises made to the press, Mentasti's emerging studio sought to diversify its activities in both distribution and production. In distribution, Argentina Sono Film continued releasing foreign titles such as *Mercedes* (dir. José María Castellví, 1933)—a "movie filmed in Barcelona, which is triumphing widely throughout Spain," whose prints were on board the steamship *Giulio Césare*—and opened an agency in the Catalan capital.[69] Directed by Octavio Barreiro, formally Metro's agent in Rosario, "This significant resolution arises from the intention by the director of Argentina Sono Film to an exchange of films with Spain."[70] Proposing to extend their activities into the production and distribution of newsreels, actuality films, and others to complement their involvement with feature films, which the company promised to expand to include six productions in 1934, Argentina Sono Film endeavored to exploit a lucrative market. This strategy, as an article in *Imparcial Film* notes, was historic, as it marked "the first time an Argentine company has established a direct agency in a foreign country."[71] The piece argues that "[a]s can be seen from the above, the activities and initiatives of the noted company and its director, señor

Ángel Mentasti, deserve the warmest applause, because they mean, for the first time, the international expansion of our cinema." In addition to allowing Argentina Sono Film inroads into Europe—soon thereafter deals to distribute *Dancing* in France, Italy, and Spain were announced—the distribution of films acquired abroad signified both an additional revenue stream and a means to continue building relationships with local exhibitors.[72] Unsurprisingly, however, *porteño* periodicals focused on the export of national cinema: "National films are starting to garner interest abroad. This constitutes conclusive evidence that Argentine cinema has left the sphere of trials and first steps."[73]

Argentina Sono Film's next production, *Dancing*, employed similar production, distribution, and exhibition strategies as *Tango!*. Even with promotion of future productions published throughout the pages of *porteño* film periodicals in late 1932 and early- to mid-1933, work on Argentina Sono Film's second movie would not commence until the success of *Tango!* was assured. In "'Tango' is a Film with Great Traction," Ángel Mentasti reshapes discourse surrounding the studio's first film and elicits interest in its second. In his typically fast-paced fashion, Mentasti tells the magazine, "I am full of satisfaction that 'Tango,' despite its technical deficiencies, if it is to be shown it is a film with great traction and . . . but look (so saying, he shows me several truly enviable *bordereaux*.)"[74] Mentasti discursively accounts for critiques of the film, to an extent, but is sure to physically gesture toward appeals to exhibitors' accounts. Gesturing toward the absence of industrialization in the emerging studio's modes of production, he also states, "Once I have fully organized commercial use in the interior and the capital, I will completely dedicate myself to preparing the next film, which, I hope, should be a new hit, thanks to the means that will be available so that it occurs—that is, will, ability, and capital." Short on details, and even shorter on facts (Libertad Lamarque, in fact, would have to wait two movies and two years to work again for Argentina Sono Film), Mentasti says that he will soon be able to talk more about the studio's next film.

By late winter 1933, production updates were regularly published in trade periodicals. Originally scheduled for a mid-September release, the newly titled film *Dancing* would not premiere until later in the spring.[75] With various reports noting its advanced production, completed shooting, and impending October release, Mentasti hosted *Imparcial Film* on set, allowing its reporter to listen to SIDE's notable work on the film's soundtrack.[76] *Dancing* was also shot on location in the Armenonville, the eponymous famous cabaret of Juan Maglio's 1912 tango.[77] Even though other periodicals such as *Revista del Exhibidor* and *La Nación* also reported that *Dancing* was nearly ready for release, adding, interestingly, that *Mercedes* was also soon on the way, its premiere was to be further delayed until November.[78] Finally, in early November, *Film* reported that it was delayed "due to causes related to the editing of the film," and its premiere would be the following week in the Porteño theater.[79] In an interview published soon before its premiere, a reluctant Luis Moglia Barth was interviewed by Athos of *Imparcial Film*.[80] Initially focusing on the director, the interview shifts to *Dancing*. Contrasted with Mentasti's bombast, Moglia Barth's circumspect response to the question of whether he thinks the film will be a success is striking. He answers, "I hope so, naturally, but even that I cannot say what will happen I am firmly convinced of having made a popular film [*un film de público*] . . . and moreover, I have accumulated another experience whose fruits will be seen in my future films." Eventually providing more conventional answers promoting the film's performances and script, Moglia Barth nonetheless tells Athos, "*Caramba!* You're inquisitive! Ok, add that filming took twenty three days in all and that this hassle has already taken too long."

Dancing premiered on November 9, 1933, at the Cine Porteño in Buenos Aires and received mixed reviews by local press. Despite being based on Alejandro A. Berrutti's successful play, which ran for five consecutive months at the Teatro Nacional, and being limited to the happenings of a single night in a *porteño* dancehall, the film was reported to be diegetically fragmented, constituted by dispersed, uneven scenes. As a series of characters shuffle in and out of scene, *Dancing* centers on the womanizing gossip of Cirilo (Severo Fernández) and Maneco (Tito Luisardo) and the travails of debuting singer Elena (Amanda Ledesma). In its largely negative review, *La Prensa* notes that the scenes are "lacking an organic nexus."[81] Much like the play, which it claims to have failed in translating the *boîte* to the stage, its filmmakers were unable to make the *dancing* cinematic. The reviewer receives the film's performances in generally positive terms—unlike other periodicals such as *Heraldo del Cinematografista* that panned the acting while praising the music, which it notes adds commercial value to the film—but singles out Moglia Barth for criticism, as he "[h]as hastily directed it, without choosing wisely subject and performers. And thus the work is halfway interesting; it does little favor to native industry." Periodicals such as *Film* remark on *Dancing*'s technical improvements, particularly its sound, and deficiencies such as the photography (even though its increased camera movement is noted by *Heraldo del Cinematografista* as adding dynamism).[82]

Strikingly, reviews of *Dancing* also meditate upon the broader implications of the film for the emerging national film industry. It is used, in a sense, as a litmus test of the current state of national cinema, but caution is expressed regarding its results. In two important reviews, *Cinegraf* and *Film* shape interpretations explaining why the film's artistic failings do not inhibit its commercial success. In a fascinating review published in *Cinegraf*, the pseudonymous author Mickey Mouse comments, "I have seen a film made in Buenos Aires: Dancing. Like another, 'Tango,' it has been filmed in the style of 'Grand Hotel' in the minimal atmosphere of our cheap theaters. It would be unfair to include the cinema in this kind of business, because it is nothing more than business, and from what I've learned out and about, a good one, that of doing similar things."[83] It later continues: "And it would be bad, but really bad, if it were said out there that this is a genuine representation of the national soul, or something like that. . . . It is not a great achievement, but anyway, it is pleasing to add a laurel to the industry . . ."[84] *Film* takes a similar line.[85] *Dancing* falls short of local filmgoers' hopes that Argentina will bestow the seventh art with a masterwork because "it cannot be because art may only reach its highest point when it has as a base an entire tradition and culture. Spontaneous generation does not exist, not in the physical nor the spiritual. The film we encountered last night has its merits and its defects . . . but [its forthcoming review] will not be in any way unfavorable from a commercial point of view." It continues, arguing that *Dancing* is "without a doubt an interesting film for audiences. Is that not already a flattering success?"

In its review of *Dancing*, *Heraldo del Cinematografista* adds further texture to the assessments found in *Cinegraf* and *Film*. Unlike the aesthetic interests expressed in the *Cinegraf* and *Film* reviews, which engage the discursive formation of national cinema, it builds upon its assessment of the narrative and formal failings of *Dancing* in a different way. It argues, "Abundant advanced publicity has been made for this film. Judging by the success of 'Tango,' this film will have a high commercial value, especially for popular cinemas and those in the interior. In spite of its deficiencies, by being an honest Argentine production, exhibitors should lend their support within reason."[86] Its expected success was not only a product of the success of *Tango!* but also the implementation of an effective marketing strategy. Much like its predecessor, Argentina Sono

Film promoted *Dancing* by publishing in *porteño* film periodicals the names of movie theaters showing the film in its initial run. For example, an advertisement published in the November 30, 1933, issue of *Revista del Exhibidor* reads: "DANCING is the most programmed film at the moment, simply because DANCING brings a bigger audience to theaters than any other film. And here we offer you proof," with a list of nearly thirty cinemas screening the movie in early December.[87] Despite this kind of promotion, *Dancing* would not reap the returns of *Tango!*. The impact of its failure on Argentina Sono Film received little attention in the press, in no small part due to the regularity of the disappearance of similarly fledgling film studios. It did, however, catch the attention of Carlos Favre and Julián Ramos, both of whom withdrew their financial support from Argentina Sono Film, leaving Mentasti to deal with the difficult task of moving his undercapitalized firm forward.

Following rhythms established by *Tango!* and *Dancing*, various articles anticipated the July 4, 1934, premiere of *Riachuelo*. With a budget that eventually inflated to nearly thirty thousand pesos, an increase of 75 percent over *Tango!*'s, *Riachuelo* took longer to complete than expected. Argentina Sono Film not only sought to film a bigger budget movie with restricted finances, but *Riachuelo* also marks a distinct commercial approach. Rather than monetizing music, the film narratively exploits comedy and romance. In addition to publishing production notes regarding script development, shooting in SIDE's new studios, and the beginnings of postproduction, among other topics, trade periodicals closely followed the development of Argentina Sono Film's distribution strategies.[88] In an interview with *La Película*, Mentasti does not reference the financial difficulties of the film's production, but rather looks toward its anticipated commercial success.[89] Mentasti, who "did not hide his enthusiasm for this new production," employs seemingly contradictory language that nevertheless signals his company's commercial strategies. He tells *La Película*, "I can assure you all . . . that 'Riachuelo' is a film that will do honor to Argentine productions, [it is] superior to what has been done in the country, [and] it will be able to rub shoulders with and be exhibited without detraction in any part of the world." To exploit the intrinsic value of the film, Mentasti proposes to further pursue commercial deals in other countries, including, notably, Mexico. With a deal in the works with a "country that has given a boost to its production, whose first films we will soon know, distributed by this Argentine company," Argentina Sono Film continues to explore ways in which it can export its films to other Spanish-speaking markets, while seeking materials to import for its own production, which is ramping up. Having reportedly already sold rights to the film in six other Latin American countries, *La Película* also notes that filming of *El alma del bandonéon* (*Soul of the Bandoneon*) will begin the following week. Continuing the modes of production from *Tango!* and *Dancing*, Argentina Sono Film makes a notable shift. Still relying on the power of stars to draw audiences into movie theaters, Mentasti's film studio moved toward different kinds of narrative to appeal to both local and foreign markets. These new strategies, more centrally incorporating comedy and romance—while still integrating popular music—were utilized throughout the early sound period. *Riachuelo* suggested their commercial viability.

Unlike *Tango!* and *Dancing*, both of which used the strategy of simultaneous screenings to turn their premieres into events, which also lessened the possibility of negative word of mouth affecting their success at the box office, *Riachuelo* was initially screened privately. Allowing the studio to receive feedback and generate publicity before *Riachuelo*'s release, this private screening was well received by *porteño* film periodicals.[90] The daily newspaper *Giornale d'Italia* even goes so far as to congratulate Mentasti in advance, describing him as the "indefatigable promotor of the film company."[91] Sustaining, if not surpassing, its prerelease positive word of mouth, *Riachuelo* was well received by critics. *Heraldo del Cinematografista* proposes that "[w]ithout being a perfect movie, it can be considered the best of all sound productions that have been produced to date in the country, and it signals for the production company and the director a true triumph.[92] *Imparcial Film* makes a similar assessment, as its review concludes, "In sum, 'Riachuelo' is a good and, above all, pleasant film, which, without being extraordinary, reveals what can be done among us when it comes to films with desire, means, and intelligence."[93] With its release coinciding with *Nueve de Julio*, the celebration of Argentina's Declaration of Independence, the critic Crayón strikes a nationalistic tone in the right-wing daily *La Bandera*: "'Riachuelo' is a nationalist triumph: Argentina Sono Film, a national production company, and national artists, really ours, children of all of the *barrios* that come to the center with their art made by pure personal effort."[94] Striking a dissonant chord compared to other periodicals, Crayón's review nonetheless draws attention to Argentina Sono Film's prudent decision to release the film on a national holiday.

Within *Riachuelo*'s broadly positive reception, debates unfolded concerning the emerging national film industry. These debates, interestingly, primarily came out of daily newspapers, whose readership represented broader sectors of the Argentine populace than the readers of periodicals like *Heraldo del Cinematografista* and *Imparcial Film*. In *La Prensa*'s review, it is argued that *Riachuelo* "is a film that can be described as good within the not great possibilities of the incipient national industry both for the excellent material employed in its filming and for the tact of its subject, direction, and performers."[95] Referring to Moglia Barth's direction of the film, but easily applicable more broadly to Argentina Sono Film, *La Razón* claims that "to persevere is to triumph or '*chi dura vince*,' as the Italian proverb says. In effect, to persevere in cinema, to insist with boldness, trying to eliminate little by little typical errors of all initiation, means to triumph with enough time."[96] Constrained by its limitations, which produced films understood to be artistic failures, Argentina Sono Film was developing new storytelling strategies better expressed through films that were more technically accomplished, particularly in cinematography and sound. It was, in fact, for these reasons that the film received a glowing review in *Cinegraf*, a magazine frequently critical of Argentine cinema.[97] Tellingly titled " 'Riachuelo,' a Manifestation of the Power of National Cinema," the review states, " 'Riachuelo now establishes the flattering reality of a significant national film and a good movie anywhere in the world because of its technique and the standards of its direction."[98]

Imparcial Film also offers, "Simple in its thematic construction, its value is in the exact reproduction of the environment and the excellent compositions that offer us that so very *porteño* corner of the Riachuelo in all of its picturesque colors."[99] Centering on the picaresque figure of Berretín (Luis Sandrini), *Riachuelo* is a story of redemption. In it, the reforming criminal Remanso (Alfredo Camiña) returns to the straight and narrow in no small part due to his love for Rosa (Margarita Solá). Berretín is also redeemed, but first through work, whose value is introduced to him by Remanso, and, later, by his true love for Juanita (Maruja Pibernat). As the film's comic star notes in the interview titled "Luis Sandrini, Stutterer by Chance," "I play the classic *criollo* pickpocket who becomes regenerated by a woman's love."[100] Berretín and Remanso atone for their pasts by foiling a plot to rob the shipyard where they had been working. Rewarded for their bravery by the shipyard's owner, who refurbishes *La vieja*, the tugboat where Berretín had been living, Berretín and Remanso also reunite with their loves. A happy ending, indeed.

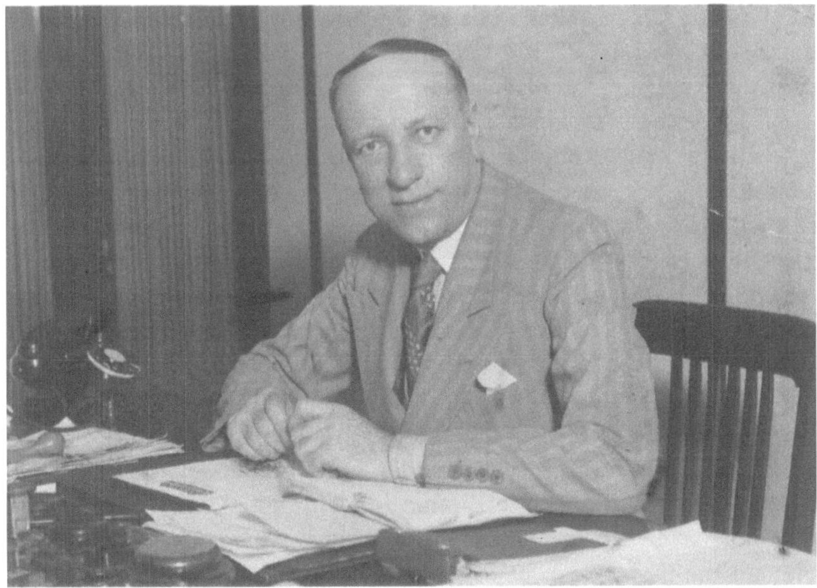

Figure 8.3. Portrait of Ángel Mentasti. Courtesy of the Museo del Cine Pablo Ducrós Hicken.

In his regular column, "What I Saw Last Night," the influential critic Néstor exclaims, "Finally! We can now say that we have a good national movie. That it is: a good national movie."[101] With a reception like that, as well as numerous reports of audiences' resounding applause at its conclusion, it is little surprising that *Heraldo del Cinematografista* heralds its commercial possibilities, ending its review by stating, "It is a production that, without a doubt, will obtain excellent reception from popular audiences, and it can be anticipated that it will be a great comic hit. It has counted on discreet publicity. Suitable, preferably in popular cinemas, for any section and day."[102] This reception is in part of its diegesis, as well as its technical execution, but it is also deeply indebted to the comic star Luis Sandrini.[103] Nearly every single review of the film examines Sandrini's performance, most arriving at similar conclusions to "Some Principal Actors of 'Riachuelo'": "Luis Sandrini, the most popular comic actor of the moment, manages to thoroughly impress in his role."[104] Even though he was disparaged by *La Prensa* as "put[ting] certain monotony in his work," other reviews praised Sandrini, such as

La Nación's, which states, "His psychology, full of undefinable *porteño* touches in his transparent mischievousness, jovially wins spirits through its naturalness, through his lively dramatic playfulness."[105] In the *Noticias gráficas* review, it is argued that "[t]his actor, whose facial expressiveness we have already praised on other occasions, possesses the gift of *photogénie,* as well as a little common agility and skill in other performers in our cinema."[106] Relying on language tied to the cinema, the review in *Noticias gráficas* allows us to understand Sandrini as the first real movie star of Argentine cinema. His performance in *Riachuelo* was not notable for its being carried out on screen, as Gardel's acting was as tango singer Carlos Acosta in *Cuesta abajo* (dir. Louis Gasnier, 1934), which would premiere a month later in Buenos Aires, but rather Sandrini's screen presence as Berretín was communicated through a truly cinematic storyworld. Effectively, this marked a shift for Argentina Sono Film. Now its "more stars than in the sky," to reference Ricardo Manetti's essay on the film studio, were not merely brought to the cinema, but rather they were fabricated through the mechanisms of national industrial film.[107]

Popular support of *Riachuelo* quickly matched, if not surpassed its critical reception. The film was an unqualified success at the box office. Published a week after the film's premiere, a note in the daily newspaper *Crítica* reports, "The resounding triumph of 'Riachuelo,' the pleasant movie being shown in the Renacimiento, would seem to be a joyous backing of our National Cinema to the national holiday, which, with extraordinary liveliness, is being celebrated in our city."[108] Attributing cinematic success to smart planning, the short article continues, "Said production by Argentina Sono Film is filling up the Renacimiento movie theater every day, and spectators' applause is the obligatory final touch of each showing." Along those lines, some five days later, in a piece announcing the film's debut in Rosario, *Imparcial Film* notes that *Riachuelo* already had been shown in 120 theaters in Buenos Aires by July 15.[109] In that same issue, the article "The Success of 'Riachuelo'" attributes the film's popular reception in no small part to Moglia Barth's direction.[110] Domestic demand for *Riachuelo* would eventually lead to foreign interest, but not before Argentina Sono Film experienced some difficulty in delivering the film to national audiences in the provinces. With an underdeveloped distribution network, Mentasti's company ran into objections from exhibitors, primarily in the interior, regarding the film's cost.[111] Perhaps to wrest control of profits from exhibitors, who would pay fixed fees to screen movies in their territory,

Argentina Sono Film suspended programming of the film from July 31 to the beginning of September.[112] *Riachuelo*'s success at the domestic box office quickly attracted the attention of distributors from abroad, as an August 15 piece in *Imparcial Film* reports. It notes that contracts were signed to distribute the film in Peru, El Salvador, Panama, and Italy, while deals were being worked out with entities in Chile, Cuba, and Spain.[113] Using as a source a piece ostensibly published in *The New York Times*, *Imparcial Films* even notes *Riachuelo*'s success in New York City.[114] The film's success was so great that rumors were printed that Sandrini might sign with one of Hollywood's Big Five, Warner Bros.[115]

By late 1934, the uncertainty with which Argentina Sono Film entered the year had been replaced by confidence. Assessments such as that of *Cinegraf*, which describes in an editorial that "'Riachuelo' can be considered, several months after its premiere, a brilliant triumph of national film. Opposite foreign productions, its power of attraction has turned out to be surprising,"[116] are especially striking when we consider that some months earlier Mentasti had written a letter published by *Imparcial Film* in which he denounced critical reception of national cinema, concluding that "[t]he public, supreme and sole judge, tells us with the facts, giving its verdict, when filling theaters in which our movies are exhibited that we are on the right track."[117] Criticizing "dilettante critics" and "pseudo critics" who do not understand that "[t]he values and knowledge of the cinema are neither bought nor improvised, they are formed by using those thousands and thousands of meters of film that we have already begun to shoot in our studios with faith and enthusiasm so that a roster of good technicians, good directors, and good Argentine artists emerge,"[118] not only does Mentasti heap scorn on these critics (whose cosmopolitan tastes for jazz and foreign films threaten the *argentinidad* to which he appeals) in his delineation of cinematic values, but he celebrates the ways Argentina Sono Film's modes of production develop Argentine national cinema. "Perfection is not obtained in a day," as the supportive editorial accompanying the letter pithily notes, and Mentasti's movement away from the ad hoc, director-centered production model of the silent period toward more modern production units is possible only with factory-like organization and sufficient labor.[119] Or, as a later profile in *La Película* would propose, "Don Ángel Mentasti is one of the living examples that 'the devil knows more because he is old than because he is the devil' and experience of commercial life is often the

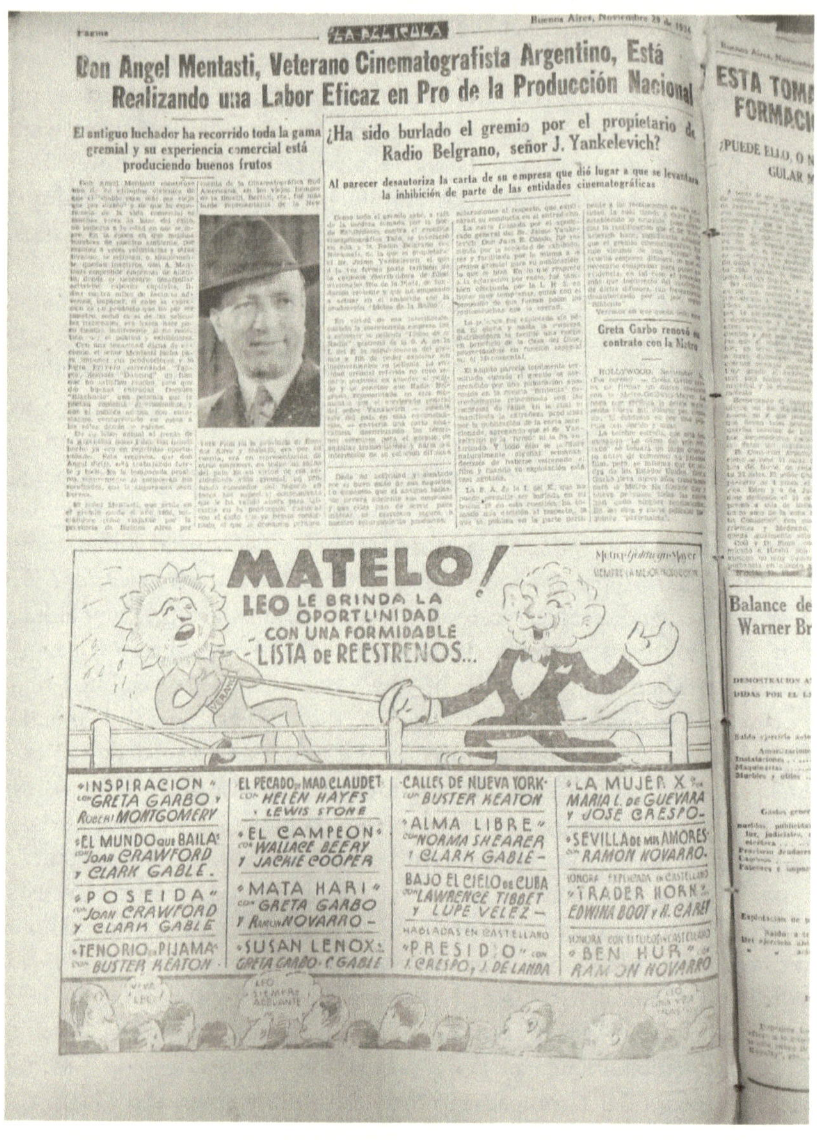

LA PELÍCULA

Buenos Aires, Noviembre 29 de 1934

Don Angel Mentasti, Veterano Cinematografista Argentino, Está Realizando una Labor Eficaz en Pro de la Producción Nacional

El antiguo luchador ha recorrido toda la gama gremial y su experiencia comercial está produciendo buenos frutos

¿Ha sido burlado el gremio por el propietario de Radio Belgrano, señor J. Yankelevich?

Al parecer desautoriza la carta de su empresa que dió lugar a que se levantara la inhibición de parte de las entidades cinematográficas

Greta Garbo renovó su contrato con la Metro

MATELO!
LEO LE BRINDA LA OPORTUNIDAD
CON UNA FORMIDABLE
LISTA DE REESTRENOS...

Metro-Goldwyn-Mayer

INSPIRACION con GRETA GARBO y ROBERT MONTGOMERY
EL MUNDO QUE BAILA con JOAN CRAWFORD y CLARK GABLE
POSEIDA con JOAN CRAWFORD y CLARK GABLE
TENORIO EN PIJAMA con BUSTER KEATON
EL PECADO DE MADELON CLAUDET con HELEN HAYES y LEWIS STONE
EL CAMPEON con WALLACE BEERY y JACKIE COOPER
MATA HARI con GRETA GARBO y RAMON NOVARRO
SUSAN LENOX con GRETA GARBO - C. GABLE
CALLES DE NUEVA YORK con BUSTER KEATON
ALMA LIBRE con NORMA SHEARER y CLARK GABLE
BAJO EL CIELO DE CUBA con LAWRENCE TIBBETT y LUPE VELEZ - HABLADAS EN CASTELLANO
PRESIDIO con J. CRESPO, J. DE LANDA
LA MUJER X con MARIA L. DE GUEVARA y JOSE CRESPO
SEVILLA DE MIS AMORES con RAMON NOVARRO
TRADER HORN con EDWINA BOOTH y H. CAREY
BEN HUR con RAMON NOVARRO

Figure 8.4. Profile of Mentasti. *La Película*, November 29, 1934.

basis of success, no matter at what age it is achieved."[120] Increasingly, as Argentina Sono Film evolved into an industrial film studio producing and distributing movies throughout each season, Mentasti would step out of the shadows.

1935, A Pivotal Year

After the success of *Riachuelo*, Argentina Sono Film began pivoting toward new modes of production and distribution. Not only did the film studio employ new directors, as Moglia Barth temporarily left and Mario Soffici and Arturo S. Mom made their feature film debuts, but Mentasti began to change the ways in which its films were made and, perhaps more importantly, distributed. Increasingly refining the processes through which its diegeses came to be framed on screen, Argentina Sono Film also began to more closely control the exploitation of its films as commercial goods. Reports concerning the 1935 film season began as early as September 1934. In addition to announcing three films for the upcoming season, *El alma del bandonéon*, *Monte criollo* (*Creole Play*), and *El circo* (The Circus), which was never released, the studio continued its typical hyperbole: "According to information that they have provided to us, the company has the firm intention of producing regularly, having already announced that beginning next season it will release a movie monthly."[121] Similar news regarding its production schedule appeared in late December in *La Película*.[122] In it, "Production to be filmed will be continued, to which end other story lines by well-known signatures are being read. Sr. Mentasti, director and soul of this company, intends to have five productions ready by the end of February for their premieres."[123] Generally speaking, as changes in the company unfolded, starting in 1935 and continuing into the next two seasons, *porteño* film periodicals were less attentive to following the stages of preproduction and more interested in distribution and exhibition news.

Parallel to the greater industrialization of its modes of production, whose increasingly commercialized storyworlds became more broadly appealing throughout the 1930s, Argentina Sono Film continued investing in its own distribution practices. By the mid-1930s, as argued in the *Imparcial Film* article "40 Productions in Spanish for 1935," which appeared at the beginning of the year, "material in Spanish is considered as a commercial force for theaters denominated as popular, thus distributors are concerned about including in their programs productions spoken in our language, which this season will be in greater quantity than the previous."[124] In addition to the U.S.-produced *films hispanos*, produced mostly by Fox Film and Paramount, but also including Columbia and Universal, the article notes that some twenty Spanish films will be distributed during the season. Most interesting, however, is the impending arrival of Mexican films, which have yet to arrive in Argentina. The article states, "With regard to Mexican production, whose activity in recent times is truly promising, we make no reference due to lacking particulars on those who introduce it in our market." It is also announced that Argentina Sono Film will release six films: *El alma del bandoneón*, *Monte criollo*, *Puerto Nuevo* (*New Port*), *La conquista de Buenos Aires* (The Conquest of Buenos Aires, which likely became *La barra mendocina*, [The Mendoza Gang]), *El circo*, and an untitled Luis Sandrini project.[125] These films, as well as those released the following year, were increasingly distributed by a more highly professionalized network of branch offices as opposed to local intermediaries. Foreign distribution continued to be of great interest not only to Argentina Sono Film, but also to *porteño* film periodicals. Appearing closely after the note in *Imparcial Film*, *Heraldo del Cinematografista* published details of a deal with Ballesteros Tonafilm of Madrid to distribute *Riachuelo*, *El alma del bandoneón*, *Monte criollo*, *La conquista de Buenos Aires*, and *Puerto Nuevo*.[126]

By the time *El alma del bandoneón* premiered at the Cine Monumental on February 20, 1935, some six months had passed since the release of *Riachuelo*.[127] It had spent, however, some time in development. Reports dating back to 1933 were published regarding Libertad Lamarque's participation in a new Argentina Sono Film production.[128] Similar notes appeared about the film's script and music, best known today for introducing Enrique Santos Discépolo's tango "Cambalache" in a fascinating montage sequence. Discépolo, a popular tango composer whose dramatist brother Armando wrote *grotesco criollo* plays such as *Mateo* (1923), *Stéfano* (1928), and *Relojero* (The Watchmaker, 1934), was reported in mid-1934 to be preparing material for Argentina Sono Film.[129] *El alma del bandonéon* centers on Fabián (Santiago Arrieta), the son of the elitist ranch owner Don Julián (Domingo Sapelli) and Elda (Libertad Lamarque), an aspiring tango singer.[130] After living in misery, rejected by Fabián's family, the couple's young daughter dies, causing them to separate. Fabián becomes a famous tango composer, while Elda awaits his return. The couple dramatically reconciles in the film's denouement at the Teatro Colón in Buenos Aires by performing together the title song.[131]

On February 20, 1935, Argentina Sono Film arranged a star-studded gala to celebrate the release of *El alma del bandoneón* at the Cine Monumental. Broadcast on Radio Argentina, much like Hollywood premieres such as *Grand Hotel* (dir. Edmund Goulding, 1932), the film studio's directors (Luis César Amadori, Mom, Soffici, and Augusto César

Vatteone) were all slated to speak.[132] The festivities were not enough to sway film critics, and the reception of *El alma del bandoneón* was largely mixed. In its ambivalent review, *Heraldo del Cinematografista* categorizes the film as *especial,* but pans its plot. Its analysis begins, "The weakest part of this production is the plot, vulgar and without consistency, and the dialogues are also lackluster. Nevertheless, it is the most 'cinematic' of the national films released to date."[133] Despite its assessment of the film's artistic merits, or lack thereof, the review nonetheless notes that "[r]eviews in newspapers have been good. It has had excellent preliminary publicity. In particular, it will interest popular audiences, being able to be included in any section and time. Technically, we repeat, this is the best of all films that have appeared in the country." Audiences ultimately agreed with this sentiment: in addition to reports of its success in Argentina, it would later become a hit in Spain.[134] According to an *Imparcial Film* note, its run at the Monumental, a four thousand spectator movie theater in Madrid, was a triumph: "This is the first Argentina Sono Film production to premiere directly in Spain, and indeed its success could not be more auspicious." Its success encouraged the release of additional Argentina Sono Film features in the country such as *Puerto Nuevo* and *Loco lindo* (*The Big Fool* or *Crazy Dandy*) in December 1936.[135]

Subverting its critiques, and also equating popular audiences and bad taste, the review in *Heraldo del Cinematografista*, a trade publication widely read by exhibitors, corresponds to those of other periodicals. *Cinegraf,* which positioned itself as an alternative publication that took cinema seriously, published a scathing review.[136] Concluding that "this film is inappropriate for the film culture of the Argentine public and an efficient contribution to the masses' preference for everything that implies an offense to good," *Cinegraf* discounts not only the broad appeal of *El alma del bandoneón*, but also the film's intermedial and intertextual connections with "[a]ll these vernacular films seem to have to revolve this alleged 'national music.'" At the end of the year, this line of reasoning is effectively integrated into a harsh critique of national cinema. In his *Cinegraf* piece, "Through a Year of National Films. Money! Watchword in Argentine Cinema," César F. Marcos argues that "'El alma del bandonéon,' constitutes the template [*modelo maestro*] of all the defects from which local cinema suffers and that we have continuously criticized."[137] Among these deficiencies, Marcos notes the exploitation of a radio star's popularity ("in certain sectors of the public"), the distortion of local color into "a succession of crude and common scenes [*escenas burdas y populacheras*]," and the vulgar abuse of sentimentality. It is an unrepentant assessment that disparages Argentina Sono Film's commerciality at the expense of artistry; *El alma del bandoneón* caters to bad taste so as to appeal broadly to spectators with little regard for anything beyond money.

As Argentina Sono Film begins to distribute its own films, fewer notes regarding domestic distribution agreements are published. Even though exceptions occasionally appear, such as one regarding the distribution of Argentina Sono Film's movies (along with those of other studios such as Lumiton, Cabildo, and Libertad Films) by Leopoldo Samper in Santa Fe, structural transformations in the ways in which national films are distributed lead to fewer reports of consummated deals.[138] In March 1935, the Madrid film periodical *Sparta* notes that Argentina Sono Film and Ballesteros Tona Films have agreed to distribute each other's movies. The agreement includes distribution throughout the entire Iberian Peninsula of *Riachuelo*, as well as six films from Argentina Sono Film's current program.[139] By mid-May, Enrique Wagenpfeil has been sent to Rio de Janeiro to establish an agency for Argentina Sono Film.[140] *Revista del Exhibidor* claims that Nicolás Proserpio will run the agency, and that *Riachuelo* will be the first film shown.[141] Later in the year, it is reported that Ángel Luis Mentasti will visit Madrid at the beginning of September 1935 to acquire films for next season. According to the *Heraldo del Cinematografista*, he will stay until February.[142] Sure enough, Ángel Luis Mentasti visits Madrid to formalize the agreement, as reported by that city's conservative evening newspaper, *La Época*.[143] According to the progressive daily *La Libertad*, "On his visit, he was accompanied by the film editors of nearly every *madrileño* newspaper and the director of the Spanish production company, CIFESA."[144]

In anticipation of the premiere of *Monte criollo*, Argentina Sono Film's fifth production, discourse surrounding the studio's films is seen to be shifting, often in relation to a banquet to be held in honor of Mentasti and the film's director Arturo S. Mom. Separating themselves from previous film criticism, which has ascribed authorship to the director in analyses of filmic texts, articles in *Imparcial Film* contend that "Argentina Sono Film, whose executive management is under the charge of Don Ángel Mentasti, is, without a doubt, the most active of our producers," and, "A good part of the success of the film upon which we are commenting owes itself—and it would be an injustice to hide it—to the activity and intelligence of Don Ángel Mentasti, true promoter of Argentina Sono Film."[145] After four productions in a little more than two years, discourse began to shift away from attributing the success of films such as *Monte criollo* to their stars or directors and toward including their film studio. With its greater industrialization, the authors of the emerging Argentina national cinema are no longer only the artistic creators of its films. Like *El alma del bandonéon*, *Monte criollo* shows that Argentina Sono Film can produce films, even successful ones, without Moglia Barth. The genius, therefore, is not the director, but the system put into place by the film studio, as signaled by Mentasti's outsized presence in the report. Tellingly, the banquet's guests are largely well-known figures in commerce and politics.[146] In another *Imparcial Film* note on the banquet, Mentasti's contributions are reiterated, saying, "Mister Mentasti is justly considered to be one of the most dynamic and intelligent promoters of our cinema."[147]

Similar to *El alma del bandoneón*, the critical reception of *Monte criollo* was initially shaped through reports of private screenings. Relating to one organized in the beginning of May 1935, *Imparcial Film* notes that *Monte criollo* is "a significant advance in our cinema, having achieved, without a fear of being denied, that it is the best film that has been made to this point in the country."[148] *Heraldo del Cinematografista*'s review continues a line of criticism seen in previous assessments of Argentina Sono Film's productions insofar as it largely focuses on the film's technical accomplishments and publicity.[149] Despite its ostensible lack of originality, although it is lauded for its cinematic action and good direction, the film is deemed to be "[a]pt for strong showings [*secciones de fuerza*], preferably in popular cinemas." In his review for *Imparcial Film*, Athos begins by lauding the movie: "Our cinema, which already counted more than one success in terms of production, has just been enriched by a film of indisputable merits that signals, within our film industry, a point at which it is definitively affirmed."[150] In no small part due to its direction, according to the review, the film is extremely well executed. Picking up some of Athos's points, but taking them in a different direction, César F. Marcos writes in *Cinegraf* that "'Monte criollo' demonstrates in A. S. Mom the possession of a broad directorial ability. Its development allows us to become familiar with the skill of the director, in the able negotiation of obstacles in a plot in which every advantage has been taken. It possesses, furthermore, agile and successful isolated moments, of careful cinematic craft that are left diminished in an ensamble whose atmosphere, anti-Argentine and little appropriate, is not at the intellectual heights of who directed it."[151] Unable to fully satisfy *Cinegraf*, *Monte criollo* was, however, a success with audiences.[152]

If the first half of the 1935 season was a resounding progression for Argentina Sono Film, the second half proved to be almost an interlude. Perhaps indicative of their initial reception, both *La barra mendocina* and the short *Pibelandia* (Kidland) are now considered lost. Delayed several times, the premiere of *La barra mendocina* took place at the Cine Monumental on August 2, 1935.[153] In its mixed review in *Heraldo del Cinematografista*, the film's plot was panned while its comedy was praised. It claimed that "there is a certain lack of continuity in the film, but despite this factor it will be pleasing to popular audiences because of the broad humor of many of its scenes."[154] Citing its excellent publicity, *Heraldo del Cinematografista* speculated that the film would be a success. Similar to *La barra mendocina*'s commercial reception, which remains unclear from the reporting of *porteño* film periodicals, very little is known about the short film *Pibelandia*. Brief notes about the short appeared in *Caras y caretas*, which described it as "a new and original attempt to dignify local cinema," and in *Heraldo del Cinematografista*.[155] Rather than premiering in the Cine Monumental like the rest of Argentina Sono Film's 1935 productions, *Pibelandia* seems to have opened on October 4, 1935, at the decidedly less fashionable Palais Bleu as part of a program that included *La barra mendocina*, *Riachuelo*, and *Monte criollo*.[156]

Even though its recent releases had garnered little attention, *porteño* film periodicals frequently reported on distribution and production developments at Argentina Sono Film. Not only was the film studio further exploring its connections with Spanish entities (a long trip by Ángel Luis Mentasti was announced in *Heraldo del Cinematografista*), but the possibility of deals with Mexican companies was increasingly becoming a reality.[157] While the Madrid press reported on Ángel Luis's business with Spanish companies, especially Estudios Ballesteros Tona Film, local outlets informed the public that Argentina Sono Film would distribute *Chucho el roto* (*Chucho, The Dandy*, dir. Gabriel Soria, 1934).[158] The news was later confirmed by *Heraldo del Cinematografista*, which wrote that "Argentina Sono Film announced to us that in 1936 it will distribute ten Spanish films and some other Mexican ones."[159] The arrival of Mexican films in Argentina marked an important moment in Latin American film history; not only did it signal the beginning of the dominance of the Mexican film industry, which was finally able to compete across key Spanish-language markets, but it marked a shift in Argentine film culture, which would eventually come to embrace certain aspects of Mexican cinema in the classical period. Several months later, it was also reported that Argentina

Sono Film would distribute a competing production company's films, SIFAL's *Crimen a las 3* (Crime at Three O'Clock, dir. Luis Saslavsky, 1935) and *Escala en la ciudad* (Layover in the City, dir. Alberto de Zavalía, 1935).[160] In addition to these important distribution developments, news about Argentina Sono Film's production and exhibition schedule was also published.[161] By the end of 1935, Argentina Sono Film had solidified its plans for the upcoming season. In a full-page advertisement taken out in the December 15 issue of *Imparcial Film*, Argentina Sono Film announces "15 big productions in the Spanish language," consisting of "6

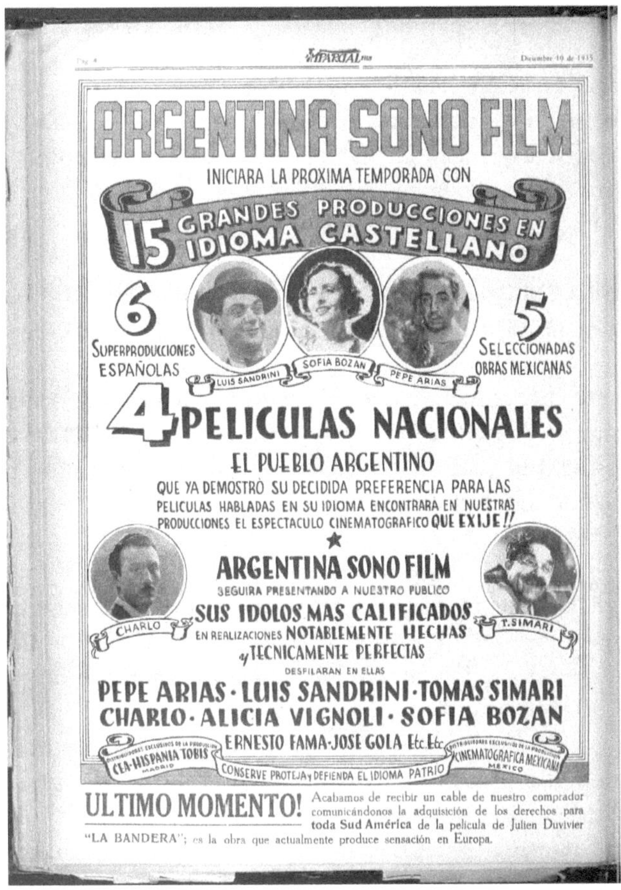

Figure 8.5. Advertisement promoting Argentina Sono Film's releases in 1936. *Imparcial Film*, December 15, 1935.

Spanish super productions," "5 selected Mexican works," and "4 national movies."[162] Including portraits of stars Luis Sandrini, Sofia Bozán, Pepe Arias, Charlo, and Tomás Simari, the advertisement reads, "The Argentine people [*pueblo*] already showed their decided preference for films spoken in their language will find in our productions the cinematic spectacle they demand." Highlighting their own national production, Argentina Sono Film also attempted to broaden the appeal of the films it distributed, as shown by the lower banner. Between the names of the Spanish (CEA Hispania Tobis) and Mexican (Cinematográfica mexicana) production companies, the banner reads, "Conserve protect and defend the national language [*idioma patrio*]." The advertisement encourages spectators to go beyond national borders, but not without holding on to their ties to Argentina (Sono Film). Curiously enough, given its strong appeal to a transnational Hispanic identity, the bottom of the advertisement, which reads, "Last minute!," publicizes Argentina Sono Film's acquisition for all of South America of Julien Duvivier's *La bandera*, "the work that currently produces sensation in Europe." Mentasti, it seems, was working all angles.

Becoming Latin America's First Industrial Studio: Argentina Sono Film in the 1936–37 Seasons

With the stability it had attained through the success of its films in the previous season, Argentina Sono Film began to emerge as the first truly industrial studio in Latin America, as increased capitalization permitted it to enlarge its production and distribution capacities. If the 1935 film season represented stabilization, if not regularization, of its feature film production, the 1936 season would see Argentina Sono Film release a then-unparalleled eight films.[163] Mentasti's efforts to industrialize production and more fully and vertically integrate the distribution of the company's movies did not go unnoticed by *porteño* film periodicals. In the March 25, 1936, issue of *Imparcial Film*, an article observes that "Argentina Sono Film, the most important national film company, has entered with the initiation of a plan of wider scope" comprising greater investment in both production and distribution.[164] Under the direction of the American (of Austro-Hungarian origins) cinematographer John Alton, newly hired as its technical director, Argentina Sono Film was finally establishing their own studios, located in the Almagro neighborhood of Buenos Aires. Alton, it was reported, would supervise the installation of "the most modern technical elements of lighting and photography, utilizing recently imported R.C.A. (High Fidelity) equipment for sound."[165] Paralleling its efforts to close in on the technical advances already integrated by other industries—not only in Hollywood, but, increasingly, those of Mexico and Spain—local laboratories also saw increased investment.[166] In addition to technical advances, Argentina Sono Film increased investment in talent, as in the return of Luis Moglia Barth as a production manager (*jefe de producción*) and the signing of actors to contracts for multiple films.[167]

Argentina Sono Film's four productions of 1936—*Puerto Nuevo*, *Loco lindo*, *Amalia*, and *¡Goal!*—were, for the first time, distributed by the company itself.[168] As specified in that year's *Anuario cinematográfico argentino*, Argentina Sono Film had established offices in Bahía Blanca, Buenos Aires, Córdoba, General Pico, Mendoza, Rosario, Santa Fe, and Tucumán.[169] In replicating Hollywood studios' distribution model, Argentina Sono Film stood to keep in house not only its distribution labor, but its profits as well. Given Ángel Mentasti's background in film distribution in the silent period, it is hardly surprising that Atilio Mentasti came to take over the Córdoba office in late 1936, according to *Heraldo del Cinematografista*.[170] As the production company sought to more vertically integrate its business practices in the domestic market, it also sought deals with foreign entities to both import and export films. Continuing the distribution of European films such as *El bailarín y el trabajador* (*The Dancer and the Worker*, dir. Luis Marquina, 1936), *La bandera* (dir. Duvivier, 1936), and *Lucrecia Borgia* (*Lucrezia Borgia*, dir. Abel Gance, 1935), Argentina Sono Film also acquired rights to distribute *Chucho, el roto* from Mexico, a country that would soon provide both opportunity and competition.[171] These foreign titles supplemented the company's own production in its domestic market, allowed their newly formed distribution network to forge relationships with local exhibitors, and provided a means to engage foreign film producers and, more importantly, distributors. In March 1936, the Madrid film magazine *Mundo gráfico* announced a deal with Hispania Tobis to distribute *Puerto Nuevo* and *Loco lindo*.[172] Even though few Argentine films had appeared in Spain, and what had been screened was claimed to have been mediocre, things were reported to be changing by the Madrid film periodical *Cine Sparta*, which assured its readers that Argentina Sono Film's industrial organization and excellent technical direction would produce films "that in Spain would achieve easy and resounding success."[173] Commercial opportunities in Spain would become increasingly difficult to pursue as the country slid into civil war, but *Cine Sparta* underscored the effects of industrialized modes of production in assembling commercial films that would resonate with audiences not only at home in Argentina but abroad as well.

Comedies with broad appeal, *Puerto Nuevo* and *Loco lindo* were early signals of the eventual disruption precipitated by the industry's development. Even though these star vehicles differed greatly from *El alma del bandonéon* and *Monte criollo*, *Puerto Nuevo* and *Loco lindo* fell into their February/May rhythms, even though the latter films were meant at one point to share very similar releases.[174] Production notes for both films—reporting that their filming had begun at SIDE's studios and, later, that foreign technicians John Alton and Fernando A. Rivero had been contracted to work on them—were published in numerous *porteño* film periodicals, often, due to their parallel production schedules, at the same time.[175] Individual reports were also published, notably regarding *Puerto Nuevo*'s music in *Imparcial Film* (La Orquesta de Francisco Canaro had

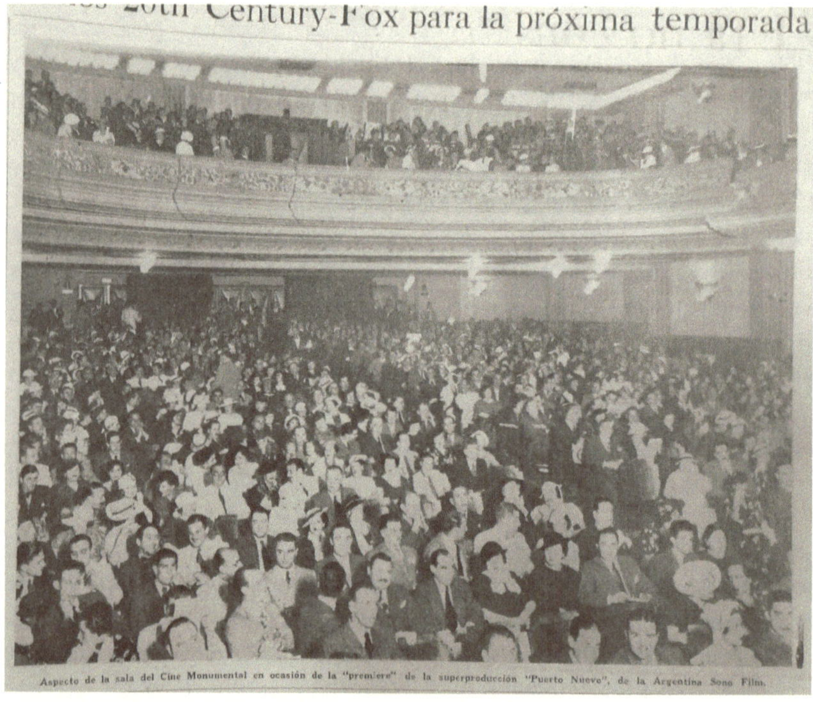

Century-Fox para la próxima temporada

Aspecto de la sala del Cine Monumental en ocasión de la "premiere" de la superproducción "Puerto Nuevo", de la Argentina Sono Film.

Figure 8.6. Scenes from the premiere of *Puerto Nuevo*. *Imparcial Film*, February 20, 1936.

been contracted to do music for *Puerto Nuevo* and Sofia Bozán would sing a *ranchera*), but Pepe Arias's and Luis Sandrini's films constituted models of commercially reliable comedies that could shore up their yearly production schedules.[176]

Initially signaled in an uneven review in *Heraldo del Cinematografista*, which noted both highlights (performances by Pepe Arias, Alicia Vignoli, Sofia Bozán, and José Gola, as well as technical elements such as cinematography, sound, and presentation) and lowlights (weak plot and Charlo's stilted acting as its protagonist), *Puerto Nuevo*'s broad commercial appeal would make it a hit with local audiences.[177] Continuing its initial run success at the Monumental, *Puerto Nuevo* was hugely successful in *los cines de barrio*, in no small part due to the resonance of Pepe Arias's Dandy. Six weeks after its premiere, an article published in *Imparcial Film* affirmed that "[w]ithout exaggerating, it can be maintained that this movie marks true programming records in the totality of the capital's cinemas. Its acceptance has not been less auspicious in the interior. In short, Argentina Sono Film has a movie for a while."[178] Disparaged critically for its lack of artistic ambition, if not complete unoriginality, it proved highly popular with local audiences. Paralleling *Puerto Nuevo* in many ways, the Luis Sandrini vehicle *Loco lindo* received somewhat mixed reviews that did not impede its commercial success. It was more well-received by *La Nación*, especially regarding its technical achievements, while *Heraldo del Cinematografista* focused on Sandrini, stating that "the sense of comedy and the attraction of the noted actor are of such standing that they absorb the attention of the spectator, and his mere appearance on screen is enough for roaring laughter to burst. And this condition is doubly visible, given that the dialogue is poor and of little inventiveness. The plot offered possibilities that were not taken advantage of."[179] In its review, *Cinegraf* harshly critiques "its tendency to exploit grotesquely" provincial local color.[180] Despite this, or perhaps because of it, the film was a hit, and was subsequently distributed in Spain and other countries. In "National Cinema Is a Game of Chance," a fictitious published dialogue, it was claimed that *Loco lindo* cost sixty thousand pesos to produce, and had produced one hundred and fifty thousand pesos in net profit to date, as it was still showing "in the majority of *barrio* movie theaters and in the interior of the Republic."[181]

In many ways, Argentina Sono Film's next production was its first serious, prestige film. *Amalia* is an adaptation of one of Argentina's foundational fictions, José Marmol's eponymous romantic novel (1851/1855).[182]

It also notably served as the source material for Enrique García Velloso's 1914 film, the country's first feature. Not only were more technical resources dedicated to its production, from initial, direct involvement of new personnel such as John Alton in their new studios in Bulnes to its final stages in the implementation of new technologies by the Tecnofilm laboratories, but Mentasti's studio invested heavily to create greater spectacle.[183] In "Back at Sono Film, Moglia Barth Prepares 'Amalia,'" a brief profile published in *La Nación*, the film's director remarks that "'Amalia' represents an artistic and industrial effort that will need for its production a deployment of considerable forces."[184] Mentasti's objective, according to Moglia Barth, was to produce a film worthy of world-wide audiences that would also contribute to the advancement of Argentine national cinema.

Even before its release, *Amalia* attracted the attention of those who wanted the Argentine film industry to produce more artistic films. In the editorial "¡Alerta, Productores Argentinos!," Chas Cruz's *Heraldo del Cinematografista* argues that "'La muchacha de a bordo' y 'Puerto Nuevo' marked commercial success of great consideration, but neither of these films can be considered to be an artistic example"; however, the piece continues, "Vernacular literature offers magnificent possibilities that to this point have not been taken advantage of, with the sole exception of Sono Film, which undertook a work of great force by bringing to the screen 'Amalia,' of imminent release."[185] Looking back to what is perhaps the touchstone of the silent period, the Humberto Cairo–produced *Nobleza gaucha*, the editorial asserts that lessons should be drawn from the past. Rather than replicating models perceived as guaranteeing safe success, "it is necessary that a greater vision of the future guides our producers' way to avoid the consummation of events so disastrous as that signaled. And, to that end, the means is simple: raise their aim." In the early transition to sound, Argentina Sono Film and other producers had found commercial success through an unsustainable model of artistically unambitious projects. If larger-scale industrial cinema were to emerge in Argentina, following the editorial's logic, it was time for a kind of brand diversification into ostensibly more serious films. *Heraldo del Cinematografista* wanted Argentina's film industry to aim higher artistically, but also commercially to seek the attention of more educated and, by extension, more affluent audiences.[186]

Breaking with the previous season's schedule, but mirroring the scheduling of *Riachuelo*, which had debuted two years earlier, *Amalia* premiered on July 8, 1936, to great critical and commercial success. In its positive review, which, interestingly, notes the film's depoliticization, *Heraldo del Cinematografista* praises the film: "It is, unquestionably, the most ambitious film to come out of Argentine studios and the best successful from an artistic point of view, deserving applause for director Moglia Barth and Argentina Sono Film for their effort and desire to evolve, to leave the already worn out field of the *sainete* or the *sainete*ized comedy in which nearly the totality of local producers live."[187] Besides citing the high quality of its production design and technical achievements, the review indicates that the film had received excellent publicity. That said, perhaps because Argentina Sono Film increasingly came to rely on popular comedies, "All of [these achievements], together with the diffusion of the novel on which the film is based, make it have a considerable commercial value, difficult to specify. For all that it means as a work of inspiration, and for the intrinsic merits of its production, it is worthy of the most honest support." *Amalia* also met with extremely positive reception in daily newspapers, so much so that the review in Bahía Blanca's *El Atlántico* is entitled "'Amalia' is the Definitive Consecration of Our National Film Industry."

Two articles published in popular magazines give insight into the evolving reception of Argentina Sono Film's movies and, more broadly, Argentine national cinema.[188] In her review of the film for *Imágenes*, which accompanies eight photographs taken at *Amalia*'s premiere (including one one of her in the company of other critics), Mary Mar first admits, "Difficult it is for the *cronista* to be forced to classify a national film. Due to a logical feeling of solidarity toward our own, we see with sympathy, and almost with emotion, everything which tends to improve itself."[189] In addition to hedging her praise somewhat, she criticizes the film's slow pacing, particularly in the love story, and says that star Herminia Franco "at times gives the feeling of being a beautiful wax doll." Continuing her ambivalent review, Mar surmises that "It is a great effort of Argentine cinema, and also an advance, if you will, of the future of the local industry," and ends her review, "we hope with time to be able to truly savor Argentine films." In his *Sintonía* review "'Amalia' Is the Best Argentine Film Presented to Date," Carmelo Santiago minimizes common critiques of national cinema by "systematically [breaking down] the many factors that have intervened in the making of this film, which we repeat, marks a step forward in the progression of the autochthonous film industry."[190] Santiago, a journalist who became Argentina Sono Film's publicist—something left undisclosed in the article—attempts to assuage persisting suspicions typical of film criticism at the time through a reading of *Amalia*, the film studio's first foray into its new series, "Selección." It is not perfect, Santiago admits in the final paragraph, but it represents the most cinematic film produced in the country.

If *Amalia* represented a step toward bringing new, more educated audiences into the movie theaters to watch national cinema, rather than Hollywood or European films, Argentina Sono Film's next feature, the Moglia Barth–directed *¡Goal!*, was a return to its popular roots.[191] (Lamentably, the film is now presumed to be lost.) The studio's first foray into soccer, a passion deeply entrenched in Argentine culture that had already been depicted in two films starring Luis Sandrini that were produced by rival Lumiton—*Los tres berretines*, released soon after *Tango!*, and *El cañonero de giles* (*The Champ*, dir. Manuel Romero), which was shot in mid-1936 and released on January 20, 1937—*¡Goal!* premiered with the Argentina Sono Film-distributed Spanish film *El bailarín y el trabajador* (dir. Marquina, 1936) on October 14, 1936.[192] Like so many Argentine films to that point, *¡Goal!*'s diegesis was drawn out of the melding of popular entertainments. Not only did the film bring the action on the pitch to the screen, but "[f]rom the national production 'Goal' a march—musical center of the film—and a foxtrot entitled 'The Green Apple' have been recorded. These two compositions have just been phonographically transcribed for Victor and performed by the Argentina Sono Film orchestra under the direction of Hans Diernhammer."[193] Tying together popular entertainments, as well as these intermedial threads, *¡Goal!* centers on mistaken identity: an office worker takes advantage of his resemblance to a well-known soccer player (both played by Severo Fernández) and suffers romantically.

In its review of the film, *Heraldo del Cinematografista* contends that *¡Goal!* falls well short of its potential due to slow pacing, clunky and unoriginal comedic situations, and lack of balance, only livening up in its final scenes in the stadium. Despite its many flaws, it is argued that its good publicity should help its success with popular audiences.[194] It should be no surprise then that *Cinegraf*, a magazine directed not at exhibitors but toward moviegoers with, ostensibly, more refined tastes (perhaps the intended target of *Amalia*), arguing that "From this peculiar rivalry [Argentina Sono Film and Lumiton] now comes a film without feet or head, with a big budget, with clumsy continuity and deficient acting. Its protagonist, following the series, is an audacious imposter that repeats situations that makers of comical movies have beaten to death in Hollywood."[195]

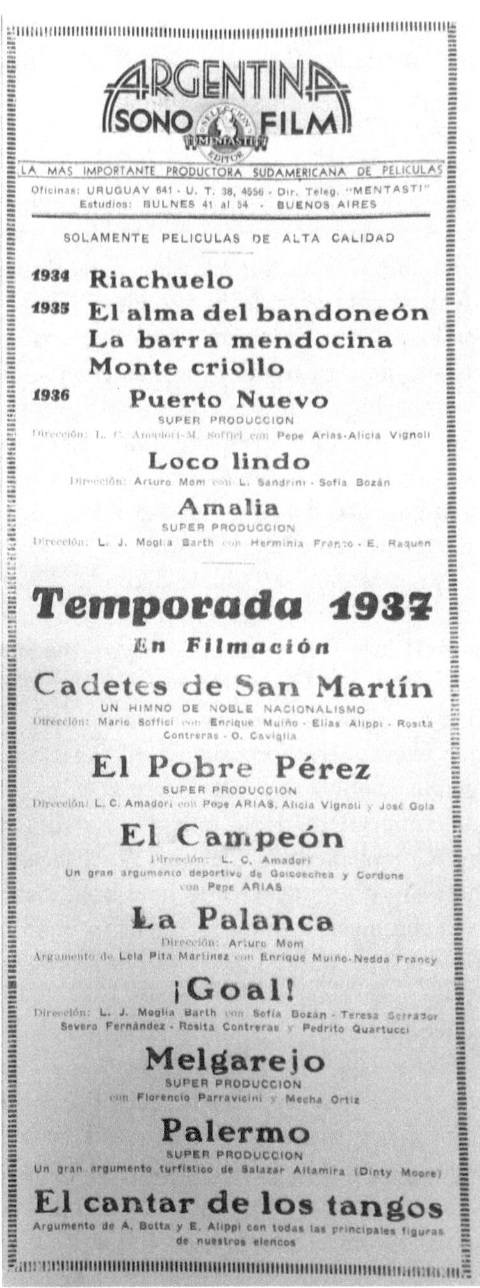

Figure 8.7. Argentina Sono Film advertises its upcoming 1937 film season. *Revista del Exhibidor*, August 20, 1936.

The review continues, claiming that *¡Goal!* is yet another opportunity to "put off even more spectators that remain faithful to the journey—here I fall, there I get up, but I am always lame (*lisiado*)—of autochthonous production." *Cinegraf* offers a critique not only of an individual film, but also of Argentina Sono Film's strategy. Unable for a myriad of reasons (artistic, financial, technical, etc.) to produce consistently films of the quality of *Amalia*, Argentina Sono Film had to also make less ambitious movies in order be able to keep on releasing films throughout the year. In this sense, Mentasti continued to realize his objective of filling out a production season in order to be able to offer exhibitors a regular product on which audiences could regularly rely for their entertainment. Argentina Sono Film was aiming higher; it was also shooting more.

In late 1936, news of the upcoming 1937 season began to appear in film periodicals. *Revista del Exhibidor* and, the following week, *Heraldo del Cinematografista* provided details of an expanding program to include *Cadetes de San Martín* (*Cadets of San Martín*), *El pobre Pérez* (*Poor Pérez*), *Palermo*, *Melgarejo*, *¡Segundos afuera!* (Out in Seconds), *El cantar de los tangos* (The Singing of Tangos), *El fantasma de Mar del Plata* (The Ghost of Mar del Plata), *El curita* (Little Priest), *Los Ranqueles* (The Ranquel Indians), *La palanca* (The Lever), and *Fragata Sarmiento* (*Soul of the Navy*).[196] In its article, which it describes as revealing "the first part of its cinematatographic production plan for the upcoming year," *Revista del Exhibidor* also reports that Argentina Sono Film will release a series of musical shorts featuring Argentine and international folklore, as well as popular *porteño* artistic attractions. Complementing the studio's reliance on music, if not film musicals, these shorts do not seem to have been made. The emphasis on music, however, continued to impact Argentina Sono Film's direction, as indicated, for example, in an interview with its representative, M. Hans Bredt, by *Cinematographie française* in January 1937.[197] In his discussion about sharing audiences and exchanging Argentine and French films, during which Mentasti is acknowledged to be "known as the 'father' of Argentine cinema" and a "pioneer," Bredt states that "[o]f 30 Argentine films, there will be a few that will interest the French public by their novelty, their musical genre." In addition to other developing aspects of its film production, music continued to play a central role in the production of films that enjoyed success both at home and abroad.

On February 10, Argentina Sono Film launched their 1937 season with *El pobre Pérez* in the Cine Monumental. Preceded by typical production news, as well as a private showing for its cast and technicians in

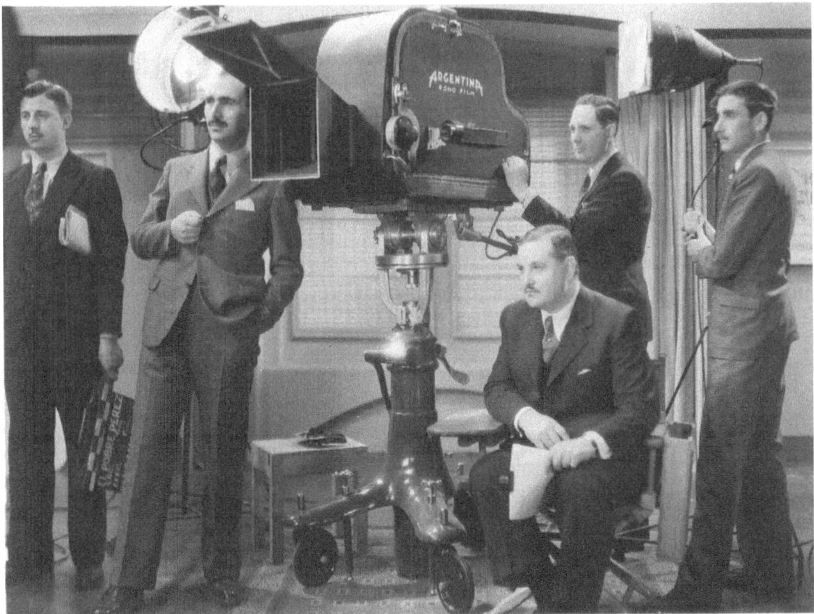

Figure 8.8. John Alton, Luis César Amadori, and others during production of *El pobre Pérez*. From the American Society of Cinematographers collection of the Margaret Herrick Library, Academy of Motion Picture Arts and Sciences.

the "elegant screening room of the Laboratorios Automáticos Tecnofilms," *El pobre Pérez* received excellent reviews from *porteño* film periodicals.[198] It was regarded, most notably, as marking an advance in Argentine film comedy. *Heraldo de Cinematografista*, for example, noted that "this new Argentine movie stands out due to its plot, superior to those of other productions" and, "[t]here's excellent humor in some situations, and there is emotion, and even tenderness, in others."[199] Argentina Sono Film's increasing investment in the technical aspects of its productions extended beyond cinematography and sound, moving into more fully developed scripts. Still relying on talent such as Pepe Arias, the stronger narrative structure and more fully developed storyworlds of these scripts more closely paralleled the classical models of Hollywood cinema, which continued to dominate at the box office in Argentina and other Latin American markets. *Heraldo de Cinematografista*'s review concludes, "The presentation is good, in varied settings reproduced with luxury and propriety. It has had good publicity. Suitable for any section, preferably popular theaters."

Following two comedies, Argentina Sono Film's next release was its first to premiere between February and May. Expanding its season was another prestige film, Mario Soffici's *Cadetes de San Martín.* Later cited by Domingo Di Núbila as the best ensemble movie made by an Argentine studio to that date, especially given the performances of Enrique Muiño, Elías Alippi, and Ángel Magaña, *Cadetes de San Martín* was long in development in no small part because of its plot.[200] In it, Julio Ortega (Enrique Muiño) is dragged into a public health scandal caused by his corrupt, womanizing partner Filomeno (Elías Alippi). With the family's reputation in tatters, his son Juan Carlos (Ángel Magaña) is expelled from the national military school. Shattered, Julio explains the situation in his suicide note, which eventually leads to his son's readmission. Given the film's delicate subject matter, as well as the somewhat fragile political situation of the time, Argentina Sono Film cooperated with General Basilio Pertiné of the Ministerio de Guerra.[201] *Cinegraf* notes that "The Ministry of War rejected the first plot of 'Los cadetes de San Martin,' a film for which the company Argentina Sono Film requested the cooperation of the Colegio Militar and its dependencies."[202] Even though filming would not be completed until late 1936, advertisements publicizing the "Hymn of Noble Nationalism" began to appear as early as August.[203]

Similar to its earlier prestige film, *Amalia*, *Cadetes de San Martín* was well received both by critics and moviegoers. In its review of the film, *Imparcial Film* continues a well-established critical trajectory by lauding the film for being yet another important step in Argentina Sono Film's development.[204] It begins by noting, "The hopes that the announced premiere of 'Cadetes de San Martin' had awakened have been amply justified. Argentina Sono Film, which not a month ago achieved a resounding success with 'El pobre Pérez,' virtually takes the lead of national production companies."[205] Assuring that its success will match, if not exceed, that of its predecessor, the reviewer cites it as a film whose artistic significance also carries social responsibility, particularly given its setting. The review continues, "Aware of such responsibility, Argentina Sono Film has sought by all means to break out of the routine, raising its sights towards purer horizons for its films." Recalling the language of the *Heraldo del Cinematografista* editorial "¡Alerta, Productores Argentinos!," *Imparcial Film* argues that Argentina Sono Film not only has aimed higher, but that "'Cadetes de San Martín' is a film that elevates our national film industry and the producer that shot it."[206] As *Imparcial Film*'s review predicted, *Cadetes de Martín* opened to huge demand on

March 3 at the Cine Monumental, and was shortly thereafter shown simultaneously at the Monumental and Renacimiento theaters (a total of 3,300 spectators).

In some ways, if *Cadetes de San Martín* was a step toward more cinematic film production, a more mature cinema, *Melgarejo* was a step backward. Or, seen differently, it constituted a more mature adaptation than those previously made in the Argentine film industry. It was, as publicity for *Melgarejo*'s May 19 premiere published in *Imparcial Film* notes, a "version of the popular piece that was one of Florencio Parravicini's greatest hits seventeen years ago. And, naturally, Parravicini is the film's protagonist." *Melgarejo* uses Parravicini's theatrical work as its source material, but, in so doing, translates its characters and their personalities to the screen. Seemingly made long after its success could be properly exploited—or, as its review in *Heraldo del Cinematografista* states, almost shrugging, "Written almost twenty years ago and performed in the theater innumerable times since then, 'Melgarejo' returns updated in its cinematic version, which permits the wide brilliance of its author and central protagonist of the work, of a little antiquated humor, but always efficient in the particular modality exploited in his long career"—*Melgarejo* received mixed critical reception.[207] It was, however, a huge hit at the box office, first in Argentina, then abroad.[208] In late October, *Revista del Exhibidor* reports, "It fits to trust that 'Melgarejo' continues its brilliant success at going to second line theaters. And nothing needs to be said of popular theaters, as the the figure of Florencio Parravicini is extremely popular without accounting for its other artists."[209] The film would later be shown throughout Latin America, as well as cities in the United States.

In early June 1937, Ángel Mentasti gave an interview with the *porteño* daily *La Razón*, which was later published as "Argentina Sono Films [*sic*] Intensifies its Production."[210] After highlighting *Melgarejo*'s success, even despite a spell of winter weather that would generally cool the interest of moviegoers, Mentasti gives detailed updates, usually including notable cast and crew, on the films *Palermo* (completed); *Viento norte* (*North Wind*), *¡Segundos afuera!*, *La casa de Quirós* (The House of Quirós), and *Maestro Levita* (*The Old Professor*) (filming); *Fragata Sarmiento* (waiting on the Ministerio de Marina), *La novia de Mar del Plata* (The Bride of Mar del Plata) and *El cantar de los tangos* (in preparation); and other projects in development.[211] Beyond his usual braggadocio, in which he promises the "public twenty big productions, all performed by the supreme artists of national cinema and theater," he also reveals that Argentina Sono Film currently occupied five soundstages, including its own, and was arranging for the construction of two more. These developments, however, were soon overshadowed by the film studio's announcement that leadership of Argentina Sono Film was being passed onto Atilio (production) and Ángel Luis (*dirección general*).[212] Even though Ángel's illness would later be described as taking everyone by surprise, this shift allowed for a less difficult transition. If Mentasti came to be a metonym representing Argentina Sono Film, eventually it signified less the single man than the family.

Palermo was the last Argentina Sono Film production to premiere in Ángel Mentasti's lifetime. Excellently shot by John Alton, whose expressive work explores the generic narrative conventions of the crime drama, and including glamour lighting, *Palermo* pivots on Ana María Nielsen (Nedda Francy). Caught between two men, her true love Adolfo Villanueva (José Gola) and the criminal Conrado Schweitzer (Orestes Caviglia), Ana María is eventually revealed to be on an undercover police assignment. Eventually, the police get their man, and so does Ana María. In its review, *Heraldo del Cinematografista* notes, "It is a film of a police character, of quick pacing and correct direction, whose resources often remind us of the American films of the genre, lacking the *porteño*ism valued in our films."[213] Rather than a national superproduction like *Amalia* or *Cadetes de San Martín*, both of which explored important aspects of Argentine society, *Palermo* marked a return to the model of *Monte criollo*. A genre movie directed at popular audiences, but not a comedy, *Palermo* set a different trajectory within Argentina Sono Film's production schedule. Also, as the review notes, "It has obtained very good reviews by the big newspapers. It was the object of very good publicity, and is apt, indistinctly, in family and popular theaters, being able to increase its commercial value." Overshadowed in *porteño* film periodicals by more dramatic developments, *Palermo* did well domestically and internationally as well, particularly in Chile.[214]

He Took the Matter into His Own Hands: Mentasti and Argentine Cinema

Soon after the rumor of his illness began to circulate in the industry, Ángel Mentasti died on July 24, 1937.[215] Described in obituaries as being "the primary champion of national film," "the most enthusiastic promoter Argentine cinema had," "its most efficient and tenacious element," and "a figure that was to decisively influence its fate," Mentasti was remembered to be not only the founder of Argentina Sono Film, but a necessary force in the emergence of the national film industry.[216] Echoed in similar language in film periodicals (even reaching the pages of *Variety*), especially those closely tied to the exhibition sector, Mentasti's obituary in *La Nación* gives insight into his importance for the Argentine film industry.[217] Referenced as the founder of Argentina Sono Film (thus eliding the roles of Moglia Barth, Favre, and Ramos), the obituary makes central his restructuring of the ways in which films were produced in the country:

> When he called someone to his side to collaborate in the field of production, he used to place his confidence in the person so consciously that, after discussing and agreeing upon the aspects of the work in germination, he would shut himself off with deliberate obstinacy in administration so as to not hinder in the slightest the collaborator's task. With him, for the first time in our country, emerged an example of the movie producer, personality of great importance, as has been demonstrated in the United States, in this peculiar industry and art.[218]

The movement away from the financially unsustainable producer/director model of the silent era toward more modern practices of unit production was not, as noted in the obituaries published in *Heraldo del Cinematografista* and *Revista del Exhibidor*, necessarily the product of imported human capital, but rather came from Mentasti's own immigrant experience in the local film industry, from working as a distributor of foreign silent films to becoming, as *Imparcial Film* notes, "what today is the most powerful film company in Argentina."[219] *Imparcial Film* underscores this point in its explanation of his success: "And it is that Mentasti was not *un improvisado* within the guild, but rather he worked in it for more than twenty years and, as a result, knew the business in its most minute details."[220] Perhaps to the detriment of competition in production and distribution, Mentasti built a business whose best days were to come.[221] *La Nación* remarks not only on past success ("Its films reached distant peoples of our language, Mexico, Cuba, Central America, Spanish, the Philippine Islands, and even the United States"), but present development ("Argentina Sono Film, which he leaves up and running, was on the path to powerful expansion").

Most importantly, Mentasti left behind organizational structures that allowed Argentina Sono Film to continue to produce films that

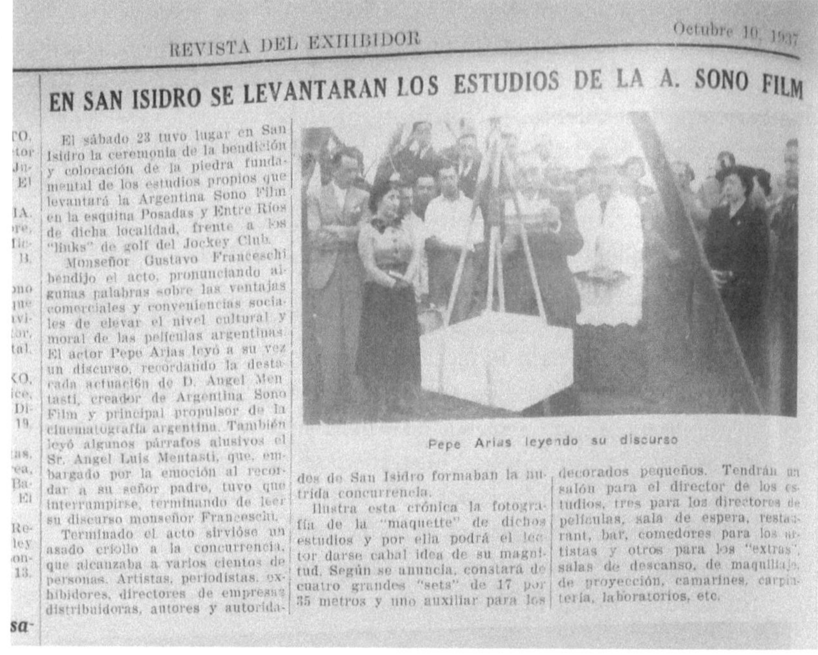

REVISTA DEL EXHIBIDOR — Octubre 10, 1937

EN SAN ISIDRO SE LEVANTARAN LOS ESTUDIOS DE LA A. SONO FILM

El sábado 23 tuvo lugar en San Isidro la ceremonia de la bendición y colocación de la piedra fundamental de los estudios propios que levantará la Argentina Sono Film en la esquina Posadas y Entre Ríos de dicha localidad, frente a los "links" de golf del Jockey Club.

Monseñor Gustavo Franceschi bendijo el acto, pronunciando algunas palabras sobre las ventajas comerciales y conveniencias sociales de elevar el nivel cultural y moral de las películas argentinas. El actor Pepe Arias leyó a su vez un discurso, recordando la destacada actuación de D. Angel Mentasti, creador de Argentina Sono Film y principal propulsor de la cinematografía argentina. También leyó algunos párrafos alusivos el Sr. Angel Luis Mentasti, que, embargado por la emoción al recordar a su señor padre, tuvo que interrumpirse, terminando de leer su discurso monseñor Franceschi.

Terminado el acto sirvióse un asado criollo a la concurrencia, que alcanzaba a varios cientos de personas. Artistas, periodistas, exhibidores, directores de empresas distribuidoras, autores y autoridades de San Isidro formaban la nutrida concurrencia.

Ilustra esta crónica la fotografía de la "maquette" de dichos estudios y por ella podrá el lector darse cabal idea de su magnitud. Según se anuncia, constará de cuatro grandes "sets" de 17 por 35 metros y uno auxiliar para los decorados pequeños. Tendrán un salón para el director de los estudios, tres para los directores de películas, sala de espera, restaurant, bar, comedores para los artistas y otros para los "extras", salas de descanso, de maquillaje, de proyección, camarines, carpintería, laboratorios, etc.

Pepe Arias leyendo su discurso

Figure 8.9. Pepe Arias gives a speech in honor of Ángel Mentasti at the cornerstone-laying ceremony for Argentina Sono Film's new studios in San Isidro. *Revista del Exhibidor*, October 10, 1937.

connected with audiences in Argentina and, increasingly, in other areas of the Spanish-speaking world. The genius of the system, to riff on André Bazin via Thomas Shatz, was to provide exhibitors with locally produced films without losing control of profits in distribution. *Heraldo del Cinematografista* also remarks that initial skepticism regarding large-scale investment in cultivating local stars eventually became admiration, and that "[d]eath surprises him in pivotal moment of his career: two films in production, two more to soon start, and various others under consideration. Our industry has suffered an irreparable loss. But his efforts have been productive: he leaves work done and a strong organization in operation at the front of which remain his sons Luis and Atilio." Soon thereafter, Ángel Luis assumed control of Argentina Sono Film and Atilio became its production director. According to *Imparcial Film*, Ángel Luis's first charge was to strictly abide by the 1937–38 production schedule, including *¡Segundos afuera!*, *Viento norte*, *Maestro Levita*, *La casa de Quirós*, and other films without definitive titles.[222] The organizational structure left behind after Ángel Mentasti's death provided his sons with processes through which theirs would continue to be Argentina's dominant film studio, as well as one of the most important in Latin America.

In the September 23, 1937, ceremony commemorating the laying of the cornerstone of Argentina Sono Film's new studios, located in San Isidro adjacent to the Jockey Club's golf course, Pepe Arias gave a speech in which he recalled the influence of Ángel Mentasti, echoing the language of his obituaries: "the creator of Argentina Sono Film and the the primary champion of national film."[223] One of a series of homages paid to Mentasti after his death, this piece in *Revista del Exhibidor* is notable not so much for its recognition, but rather because of its image of Pepe Arias reading his remarks, looking toward the studios' dangling cornerstone, which, along with the solemn-looking participants, awaits its laying.[224] Though our attention, as cinephiles and critics, may be drawn initially to the image of the star, Mentasti has come to be seen as forming the base of Argentina Sono Film and, in many ways, Argentine national cinema. By regularizing Argentina Sono Film's mode of production and, concurrently, assuming control of the distribution of its films, as well as others from home and abroad, Ángel Mentasti helped to write the future of an increasingly integrated Argentine film industry.

9

"A Man Expert in the Needs of the Set"

Tito Davison, an *Éminence grise* in the Argentine Film Industry of the Late 1930s and Early 1940s

Monday, May 2, 1983. An event was held in Guadalajara, Mexico, as part of the Foro de Consulta Popular de Comunicación Social, which was also convened on separate dates in Hermosillo, Monterrey, and Mérida, to reflect upon the media in Mexico, in accordance with recent reforms of Article Six of the Constitution (which guarantees the right to information) made by the government of José López Portillo. Along with the press, radio, and television, cinema was examined through various thematic lenses, including "professional preparation."[1] A seventy-year-old man delivered a short paper (some 473 words) on "Preparación profesional cinematográfica" ("Professional Preparation in the Cinema"). Having obtained a college degree, according to the old man, graduates seek out opportunities to practice what they have learned. Theory becomes praxis. "This professional preparation exists in all activities and trades, except in cinema." Whatever students may learn about making films in college, he (somewhat strangely) argued, is purely theoretical.[2] Less strangely, he contended that film workers acquire the skills needed to carry out their jobs "through the preparation, the filming, and the completion of a film." A film electrician gains knowledge on set, as stagehands and prop workers "learned 'looking and asking.'" All film workers are important, and require mastery, practice, and technique, but the director possesses authority "like a ship captain during a voyage." He continued, "And now, how does a director learn cinema? Preparing professionally. Studying every aspect that intervenes in a film." Professional preparation in all fields, the man concluded, is essential for the enhancement of all countries, including Mexico.

Seven years earlier, on Wednesday, August 25, 1976, the same man gave an extensive interview to María Isabel Souza, as part of the Programa de Historia Oral (Oral History Program), a joint initiative of the Instituto Nacional de Antropología e Historia (National Institute of Anthropology and History) and the Departamento de Etnología y Antropología Social (Department of Ethnology and Social Anthropology) of the Universidad Nacional Autónoma de México.[3] In it, he described his own professional trajectory, beginning as a thirteen-year-old cameraman in Chile, then a fifteen-year-old extra in Hollywood, a twentysomething working actor in Spanish-language productions (with corresponding odd jobs, from dishwashing to film journalism), a thirtysomething film worker in Argentina, until, finally, from his forties on, a director in Mexico. But he detailed not only his own formation, but the shaping of what underpins his professional praxis:

> In the field of those who make movies, one must know the obligation one has: we have always understood cinema as an industry, so I think of that spectator who forms a being that is called the public. I look for my movies to please, entertain. I have always thought that the cinema a window into fantasy, and that we want a little *distracción* [distraction, entertainment]. As time passes, life is more difficult. It is full of anxiety, worries. Why dramatize life on the screen more? At least watch, have fun. And this does not mean that all movies must be sugary. In our cinema there are different types of stories, which speak a lot about their times: *cabareteras*, rurals, films of the Revolution, the so-called trivial comedies, or historical films. Variety is the spice of life, right? Thus, it is in one's interest to do it all, you cannot load up on one kind of films because I fear the public will grow tired.[4]

Separated by a little more than seven years, and representing two Tito Davisons (for that is the man's name), these scenes give us insight into his views of the relationship between labor and film industries throughout Latin America from the silent period to commercial cinema of the 1970s. In their own ways, they also inform two central topics—work and diegesis—of this chapter.

The limiting imagination of National Cinema, to borrow Andrew Higson's expression, has led to a selective memory in Latin American film history, one in which certain kinds of domestic film workers and technicians are remembered, if not revered, while others slip further into obscurity, if not oblivion. This selective memory is exacerbated by another pervasive critical disposition, the perception of the inaccessibility of certain kinds of film work. "Sometimes these separate texts—those of the cameraman or the actors—may force themselves into prominence so that the film becomes an indecipherable palimpsest. This does not mean, of course, that it ceases to exist or to sway us or please us or intrigue us; it simply means that it is inaccessible to criticism."[5] Peter Wollen and other film critics might not today adhere to the strict auteurism of these words,

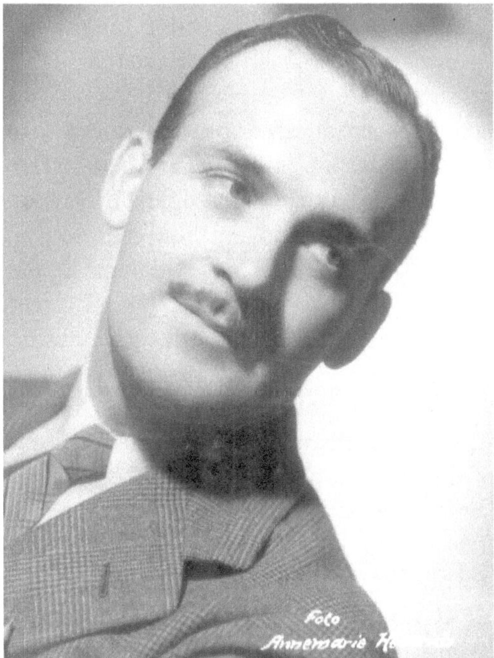

Figure 9.1. Portrait of Tito Davison taken by Annemarie Heinrich, a German-born naturalized Argentine photographer. Courtesy of the Museo del Cine Pablo Ducrós Hicken.

originally published in his 1969 book *Signs and Meaning in the Cinema*, but too few are willing to do the work of examining those separate texts. A film may be a palimpsest, but critics must be open to deciphering the traces left by its workers. However faint, the contributions of these film workers are, indeed, accessible, even though criticism might be, initially at least, incomplete or somewhat speculative. Among the host of foreigners in Latin America during the early sound period, whose work led them to circulate between different film industries, seeking out various kinds of opportunities to ply their trade, and who became largely forgotten in national, or even compartivist, historiographies is the Chilean Tito Davison.

Like so many who aspired to work in the film business, Davison initially sought success in Hollywood. Unable to achieve that success, he returned to Latin America: he then took jobs in Buenos Aires and, later, in Mexico and beyond.[6] In this chapter, I examine his film work in Argentina (1937–1943)—where he labored in different aspects of the film industry, earning credits as director and writer—focusing on the ways in which his labor, specifically, can be seen projected onto the screen in the films on which he worked. By discussing his role as a worker who practiced various forms of increasingly specialized film labor—for instance, as a screenwriter, particularly of adaptations but also originals (albeit in collaboration), and as a co-director, assistant director, and, in the case of the 1942 animated short *Upa en apuros* [Upa in Trouble], director "de diálogos y montaje"—I aim to shed light on Davison's role as what Argentine film historian Gregorio Anchou calls an *éminence grise*, as well as his modest efforts as a director.[7] Although he has received little attention in Argentine film historiography, Davison's career in the country dovetails with the emergence of the national film industry as a promising regional power that threatened to challenge its Mexican counterpart until its virtual collapse (due to geopolitical and economic factors). Furthermore, his exit to Mexico coincided with the end of the early sound period and the beginning of the classical period and the *Época de oro* or Golden Age of Mexican Cinema. In the 1976 interview, which we should not trust unduly, Davison reflects, "I thought of myself as prepared. Later we would see if I was, or not. The truth is that I should have come to Mexico at that time. All of my friends told me, 'An industry is starting there. Besides, they are missing known people.'"[8] It would take some time for Davison to become fully integrated within the Mexican film industry, but throughout he would apply lessons he had learned working in Argentina.

Before and Beyond Hollywood

By the time Davison arrived in Buenos Aires in February 1937, he had worked in many trades in Hollywood and on the fringes of the film industry. Along with his new wife June Marlowe—not the semi-successful actress of that name best known for playing Miss Crabtree in Hal Roach's *Our Gang* shorts such as "School's Out" (dir. Robert F. McGowan, 1930), but the June Marlowe who was Helen in *Riddle Ranch* (dir. Charles Hutchison, 1935), a film whose title credit notes that it stars "Black King, the horse with the human brain"—Davison sought out greater professional opportunities in Argentina. *Ecran*, the influential and long-running Chilean film magazine, notably remarks that the couple was heading to the Argentine capital because "*miss* Marlowe had been contracted" and "For his part, Tito Davison has received various offers from the Argentine film industry and will take advantage of his stay to exhibit the movie he filmed aboard the training ship, frigate 'Presidente Sarmiento,' during his visit to California."[9] Shot with midtier Argentine radio personality José María Reynal, and unrelated to the long-in-development Argentina Sono Film project that Carlos Borcosque would eventually direct (*Fragata Sarmiento*, 1940), the training-ship film evidenced Davison's desire to seek opportunities to get behind the camera.[10]

Davison was born on November 14, 1912, in Chillán, located south of Santiago in the Bio Bio Region. His mother (Amanda Davison de Herman) and father (Julio Herman Davison) were both second-generation Chileans, children of immigrants who had arrived in the mid-nineteenth century, which led Davison to, curiously, note in his interview with Souza that "I am not mixed, my origin is as German as it is Scottish, but that does not take away from my feeling the most Chilean of Chileans."[11] His family, as he somewhat anachronically describes it, was middle class, but Davison was afforded opportunities unavailable to most new arrivals through his grandfather's success selling, first, carriages, then automobiles, and his father's work in insurance. In Tito's teens, the family moved to Santiago, where he studied at the prestigious Instituto Nacional. From his earliest memory, he was a cinephile. Although he would not direct a film in Chile until 1956's *Cabo de Hornos* (*Cape Horn*), Davison's career began in earnest as Borcosque's assistant on the 1923 feature *Traición* (Betrayal). With a relative planning a trip to the United States, where he would be named Vice-Consul of Los Angeles, Davison convinced his father to allow him to postpone his studies for a year to "test his luck." Davison followed Borcosque north to Hollywood, arriving in mid- to late 1927.[12]

Initially, Davison aspired to act. Limited somewhat by his age—he was only fifteen at the time—he began working as an extra, eventually appearing in some "sixty or eighty movies" or "a hundred" by his own estimation.[13] In "The Life of Extras," a 1935 piece published in the *porteño* magazine *Aconcagua*, he wrote, "I walked—without leaving Hollywood—through Parisian streets, through humble Soviet settlements, through battle fields. I've been American, Mexican, Indian, and even Oriental, naturally with the help of the *make-up man*."[14] He detailed the inner workings of the Central Casting Office and the experience of working as an extra in this pedagogical piece. Later, he asks, "Now, of what does film work consist? The labor of the extra is really simple: follow the orders of the assistant director. Cross a street. Go through a room. Walk up stairs or through a hallway. The only thing asked of one is to be natural and to never look toward the camera."[15] Instead of glossing over implicit difficulties of working within an inequitable system, Felipe de Leiva (Agustín Aragón Leiva) revealed some of the injustices endured by these film workers in two articles for *Cinelandia*, "Memoirs of an Extra" and "Memoirs of an Extra, Day Two."[16] Davison might have tempted readers into believing that "being an extra is not a degrading profession. Each one is a star in waiting," but Leiva argued that "the extra is a pariah, who has to beg for his supper seeking work from studio to studio" and, "the extra is an idler. Those who have failed in action, those with no profession, the good-for-nothings, are extras." Being an extra, however, allowed Davison to experience the film industry and, notably, folded him into a vibrant community of Latin Americans—principally, but not exclusively Mexican, as "The conquest of Hollywood by Latinos is a fact. . . . They are the ones who work cheaply, they are the ones who provide greater efficiency, they are the ones who make directors shout less. The use of Mexicans means a savings of hundreds of thousands of dollars for the producers, year after year. Argentines, Chileans, Colombians, fill out the ranks." Collapsing soon thereafter as a result of the transition to sound and studios' movement away from producing Spanish-language films, this community would soon disperse. Like others who would later ply their trades in Latin American film industries, Davison filled out the ranks as an extra in Hollywood, but was unable to sufficiently fill his bank account, so he supplemented his income by washing dishes, among other odd jobs.[17] Like John Carradine and Helen Troy, the subjects of his 1936 piece "Extras yesterday," he waited, hoping that "Hollywood is similar to roulette. The numbers are the extras and the ball, the opportunity, which sooner or later will fall into them."[18]

Working as an extra opened possibilities, as Davison observed in "The Life of Extras": "In 1929, I got the much dreamed-about opportunity when I was selected for a supporting role in the first film to be produced spoken in our language, *Sombras de gloria* with José Bohr."[19] Within the next seven years, Davison would appear in at least seven *films hispanos*.[20] Though these films are all lost, dialogues taken from screen used by censors reveal among them the existence of small or bit parts whose function was to support stars such as Bohr, George J. Lewis (Jorge Lewis), Delia Magaña, Conchita Montenegro, Antonio Moreno, Raul Roulien, and Ernesto Vilches. Davison's biggest role came in *El presidio*, MGM's Spanish-language version of *The Big House* (dir. George Hill, 1930). Opposite José Crespo's Morgan and Juan de Landa's Butch, Davison plays Kent Marlowe, a man sent to prison for manslaughter who helps thwart Butch's escape, while Morgan is given a pardon and later reunites with Kent's sister, Ana (Luana Alcañiz). Anticipating, perhaps, success that never quite arrived, Borcosque's January 27, 1931, *Ecran* article "Chile Has a Star in Hollywood" described the reception of Davison's performance, noting, "The entire Hollywood and Los Angeles press has been unanimous in referring to the definitive success of the young Chilean actor."[21] Even though Davison was never cast in anything more than small or bit parts, he appeared regularly in magazines such as *Cinelandia* and *Ecran*, which published reports on his roles, gossip on his friendships and relationships, and letters from fans. But because these parts dried up, in no small part due to a movement away from Spanish-language productions by Hollywood studios first in 1931 and, more definitively, in 1935, he would come to be known by readers of *Ecran*, at least between 1932 and 1936, not so much for his acting in *films hispanos*, but for his writing from Hollywood.[22]

In the mid-1930s, Tito Davison wrote for film magazines in Chile, the United States, and Argentina, leveraging his position as a Hollywood insider. Similar to other kinds of film work in which he engaged, Davison's film writing was both credited (under his byline) and uncredited (as an unattributed correspondent who regularly dispatched information).[23] Pieces credited to Davison generally fall into four categories: articles, gossip columns, pedagogical pieces, and profiles on the inner workings of Hollywood. He began writing for *Ecran* as early as 1932, publishing a

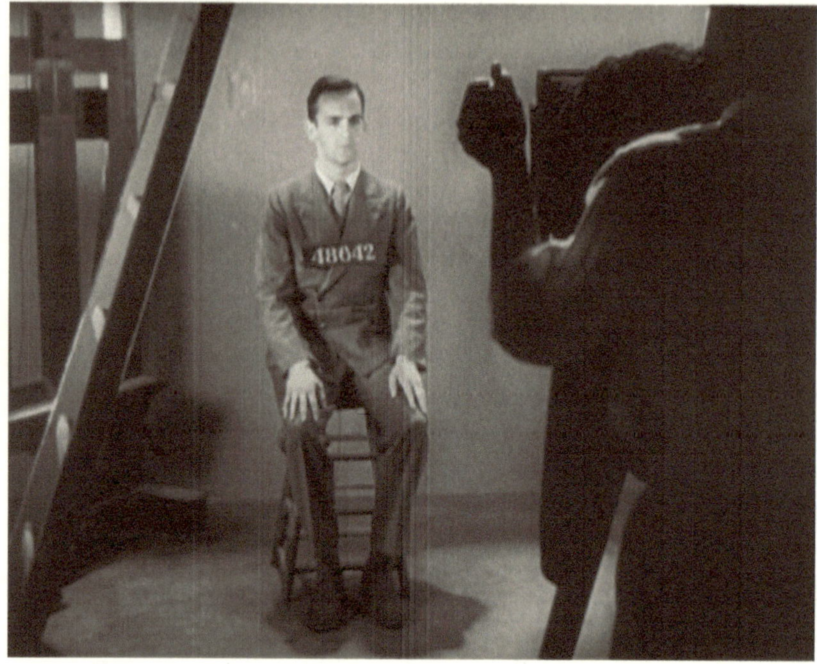

Figure 9.2. Davison's Kent Marlowe being processed into the prison system in *El presidio*.

profile on the actress Ruth Hall (Ibáñez) and the article "In Hollywood, Where Proverbs Become Inverted: The Luck of the Pretty Girl, the Ugly One Can Only Envy."[24] For *Ecran*, he wrote profiles on figures such as Sylvia Sidney, Chester Morris, and Carlos Borcosque, as well as articles such as "Gentlemen Prefer Blondes," "Preparing Future Stars," and "The Foreign Phalanx in Hollywood"; the recurrent gossip column "Hollywood Through the Keyhole"; and pedagogical pieces like "Writing to the Stars," "The 'Affectation' of Cinematic Performer," and "Beauty is Fabricated."[25] For *Cinelandia*, Davison's contributions were as a columnist and a profile writer. In July 1934, Davison began writing "Laughing With the Stars," a regularly published column running until September 1936, in which he recounted anecdotes and gossip about Hollywood. He would also occasionally fill in for Galo Pando's column "Gossip and Stories."[26] In June 1935, profiles written by Davison featuring Hollywood's biggest stars started to be published. In successive months, Davison interviewed

Gary Cooper, Franchot Tone, Jean Harlow, Robert Montgomery, Claudette Colbert, Carol Lombard, Bette Davis, Kay Francis, and finally, in March 1936, Shirley Temple.[27] He also contributed the articles "Stars of 1940 (?)" and "A Cinematic Pioneer" (on D. W. Griffith).[28] Toward the end of 1934, Davison also began to write for Argentine magazines.[29] His work in *Aconcagua*, for example, followed patterns seen in his writing for Chilean and U.S. publications. He wrote articles such as "Private Life of Cinema Artists," "The Life of Extras," "They Are the Ones in Charge," and "What 'Aconcagua' Sees in Hollywood."[30] Earlier than the one published in *Cinelandia*, he also wrote a profile of Shirley Temple.[31]

Davison's formative years working on the margins of Hollywood made possible his subsequent incorporation into the emerging Argentine film industry. He familiarized himself with motion pictures first as an actor, as an extra and later in supporting roles in Hollywood's Spanish-language films, and later as a writer. His work in the movies, however, was not

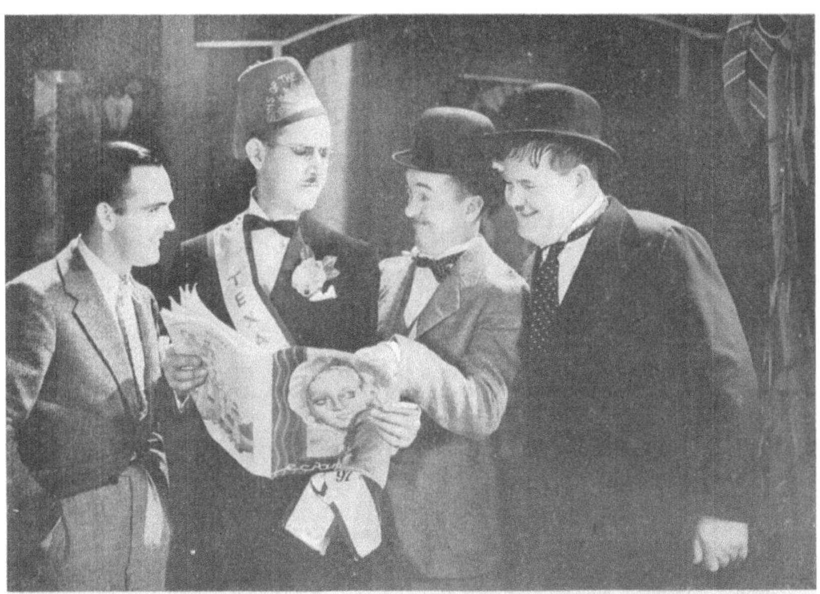

Figure 9.3. On the set of the feature *Sons of the Desert* (dir. William A. Seiter, 1933), Davison joins its comic stars for a promotional photograph. *Ecran*, February 27, 1934.

limited to acting and writing, and he also began to work off-screen in a variety of roles. He would later describe these experiences in interviews, and they were also occasionally noted in film periodicals such as *Cine-Mundial*, which, for example, reported as early as September 1933 that Davison, "who renounced his artistic career on-screen to devote himself to the megaphone," was contracted to Fanchon Royer Pictures, Inc., and, in December 1935, "is currently a technical advisor on 'The Robin Hood of El Dorado,' where Warner Baxter plays the famous bandit Joaquin Murieta [*sic*], hero of California."[32] In his interview with Souza, he reminisces about working as a technical advisor on films such as "*Robin Hood el dorado*" with an *ambiente hispano*, and also mentions, "I dedicated myself from then on to learn different trades such as director's assistant, script supervisor . . . I also learned editing."[33] Even had he wanted to continue working as a technical advisor on cultural issues, Davison recalls, "But I had to making a living in another way and I split my time between journalism and these advising and training jobs." With relatively limited opportunities in Hollywood, as well as the couple's desire for fresh possibilities as newlyweds, Tito Davison and June Marlowe moved to Buenos Aires. He was ultimately unable to become established as a director, but his development as a filmmaker would continue, primarily as an adaptor, screenwriter, and technical director.

An *Éminence grise*: Davison's film work in Argentina in the Late 1930s and Early 1940s

Writing in a foundational issue of *Heraldo del Cinematografista* in which more than seventy key figures in the Argentine film industry, such as Israel Chas de Cruz, Libertad Lamarque, and Mario Soffici, discuss topics like "Cinema is Talent, Experience, and Money," "We Stars Have Limited Life," and "The Error of 'the Self' in Cinema," among many others dealing with various aspects of production, distribution, exhibition, and reception, Tito Davison discusses the crafting of commercial diegesis in "Better Plots Must Be Sought."[34] In its short existence, Davison writes, national cinema has touched on "almost everything . . . from the historical drama to the sophisticated comedy, following, in a way, the Hollywood formula, in the sense that to interest spectators [*público*] they must be given a varied program." Taking advantage of the fact that "spectators [*público*] are benevolent and accept everything," the Argentine film industry produces too many films that "do not demand any artistic concern nor strength of imagination." This, Davison continues, will not likely be the case forever; the industry must adapt. Noting that everyone agrees that the industry needs better plots, better storyworlds, Davison concludes his short piece by remarking, "To say cinema is to say renewal. Why not do it then?"

Much of Davison's film work in Argentina pivoted on the visual framing of a broadly appealing commercial diegesis in preproduction. He would, as I discuss in the next section, also direct films, but most of his credits acknowledge his work as part of a team who sketched the initial form of what would eventually be projected on screen. Unlike adaptors or screenwriters, who are tasked with assembling a film's narrative through action, characterization, and dialogue, among other tools, Davison supervised the *encuadre* (framing) of *El haragán de la familia* (*The Family Loafer*, dir. Luis César Amadori, 1940), *Hay que educar a Niní* (Niní Must Be Educated, dir. Amadori, 1940), *Locos de verano* (Crazy About Summer, dir. Carlos Hugo Christensen, 1942), *Canción de cuna* (*Cradle Song*, dir. Gregorio Martínez Sierra, 1941), *En el viejo Buenos Aires* (*In the Old Buenos Aires*, dir. Antonio Momplet, 1942), *Tú eres la paz* (You Are Peace, dir. Martínez Sierra, 1942), and *Los hijos artificiales* (Artificial Children, dir. Momplet, 1943). In an industry in which labor was increasingly specialized, but had not fully stabilized or become totally institutionalized, the *encuadrador* or *encuadernador* was tasked with working with writers' *libros* by providing technical directions that temporalized the diegesis within scenes and spatialized it within mise-en-scène and through camera movement.[35] These technical directions anticipated the assembling of a film through production to postproduction. It is impossible to isolate Davison's contributions to these films, especially given the inextricably collaborative nature of his position, compelling him to liaise with writers, the director, and editors, among other film workers. Enmeshed within the labor of others, examining Davison's work in control of *encuadre* gives us partial but important insight not only into his contributions to individual films, but to an increasingly specialized Argentine film industry.

Throughout the 1930s and pushing into the 1940s, Argentine national cinema witnessed the emergence of new modes of production driven by increasing industrialization. Following the Hollywood model, as Davison noted, production companies (most of them fleeting) incorporated ever more specialized workers into creating their films. Increased specialization was a process that continued to develop throughout the early sound period as it transitioned into classical cinema. Part of this process included shifting

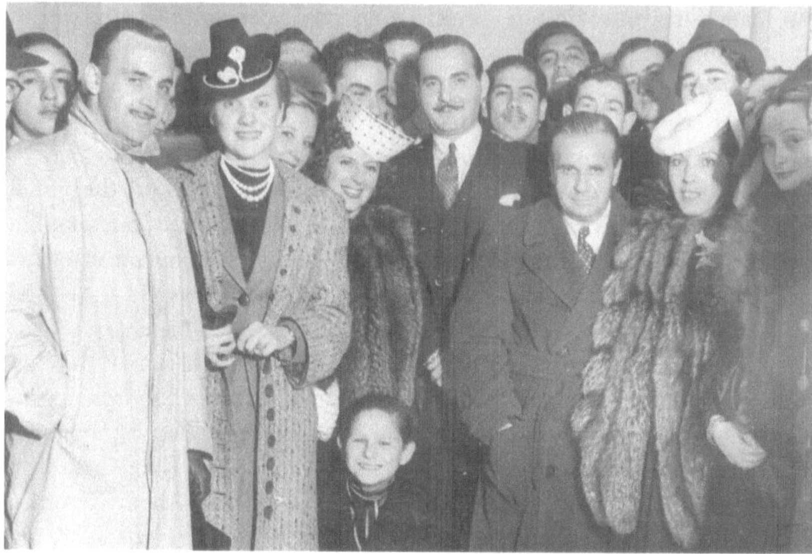

Figure 9.4. Davison among other figures of Argentina's film industry, some more important than others. In foreground from left: Tito Davison (first, with hand in light overcoat) and his wife, the actress June Marlowe (second, with dark hat); the singer and actress Dora Davis (third, with fur coat and geometric hat); the actor Vicente Padula (fifth, with mustache); the director Carlos Borcosque (sixth, with hand in dark overcoat); and the actress Anita Lang (eighth, with fur coat and thin hat). Courtesy of the Museo del Cine Pablo Ducrós Hicken.

responsibilities for distinct aspects of assembling a film. In the first few years of the transition to sound, a film's technical direction was controlled by its director, as an extension of the silent period's director system. Without sufficient knowledge within the national film industry at the time of how to make a film more cinematic, to go beyond what Nataša Ďurovičová calls a "canned theater production," these responsibilities were then given to a worker credited with the *encuadre*.[36] By the mid-1940s, as the Argentine film industry came to more closely correspond to Hollywood's classical mode of production, the *encuadre* was folded into the responsibilities of the director and his assistant, something Domingo Di Núbila describes in his 1948 short pedagogical book *Cómo se hace un film*.[37]

In the late 1930s and early 1940s, however, the shaping of the *encuadre* was evolving. Evident in references to the role in contemporaneous film periodicals, supervision of the *encuadre* was increasingly seen as being an important element in a movie's production. Despite this, there were few clear explanations of what the role entailed, particularly in relation to the crafting in preproduction of the diegesis. A brief letter published in "Questions and Answers," a regular column in *Radiolandia*, conveys this confusion. In it, A. D. asks a deceivingly simple question: "How is a movie plot written? Like a novel? Or with special technique?"[38] Its implications, however, are much more complex. A. D. not only seems to intuit that the off-screen writing of a film's plot is somehow different, somehow special, but also that it is distinct from the diegesis on-screen. A film's storyworld is much more than its plot. The *Radiolandia* columnist responds by writing, "In yours, we reply to many. Those who do not have the technique of framing write their plots as a novel. For that matter, some only sketch the central idea. Studios have experts that later give it shape by framing it." Both question and answer betray some confusion surrounding, narrowly, the creation of a film's diegesis and, broadly, increasing specialization in the film industry.

Davison's first forays into the technical supervision of the *encuadre* were collaborations with Luis César Amadori, one of the most important directors of the early sound period in Argentina. In *El haragán de la familia*, featuring Pepe Arias ("an unquestionable star of our cinema," according to *Radiolandia*), Davison is credited as assistant director, even though he was reported earlier by *Heraldo del Cinematografista* to be in charge of the *encuadre*.[39] Davison would be credited as directing the *encuadre* in the second of these collaborations with Amadori, the 1940 film *Hay que educar a Niní*. Another Argentina Sono Film vehicle for a star comic—this time, Niní Marshall, who successfully spun radio success into film stardom, having previously appeared on screen as her characters Catita and Cándida in films produced by Lumiton and EFA.[40] Shifting credits not only represented the instability of increasingly specialized film labor, but also the importance of the *encuadre* in the construction of the diegesis in the early 1940s. Signaled by increased press coverage, as several notes cited Davison's participation in the film in charge of the *encuadre* during its preproduction, the credit also reflects Davison's more important role in *Hay que educar a Niní*. Working with Amadori, Davison shaped the visual framing of the film by factoring in the efforts of a wide range of technicians and talent such as writer René Garzón, cinematographer Alberto Etchebehere, and star performer Niní Marshall. Even though Davison would not have worked directly with many members of the film's cast and crew, he would have needed to understand the ways

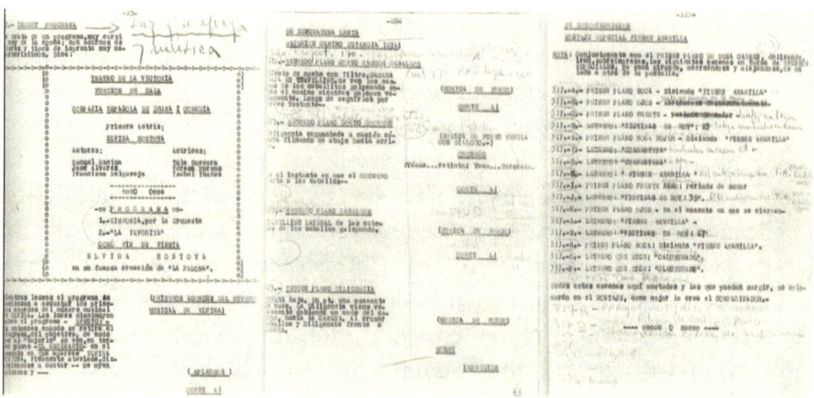

Figure 9.5. Pages of the *libro cinematográfico* of *En el viejo Buenos Aires* belonging to assistant director Alicia Miguez Saavedra. Courtesy of the Museo del Cine Pablo Ducrós Hicken.

in which preproduction efforts had to be shaped for production. In the construction of a technical script, Davison was tasked with anticipating the film's assembling in postproduction editing.

After working with Amadori, an experienced director whose previous box office successes such as *Puerto Nuevo* (1937), *Madreselva* (*Honeysuckle*, 1938), and *Caminito de gloria* (The Road to Glory, 1939) left him firmly entrenched within the Argentine film industry, Davison was employed to support the adaptation of literary works by two inexperienced cineastes, Gregorio Martínez Sierra and Antonio Cunill Cabanellas.[41] Assigned to adapt projects such as *Tú eres la paz*, Davison worked on making them less theatrical and more cinematic. Like *Canción de cuna* and *Locos de verano*, Davison's next film was a period picture. In Antonio Momplet's *En el viejo Buenos Aires*, starring Libertad Lamarque and produced by Estudios San Miguel, Davison participated in framing an earlier time. In its *libro cinematográfico*, a technical screenplay that situated dialogue in particular scenes within predetermined framing, the process of Davison's work with Momplet (among others) emerges.[42] In one sequence, Lamarque's Elvira performs at a gala at the Teatro de la Victoria. In the technical screenplay, the entire playbill is written. It appears slightly modified in the film, and is on-screen but for matter of seconds. What seems designed in the technical screenplay to occupy much more of the viewer's attention becomes only an establishing shot after the film has gone through editing. Elvira's appearance onstage in a long shot, however, is consistent with the technical screenplay, where she is described as *ricamente ataviada* ("richly dressed"). The audience's applause, as mentioned in the *libro cinematográfico,* is seen rather than heard, as the soundtrack is dominated by Libertad Lamarque's famously beautiful voice as she sings "La paloma" ("The Dove," also known in English as "No More"). Elvira's performance is quite different than the one sketched out in preproduction, but this short sequence helps us better understand how Davison worked to shape a cinematic experience for audiences of *En el viejo Buenos Aires.* He later worked on the *encuadre* of another film directed by Momplet, *Los hijos artificiales.*

Through his work on films such as *Hay que educar a Niní* and *En el viejo Buenos Aires*, Davison applied the lessons of his previous film experience in the United States and Argentina to help shape more cinematic commercial movies. By examining his role in charge of the *encuadre,* we gain insight into the ways shifting labor practices were reflective of increasing industrialization in a maturing Argentine film industry, leading to films that more closely reflected the aesthetics and diegeses of Hollywood classical cinema. The industrial and commercial particularities of Argentine cinema, however, gave rise to local expressions of what was becoming classical cinema. Framing more cinematic storyworlds was an important way in which Tito Davison impacted this emergent classicism, but it was not the only role he would play, nor was it, ultimately, his sole ambition.

A Director on the Margins

Tito Davison's primary contribution to the Argentine film industry might have been as an *éminence grise*, but he also directed (in some form or fashion) movies at the beginning and end of his time in the country. Forced to operate within a range of different production conditions, Davison's talents were employed in very different ways. These films, however, allow us to better understand his place as a filmmaker within the broader context of the Argentine film industry, both as an individual and a foreigner. *Murió el Sargento Laprida* (*Sergeant Laprida*, 1937) was the first film on which Davison worked in Argentina. The sole production of Lucantis Film, one of the period's many transitory production companies, *Murió el Sargento Laprida* was an adaptation of the Alberto Vacarezza *sainete.*[43] In addition to directing the film, Davison is also credited with its "film script" (*guión cinematográfico*).[44] Premiering on December 23, 1937, at the Cine Opera in Buenos Aires, *Murió el Sargento Laprida* brings together two popular figures from radio and the stage, Celia Gámez and Julio de Caro.[45] The film was anticipated by modest production news, especially in *Radiolandia*'s regular column "Light, Camera, Sound!," and met with a tepid reception.[46] Its review in *Heraldo del Cinematografista* finds fault in its slow pacing and theatrical staging, but notes that it is "technically very good, especially as far as its photography is concerned, [and] has wise shot choices in general, highlighting the race of fire trucks through dark streets and firefighters' maneuvers to put out the fire."[47] Davison's *Murió el Sargento Laprida* entwined these two well-known modes of spectacle: one safe (depicting popular forms of entertainment) and one dangerous (depicting fire).

Not only enlisting radio stars to perform, but also prominently featuring popular music, *Murió el Sargento Laprida* draws from what Ana M. López has called the radiophonic imaginary.[48] Focusing her attention on early sound cinema, López argues that diegetic presence and imprint of radio, both as a presentational and performative practice, exploit radio's popularity, which at that time challenged if not surpassed that of national cinema, and generated representational alternatives. Despite being based on Alberto Vaccarezza's *sainete*—or, perhaps, *because* it was based on his popular play—Davison's adaptation relied on the radiophonic imaginary to broadly appeal to spectators as well as to diegetically fuse together seemingly disparate modes of spectacle. Similar to many other films of the period, but especially those from the early transition, *Murió el Sargento Laprida* uses song both to broaden its transmedial appeal and to convey meaning central to its narrative. Tellingly, it relies on the tango "Fuego" ("Fire").[49]

"Fuego" is performed twice in the film to distinct effects. The first rendition of the song follows the establishment of the film's love triangle: the inherently good Sergeant Laprida (Mario Danesi), his provocatively named wife La Tigra (Gámez), and their *conventillo* neighbor Corporal Goyena (Alberto Mendoza), who is also a firefighter. In a sequence that is framed well by Davison, especially in La Tigra and Goyena's embraces, but ultimately disappoints by failing to follow conventional shot/reverse shot editing, the viewer is sufficiently placed within the storyworld to understand the affective distance between La Tigra and Laprida in the next scene. Now emotionally inhabiting the characters' Buenos Aires, the viewer (and the camera) follows La Tigra as she turns on the radio. Transposed via a dissolve to a shot tilting down a radio mast, the scene cuts to a broadcast booth manned by attentive technicians. Cutting to an on-air light flashing "*transmite*" (broadcasting), the scene finally takes the viewer via a diagonal wipe to the studio, where Julio de Caro's orchestra performs "Fuego." Breaking away from the singular perspective represented by the love triangle, the performance of "Fuego" presents the viewer with no fewer than twelve different angles whose gravitational force centers on the conductor (not the singer, whose face is curiously often obscured by a violinist). Dynamically assembled, the performance brings together camera movement (primarily through panning) and varying shots. In many ways, it is a kind of proto–music video whose diegetic aim is to temporarily suspend the emotional anxiety of *Murió el Sargento Laprida*'s melodramatic love triangle. "Fuego" is used somewhat punctuatively, as songs "can not only modulate the meaning and rhythm of a text but actually determine it as well."[50] It is a pause that is not to last, however, as, following nearly the same sequence of shots, the viewer soon is returned to the *conventillo*, where Laprida and La Tigra dine and are unable to find the words to say what they mean.

The imprint of radio is felt in the second performance of "Fuego," which is sung by La Tigra at a dinner held in honor of Laprida "*con motivo de su condecoración*" ("for his award"), which he receives for having earlier bravely saved a young child.[51] A crane shot, or perhaps one from a balcony, looks down onto a large party gathered to celebrate Laprida, including dignitaries such as Lieutenant Zárate (Rodolfo de la Serna). After a toast, the comic relief Private Rafael (Tomás Simari) invites La Tigra to perform a tango to enliven the party. Slow to accept, she asks to sing "Fuego." Her reticence seems justified, as her repressed public emotions for Goyena are all too evident. Singing lyrics that begin "*Te llevo en mi vida como una esperanza, / como una esperanza que debo olvidar; / te sueño en mis noches de dulce bonanza / que luego se pierden con mi despertar*" ("I carry you in my life as a hope, / as a hope that I should forget; / I dream you in my nights of sweet blessing / that are soon lost with my awakening"), La Tigra quickly betrays the object of her affection through her glance. She sings "Fuego" not to Laprida, but to Goyena. Although a somewhat similar strategy is employed by Davison in its second rendition—even if its cutting and panning draws attention away from more subtle touches such as Mendoza's reactive performance—"Fuego" here underscores rather than suspends, given its refrain even more diegetic weight. "*¿Quién pudiera calmar este fuego?*" ("Who could calm this fire?"), it asks with resignation, which, following the strategy established in the song's previous performance, soon leads to relationship-defining conversations, first between Laprida and La Tigra (interrupted numerous times) and later between Goyena and La Tigra. Borrowing from the radiophonic imaginary, and not dissimilar to the affective twists and turns of a *radionovela*, "*Fuego*" is one of the primary means through which *Murio el Sargento Laprida*'s characters navigate their tense relationships.

The spectacle of *Murió el Sargento Laprida* is not only a melodramatic plot about a suffering husband who unintentionally redeems the infidelity of his wife by perishing within flames (a professional hazard), but, rather, it is fire itself. The film's pacing issues—both aural and visual, as it is sporadically underscored by and filled with interstices of silence, and is shot by a single, rooted camera, which pans but does not really move—are forgotten in high-stakes scenes of men battling fires. Equipped with the latest technology (e.g., modern fire trucks driving through *porteño* streets in the film's initial sequence), these firefighters represent the safety net provided by a well-functioning government. Laprida exemplifies the most principled public officials—in one scene early in the film, he complains to his superior Captain Almagro (Juan Sarcione), "If we could get the cooperation of the public to give us warning, great disasters would be avoided. Pardon me, my Capitán."[52] "The public" is depicted as being negligent, however, as the massive fire that provides *Murio el Sargento Laprida*'s denouement is started by a man who lights a cigarette, tosses the match into a wastebasket, and then nonchalantly exits the room.

Briefly interrupted by a final conversation between Laprida and Goyena, in which they talk as Apolinario and Bernardo and not Sergeant and Corporal, which ends with Laprida asserting, "Love is God's law and whoever opposes it is a villain," the subsequent (lengthy) sequence shows the firefighters' frenzied reactions (accelerated through editing in several shots) to the fire's growth. Like the fatalistic tango, Laprida is unable to forever hold off the forces of nature. Shot in a similar style to "Fuego," the fire sequence is dynamic, and features the rushing of firefighters in various roles responding to flames consuming a building, as well as the reaction of the gathered crowds. After again demonstrating his valor by saving the building's tenants, shot cleverly with big flames in the foreground and more in the background, Sergeant Laprida dies when the roof collapses upon him. Spectacle is not only private in *Murió el Sargento Laprida*—as he dies in Goyena's arms, Laprida utters, "Leave me. Save yourself, Capitán. Take care of her"—but also public, as new cadets complete their training to become firefighters "whose heroic tradi-

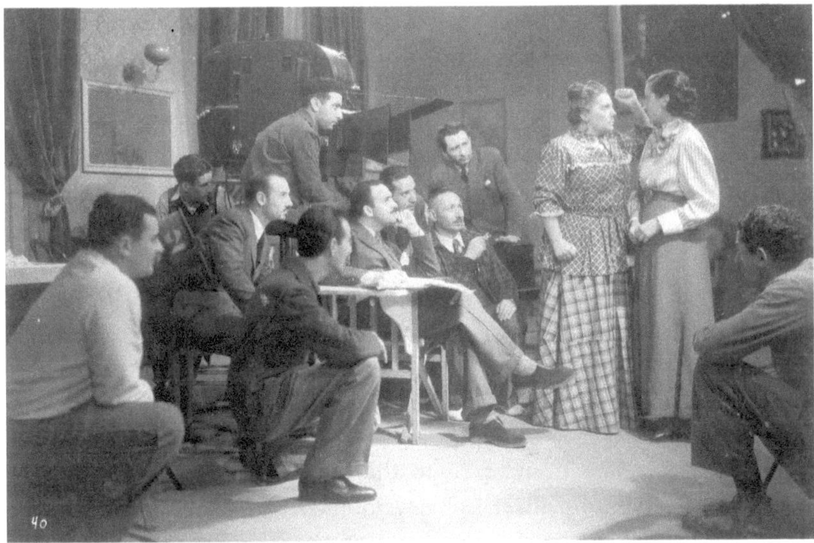

Figure 9.6. On the set of *Las de Barranco*. Seated with his hand on his chin, Davison directs Olinda Bozán and Tulia Ciámpoli. Many of the film's technicians surround them. Courtesy of the Museo del Cine Pablo Ducrós Hicken.

tion is upheld by an infinity of lives sacrificed in the fulfillment of duty," according to their superior, while a slow dolly shot (one of few in the film) reveals the name of one of the firetrucks to be "Sargento Laprida."

Soon after the premiere of *Murió el Sargento Laprida*, Davison began working on a film with another independent producer: *Las de Barranco* (*Mary Had Three Daughters*), an adaptation of Argentine playwright Gregorio de Laferrère's work, was produced by Productora Argentina de Films (PAF), a company established by film veteran Juan La Rosa that produced six films in the mid-1930s.[53] Unlike other independent production companies such as Lucantis Film, however, PAF adequately responded not only to growing demand for certain levels of technical quality, but also to the necessity for (at least somewhat) regular production. Anchou, consequently, asserts that "PAF is the first company of those we now call independents that at the time of its activity was worthy of the respect and consideration of its peers in the industry."[54] Similar to other PAF productions such as Daniel Tinayre's *Sombras porteñas* (Shadows of Buenos Aires, 1935) and *Una porteña optimista* (An Optimistic Porteña, 1936), *Las de Barranco* attached a star (Olinda Bozán) to a project with strong local appeal. Often surrounding Bozán, a popular comic actress, the film counted on modest press during its production, including "For 'Las de Barranco' a Typical Beginning of the Century Courtyard Was Reproduced," an intriguing piece on its set design published in *Film*.[55] Unfortunately now presumed lost, *Las de Barranco* premiered on June 29, 1938, at the Cine Monumental in Buenos Aires.

Las de Barranco received mixed reviews in *porteño* film periodicals. Even though "an evocative scent runs throughout the film," as *Radiolandia*'s "'Las de Barranco' is a Film Ennobled with Emotion" argues, it was widely disparaged for being overly theatrical.[56] *Proyecciones* claims that the "opinion of the public" is that the film "entertains," but concludes "It is not for cinema. This is another Argentine film based on a famous play that offers few cinematic possibilities."[57] *Heraldo del Cinematografista* contends that it "has been taken to the screen with few modifications, preserving its typically theatrical development, which is shown in the characters' continuous entrance and exit on the same stage, a rushed end that could have been better to the demands of the screen, and the asides, unforgivable in the cinema."[58] It argues that "the actors' work surpasses that of the director, who has limited himself to transferring a made work to the screen." In many ways, *Heraldo del Cinematografista*'s review encapsulates the film's critical reception: it was a well-acted version of Laferrère's play that failed on-screen. This failure, initially at least, saw Davison's direction receive less harsh reviews in *Radiolandia* ("The directing is correct. Behind this term it is understood that there is a lack of wise directorial decisions and that this absence is taken place by common sense in when it comes to cinematic description") and *Proyecciones* ("He has realized a more or less felicitous task"). However, the canned theatricality of *Las de Barranco* would lead it to be quickly panned as one of 1938's failed adaptations, which according to *Radiolandia*'s "Halfway Through the Season of Argentine Cinema" included NIRA Film's *El casamiento de Chichilo* (Chichilo's Wedding, dir. Isidoro Navarro), Cinematografía Julio Joly's *El cabo Rivero* (*Corporal Rivero*, dir. Miguel Coronato Paz), and Argentina Sono Film's *Con las alas rotas* (*With Broken Wings*, dir. Orestes Caviglia).[59]

Along with other new talent such as Niní Marshall, Paulina Singerman, and Ernesto Vilches, *Radiolandia* also reviewed Davison's debut on the Argentine silver screen in "Halfway Through the Season of Argentine Cinema."[60] While not accorded the praise heaped on Marshall and Singerman, Davison escaped the seething criticism suffered by Vilches, a

Spanish actor who had also appeared in Spanish-language films produced in Hollywood. Its insouciant assessment: "Tito Davison: so-so with 'El sargento Laprida' [*sic*] and 'Las de Barranco.'" Less than impressive on two feature films made by independent production companies, neither of which would survive beyond 1938, Davison sought out other kinds of work within the Argentine film industry. After helming *Murió el Sargento Laprida* and *Las de Barranco*, Davison would become a kind of what Anchou calls *éminence grise*, working primarily as the director of the *encuadre*. Without necessarily receiving credit commensurate for his influence on Argentine cinema of the late 1930s, and especially the early 1940s, Davison nonetheless was an important advisor working primarily behind the scenes. He would, however, eventually return to positions of greater public control, as he is credited as the director of two films, the animated short *Upa en apuros* and the feature *Casi un sueño* (*Almost a Dream*, 1943). Relegating these roles to mere expansions of technical supervision not only minimizes Davison's contribution in filming these movies but also does little to problematize shifting roles in the production of Argentine industrial cinema.

Following four years working behind the scenes, Davison made a somewhat unconventional return to directing in the short *Upa en apuros*, a film adaptation of Dante Quinterno's comic strip *Patoruzú*. Originally appearing in the daily *Crítica* in 1928, and gaining widespread popularity in the mid-1930s, Patoruzú is one of the most influential characters in Argentine comics.[61] Unsurprisingly, given its creator's formation of the Sindicato Dante Quinterno (on the model of King Features Syndicate) in order to more widely exploit commercial possibilities, *Patoruzú* was reportedly going to be brought in color to the silver screen (by "a powerful German company") as early as 1939.[62] As the Sindicato Dante Quinterno took the opportunity to license various kinds of *Patoruzú* merchandise, its film adaptation worked its way slowly through development.[63] As noted in October 1942 in a brief report in *Heraldo del Cinematografista*, "After three years of meticulous trials and patient tests, Dante Quinterno will present his first cartoon, in color."[64]

On the program of the premiere of *La guerra gaucha* (*The War of the Gauchos*, dir. Lucas Demare, 1942), *Upa en apuros* was first widely screened at the Cine Ambassador on November 20, 1942.[65] Its review in *Heraldo del Cinematografista* is representative of its positive reception by the *porteño* press: "It surpasses what little has been done in the country in the genre, this first cartoon in Technicolor counts on good technical realization, both in the movement of the figures and in the use of color ('Alexcolor' system), allowing for hope the experience will be repeated in an increasingly perfected way."[66] Credited as the film's "Director of Dialogues and Editing," Davison collaborated with a team of animators under Quinterno's supervision.[67] He received recognition in the review, which states, "Tito Davison was the technical director of the film, which has measured dialogue and an animated musical background by Melle Veersma. Knowing the difficulties of all kinds that are against the making of films of this nature, the work of illustrator Dante Quinterno is deserving of great praise and worthy of union support. It has had good publicity." Unsurprisingly, Quinterno draws much of the attention in pieces like *Sintonía*'s "Patoruzú Begins in the Cinema," but Davison left indelible marks on the short.[68] Not only did he help structure its minimal dialogue, but he also helped to adapt a static comic strip into an energetic short film. The dynamism of *Patoruzú*'s adaptation to the screen is seen throughout the short, but one notable scene occurs when Patoruzú bumbles up and around a hill with Upa in his stroller. As they round a corner in the foreground, a sign occupies the center of the frame in the background. Patoruzú and Upa step out of frame, and the frame pauses briefly. It then zooms toward the sign, which reads "Wanted. The Gypsy Juaniyo. Child thief. Reward $10,000." Ominous music underscores a quick read for adults and a (relatively) long take of the bad guy for children. Following a dissolve from the wanted poster to Juaniyo on his wagon drinking wine and talking of his plans to kidnap a child for an evil circus owner, the viewer waits for the inevitable as the wagon (with his pet bear following close behind) winds down a road: Patoruzú and Upa encountering the notorious kidnapper. But, familiar with the comic, the viewer also knows who will be defeated (sent to jail) and who will triumph (and, later, perhaps, collect the reward).

Days after the premiere of *Upa en apuros*, Davison would reportedly already be on the set of *Casi un sueño*.[69] Produced independently by Carlos Gallart (another fleeting company) and distributed domestically and internationally by EFA (Establecimientos Filmadores Argentinos), *Casi un sueño* is a light melodrama whose commercial aspirations were inextricably tied to its young star, María Duval.[70] It marked Duval's second film for Carlos Gallart, as she had starred two years earlier in *Canción de cuna* (whose *encuadre* had been entrusted to Davison).[71] The Argentine Deanna Durbin, Duval was an *ingénue* who, it once seemed, would conquer Argentine cinema.[72] Production notes about the film began to emerge in early September 1942.

Heraldo del Cinematografista reported that "Carlos Gallart will produce a film with María Duval with a team [*en equipo*]. Tito Davison will be in charge of the technical part with it being possible that Enrique Amorim will collaborate on the film."[73] (Amorim was a noted Uruguayan author associated with the Boedo literary group.) *Radiolandia*, a fan magazine that reported on industry news from a very different perspective, focused its attention on Duval, but also made references to its cast. On November 21, for example, it ran the piece "María Duval Directed by Amorim," which does not mention Davison but does note that the film's title is *Negrita* (its eponymous protagonist). In December, reports emerged with information about the film's cast and crew. In a detailed piece on *Casi un sueño*, its new title, Duval is described as "one of the happiest discoveries of the *cinematografía criolla* [national cinema] in recent years."[74] Also, "[t]he technical direction will be Tito Davison's, a man expert in the needs of the set, as he will prove in 'Canción de cuna,' his last work." Among other details, *Film* notes, "It will be directed by Enrique Amorin [*sic*] with the *asesoramiento* [supervision] of Tito Davison."[75] *Heraldo del Cinematografista* gave nearly the same details, only to amend them ("la colaboración de Enrique Amorim and Tito Davison") in its next issue.[76] With Duval clearly defined as the star of *Casi un sueño*, its direction, well, was a little more complex. Instead of clarifying the division of labor, the film's credits blurred them even more, as they read: "Dirección de Fotografía, José M[aría] Beltrán; Dirección artística, Enrique Amorim; and Dirección técnica y encuadre, Tito Davison." Anchou, and other Argentine film historians, credit Davison with co-direction (with Enrique Amorim, but, curiously, not with Beltrán, another itinerant foreign film worker).

Premiering on April 21, 1943, in the Cine Monumental, *Casi un sueño* was met with decidedly mixed, if not negative, reviews. In its review of the film, which appeared the week after the film premiered and, notably, does not explicitly mention Davison (but does so implicitly, both disapprovingly and with praise), *Heraldo del Cinematografista* focuses its attention on Duval, stating, "Deliberately, we leave for the end the analysis of María Duval's work. The extraordinary strength of this young actress—without dispute, the supreme *ingénue* of Argentine cinema—and her charm and grace conquer the viewer's spirits and gives value to the film."[77] The *simpatía y gracia* of the ingenue is, of course, performed by the actor—and, in this case, quite well—but it is also constructed diegetically and formally in *Casi un sueño*. *Variety*'s Argentine correspondent, Ray Josephs, notes this in his review of the film:

> Unlike most pix here this one had a producer, Carlos Gallert, and both an artistic and technical director. Enrique Amorim handled former role, but steady hand of Tito Davison, who gets credit for technical direction, is apparent. Davison has contributed some smoothness but hasn't been able to overcome all the somewhat faulty continuity.[78]

Unlike Argentine film historiography—which, usually affected by Amorim's place within the letters and politics of the River Plate, has been kind to the author's work on *Casi un sueño*—Josephs notes not only the technician's importance, but that his work is inscribed within the film. Perhaps more kind than other reviewers, Josephs remakes that "this one did an o.k. opening biz and seems slightly better than average for second runs in the interior. Will need plenty of build-up, though."

As what might be considered to be the peak of what *ingénue* cinema could have been in Argentina, *Casi un sueño* is an (at times) strange Cinderella story, whose diegetic force revolves not so much around its protagonist Negrita, but rather the performance of the starlet María Duval.[79] Despite this, the film does not begin in the orphanage where Negrita is being raised, but rather at a well-to-do house. There, Doña Sabina (María Santos) sees off yet more domestic servants. Her friend Don Ramiro (Miguel Gómez Bao), who arrives just as two disgruntled (and probably understandably so) women are being fired, suggests that she do a charitable work to solve two problems: her domestic work issue and the pending matter of a pension from the state. He tells her, "You could adopt a girl, use her as a servant. Your nephew will approve, I suppose." At the orphanage, they review the girls (in a way that recalls cinematic representations of selecting a prostitute or a puppy). Reviewing the line of teenage girls, and having already caught Don Ramiro's eye, Doña Sabina chooses "*esta*," "this one." Negrita moves in with Doña Sabina, and begins to clean the house. To her surprise, her cleaning is interrupted by a group of schoolboys who ascend the beautiful staircase to the second floor. Cautiously, Negrita follows, eventually entering a room where a handsome young man is at the piano. Eduardo (Ricardo Passano, hijo) is rehearsing a song with his boys' choir. Confusion heightens with the arrival of Panchito (Tito Gómez), Eduardo's friend (and the film's comic relief). As Negrita attends to the family's affairs, she comes to have an idea of their situation.

Later, Eduardo visits Panchito, who is dancing with Fanny (Marga Landova). The three begin to talk about a prize for which Eduardo is a finalist. Eduardo describes to Fanny, his increasingly distant love interest, his desire to win the competition on his own merits. Slowly but surely, Negrita becomes a part of the family's lives, even drawing nearer to the boys' choir. If what Eduardo and Fanny shared is slipping into the past, Eduardo and Negrita are growing increasingly closer. In one sequence, Negrita, an observer when Fanny comes to visit, watches as she leaves. Some time later, Eduardo asks her to take a trip with him . . . to the amusement park. Negrita happily accepts, and the two enjoy the park's attractions and a kiss in the *Canal misterioso* (The Canal of Mystery). Negrita later visits Don Ramiro and expresses the impossibility of her situation. A girl like her cannot hope for a man like Eduardo. Don Ramiro expresses his doubts, and Negrita eventually comes to accept what she thinks is reality. In a series of sequences, the family's problems—financial, romantic, etc.—are shown. The rhythm of this daily life is broken up by a phone call (as, tellingly, Negrita holds Fanny's portrait in her hand): Negrita is informed that Don Ramiro is not feeling well. He eventually dies. As fate would have it, the seemingly poor Don Ramiro was, in fact, quite wealthy, owning twenty-two houses throughout Buenos Aires. Negrita inherits everything. She comes under the protection of a new guardian, Garay (Rafael Frontaura). Eduardo, meanwhile, wins the competition and, with it, a trip abroad. It seems that the love that Eduardo and Negrita share may, after all, be nothing more than a dream, until the final scene when Eduardo is met at the train station by his true love. Eduardo tells Negrita that he will live at the *Canal misterioso.* The film ends as Garay tells Negrita, "He will return. Men always return to those who most inspire them."

Keeping in mind that reconstructing Davison's specific work is not only a historical impossibility, but also theoretically impossible, as a film (as an assemblage) cannot be minimized to an aggregation of its components, I offer a reading of a single, pivotal sequence of *Casi un sueño.* As technical director, Davison would have been charged with assembling the sequence's pieces so as to allow it to become a more coherent whole. In it, Negrita discusses the complex problem she faces: an orphan taken in to a family basically as a domestic servant, she has developed a romantic relationship with Eduardo, culminating in a kiss (shot entirely in black) in the *Canal misterioso* at an amusement park. The exposition of the primary tension of the film's storyworld not only serves the obvious, to exteriorize Negrita's inner conflict, but also functions as a melodramatic excess, a means through which the viewer may wallow in her difficulty. Her predicament, however, is as quotidian as her dress or even the bows tying her pigtails. Don Ramiro, whose role shifts from suggesting the effective imprisonment of an orphan girl (to solve his friend's difficulty maintaining domestic help) to acting as the girl's counselor and, post mortem, her benefactor, helps her (and the viewer) work through the problem. This work is enacted through dialogue, but also through Miguel Gómez Bao's ability to fully inhabit the role of an inoffensive, caring, grandfatherly figure. The sequence is effective, in no small part, because he affectively draws in Negrita and the viewer. Constructed primarily through dialogue, the melodrama faced by the *ingénue* is also expressed through camera movement, lighting, editing (particularly as the scene shifts from proscenium staging to shot/countershot), and, quite importantly, underscoring that underlines the expression of the central problem of the film, and its title. Fading to black, the scene ends with evanescent strings.

A Dream Finally Realized

As Negrita tells Don Ramiro, "I understand now. It cannot be. It is a dream. Almost a dream." Having almost realized his return to the director's chair with *Upa en apuros* and, more so, *Casi un sueño*, Tito Davison would not direct again in Argentina. Even though his professional preparation had given him knowledge of every stage of commercial film production and he had developed a greater understanding of the artistic demands of the film industry, Davison's future in the Argentine film industry crumbled away, due to geopolitical shifts. In Argentina, Davison continued studying what he would discuss decades later in "Professional Preparation in the Cinema": every aspect of filmmaking, including, but not limited to "basic principles of dramaturgy, performing art, film adaptation, architecture, set design, sense of dialogue, knowledge of rhythm, a broad affinity for camera lenses and, a wide knowledge of editing."[80] Davison's specialized work in different aspects of the film industry impacted Argentine cinema of the late 1930s and early 1940s in ways both visible and invisible, then and, after some eighty years, now. In a group with many others, Davison was always a step behind people such as Libertad Lamarque who occupied the foreground of Argentine cinema. But in the background Davison acted as a kind of *éminence grise* who exerted influence over the shaping of the Argentine film industry from a distance. Through specialized film labor as a screenwriter, technical supervisor, assistant director, technical director, and director, Davison helped define emerging new modes of production. Increasingly industrialized, Argentine film distanced itself from the theatricality of the transition to sound and moved toward the commercial model of what would later be called classical Hollywood cinema. In order to become more cinematic, Argentine cinema needed technicians who were experts in the needs of the set. Tito Davison was one.

Argentina's refusal to join the Allies in World War II led to retaliatory measures by the United States, which included limiting the exportation of film stock and equipment. Coupled with "preexisting currency and trade restrictions that made the film industry favor Europe over the United States during the interwar period," as Nilo Couret notes, Argentine studios produced fewer and fewer films from 1942 until 1946.[81] The Argentine film industry would have to wait until 1946 for limits on film stock to be relaxed; that year, the recently elected Juan Domingo Perón would also enact the *Ley de cine*. Argentine cinema would find not only stable but fertile ground again soon. In his 1976 interview with Souza, Davison

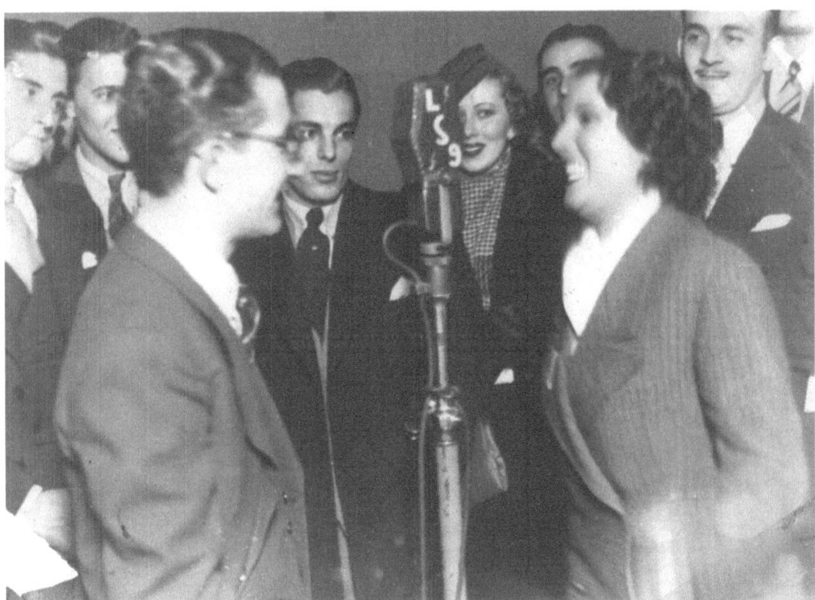

Figure 9.7. Tito Davison, as well as many others, in the background. In the foreground, Libertad Lamarque is being interviewed by Carmelo Santiago. Courtesy of the Museo del Cine Pablo Ducrós Hicken.

says, "It was war time and Argentina suffered a crisis in relation to virgin material [film stock], so they cancelled my contract. So, I thought, 'I should go to Mexico, as I originally wanted.' Only now it is not in my interest to do it from Argentina. I am going to try to do it from the United States, to see if I can do it."[82] Eliding his own personal history, not least of which was his American wife June Marlowe and their son, Davison fashions his arrival to Mexico as greater experience. He would again work on the margins of Hollywood. In its May 5, 1943, issue, *Heraldo del Cinematografista* reports that "Personal reports allow us to signal that Tito Davison, connected to the Argentine industry, was appointed as Latin American consultant at the 20th Century-Fox studios in Hollywood."[83] He later also worked for Paramount.[84] Davison and Marlowe would stay in Hollywood only briefly, as they were in Mexico by 1944. There, again, he began on the fringes as an adaptor, screenwriter, and technical director. Between 1945 and 1947, he adapted twelve films for director Roberto Gavaldón. His break came from the success of one of these adaptations, *El socio* (*The Partner*, 1945), as he was nominated for an Ariel in Best Adaptation. With more exposure and success, Davison finally directed again in 1947. Starring María Antonieta Pons, Juan Orol's (first) Cuban muse, his Mexican debut was *La sin ventura* (*The Unhappy One*). Davison's luck had finally changed. He would eventually direct more than eighty features.

10

Foreign Film Workers and the Emergence of Industrial Sound Film in Latin America

Foreign film workers were integral to the emergence of industrial sound film production in Latin America. Fledgling film industries throughout the region incorporated foreign workers who provided the creative capital, usually in the form of technical or artistic expertise, necessary for the production of talkies. Whether hired abroad to fulfill a short-term contract or employed locally in a more incidental and indeterminate way, foreign film workers made specific contributions to film industries in distinct national contexts. The only way foreign film workers' contributions to national cinema can be understood is by historically contextualizing their labor and, more speculatively, examining how they helped to form the cinematic imaginaries projected onto the screen. Indelibly or fleetingly, foreign workers' labor is inscribed within national cinemas. Foreigners might disrupt the narrative unity of national cinema in film history, but they played varying characters in its story. Sometimes protagonists, sometimes secondary players, and sometimes extras, these foreigners are too often ignored, especially those who were not actors. The genesis amnesia of film historiography convinces us that the rise of film industries, of national cinemas, is fated. But the determined conclusions of these stories of film history—for example, the end of Spanish-language production in Hollywood and the *épocas de oro* in Mexico and, to a lesser extent, Argentina—do not match the unboundedness of historical possibility. Things might very well have become something else. By examining specific case studies in *Alton's Paradox*, I do not mean to suggest that these specific foreigners were necessary conditions for the emergence of Latin American film industries, but rather that their historical contributions to the cinemas of Hollywood, Mexico, and Argentina necessitate greater attention and understanding. Through introducing the involvement of other foreigners in these labor markets, I also aimed to show that film industries throughout Latin America incorporated foreign labor in different ways for multiple reasons. Every nation has a particular history that must be recovered. By briefly tracing the emergence of sound film in Brazil, Uruguay, Peru, and Chile, we might come to have a better feeling for the unevenness of their specific industrial contexts as well as the disjointedness of the rise of national cinemas.

On November 23, 1931, *Coisas nossas* (*Our Things*), the first Brazilian *filme-revista*, premiered at the Cine Eldorado in Rio de Janeiro.[1] *Coisas nossas* was shot in the spirit of films like MGM's 1928 *Broadway Melody* (dir. Harry Beaumont). Now lost, it was not driven by plot, but by music. "The first film spoken and sung made in Brazil," according to a *Cinearte* advertisement published soon after its release, Byington & Cia.'s *Coisas nossas* delivers "our customs, our music, our songs, our artists! A Brazilian film, spoken and sung, done in Brazil."[2] Conspicuously absent from the ad is the name of the film's director. Left unmentioned in film periodicals from the early "Brazilian Cinema" (published in the February 17, 1932 issue of *Cinearte*) to later ones like Paulo Amarante's "A New Point of Departure in National Cinema" (appearing in *A Scena Muda*'s July 9, 1946, issue), later critics and film historians such as Antônio Moreno would conclude, "Ironically, the discovery of the vein [a geological metaphor] was made by the American Wallace Downey."[3] But Wallace Downey—born in New York, died in New York—was part of a changing scene of a new art. After working for several years in the recording industry in the United States, Downey arrived in Brazil in 1928 as an artistic director for Columbia Records. Three years later, in partnership with Alberto Byington, he established the company Byington, which produced and distributed *Coissas nossas*. Jurandyr Noronha describes:

> With increasing interest in the film industry, he founded Waldow Filmes (and later, more importantly, Sonofilmes), which produced various *filmes-revistas* and was a pioneer in Brazilian musicals that gave origin to the *chanchadas,* of enormous popular success in the 1950s. He invented the careers of Aurora and Carmen Miranda, Oscarito, and other artists that would come to have great prominence in Brazilian cinema.[4]

Unlike other U.S. workers in Brazilian cinema, who largely brought technical and creative expertise, Downey contributed to its industrial development.[5] Not only did he import an industry standard Bell & Howell camera, but he also brought advanced technologies such as sound equipment and color [used in a sequence of his feature *João ninguém* (Johnny Nobody, 1936)]. Like so many pioneers of the early sound period, especially in Latin America, Downey's career as a director and a producer was relatively short-lived, spanning only some thirteen years until his final film, *Abacaxi azul* (Blue Pineapple, 1944), flopped, but his work in the 1930s suggested that national cinemas like that of Brazil should mirror other forms of industrial development through relying on foreign capital, both human and monetary.

Downey's films gesture toward the tension between "local" and "foreign" that so marked the early sound period not only in Latin America but throughout world cinema. Inspired by films produced in Europe and, especially, Hollywood, the national cinema emerging in Brazil also integrated elements of local popular culture. The circus and popular theater, among other forms, infused the films of important production companies of the 1930s and early 1940s such as Cinédia, Brasil Vita Filmes, and Sonofilmes, leading to backstage musicals and the *chanchada,* the defining musical film genre of the golden age of Brazilian cinema. However, as Nilo Couret succinctly contends, "The chanchada was neither national nor cinema before being reappropriated as the paragon of national cinema."[6] The term evolved, but the musical films of the early sound period sought to appeal to local audiences, while incorporating a wide range of film workers who came from other lands.[7] Appearing in these *chanchadas,* two of the most important performers its film industry ever produced were the comic actor Oscarito and the "Brazilian Bombshell" Carmen Miranda. Born in Spain and Portugal, respectively, these actors indelibly marked Brazilian cinema. The Portuguese actress Violeta Ferraz and the Polish actor Zbigniew Ziembiński made long-lasting impressions.[8] Spanish star Conchita Montenegro appeared in *O grito da mocidade* (The Cry of Youth, dir. Raúl Roulien, 1936).[9] There were few foreign directors in the 1930s and early 1940s in Brazil: the most important were the Portuguese-born Ruy Costa and Mesquitinha.[10] Joining them on the sets of Brazilian films were the cinematographers Jiří Dušek and Adam Jacko (Czechoslovakia), George (Gÿorfy) Fantö (Hungary), Aquilino Mendes (Portugal), and John Reichenhein (Germany).[11] Other important film workers during the period include the production designer Alcebíades Monteiro Filho and the director's assistant Fernando de Barros, both from Portugal, as well as the sound engineers Genaro Ciavarra (Argentina) and Ludovico Berendt (Poland). Juanita Jacko, the Argentine wife of Czech Adam Jacko, "was one of the first professionals in the country in the area of editing."[12] Brazilian cinema was not able to fully industrialize until much later, in no small part due to "structural problems at the level of distribution and exhibition. But, at this stage, the protagonists of Brazilian cinema believed that the keystone of the latter was the creation of an industrial production infrastructure."[13] This infrastructure was strengthened by the establishment of the studio Atlântida Cinematográfica in 1941; however, the Brazilian film industry was unable to regularly produce more than twenty films per year until 1949.

Sound film production arrived in Uruguay in fits and starts—or, more specifically, it experienced two separate starts followed by two distinct fits. *Dos destinos* (Two Destinies, dir. Juan Etchebehere, 1936) was the first (part-)talkie produced in the country. Relying on technical support from figures existing on the periphery of the Argentine film industry and local talent drawn from the radio, *Dos destinos* presents the divergent fates of two brothers from the country who come to the big city, Montevideo.[14] Writing two decades later, José Carlos Álvarez contends, "Our talking cinema is born and continues to live subject to improvisation, audacity, chance. Those who make films do not know what to say or how to say it. In general, foreign imitation predominates, and the worst example comes from Argentina."[15] Similar to *Dos destinos*, the subsequent wave of films was produced by short-lived film companies, employed technicians from Buenos Aires (as well as locals who had gained experience working on newsreels), and featured largely Uruguayan casts and writers. In addition to comedies centering on radio culture—*Soltero soy feliz* (I'm Happy Single, dirs. Juan Carlos Patrón and Edmundo Bianchi, 1938) and *Radio Candelario* (dir. Rafael Jorge Abellá, 1939)—the country's fledgling industry produced two notable features in 1938: Rina Massardi's *¿Vocación?*, the country's first film directed by a woman, and *Lucerito* (dir. Jorge César Buzio), animated in Technicolor (16mm). "[T]hese brief heights were followed by a long step backward: production was paralyzed for eight years, until some Argentine businessmen began filming in Uruguay, where costs were lower and there was no union control."[16] With the aid of Cinelate, a local confectionary, Argentine brothers Alberto and Juan Roca agreed to move their facilities to Montevideo.[17] Before their new company Orión Sociedad Cinematográfica Uruguaya was established, they were forced to overcome the destruction of their equipment in a fire. "There was no capital to import what they had lost, but there was will, tenacity, technical ability, and inexhaustible inventiveness to rebuild here what was necessary."[18] Orión's studios and laboratories would eventually produce a (relative) flurry of films in the late 1940s and early 1950s, including *Los tres mosqueteros* (Three Musketeers, dir. Julio Saraceni, 1946) and *El ladrón de sueños* (Dream Thief, dir. Kurt Land, 1949). With transnational casts, crews, and capital, these movies fleetingly brought the film industry across the River Plate.[19] By 1953, however, a new step backward had been taken.

Talkies dramatically altered the cinema in Peru. "The arrival of sound drove the construction of new movie theaters. Seventeen new cinemas were opened in the *Cercado de Lima* [an area within its historic center] during the 1930s."[20] The building craze also extended out into the metropolis to places such as Miraflores, Chorrillos, and Callao. Increasingly showing more films in Spanish, these cinemas drastically changed *limeño* and, by extension, Peruvian film culture.[21] Hollywood's Spanish-language films and, later, Argentine and Mexican imports inspired local filmmakers. Many short-lived production companies made films during this period—one notable project was Ollanta Film's *El vértigo de los cóndores* (Vertigo of the Condors, 1939), which was directed by the Chilean Roberto Saa Silva, who later directed *Allá en el trapiche* (Over at the Sugar Mill, 1943) and *Anarkos* (1944) in Colombia—but Amauta Films ambitiously sought to establish Peru's first film studio. "The film and business project of Amauta Films set the objective of making sound films continuously and permanently, aiming at the consolidation of an industry. This goal coincided with companies established in other countries in the region."[22] Delineated in ten points in a July 22, 1937, advertisement in the magazine *Radiocine*, "The intentions of Amauta Films were impressively ambitious, aiming to 'conquer' not only the national market but . . . international markets as well."[23] Financed by Felipe Varela La Rosa, Amauta Films was formed around four men with diverse transnational relationships with the cinema: Manuel Trullen, a cameraman with Spanish roots who had lived in Argentina and Chile; Ricardo Villarán, a Peruvian director who had worked in the Argentine film industry; Francisco (Pancho) Diumenjo, an Argentine sound designer with Spanish roots; and Sigifredo Salas, a Chilean cameraman and, later, director. "They provided the indispensable base of money, *industria* [expertise], work, and technical knowledge that allowed for the company's film activity."[24] Building upon its success, the production company invested in its industrial infrastructure (equipment, sets with improved acoustics, etc.).

"In producing 14 films in less than four years (1937–1940), Amauta Films is the most successful film production company in Peruvian history."[25] Like the films of emerging industries in other countries, Amauta Films productions express tensions between the local and the global, the national and the transnational. Casting was one way in which these tensions were manifested. Often with experience gained abroad, usually in Argentina and Chile, foreign actors and musicians such as Carmen Pradillo (Spain), Silvia Villalaz (Panama), José Muñiz (Uruguay), Alejo López (Argentina), and Venturita López Piris (Chile) were incorporated into Amauta Films' productions.[26] Many worked on multiple films, and some, such as Cuban-born actor Óscar Ortiz de Pinedo (in Mexico), later had a long careers elsewhere. Amauta Films' movies expressed this tension in complex ways. In *De doble filo* (Double-edged, dir. Villarán, 1937), "Argentina, Ecuador, Mexico, Chile, and Peru parade through an uninterrupted chain of music, songs and sensual and picaresque dance moves. . . . And in competition with the gaucho tangos, *Evocación*, an Incan tango that contains all of the infinte sadness of the indian," according to a note published in *Universal*.[27] This transnationalism might have targeted foreign audiences, as Amauta Films' sought to distribute beyond Peru, but it also would have appealed to local spectators, who wanted to see themselves, as well as others, on screen. It represented a cinematic cosmopolitanism for domestic and foreign consumption. In films like *El miedo a la vida* (Fear of Life, 1938), Villarán's movement away from specificity distanced spectators in Lima and beyond, despite positive reviews.[28] A later *Universal* piece claimed that its failure to connect with audiences was similar to other quality films such as William Wyler's *Callejón sin salida* (*Dead End*, 1937), as well as Jean Renoir's *Bajos fondos* (*Les bas fonds*, 1936) and *La gran ilusión* (*La Grande Illusion*, 1937), unlike "the unconditional acceptance of certain Mexican production, weepy and tacky [*llorona y ramplona*]."[29] Amauta Films would pivot back toward a cinema that was "ingenuously lyrical and movingly *criollo*" in *Palomillas del Rímac* (The Rímac Rascals, 1938). It would, however, localize similar foreign archetypes. A review in *Universal* states, "Until now, *el palomilla,* genuine product our our coast, had not taken part in the cinema. France has its *gavroche,* master and minuscule lord of Paris; Madrid its *golfillo*; Chile, its *patacalata santiaguino*; Buenos Aires its *canillita*."[30] It might be that contemporaneous periodicals such as *Ímpetu* were able to affirm, "The film industry in our country confronts a fundamental problem, and it is to finally to elucidate what IS national cinema"; however, without the establishment of strong, lasting industrial structures in Peru, this polemic could be asked but never answered. As Peruvian film historian Ricardo Bedoya concludes, "After the unexpected sprouting of film production inspired by Amauta Films, the downturn arrived."[31] With production interrupted by the censorship of *Barco sin rumbo* (dir. Salas, 1940) and scarcity of film stock due to World War II, Amauta Films eventually collapsed, taking with it for some time the promise of a film industry in Peru.[32]

In the early 1940s, a project supported by the Chilean state made possible the development of the country's film industry. "The creation and operation of Chilefilms in the 1940s was, without a doubt, a singular event in the history of Chilean cinema. The emergence of the company in 1942 was part of a specific national project linked to nationalist discourses typical of the cultural, economic, and political environment of Chile in the 1930s and 1940s."[33] Following a model of *desarrollo hacia adentro* [inward development], the Corporación de Fomento de la Producción (Production Development Corporation or CORFO) was established in 1939 to diversify the Chilean economy. Among many sectors of the economy in which import substitution policies were implemented was the film industry. Despite vibrant local film cultures, production in the early sound period in Chile was nearly nonexistent. On July 10, 1935, the melodrama *Norte y sur* premiered in Santiago's Cine Central. Partially financed by the Caja de Crédito Minero, the film was made by its director Jorge Délano and his partner Emilio Taulis with locally built equipment.[34] Like his compatriots José Bohr, Carlos Borcosque, and Tito Davison, "Coke" (as Délano was often called) had spent time in Hollywood. Tellingly compared to the early Argentine sound film *Tango!* in a review published in *Revista Hoy*, *Norte y sur* presents a love triangle in which a beautiful young woman (Hilda Sour, "the Chilean Kay Francis") is torn between Chilean and American suitors (Alejandro Flores and Guillermo Yánquez). However, "After *Norte y Sur* things did not change for national cinema. One swallow does not a summer make."[35] Less isolated efforts began in 1939, and revolved around Délano, Eugenio de Liguoro, and, finally, Bohr. Having arrived a few years earlier, the Italian de Liguoro directed ten films in Chile, beginning with *El hechizo del trigal* (Spell of the Wheatfield, 1939). After periods in Hollywood and Mexico, Bohr returned to Chilean cinema with *P'al otro lao* (To the Other Side, 1942).[36] Filmed in Argentina with a largely Chilean cast, but featuring Argentines Tita Merello and Tono Andreu, it opened in Buenos Aires as *27 millones*

(27 Million). With *El relegado de Pichintún* (Pushing Pichintún Into the Background, 1943), Bohr fully returned to Chile, where he would work until 1970's *Sonrisas de Chile* (Smiles from Chile). These three directors shot films with casts and crews with varying transnational ties.[37]

The unprecedented industrialization of Chilean cinema in the 1940s cannot be disentangled from Chilefilms. In late 1941, a proposal was put forward to the CORFO for the creation of a national film studio to be supported within the framework of its *Plan de industrias*. The president of Argentina Sono Film, Ángel Luis Mentasti, traveled to Santiago to sign a contract providing his company's "technical consultancy in the construction of a great studio."[38] Quickly reported in Buenos Aires' *Heraldo del Cinematografista*, news also reached Hollywood, as *Variety* detailed the new company's corporate and financial structure.[39] Chilefilms would eventually produce nine films from 1944–47.[40] Its initial offerings were prestige dramas directed by three Argentines (Luis Moglia Barth, Carlos Schlieper, and Carlos Hugo Christensen) and one Chilean (Carlos Borcosque). Also imported from Argentina to work on these films were composer George Andreani, makeup artist César Combi, sound engineer Jorge Di Lauro, and cinematographers Antonio Merayo, Fulvio Testi, and Alfredo Traverso.[41] Chilefilms also produced three flops directed by lesser-known directors who had worked in Buenos Aires, Roberto de Ribón and Mario Lugones.[42] Starring in the enigmatic Ribón's *El diamante del Maharaja* (The Maharaja's Diamond, 1946) was none other than Luis Sandrini, the Argentine comic star who "was never quite as bounded by the nation as film histories would have us believe."[43] In supporting roles, Argentines Guillermo Battaglia and Paul Ellis (Manuel Granada) also appeared. Encouraged by Germán Picó Cañas, the new CORFO vice-president, Chilefilms pivoted toward "nationalizing" its productions. In Délano's *El hombre que se llevaron* (The Man They Took Away, 1946) and Bohr's *La dama de las Camelias* (The Lady of the Camellias, 1947), foreign film workers involved in previous productions contributed to films whose diegeses were more recognizably directed toward local audiences. Despite investing heavily in its productions, not only in terms of workers but also technology, Chilefilms ultimately was never able to sufficiently connect with moviegoers at home and abroad. "Experts in the size of our internal market, the bet was directed not at rivaling Argentine production, recognizedly solid despite the celluloid blockade, but rather to build commercial relationships that would stimulate the region."[44] Unable to sufficiently develop (inter)national distribution, its ostentatious, cosmopolitan films proved to be both too expensive to produce and insufficiently profitable to warrant continued financing by the Chilean state. Despite the ultimate failure of Chilefilms, Chilean cinema of the 1940s would be unmatched in terms of activity until the 1970s.

Alton's paradox is an invitation to reconsider the ways in which foreign film workers impacted the emergence of national film industries in Latin America. Alton's call in *International Photographer* may never have been fully realized—foreign technicians never fully took matters into their own hands, and organization was never entirely entrusted to foreigners—but foreigners helped to develop the enormous possibilities presented by new sound technologies that transformed the cinema, including film production. The history of national cinema in Latin America varies widely. Or, perhaps better put, the histories of national cinemas in Latin America vary quite widely. Countries with greater industrial organization and larger domestic markets employed individuals who created structures that allowed for regular production on an industrial scale. Similar to other industries, other countries saw promising moments of industrial growth, only to see decline before maturation. Still others were prohibited from forming a local film industry for decades due to cost, competition, and many other factors. In each of these situations, however, foreign capital was incorporated to produce films that would resonate meaningfully with local audiences. Competing with Hollywood, as well as European and, increasingly, other Latin American cinemas (especially Mexico and Argentina), local film industries branded their films as national cinema. Much like other works of other media industries, these industries' films do not often easily fit into the categories that have been imposed upon them. The differentiation of local production is more complex and nuanced than film historiography often suggests. National cinema never exists by itself. The genesis amnesia of national cinema has obliterated, unintentionally or not, that that which does not fit into accepted forms of scholarly differentiation. Among other forms of foreign capital employed in emerging film industries in Latin America, film workers helped produce films that were not neatly national, but were also not always clearly transnational. Foreign film workers—from writers to producers, from extras to stars, from set designers to editors—may not always be remembered, but they made their mark upon the emergence of national film industries throughout Latin America.

Notes

*Note on translations of film titles: those in italics correspond to commercial or festival releases, usually in the United States, while those without italics are my own.

Chapter 1

1. John Alton, "Motion Picture Production in South America," *International Photographer*, May 1934, 14, 27.

2. Capitalization is original to the quote. The epigraph appeared in issues of *International Photographer* from its inception in February 1929 (1.1) to March 1933 (5.2). The quote reappears on the front cover of a curious special issue (7.1) in February 1935, celebrating "The Birth Month of Father Abraham." In his First Annual Message, given on December 3, 1861, Lincoln remarked that "[l]abor is prior to and independent of capital. Capital is only the fruit of labor, and could never have existed if labor had not first existed. Labor is the superior of capital, and deserves much the higher consideration." The American Presidency Project. www.presidency.ucsb.edu/ws/?pid=29502. International Photographers of the Motion Picture Industries was Local No. 659 of the International Alliance of Theatrical Stage Employees and Moving Picture Machine Operators of the United States and Canada (I.A.T.S.E. and M.P.M.O.).

3. Patrick Keating notes that *International Photographer* never fully established a distinctive voice, particularly from a union perspective, as its interest in labor dissipated after Silas Snyder, twice editor of *American Cinematographer*, took control of the magazine. *Hollywood Lighting from the Silent Era to Film Noir* (New York: Columbia University Press, 2010), 111.

4. Local and international film periodicals detailed the wiring of movie theaters in Latin America, as well as throughout the world. Of particular use are the *Film Daily Year Book of Motion Pictures* volumes from 1929 to 1943.

5. Paulo Antônio Paranaguá, *Cinema na América Latina: longe de Deus e perto de Hollywood* (Porto Alegre: L & PM Editores, 1985), 9.

6. In her landmark essay "Early Cinema and Modernity," López discusses the cinema's uneven relationship with the modern as idea and process in the silent

period. *Cinema Journal* 40, no. 1 (2000): 48–78. Other scholars who comment upon the role of foreign filmmakers in this period include Aurelio de los Reyes, Jurandyr Noronha, Paul Schroeder Rodríguez, and Andrea Cuarterolo.

7. In "Early Cinema and Modernity in Latin America," López lists initial screenings throughout the region of the two apparatuses. Here, I refer indirectly to Pierre Bourdieu's "The Forms of Capital," in *Handbook of Theory and Research for the Sociology of Education*, ed. John G. Richardson (Westport: Greenwood, 1986), 241–58.

8. For Bourdieu, genesis amnesia is the phenomenon in which history is taken to be an *opus operatum* or a fait accompli. In *Outline of a Theory of Practice* (Cambridge: Cambridge University Press, 1977), he argues, "Yet we do not sense this man of the past, because he is inveterate in us; he makes up the unconscious part of ourselves. Consequently we are led to take no account of him, any more than we take account of his legitimate demands." (79) He expands upon the idea of genesis amnesia in an important footnote. He contends, "The antigenetic prejudice leading to unconscious or overt refusal to seek the genesis of objective structures and internalized structures in individual or collective history combines with the antifunctionalist prejudice, which refuses to take account of the practical functions which symbolic systems may perform; and together they reinforce the tendency of structuralist anthropology to credit historical systems with more coherence than they have or need to have in order to function. In reality these systems remain, like culture as described by Lowie, 'things of shreds and patches,' even if these patches are constantly undergoing unconscious and intentional restructurings and reworking tending to integrate them into the system" (218n1).

9. *Porteño* refers to someone from the city of Buenos Aires. "Viene a filmar a nuestro país un operador americano," 11. A piece published the following day in *La Película* reveals that he has traveled with László (or Ladislao) Kish, another itinerant film worker with Hungarian roots. April 21, 1932, 5. Kish directed or co-directed six films in Italy, largely in the early 1940s.

10. "John Alton in Argentine for Making of Productions," *International Photographer*, June 1932, 37.

11. Domingo Di Núbila, *Historia del cine argentino.* Vol. 1 (Buenos Aires: Cruz de Malta, 1959), 43.

12. Since 1944, a monolith in the Plaza Mariano Moreno in Buenos Aires has marked kilometer zero in Argentina. It was originally placed slightly more to the east in the Plaza Lorea in 1935. Both are located adjacent to the Plaza del Congreso.

13. Produced by Argentina Sono Film, Latin America's most important industrial film studio in the classical period; starring Pepe Arias, a comedian and one of Argentina's earliest film stars; directed by Soffici, one of the principal filmmakers of the classical period; and shot by Antonio Merayo, the first legendary Argentine cinematographer, *Kilómetro 111* marks a decidedly more mature cinema than the country's earliest sound films. Through his work as a cinematographer

and, later, the technical director of Argentina Sono Film, Alton's work explicitly and implicitly influenced its production.

14. Nicolas Poppe, "John Alton in Argentina, 1932–1939," in *Cosmopolitan Film Cultures in Latin America, 1896–1960*, ed. Rielle Navitski and Nicolas Poppe (Bloomington: Indiana University Press, 2017), 217–40.

15. Alton details some of these developments in his article "Motion Picture Production In South America Up to Date," including the purchase of new film equipment from Tom White, a peripatetic American production manager, and Max Factor makeup from the "imported makeup artist" Bruno Boval. *International Photographer*, March 1937, 29.

16. Chris Cagle reminds us of how Hollywood studios' house styles were dependent on a range of production and postproduction practices. "Classical Hollywood, 1928–1946," in *Cinematography*, ed. Patrick Keating (New Brunswick: Rutgers University Press, 2014), 47–50.

17. From the first sound films in Mexico and Argentina, efforts were made to distribute films beyond national borders. While initially concentrated in Spanish-language markets, including Spain, producers sought to also make inroads in other countries. One early strategy involved emerging film festivals. Work is now being done on the early reception of Latin American industrial cinemas in other regions of the world. One example: Dubravka Sužnjević and Robert McKee Irwin, "'Vedro Nebo' in Far-Off Lands: Mexican Golden Age Cinema's Unexpected Triumph in Tito's Yugoslavia," in *Global Mexican Cinema: Its Golden Age 'el cine mexicano se impone,'* ed. Maricruz Castro Ricalde and Robert McKee Irwin (London: Palgrave Macmillan; British Film Institute, 2013), 183–97.

18. Charles Ramírez Berg, *The Classical Mexican Cinema: The Poetics of the Exceptional Golden Age Films* (Austin: University of Texas Press, 2015).

Chapter 2

1. The first talkies to arrive in Uruguay were English-language. Spectators in Montevideo were first exposed to Vitaphone's sound-on-disc technology on September 25, 1929, in the Rex, with George Fitzmaurice's *El amor no muere* (*Lilac Time*, 1928). Max Glücksmann, one of the most important figures in the region's early film cultures, distributed and exhibited it. Some seven weeks later, Friedrich Wilhelm Murnau's *Los 4 diablos* (*The Four Devils*, 1929) opened at the same theater. The November 14, 1929, screening marked Movietone's sound-on-film debut in Uruguay. All subsequent data regarding premieres in the country are taken from the website "Cinestrenos. El cine en Montevideo desde 1929." UruguayTotal.com. http://www.uruguaytotal.com/estrenos/; accessed January 6, 2020.

2. By mid-1934, spectators in Montevideo had seen both multilinguals produced by UFA in Germany with Spanish casts such as *El profesor de mi*

mujer (an alternative title of *El amor solfeando*, [Love's Humming, dirs. Armand Guerra and Robert Florey, 1930]) and Spanish films sonorized in France such as *El embrujo de Sevilla* (*The Charm of Sevilla*, dir. Benito Perojo, 1931). Before the April 27, 1937, premiere of *Allá en el Rancho Grande* (dir. Fernando de Fuentes, 1936), only three Mexican films had been distributed in Uruguay. Opening with Cantinflas's *¡Así es mi tierra!* (*Such Is My Country*, dir. Arcady Boytler, 1937), 1938 saw the arrival of seven Mexican movies.

3. *Hollywood*, of course, is a slippery term. Throughout this book, Hollywood is regularly used to refer to production companies based in the United States.

4. Its "Cinestrenos. El cine en Montevideo desde 1929" entry reads: "Curiosity: This was the first film of the *cine hispano* exhibited in Montevideo; locally, 85 feature- and medium-length films were premiered and a great quantity of shorts of the kind, until the beginnings of the '40s."

5. Antonio Moreno spent his infancy in Andalusia. Adopted at the age of twelve by American tourists, Moreno moved to the United States. In his mid-twenties, he began acting. In his long career, he worked as an extra, a star, and everything in-between. He is perhaps most well-known as the director of the first Mexican sound film, *Santa* (1932). Ramón Pereda was also born in Spain, but eventually made his mark as both an actor and a director in Mexico. He also directed his Cuban-born wife María Antonieta Pons, who was once married to Juan Orol, in *Romance en Puerto Rico*, a 1962 Mexico/Puerto Rico co-production. Barcelona-born María Alba appeared in a number of the *films hispanos,* as well as two Mexican films. Born as Alfredo Carlos Birabén in Buenos Aires, Barry Norton's career was somewhat similar to those of Moreno and Alba. The most successful period of his career was in the 1930s, during which time he acted in both English- and Spanish-language films.

6. Nicolas Poppe, "Made in Joinville: Transnational Identitary Aesthetics in Carlos Gardel's Early Paramount Films," *Journal of Latin American Cultural Studies* 21, no. 4 (2012): 482.

7. Like many other films of the period, a silent version of the film was also cut for theaters that had not yet been wired for sound. *Drácula* opened at the Colonial and Grand Splendid theaters in Montevideo on September 14, 1932. Browning's *Dracula* would also show in the Uruguayan capital, albeit as part of a double bill a decade later. On February 15, 1945, it was shown at the Cine Rex alongside its Spanish-language counterpart.

8. Starring José Bohr, *Hollywood, ciudad de ensueño* was produced by Fenix Films, shot in Universal City, and distributed by Du World Pictures. It is one of a few of these films that is not totally lost, even though the UCLA Film & Television Archive has been unable to restore the film "due to the poor condition of the surviving elements." Roberto Green Quintana, "Buried in the Vault: The Restoration of Hollywood's Spanish-language Films," In *Hollywood Goes Latin: Spanish-Language Cinema in Los Angeles*, ed. María Elena de las Carreras and Jan-Christopher Horak (s.l.: FIAF/UCLA Film & Television Archive,

2019), 58. The copy of the film I viewed at the archive in January 2015 was missing reels one and four. It ran fifty-three minutes rather than the listed sixty-eight.

9. Lisa Jarvinen examines differing strategies of these independents, including originals such as Hispania Talking Film's *Sombras habaneras* (Havana Shadows, dir. Cliff Wheeler, 1929) and Hollywood Spanish Pictures' *Charros, gauchos y manolas* (dir. Xavier Cugat, 1930). *The Rise of Spanish-Language Filmmaking: Out from Hollywood's Shadow, 1929–1939* (New Brunswick: Rutgers University Press, 2012), 28–30. The distribution and exhibition of these films throughout Latin America was uneven, but many such as *Charros, gauchos y manolas* (October 3, 1930 in the Cervantes) were shown in Montevideo.

10. And Europe, too. In many ways, European film production (even by Hollywood studios such as Paramount) should be disentangled from that done in Los Angeles and New York.

11. In his "The War of the Accents: Spanish Language Hollywood Films in Mexican Los Angeles," Gunckel gives a local example of a debate that raged (in different ways) throughout the Spanish-speaking world. *Film History* 20 (2008): 325–343. Jarvinen also dedicates her chapter, "Language Controversies: 1930–1931," to it, 60–82. Also, see Jarvinen for uneven reception, 114–18.

12. Ibid., 115.

13. Other studios continued to produce Spanish-language films, albeit many fewer of them. Columbia, for example, produced the Lupe Vélez vehicle *Hombres en mi vida* (*Men in Her Life*, dir. Selman, 1932), which also featured Gilbert Roland, and Ramón Pereda. Enrico Caruso Jr. starred in two 1934 films: First National's *La buenaventura* (The Fortune Telling, dir. William McGann) and Warner Bros.'s *El cantante de Nápoles* (dir. Howard Bretherton). Franchon Royer, one of Hollywood's few female producers at the time, released *Dos noches* (dir. Carlos F. Borcosque, 1933), with José Crespo and Conchita Montenegro. Unlike other stars in the period, Crespo was not closely tied to one studio. In addition to the three films he shot with Fox—*La ciudad de cartón* (The Cardboard City, dir. Louis King, 1933), *Señora casada necesita marido* (Married Woman Wants a Husband, dir. James Tinling, 1934), and *Angelina o el honor de un brigadier* (Angelina, or the Brigadier's Honor, dir. King, 1935)—Crespo also appeared in two features for Universal—*Tres amores* (Three Loves, dir. Aubrey Scotto, 1934) and *Alas sobre el Chaco* (*Storm Over the Andes*, dir. Christy Cabanne, 1935) and Columbia's *La última cita* (The Last Date, dir. Bernard B. Ray, 1935).

14. Ibid., 119.

15. News about the closure abounds in trade publications of the day. One example: "Fox to End Spanish Production on Coast," *Motion Picture Daily*, June 26, 1935, 6. Somewhat tellingly, a note published below ("Fox Foreign Personnel Shifts") reports that John Lindsay, formerly sales manager of the Spanish office, was transferred to head its Venezuelan exchange. Efforts were shifted away from production toward distribution.

16. Imperio Argentina's two shorts (*La casa es seria* [The House Is Serious, dir. Lucien Jaquelux, 1933] and *Buenos días* [Good Day, dir. Florián Rey, 1933]) and five features (*Su noche de bodas* [*Her Wedding Night*, dir. Louis Mercanton, 1931], *Lo mejor es reír* [*Laughter*, dir. E. W. Emo, 1931], *¿Cuándo te suicidas?* [When Will You Kill Yourself, dir. Manuel Romero, 1931], *El cliente seductor* [The Smiling Client, dir. Richard Blumenthal, 1931], and *Melodía de arrabal* [*Suburban Melody*, dir. Louis Gasnier, 1933]) were all shot in Joinville. There, Carlos Gardel also shot *Las luces de Buenos Aires* (*The Lights of Buenos Aires*, dir. Adelqui Millar, 1931), *Esperáme* (Wait for Me, dir. Gasnier, 1933), *Melodía de arrabal*, and his only short, *La casa es seria*. After negotiations with Fox failed, Gardel worked out a new deal with Paramount. Produced by Exito, his own production company, and distributed by Paramount, *Cuesta abajo* (The Downfall, dir. Gasnier, 1934), *El tango en Broadway* (dir. Gasnier, 1934), *El día que me quieras* (dir. John Reinhardt, 1935), and *Tango Bar* (dir. Reinhardt, 1935) were all shot in Paramount's Eastern Service Studios in Astoria. Today, they are known as the Kaufman Astoria Studios.

17. Jarvinen, 8. Jarvinen argues this turn was due to "economic pressures of the mid-1930s and producers' increasing awareness of the need to compete with growing sound film industries in Mexico, Spain, and Argentina."

18. *Mis dos amores* (My Two Loves, dir. Nick Grinde, 1938) was the only film ever produced by Cobian Productions Inc. *El trovador de la radio* (*Radio Troubadour*, 1938), *Papá soltero* (*Bachelor Father*, 1939), *El otro soy yo* (*I Am the Other One*, 1939), and *Cuando canta la ley* (*When The Law Sings*, 1939) were all produced by Dario Productions and directed by Richard Harlan. Jarvinen briefly discusses them, 157–58.

19. Juan B. Heinink and Robert G. Dickson, *Cita en Hollywood: antología de las películas norteamericanas habladas en castellano* (Bilbao: Mensajero, 1990). A list of Spanish-language films produced by Hollywood studios based on *Cita en Hollywood* is included in *Hollywood Goes Latin: Spanish-Language Cinema in Los Angeles*, a volume published nearly thirty years later, 198–204. A mere two titles—one feature and one short—were added to the filmography.

20. Florentino Hernández Girbal, *Los que pasaron por Hollywood*, ed. Juan B. Heinink and Robert Dickson (Madrid: Verdoux, 1992). Jesús García de Dueñas, *¡Nos vamos a Hollywood!* (Madrid: Nickel Odeon, 1993). Álvaro Armero, ed., *Una aventura americana: españoles en Hollywood* (Madrid: Compañía Literaria, 1995). Unsurprisingly, these books tell the story of Hollywood's Spanish-language production in way that is decidedly Peninsular.

21. Colin Gunckel, *Mexico on Main Street: Transnational Film Culture in Los Angeles Before World War II* (New Brunswick: Rutgers University Press, 2015).

22. Colin Gunckel, Jan-Christopher Horak, and Lisa Jarvinen, ed., *Cinema between Latin America and Los Angeles: Origins to 1960* (New Brunswick: Rutgers University Press, 2019). María Elena de las Carreras and Jan-Christopher Horak, ed., *Hollywood Goes Latin: Spanish-Language Cinema in Los Angeles* (s.l: FIAF/UCLA Film & Television Archive, 2019).

23. Gunckel, Horak, and Jarvinen, "Introduction," in *Cinema between Latin America and Los Angeles*, 1.

Chapter 3

1. In *Making Cinelandia*, Laura Isabel Serna examines Navarro's serialized novel. Laura Isabel Serna, *Making Cinelandia: American Films and Mexican Film Culture Before the Golden Age* (Durham and London: Duke University Press, 2014), 212–13. Navarro also put together an elaborate *revista* for *La ciudad de irás y no volverás*. Nicolás Kanellos, *A History of Hispanic Theatre in the United States: Origins to 1940* (Austin: University of Texas Press, 1990), 51–52. Arriving in Los Angeles in 1922, Navarro would return to Mexico in 1942. Gunckel describes the going-away gala Frank Fouce organized for him in the Teatro California. Colin Gunckel, *Mexico on Main Street: Transnational Film Culture in Los Angeles Before World War II* (New Brunswick: Rutgers University Press, 2015), 187. The full lineup for the event was published in *La Opinión*. Empresa Francisco Fouce, Advertisement, *La Opinión*, March 16, 1942, 4.

2. Gabriel Navarro, "El Cine de Aquí y de Allá," *La Opinión*, June 19, 1938, 6 (segunda sección). *La Prensa*, June 26, 1938, 2 (segunda sección).

3. Miguel de Zárraga, "Las películas españolas hechas en Hollywood," *La Opinión*, July 3, 1938, 6 (segunda sección). Jan-Christopher Horak discusses *Verbena trágica* in "Cantabria Films and the LA Film Market, 1938–1940," in *Cinema between Latin America and Los Angeles: Origins to 1960*, ed. Colin Gunckel, Jan-Christopher Horak, and Lisa Jarvinen (New Brunswick: Rutgers University Press, 2019), 97–118.

4. Gunckel examines the Navarro/Zárraga debate (177–80), 180. Zárraga, "Las películas españolas hechas en Hollywood," *La Opinión*, June 19, 1938, 6 (segunda sección). Navarro, "Lo que olvidó el Señor de Zárraga," *La Opinión*, June 26, 1938, 6 (segunda sección). Zárraga, "Punto final: El defensor del cine hispano en Hollywood halla el camino de Damasco," *La Opinión*, July 10, 1938, 6 (segunda sección). Navarro, "'Verbena trágica: La vida en su peor tragedia; La deslealtad," *La Opinión*, August 28, 1938, 6 (segunda sección).

5. These workers did not come to Hollywood only from Latin America and Spain; they also included many from the United States.

6. Lisa Jarvinen, *The Rise of Spanish-Language Filmmaking: Out from Hollywood's Shadow, 1929–1939* (New Brunswick: Rutgers University Press, 2012), 10. Gunckel also discusses Mojica and Gardel together, 117–18.

7. There are a few serious treatments of Mojica. Jarvinen, *The Rise of Spanish-Language Filmmaking*, 121–27. Rosario Vidal Bonifaz, "José Mojica: The Tenor from Jalisco, Mexico, Who Conquered Hollywood," in *Hollywood Goes Latin: Spanish-Language Cinema in Los Angeles*, ed. María Elena de las Carreras and Jan-Christopher Horak (s.l: FIAF/UCLA Film & Television Archive, 2019), 143–51.

8. Mojica's remaining films are presumed lost. Roberto Green Quintana, "Buried in the Vault: The Restoration of Hollywood's Spanish-language Films," in *Hollywood Goes Latin: Spanish-Language Cinema in Los Angeles*, ed. María Elena de las Carreras and Jan-Christopher Horak (s.l.: FIAF/UCLA Film & Television Archive, 2019), 59.

9. Martin Shingler, *Star Studies: A Critical Guide* (London: Palgrave Macmillian; British Film Institute, 2012), 111–12.

10. It might be argued that one of the reasons Spanish-language production ultimately failed was Hollywood's lack of full commitment to developing a parallel star system. The paths of the would-be stars of Spanish-language films, as well movies shot in languages other than English, were not built in the same systematic way as those described in Jeanine Basinger's *The Star Machine* (New York; Knopf, 2007).

11. Along with "persona," "star image" is one of the more slippery terms in star studies, as noted by numerous scholars. Though I do not mean to directly apply Richard Dyer's semiotic approach in *Stars*, I do draw from his insights into stars as being ideologically contradictory, as well as their structured polysemy ("the finite multiplicity of meanings and affects they embody" in which some "are foregrounded and others are masked or displaced") (London: British Film Institute, 1998), 3. My approach is influenced by a number of theorists working in star studies, but especially draws from Christine Gledhill's "Signs of Melodrama," in *Stardom: Industry of Desire*, edited by Christine Gledhill (London; New York: Routledge, 1991), 207–29. Much like stars themselves, the structured polysemy of "star image" allows us to have more capacious understandings of these very important public figures, especially ones like Mojica who do not easily fit into our intellectual categories.

12. Koegel, John. "Mexican Musicians in California and the United States, 1910–50," *California History* 84, no. 1 (2006): 9.

13. Shingler, 21.

14. "Por las distribuidoras," *Imparcial Film*, September 25, 1933, 11.

15. "Murió en Perú José Mojica," *La Opinión*, September 21, 1974, 1.

16. "Duelo en Perú por la muerte de José Mojica," *La Opinión*, September 22, 1974, 1, 3. "El funeral de José Mojica fue tumultuosa manifestación de duelo," *La Opinión*, September 23, 1974, 1, 2. "Homenaje en Arequipa a José Mojica," *La Opinión*, September 24, 1974, 2, 4. "Frei Mojica morreu omtem aos 78 anos," *Folha de São Paulo*, September 21, 1974, 1. A day later, *Folha de São Paulo* ran his obituary. "Mojica, do cinema à religião," *Folha de São Paulo*, September 22, 1974, 53 (caderno de domingo). "Jose Mojica, Mexican Film Star Who Became a Friar, Dies at 78," *New York Times*, September 22, 1974, 57. "Star José Mojica, Quit Stage for Monastery," *Washington Post*, September 22, 1974, C6.

17. "Homenaje en Arequipa José Mojica," *La Opinión*, September 24, 1974, 2, 4.

18. In this paragraph I parenthetically cite the following sources: Vidal Bonifaz, 144–45; Jarvinen, 121–23; Koegel, 14–20; and José Mojica, *I, A Sinner* (Chicago: Franciscan Herald Press, 1963), 340–41.

19. It is also common to see his birth year listed as 1894 or 1896. José Díez Martín, *Memorias del ídolo José Mojica* (Madrid: Alco, 1975), 21.

20. "Don José Mojica," *Cinearte*, July 8, 1931, 6.

21. Mojica, 341.

22. In addition to his passion for painting, which was often highlighted in profiles, Mojica enjoyed photography. Ralph Wilk, "A Little from 'Lots,'" *The Film Daily*, October 8, 1929, 4.

23. Koegel, 14. For more on Tito Guízar, see my essay "Tito Guízar on Radio Row: Intermediality, Latino Identity, and Two Early 1930s Vitaphone Shorts," in *The Routledge Companion to Gender, Sex, and Latin American Culture*, ed. Frederick Luis Aldama (New York: Routledge, 2018), 91–100.

24. Pierre V. R. Key, "Music and Musicians. Gossip from New York," *San Diego Union*, February 19, 1922, 9.

25. Mojica, 204, 180. Caruso sang *Rigoletto* at New York's Metropolitan on February 7, 1917, and December 29, 1917. These dates may have coincided with Mojica's time in New York. Pierre V. R. Key and Bruno Zirato, *Enrico Caruso: A Biography* (Boston: Little, Brown, 1922), 432, 435.

26. Mojica, 204–205. Key and Zirato. *Enrico Caruso*, 438–39. Mojica's performances in *Pagliacci* and *Manon Lescaut* would have taken place on October 23 and October 30, 1919, respectively.

27. Mojica, 206.

28. Luis Lara Pardo,"José Mojica, legitima gloria mexicana," *Excélsior*, March 27, 1921, 18. It was reproduced the next month in Los Angeles' *El Heraldo de México*. "José Mojica," April 16, 1921, 7–8.

29. "El Tenor Mexicano José Mojica, se Distinguió en el Estreno Mundial de la Opereta 'El Amor de las Tres Naranjas," *Excélsior*, January 15, 1922, 8 (tercera sección).

30. Compañía Mercantil Nacional Mexicana, S.A., Advertisement, *El Universal*, May 17, 1922, 2 (segunda sección).

31. Eduardo Guaitsel, "Hollywood al día," *Hispano-América*, May 9, 1931, 3–4.

32. "'Sheik of Opera' Tells Life Story," *Sunday Star*, April 12, 1925, 13 (part one).

33. Eleanor Clarage, "Main Street Meditations," *Cleveland Plain Dealer*, February 24, 1926, 14.

34. Edgar Morin, *The Stars* (Minneapolis: University of Minnesota Press, 2005), 73. This is a key aspect of Mojica's stardom that requires detailed scholarly attention. Mojica's sexuality, for example, was subtly commented upon in gossip columns, especially Spanish ones. Homophobic touches persisted, for example, in Mojica's entry in Jesús García de Dueñas's *¡Nos vamos a Hollywood!* (Madrid:

Nickel Odeón, 1993), 174, 207n.74. Recent scholars such as Koegel counteract this homophobia when discussing Mojica's sexuality, 18–19.

35. From a correspondent, "My Operatic Career," *Times*, March 16 1960, 14.

36. "Big First Run Presentations," *Motion Picture World*, August 8, 1925, 642.

37. In his "Mexican Musicians in California and the United States, 1910–50," John Koegel describes Mojica's singing on these records, arguing that "Mojica's recordings of Italian and French opera arias made in the 1920s reveal a voice that is fresh, flexible, and more than capable of navigating quickly moving melodic passages," and, "His recordings from the 1920s and 1930s of some of the best Mexican popular songs of those decades show a dramatic approach to the popular repertory, but one that also includes a lighter touch when appropriate. The same fine musical attributes heard in his operatic recordings can also be heard in his evocative and charming recordings of popular songs," 15, 17.

38. "Chicago Opera Season Opens," *Cleveland Plain Dealer*, November 4, 1927, 25.

39. Jarvinen, 121. Mojica later was reported to be earning $18,000 a week as a contracted player for Fox. *Motion Picture Daily*, March 21, 1936, 4.

40. "Don José Mojica, Well Known Tenor, Signs for Fox," *Hollywood Filmograph*, July 13, 1929, 29.

41. "Opera Tenor Goes 'Talkie,'" *Morning Oregonian*, July 18, 1929, 8.

42. Jennifer Fleeger, *Sounding American: Hollywood, Opera, and Jazz* (Oxford: Oxford University Press, 2014), 4. After discussing Vitaphone's opera shorts, Fleeger notes, "A similar preference for the male voice can be found in the output of the other studios: seven of nine films produced by Fox, MGM, and Paramount feature men," 70.

43. "Songbirds in Favor," *Picture Play*, December 1929, 92. In a later account, the Chicago Civic Opera's performers were reported to be hesitant to sign with a Hollywood studio because Mojica had yet to appear on-screen. "Wabash Ave.—South," *Motion Picture News*, June 28, 1930, 78.

44. "Opera More Concerned Over Losing Choruses Than 'Names' to Pictures," *Variety*, February 5, 1930, 1, 46.

45. Fleeger, 65.

46. Fox would only release two opera shorts, Movietone Numbers starring the baritone Ricard Bonelli. Fleeger, 64.

47. Ginette Vincendeau, "Hollywood Babel: The Coming of Sound in the Multiple-Language Version," *Screen* 29, no. 2 (1988): 30.

48. Evelyn Ballarine, "The Flapper Fan's Forecast," *Screenland*, October 1929, 4. "Don Jose [*sic*] Mojica. Fox Movietone Artist," *Gráfico*, November 23, 1929, 8. "Don Jose [*sic*] Mojica and Mona Maris, Fox Movietone Artists," *Gráfico*, December 21, 1929, 7.

49. Clayton Sheehan, "Internationalizing," *The 1930 Film Daily Year Book of Motion Pictures* (New York: The Film Daily), 997. One of the focuses of Sheehan's arguments is Grandeur Film, a briefly utilized 70mm widescreen film format.

50. Evelyn Ballarine, "Forecasting the Picture Program," *Screenland*, March 1930, 6. Ballarine writes, "Seven foreign nationalities, a whole League of Nations, are presented in 'One Mad Kiss.' Don Jose [*sic*] Mojica, the star, is Mexican; Mona Maris, leading lady, is a native of Argentine [*sic*]; Tom Patricola is of Italian birth, [*sic*] Antonio Moreno was born in Spain; Marcel Silver, director, is a native of France; Frank Merlin, stage director; [*sic*] was born in Ireland; and Alexander Kahle, cameraman, was born in Prussia. And yet it has been said that the talkies were eliminating foreigners!"

51. See, for example, "Better Talking Movie Week Gets Response from Public," August 30, 1930, 3. It grossed only $3,448 in a week at the Boulevard, a Los Angeles neighborhood theater.

52. "Inside Stuff—Pictures," *Variety*, February 26, 1930, 20.

53. "Opinions on Pictures," *Motion Picture News*, July 26, 1930, 61. It did, however, receive a very favorable (albeit not impartial) review in *Talking Screen*. "Talking Screen Reviews," May 1930, 57.

54. "José Mojica," *Cinearte*, August 15, 1941, 16–17. José Mojica, *I, A Sinner*, 297–98.

55. "José Mojica," 17.

56. Some examples of profiles written on Mojica in the 1920s to early 1930s include: Luis Lara Pardo, "José Mojica, legitima gloria mexicana," *Excélsior*, March 27, 1921, 18; "Una gloria mexicana. José Mojica," *El Heraldo de México*, April 16, 1921, 7–8; Eduardo Guaitsel, "Hollywood al día," *Hispano-América*, May 9, 1931, 3–4; "Don José Mojica," *Cinearte*, July 8, 1931, 6–7; "José Mojica. Gran actor y gran mexicano," *El Imparcial*, November 20, 1931, 4; Hortensia Elizondo, "De charla con José Mojica," *La Prensa*, June 8, 1932, 6; Gilberto Souto, "Uma tarde em casa de Don José Mojica," *Cinearte*, September 14, 1932, 14–15, 38; El Cameraman Vito, "Astro de nuestra raza: José Mojica," *Ecran*, July 25, 1933, 6; and "Francisco J. Ariza, "La Jira de Mojica por Oriente," *Cine-Mundial*, September 1933, 537, 547. Like so many important figures of the day, Mojica's travels were noted in quick references in gossip columns as well as feature stories. Two examples: General Crack, "Mojica y el pueblo hispano americano," *Ecran*, February 13, 1934, 2–4 and "Facetas íntimas de José Mojica," *Filmográfico*, March 1934, 14.

57. Elizondo, 6.

58. Curiously, *Variety* reports that Mojica had signed a combination contract. "Mojica is with Fox and Metro for two pictures each." "'Variety's' Bulletin Condensed," *Variety*, June 4, 1930, 42. Mojica never filmed for Metro.

59. Jarvinen, 123.

60. *Cuando el amor ríe* was adapted from the 1922 John Gilbert film *The Love Gambler* (dir. Joseph Franz). *Hay que casar al príncipe* and *La ley del harem* drew from two Howard Hawks films: 1927's *Paid to Love* and 1928's *Fazil*, respectively. *El caballero de la noche* was adapted from *Dick Turpin* (dir. John G. Blyston, 1925). Curiously, after the success of Mojica's version, it would later be

remade in English as *Dick Turpin* (dirs. W. Victor Hanbury and John Stafford), 1934. *Mi último amor* was the Spanish-language version of *Their Mad Moment* (dirs. Hamilton McFadden and Chandler Sprangue, 1931).

61. "Fox Organizes Unit to Make Spanish Versions, *Motion Picture News*, July 5, 1930, 29 and 33. Curiously, the note was published twice in the same issue. A late-1930 article, published after the production of *Cuando el amor ríe*, reports, "Under a new long term contract, Don Jose [*sic*] Mojica will continue to play leading roles for Fox Films in original Spanish productions." "Fox Signs Mojica for Spanish Versions," *Exhibitors Daily Review and Motion Pictures Today* (later *Motion Picture Daily*), November 11, 1930, 11. Furthermore, "Before starting his new contract, he will make a four months' concert tour in Spain, Italy, and France."

62. Jarvinen, *The Rise of Spanish-Language Filmmaking*, 123.

63. It appears that Mojica shot these six films under two contracts. In "Hollywood," "[b]riefly rewritten extracts from 'Variety's' [*sic*] Hollywood Bulletin," *Variety* reports, "Revival of direct-shot Spanish at Fox. Jose [*sic*] Mojica is engaged for three besides his domestic musical assignment." May 17, 1932, 6. Production notes on *El rey de los gitanos* were sporadically (and sometimes asynchronously) published in Spanish-language film magazines and newspapers, and often touched upon Mojica, the film's cast, and its music. "Noticias de los estudios," *Cinelandia*, August 8, 1933, 40. "Producciones en Español," *Cine Mundial*, November 1933, 625. Don Q., "Centelleos," *Cine Mundial*, November 1933, 665. "José Mojica baila en 'El rey de los gitanos," *La Prensa*, December 20, 1933, 8.

64. Souto, 17. Incidentally, as was the case with many interviews Mojica gave, his mother was also present when he talked to Souto.

65. Mary A. Roberts, "The Rolling Stone that Gathered Moss," *Movies*, 10. Aubrey Soloman notes that "John Stone, who had been working his way up the ladder from writer to story editor then to producer for the previous 11 years had never held a contract. Having been brought in under his original name of Jack Strumwasser by Sol Wurtzel in early 1921, he wrote 22 scenarios between that year and October 1923, many of them for Buck Jones, Dustin Farnum and then Tom Mix. Then the efficient Strumwasser reportedly ran into a problem, most likely with Winfield Sheehan, who insisted on his termination. In an anecdote recounted by Sol Wurtzel's son, Paul, shortly after Wurtzel carried out these orders, a new writer appeared on the lot named John Stone (really Strumwasser) who continued his writing career on Tom Mix films. Under Wurtzel's personal guidance, Strumwasser/Stone remained on the lot but without a contract. The lack of a contract continued for 11 years until Sheehan left on vacation and suddenly, Stone was handed a long-term deal by Sol Wurtzel. It is only speculation, but there may have been some connection between Sheehan's declining importance at Fox and Wurtzel's ascendancy, that the time was right

to offer Stone a contract." *The Fox Film Corporation, 1915–1935* (Jefferson and London: McFarland, 2011), 199.

66. Koegel, 18.

67. In the interview with Souto, Mojica also refers to Brazil's Latin spirit, "I receive many letters from Brazil, and I answer them all, as I am immensely attached to the Latin audience. I feel that they think like us, that they feel like us—Mexicans, *latinos,* anyway!," 17.

68. One example of press on "The Gypsy King": "A eleicão do 'rei dos ciganos polonezes' acabou em tumulto," *Correio da Manhã,* May 30, 1931, 1. "El Rey Gitano" was publicized in U.S.-based press. Burke Furniture Co., Advertisement, *La Prensa,* January 5, 1930, 2.

69. Lubitsch's presence looms large, but it is conceivable that *El rey de los gitanos* was also influenced by the cultural understandings of its largely Spanish cast and Spanish screenwriter José López Rubio. In *White Gypsies: Race and Stardom in Spanish Musicals* (Minneapolis: University of Minnesota Press, 2012), Eva Woods Peiró examines class, gender, and ethnicity in Spanish cinema before and after the 1930s.

70. Martin Shingler, *Star Studies: A Critical Guide* (London: British Film Institute; Palgrave Macmillan, 2012), 165–66.

71. Ibid., 166.

72. "Ecos y noticias," *La Vanguardia,* May 23, 1933, 21. "Espectáculos," *La Vanguardia,* May 23, 1933, 22. Heinink and Dickson incorrectly list its release in Barcelona as May 5, 1933. It was distributed by Hispano Fox Film, 213–14.

73. "'El Rey de los Gitanos' irá hoy a la pantalla en una función de Gala," *La Opinión,* May 26, 1933, 4.

74. Ibid.

75. "El estreno de 'El rey de los gitanos' en el Ambassador," *Film,* July 14, 1933, 7. It is noted that of the main actors, three are Mexican and three are Spanish. Also, "The Hungarian master D. J. Vecsei composed six beautiful songs, which are sung by Mojica." Notably, it was followed up at the Ambassador by *Huérfanos de Budapest* (*Zoo in Budapest,* dir. Rowland V. Lee, 1933).

76. "Notas de interés," *Film,* July 28, 1933, 4.

77. See listings in *Correio da Manhã.* It played, irregularly, at the following movie theaters on the following dates: Cinema Modelo (11/18), Cine Fluminese (11/23), Mascotte (11/30), Paris (1/16), Primor (1/18), Paris (1/19), Nacional (1/23–28), Haddock Lobo (1/31), Popular, Cinema Floresta (2/7), and Guarany (2/18). The Popular, Mascotte, Primor, Paris, and Haddock Lobo were all part of the Vital Ramos de Castro circuit.

78. "Nos theatros," *Correio da Manhã,* October 28, 1933, 9. Interestingly, not only was Mojica's role transformed ("Clara Weiss plays the leading role in the operetta's plot and Mujika, a gypsy"), but also the article focused on his

costar, Rosita Moreno, who had recently performed in the then Brazilian capital. According to the article, it was written by "the masters Valente and Tagliaferri."

79. "José Mojica baila en 'El rey de los gitanos,'" *La Prensa*, December 20, 1933, 8.

80. "Se exhibirá 'El rey de los gitanos,'" *La Prensa*, January 14, 1934, 7.

81. María Luisa Amador and Jorge Ayala Blanco, *Cartelera cinematográfica, 1930–1939* (Mexico City: Filmoteca, UNAM, 1980), 102.

82. Correspondence from H. G. [Hettie Gray] Baker to Gentlemen, April 26, 1934, Casefile Number 27361, Box 295, New York State Motion Picture Division License Application Case Files, New York State Archives, Albany, New York, United States. The twenty-four dollar fee to receive a license from the Motion Picture Division of the State of New York Education Department was returned.

83. Writing for *Variety*, E.P. Jacobi reports "Fox' Spanish-language picture, 'Gypsy King,' starring Jose Mojica, looked familiar here because all soldiers figuring in the fictitious kingdom where it set wear regulation Hungarian uniforms, even down to the trapping and decorations." "Budapest," May 8, 1934, 60. It was also shown in other areas of the country such as Nyíregyháza. Apollo "A Cigány Kilárly," Advertisement, *Nyírvidék—Szabolcsi Hírlap*, September 28, 1934, 5.

84. Listed as *El rey de los gitanos* o *El zíngaro vagabundo* in Peru, the film was distributed by Leon's Films. Violeta Núñez Gorritti, *Cartelera cinematográfica peruana, 1930–1939* (Lima: Universidad de Lima, Fondo de Desarrollo Editorial, 1998), 126.

85. It is important to note that, much like his looks, Mojica's voice was mediated by recording technologies (as it had been, albeit differently, since the mid-1920s in recording and, later, broadcasting studios).

86. "'El rey de los gitanos' en el Kursaal," *La Vanguardia*, May 26, 1933, 14. "Tabloid Reviews of Foreign Films," *The Film Daily*, May 31, 1933, 7. In the latter, *El rey de los gitanos* was reviewed alongside *Pol de carotte* (*The Redhead*, dir. Julian Duvivier, 1932) and *Die Lustigen Musikanten* (also known as *Laubenkolonie*, *The Merry Musicians*, dir. Max Obal, 1930).

87. "Noticias de España," *Imparcial Film*, July 10, 1933, 4. This language is mirrored in its review in Rio de Janeiro's *Cinearte*: "You cannot say it is bad, but you also cannot call it excellent. It is simply something fun." "A tela em revista," November 15, 1933, 11.

88. "El rey de los gitanos," *Heraldo del Cinematografista*, July 19, 1933, 482.

89. "Al margen de los estrenos," *Heraldo del Cinematografista*, July 19, 1933, 479.

90. "At the moment in Rosario" reports that audiences "[like] films spoken in Spanish more, and even more if they are in 'our language,' as we do not speak a precisely pure Castillan. *Melodía de arrabal*, *Caballero de la noche*, *Rey de los gitanos*, and *Tango* have triumphed. Some theaters have even shown *Tango* more than fifteen times." "La actualidad rosarina," *Heraldo del Cinematografista*,

October 18, 1933, 545. In an interview with *Imparcial Film* the owner of the Cine Belgrano, Francisco Iaria, states that two Mojica films (*Caballero de la noche* and *El rey de los gitanos*) are among thirteen (relative) hits in the theater. Others include *King Kong*, *The Sign of the Cross* (dir. Cecil B. DeMille, 1932), and the Laurel and Hardy film *Hermanitos del diablo* (*The Devil's Brother*, dirs. Hal Roach and Charley Rogers, 1933). "The relative success that I award to the films is comparing cost with performance." "Ha sido una de las peores temporadas desde varios años," December 31, 1933, 6–7.

91. Miguel de Zárraga, "Los estrenos. 'El zíngaro vagabundo' (Fox)," *Cine-Mundial*, June 1933, 320.

92. "A tela em revista," *Cinearte*, November 15, 1933, 10–11. This was, however, more imaginative than *A Scena Muda*'s summary told through a distilled narrative of the plot and publicity stills. "O rei dos ciganos—(José Mojica e Rosita Moreno)," October 3, 1933, 20–21, 29.

93. "No mundo da téla," *Correio da Manhã*, September 27, 1933, 7.

94. Ibid.

95. "D. J. Vecsei, well known concert pianist, has crashed Tin Pan Alley with a successful song hit, 'Still Was the Night.' Irving Bibo, prolific ace lyricist, is the other end of this new words and music team." Woody, "Music," *Inside Facts of Stage and Screen*, February 7, 1931, 13.

96. "Delayed 'Hypnotized,'" *Variety*, November 15, 1932, 8.

97. *No dejes la puerta abierta* was a version of *Pleasure Cruise* (dir. Frank Tuttle, 1933).

98. In *No dejes la puerta abierta*, the following songs appear: "Esta noche en casa los dos" ("Spend an Evening at Home"); "Hace un año que me casé" ("It's Our Anniversary Day"); "Beber para olvidar" ("Sing a Song of Sin"); and "Luna turbadora" ("Cupid in the Moonlight"). All song titles come from the *The 1934 Film Daily Year Book of Motion Pictures*. "Song Writers. 1933 Work," *The 1930 Film Daily Year Book of Motion Pictures* (New York: The Film Daily, 1934), 502.

99. "Mojica," *Cinelandia*, November 1932, 47.

100. Estcban V. Escalantc, "Rosita Morcna al natural," *Filmográfico*, May 1933, 8–9. Morena tells Escalante, ""Pepe is a guy who, instead of trying to 'steal' scenes like others I know, helps and makes sure that those who are in front of the camera with him enjoy the same privileges. I do not think that there is a colleague on par with Mojica in Hollywood. Tell him, please, because with me he has been very good, and in general with everyone."

101. In a short entry on the film, Harry Waldman writes, "It is now lost." *Hollywood and the Foreign Touch: A Dictionary of Foreign Filmmakers and Their Films from America, 1910–1995* (Lanham and London: Scarecrow Press, 1996), 245.

102. Similar topically, the two varied only in development; objects that were flashed with light in the former were given greater exposure in the latter. Originally, it seems, a pseudonym of Baltasar Fernández Cué, Don Q. was used in

Cine-Mundial from 1927 to the end of the magazine's run in 1948. In an interview in the 1970s, Mexican filmmaker Ramón Pereda recalls, "So, between Baltasar Fernández Cué, who was Don Q., and some of those who were there, we formed the cast [of Paramount's *El cuerpo del delito* (dir. Cyril Gardner and A. Washington Pezet, 1930), the Spanish-language version of *The Benson Murder Case* (dir. Tuttle, 1930)] at Henry's." Fernández Cué's first piece published in *Cine-Mundial* was the October 1926 piece "How to Quickly Make a Star" ("Cómo se hace pronto un astro"), 642, 676–680. His big break came the next month with "Mi última visita a Valentino," November 1926, 718–19, 768–70. By 1933, however, Fernández Cué was living in Madrid, having been deported from the United States.

103. Don Q., "Centelleos," *Cine-Mundial*, February 1932, 97. "Centelleos," *Cine-Mundial*, January 1933, 15. "Centelleos," *Cine-Mundial*, March 1933, 153.

104. As it became a more prominent feature of *Cine-Mundial*, "Centelleos" grew in length, leading to lesser differentiation with "Hollywood."

105. Don Q., "Hollywood," *Cine-Mundial*, February 1932, 107–108. Medea de Novara would later move to Mexico, where she would act in films such as *Juárez y Maximiliano* (dirs. Miguel Contreras Silva and Raphael Sevilla, 1934) and *La emperatriz loca* (The Mad Empress, dir. Contreras Torres, 1939). "Hollywood," *Cine-Mundial*, August 1932, 547–548. "Hollywood," *Cine-Mundial*, October 1933, 581–583.

106. Don Q., "Hollywood," *Cine-Mundial*, December 1933, 705.

107. It appears that an alternate title was considered, *Oro de California* (*California Gold*). Gabriel Navarro, "Este Hollywood," *La Opinión*, November 19, 1933, 7 (segunda sección).

108. In addition to contracting labor whose cultural and linguistic competency allowed them to make movies with which spectators could more easily identify, John Stone and Fox's Foreign Department also embraced an initiative launched by U.S.-based, Spanish-language press, "Caras nuevas," through which Anita Campillo would be cast. Gabriel Navarro, "El primer triunfo," *La Opinión*, October 15, 1933, 3, 8 (segunda sección) and "Este Hollywood," *La Prensa*, October 15, 1933, 7 (segunda sección). Fox tested "four new figures, coming from our scenes and our society: Carmen Samaniego, Anita Campillo, Lilia Esparza y María Luisa Castañeda." Samaniego, one of Ramón Novarro's sisters, was originally cast. "Carmen Samaniego ingresa a la pantalla," *La Opinión*, September 19, 1933, 3 (segunda sección) and "Una hermana de Novarro en el cinema," *La Prensa*, September 22, 1933, 1–2. Even though it was front-page news in San Antonio, Samaniego "had the bad luck that the photogenic tests that were done did not favor her." She was replaced by Anita Campillo. Don Q., "Centelleos," *Cine-Mundial*, January 1934, 33.

109. "Fox mantiene la supermacia de las películas hispanas," *Filmográfico*, 1933, 1. On the opposite page (the inside cover), a full page ad ran for Fox's films to premiere in Mexico in the new year, 1934.

110. Heinink and Dickson, 220–221.

111. Gunckel, 19. "The Spanish Feeling Predominates in the Fox-Arlington Theater, Santa Barbara," *The Architect and Engineer* 118, no. 3 (1934): 46. This caption, accompanying a photograph of the movie palace, attributes the building to William A. Edwards, whose Santa Barbara firm Plunkett and Edwards is credited for its design. In her *The Show Starts on the Sidewalk*, Maggie Valentine places the Fox-Arlington within the context of the rise of exotic rivals in the 1920s and 1930s. Beyond the Egyptian Theater, inspired by the discovery of King Tutankhamun's tomb in November 1922, and Grauman's Chinese Theater in Los Angeles, "[i]n Southern California, this quest for exoticism often took the form of Spanish Colonial, because it was thought to be historically accurate and geographically appropriate." Valentine notes that the Fox, the Fox-Florence, and the Fox-Arlington all were built in Spanish Colonial style. Valentine, *The Show Starts on the Sidewalk* (New Haven: Yale University Press, 1994), 72.

112. "Fue brillantísima la fiesta en Santa Barbara, con motivo de la restauración de "Santa Inés,'" *La Opinión*, December 8, 1933, 4.

113. Heinink and Dickson, 220. "Calendar of Current Releases," *Variety*, February 13, 1934, 31. "Calendar of Current Releases," *Variety*, March 34, 1934, 34. It was reviewed by H. T. S. (Harry T. Smith) for *The New York Times*. "In Old California," February 5, 1934, 19.

114. "'La cruz y la espada'" *La Vanguardia*, February 25, 1934, 14. *La Vanguardia* was not published on Mondays between February 2, 1920 and April 12, 1982.

115. Alhambra, Advertisement, *Correio da Manhã*, March 27, 1934, 16. Alhambra, Advertisement, *Correio da Manhã*, April 8, 1934, 24.

116. M. D'Avril, "Los últimos estrenos," *Ecran*, March 27, 1934, 10.

117. Curiously, especially given its coverage in *La Prensa*, it does not seem to have been ever shown in San Antonio.

118. Núñez Gorritti, *Cartelera cinematográfica peruana, 1930–1939*, 121. It was also distributed by Leon's Films. In "Hollywood's Spanish-Language Movies in Buenos Aires, Lima, Montevideo, and Mexico City," Núñez Gorriti argues, "We believe that the delay in exhibition of Mojica's films is Lima was due to the fact that Fox opened a subsidiary as early as 1933, so Fox films still maintained the pattern established by the 'cinematographic program.'" In *Hollywood Goes Latin: Spanish-Language Cinema in Los Angeles*, edited by María Elena de las Carreras and Jan-Christopher Horak (s.l.: FIAF/UCLA Film & Television Archive, 2019), 40.

119. "¿Estamos por fin al principio de una nueva era Cinefónica?," *La Opinión*, December 10, 1933, 3, 8 (segunda sección) and "La Película 'La Cruz y la Espada' en Español, ha sido un Gran Exito," *La Prensa*, December 10, 1933 (segunda sección).

120. Francisco J. Ariza, "Los estrenos. 'La Cruz y la Espada' (Fox)," *Cine-Mundial*, March 1934, 124.

121. Ibid. In a later piece, Ariza again recognizes Mojica, mentioning him alongside other performers with notable recent work such as May Robson,

Warner Baxter, Mae West, Charles Laughton, and John Barrymore. He also attributes more of *La cruz y la espada*'s success to Zárraga's script. "Corte de caja," *Cine-Mundial*, March 1934, 134, 168–71.

122. "¿Estamos por fin al principio de una nueva era Cinefónica?," 8 (segunda sección) and "La Película 'La Cruz y la Espada' en Español, ha sido un Gran Exito," 7 (segunda sección). This mirrors language in an earlier piece Navarro wrote. After reading the script, Navarro expresses hope that the filmmakers are allowed to make their own film. If they are, "the work will become without dispute the best that has been done in Spanish in any of Hollywood's big studios." Notably, Navarro reports an English-language adaptation is also being considered. "Este Hollywood," *La Opinión*, November 10, 1933, 6.

123. Ibid. Because the term *Hispanic* was little used at the time in English-language U.S. publications, I have not translated the term into English.

124. H. T. S. (Harry T. Smith), 19. It is possible that Smith is alluding to D. W. Griffith's 1910 film of the same name. Smith's lede is reminiscent of two other brief English-language reviews of *La cruz y la espada*. "Tabloid Reviews of Foreign Films," *The Film Daily*, February 6, 1934. "Feature Films. The Cross and the Sword." *Motion Picture Reviews*, August 1934, 5.

125. Sabine Hake, *Popular Cinema of the Third Reich* (Austin: University of Texas Press, 2001), 143. Even though Smith is referenced in studies on films in many languages (French, German, Russian, Spanish, etc.), there do not to be any academic studies dedicated to his work for the *New York Times*.

126. "La cruz y la espada," *La Película*, March 22, 1934, 6. "La cruz y la espada," *Heraldo del Cinematografista*, March 21, 1934, 657. *Heraldo del Cinematografista* categorizes the film as "especial," and gives it the following scores (out of five): three (commercial value), three (artistic value), and two (plot value).

127. A similar observation would be made by *Imparcial Film*. "Bolsa de estrenos," *Imparcial Film*, March 25, 1934, 6. *Imparcial Film* offers less of a review and more of a summary of how to market it to theaters in the *barrios* of Buenos Aires or the provinces. It is described as "made with elevated artistic dignity and one of the best works of José Mojica."

128. Both *A Scena Muda* and *Cinearte* published illustrated plot summaries, likely to help local spectators better understand the Spanish dialogue. Accompanied by beautiful publicity stills from the film, the summaries are not wholly accurate. "Entre a Cruz e a Espada—(José Mojica, Anita Campillo e Juan Torena)," *A Scena Muda*, March 27, 1934, 23–25, 35. "Entre a Cruz y a Espada," *Cinearte*, April 1 1934, 16–17.

129. *A tortura da fé* (*Zwei Menschen*, dir. Erich Waschneck, 1930) and *Filha de Maria* (*Cradle Song*, dir. Mitchell Leisen, 1933) also ran during Holy Week in 1933.

130. *O martyr do calvário*, Advertisement, *Correio da Manhã*, March 27, 1934, 16.

131. "Entre a cruz e a espada," *Correio da Manhã*, March 25, 1934, 14.

132. "A tela em revista," *Cinearte*, May 1, 1934, 39.

133. Among the shots included in the monologue are the Misión San Luis Rey de Francia in Oceanside, Misión San Gabriel Arcángel in San Gabriel, and the Misión Santa Bárbara.

134. *La cruz y la espada*'s *hispanismo* is indebted to discourses prevalent throughout the Spanish-speaking world, which imaginined the cultural reconscription of the Americas to the Spanish empire, but it is also reflective of local racial hierarchies in Los Angeles in which whiteness was defended, particularly by the upper classes. "If Mexicans typically possessed an advantage over African Americans in at least some of the the city's industries in the first decades of the twentieth century, distancing them from denigrating or blackening images also represented a rhetorical attempt to protect or enhance the status of Mexicans within local racial hierarchies." Gunckel, 38. The status of upper-class Mexicans within local racial hierarchies was also threatened by recent immigrants whose ethnic difference, their indigeneity, imperiled the former's whiteness, thus making *hispanismo* all the more attractive.

135. Tellingly, the film's first song "Canción de los vendimiadores" ("The Grape Pickers' Song") is followed by "Canción de la taberna" ("Tavern Song").

136. In this quote, Couret explicitly references *Los tres berretines* (The Three Whims, dir. Equipo Lumiton, 1933), but the argument can be made more broadly regarding how songs functioned within certain kinds of film musicals in the early 1930s. Couret argues against my own use of Michel Chion's work in "Sounding Out Temporality in the Argentine Film Musical of the 1930s," *Arizona Journal of Hispanic Cultural Studies* 16 (2012): 211–226.

137. Mojica performs "Gratia plena" ("Full of Grace"), whose lyrics were written by celebrated Mexican poet Amado Nervo; "Jota número 3," which Francisco sings for a town party, exalting God's desire to see himself reflected ("And so California was born / Flower of Mexico and Spain"); and "Carmen Carmela," a traditional folk song in which Francisco is joined by superimposed images of Carmela. "Versos de Amado Nervo en una película Fox," *Filmográfico*, January 1934, 27.

138. Vidal Bonifaz observes that there is "a series of iconographic references to classical Spanish paintings" in *La cruz y la espada*. The cave sequence is one example, but so is "Gratia plena," which evokes Francisco Goya's *Retrato de Joaquina Candado* (c. 1802–04). As well as noting Zárraga's influence in creating the film's mise-en-scène, she also argues that Strayer "took advantage of *La cruz y la espada* to demonstrate an extraordinary visual sense . . . recalling some paintings of Joaquín Mir, Daniel Vázquez Díaz, Benjamín Palencia and Ignacio Zuloaga." In *Hollywood Goes Latin*, 149–50.

139. Navarro, "La Cruz y la Espada. ¿Estamos por fin al principio de una nueva era Cinefónica," 3, 8 (segunda sección) and "La Película 'La Cruz

y la Espada' en Español, ha sido un Gran Exito [*sic.*]," December 10, 1933, 7 (segunda sección).

140. *La cruz y la espada*, Advertisement, *Filmográfico*, April 1934, back cover. The same still was used in its Argentine publicity. "'La cruz y la espada,'" *Imparcial Film*, March 5, 1934, 2. Notably, the next issue of *Filmográfico* does not use the still, but rather an image of a large cross and a sword. *La cruz y la espada*, Advertisement, *Filmográfico*, May 1934, back cover.

141. Correspondence from Irwin Esmond to Gentlemen (Attention: Miss Hettie Gray Baker), September 6, 1934, Casefile Number 27426, Box 298, New York State Motion Picture Division License Application Case Files, New York State Archives, Albany, New York, United States. It was ordered to be removed by New York's Motion Picture Division for being "Inhuman" and "Will Tend to Incite Crime."

142. "El hábito no hace al monje . . . ," *Cinelandia*, February 1934, 48.

143. Much like Carlos Gardel, Mojica always overshadowed the B movie directors with whom he had to work. He lamented to *Cinearte* in 1941 that "I never realized my biggest wish in the cinema, which was to sing old melodies in a big production with a symphony orchestra directed by Lubitsch or Korda." He notes that his greatest artistic achievement was singing *Pelléas et Mélisande* alongside Mary Garden at the Chicago Opera. "José Mojica," August 15, 17.

144. Eduardo Guaitsel, "Hollywood al día," *Hispano-América*, May 9, 1931, 3–4.

145. "Mojica," *Cinelandia*, November 1932, 47.

146. Ralph Will, "Hollywood Speaking," *Film Daily*, July 9, 1940, 7.

147. Mojica's definitive entrance into the Franciscan Order has often been connected to the death of his mother. In an April 1943 interview with the right-wing film periodical *Primer plano*, for example, Spanish actor Miguel Ligero recounts, "And all of his hopes came down to love for his mother. That is why I was not surprised that when she died he went into a monastery." Qtd. in Álvaro Armero, *Una aventura americana: españoles en Hollywood* (Madrid: Compañía Literaria, 1995), 204.

Chapter 4

1. "De sobre mesa," *Filmográfico*, April 1932, 3.

2. In Mexican film historiography, foreigners play a similar role: they are present throughout, but infrequently are they given the spotlight.

3. What follows draws from contemporaneous film periodicals as well as later film historiography. Emilio García Riera's shadow looms large here, as well as in other texts that informed this brief history.

4. Emilio García Riera, *Breve historia del cine mexicano* (Zapopan, Jalisco: Ediciones Mapa, 1998), 79–80.

5. Emilio García Riera, *Historia documental del cine mexicano*, Vol. 1 (Guadalajara: Universidad de Guadalajara, 1993), 163.

6. At the time of its founding, the Unión de Directores Cinematográficos de México had twenty-six members (with provisional leadership): Rolando Aguilar, Carlos Amador, Adolfo Best Maugard, José Bohr, Arcady Boytler, Juan Bustillo Oro (*primer vocal*), Guillermo Calles, Miguel Contreras Torres, Robert Curwood, Fernando de Fuentes (president), Boris Maicon, Roberto Montenegro, Carlos de Nájera, Carlos Navarro, Rubén C. Navarro, Manuel R. Ojeda, Juan Orol, Ramón Peón, Alex Phillips, Rafael E. Portas, Gustavo Sáenz de Sicilia, Manuel Sánchez Valtierra, Raphael J. Sevilla, Gabriel Soria (secretary), Chano Urueta, Miguel Zacarías. García Riera, *Fernando de Fuentes (1894/1958): trabajo colectivo* (México: Cineteca Nacional, 1984), 42. Seven of them were foreigners.

7. Perhaps due to Carlos Monsiváis's essay "Mexican Cinema: Of Myths and Demystifications," this is particularly true in film historiography written in English. In *Mediating Two Worlds: Cinematic Encounters in the Americas*, ed. John King, Ana M López, and Manuel Alvarado (London: British Film Institute, 1993), 139–46, Monsiváis marks 1955 as the end of the Golden Age, while many others use Pedro Infante's death in an airplane accident in 1957 as its conclusion.

8. Francisco Peredo Castro, *Alejandro Galindo, un alma rebelde en el cine mexicano* (Mexico City: Editorial Miguel Ángel Porrúa, 2000), 38. Galindo has credits as an actor, director, producer, and screenwriter.

9. Dada and Quigley began their careers in Mexico by writing and, eventually, they came to direct.

10. Other foreign actors who made appearances in Mexican films of the period include Blanquita Amaro, Salvador Aponte, Miguel Arenas, Elisa Asperó, Anita Blanch, Isabel(ita) Blanch, Antonio Bravo Sánchez, Enrique Herrera Rodríguez, Carlos Martínez Baena, Barry Norton, Matilde Palou, Ramón Pereda, and Vilma Vidal.

11. García Riera, *Historia documental del cine mexicano*, Vol. 1, 253.

12. Esperanza López, "El cine: sus problemas y sus posibilidades," *Cine*, November 6, 1938, 50.

13. Roberto Cantú Robert, "Puntos de vista," *Cinema Reporter*, July 22, 1938, 1.

14. Roberto Cantú Robert, "Año de oro del cine mexicano," *Directorio cinematográfico de Cinema Reporter*, 1940, 62.

15. Roberto Cantú Robert, "Palabras del editor," *Directorio cinematográfico de Cinema Reporter*, 1940, 7

16. Alfonso Pulido Islas, *La industria cinematográfica de México* (Mexico City: Editorial México Nuevo, 1939), 94.

17. These projects might reveal the presence of new tensions: no longer challenged at the box office by Hollywood's Spanish-language films, the Mexican film industry began to worry about imports from Argentina.

18. Other actors to appear included Luis Alcoriza, Luis Aldás, Miguel Arenas, Rafael Banquells, José Baviera Navarro, Carmelita Bohr, Antonio Bravo, María Calvo, Fernando Cortés, Ángel Garasa, Prudencia Grifell, Eugenia Galindo, Marcus Goodrich, Irving Lee, Mary López, José Mora (Pal), Margarita Mora, Mercedes Soler, Alfonso Torres, and Estela Zarco.

19. Until this point, del Diestro had acted. Notably, Michelena and Rowland worked on films made by foreign production companies, CIFESA (Compañía Industrial de Film Español, S.A.) and RKO, respectively.

20. Emilio García Riera, *Breve historia del cine mexicano* (Zapopan: Ediciones Mapa, 1998), 79–80.

21. These three companies included influential producers such as Gregorio Wallerstein and Sam (Simón) Wishñack (Filmex), Agustín J. Fink (Films Mundiales), and Russian-born Jacques Gelman and Santiago Reachi (Posa Films).

22. Carl J Mora, *Mexican Cinema: Reflections of a Society, 1896–1980* (Berkeley: University of California Press, 1982), 59. Mora notes that the nine companies were Grovas, S.A., Films Mundiales, América Films, Ixtla Films, CLASA, Juan Bustillo Oro, Cinematografía Miguel Zacarías, Vicente S. Piques, and Producciones Fernando de Fuentes. Some twenty-one companies did not receive credit from the Banco Cinematográfico.

23. For more on the repercussions of Mexico's joining the Allies in World War II after two Mexican oil tankers were attacked by the Germans, see Seth Fein's work, including, but not limited to: "Myths of Cultural Imperialism and Nationalism in Golden Age Mexican Cinema," in *Fragments of a Golden Age: The Politics of Culture in Mexico, 1940–2000*, ed. Gilbert Joseph, Anne Rubenstein, and Eric Zolov (Durham: Duke University Press, 2001), 159–98 and "Transnationalization and Cultural Collaboration: 'Mexican' Cinema and the Second World War," *Studies in Latin American Popular Culture* 17 (1998): 105–28.

24. Also debuting between 1941 and 1943 were foreign actors Ricardo Adalid, Augusto Bendicio, Alejandro Ciangherotti, Luis Coto, Andrés Falgás, Pituka de Foronda, Consuelo Guerrero de Luna, Francisco Llopis, Gloria Lynch, Bill Miller, Consuelo Monteagudo, Gustavo Rojo, Pilar Sen, Ángel di Stefani, and Jesús Valero.

25. Wallace, a Peruvian, had actually been working in Mexico since 1934. I am uncertain of their relationship, but the Peruvian Noemí Wallace also worked as a make-up artist in the Mexican film industry.

26. Not without its own twists and turns, *Filmográfico/Cinema Reporter*'s success recalls a cry from its first editorial: "United with *la Empresa cinematográfica* (the film Enterprise), we will fight for the improvement and intensification of the celluloid industry, for the coming together of all those who have contributed

their force to the stabilization of the National Industry." "De sobre mesa," *Filmográfico*, April 1932, 3. It was published, for example, as a section of the magazine *Continental* from mid-1936 to mid-1937. First promised in an editorial published in the April-May 1937 issue of *Filmográfico*, the self-styled *Hollywood Reporter* of Mexico would not appear until July 22, 1938. "Cinco años," n.p. Film journalism, too, had also become industrialized. *Cinema Reporter* was a much more robust enterprise, publishing both weekly and monthly issues in 1942.

Chapter 5

1. "Nuestros técnicos y el porvenir de la cinematografía mexicana," *Revista de Revistas*, October 8 1933, 24–25. Quote appears on page 24.

2. Patrick Keating, *Hollywood Lighting from the Silent Era to Film Noir* (New York: Columbia University Press, 2010); Keating, ed., *Cinematography* (New Brunswick: Rutgers University Press, 2014); and *The Dynamic Frame: Camera Movement in Classical Hollywood* (New York: Columbia University Press, 2019). Perhaps it would have been possible to reach a deeper understanding of Phillips's craft had the manuscript he was working on before his death, *Manual de fotografías y alumbrado* (*Manual of Photographies and Lighting*), not been lost to oblivion. Phillips might have left a legacy like John Alton's *Painting with Light* (New York: Macmillan, 1949). Or perhaps not.

3. Christopher Beach, *A Hidden History of Film Style: Cinematographers, Directors, and the Collaborative Process* (Berkeley: University of California Press, 2015), 5.

4. Ibid., 1.

5. María Alba Fulguiera, "Alex Phillips," in *Testimonios para la historia del cine mexicano Vol. 1*, ed. Eugenia Meyer (México, D.F.: Cineteca Nacional; Instituto Nacional de Antropología e Historia, 1975), 21–29.

6. Numerous later documents in his personnel records indicate that Pelepiuk lied in his attestation form. He seems to have been born in 1900.

7. Built a mere four years earlier, S.S. *Missanabie* was torpedoed by German submarine U87 on September 9, 1918. Forty-five people lost their lives.

8. In "Medical History of an Invalid," taken April 17, 1919, his next of kin is listed as "Mrs. Kathleen Pelepink. 700 1st Ave West, Long Beach, California." Her relationship is listed as "Stepmother." In "Particulars of Family of an Officer or Man Enlisted in C.E.F.," dated March 1, 1916, Alex answers that both of his parents—"Nicholas" and "Catherine"—are alive and living in Russia.

9. Claudia Negrete Álvarez, "Historias narradas con luz. Tres décadas de labor cinematográfica de Alex Phillips," PhD diss., Universidad Nacional de México, 2009, 98.

10. Fulguiera, 21.

11. *La magia entre la luz y la sombra*, dir. Ernesto Medina, 1998.

12. Fulguiera, p. 22.

13. *La magia entre la luz y la sombra.*

14. In the interview with Fulguiera, Phillips claims it was on the set of *La isla del diablo* (*Hell's Island*, dir. Edward Sloman, 1930), but it seems more likely that Phillips is referring to *The Devil to Pay* (dir. George Fitzmaurice, 1931).

15. Fulguiera, 22. Also, *La magia entre la luz y la sombra.*

16. Fulguiera, 23.

17. "Un gran fotógrafo llegó ayer a México," *El Universal*, November 8, 1931, segunda sección, 1.

18. It seems unlikely that Phillips worked on all of Swanson's films, but he almost certainly helped shoot *The Trespasser* (dir. Edmund Goulding, 1929). He remained on the periphery of Hollywood, unable to obtain a position, such as the one at Paramount, or much visibility from a publication like *Film Daily*. Like so many film workers, he was left to work in obscurity.

19. "Motion Picture Production in South America," *International Photographer*, May 1934, 27. Alton asserts that "[t]he gorgeous countryside lends itself wonderfully to background of even a Hollywood made picture. Some of these days some smart producer will realize the gold mine that no camera has touched as yet."

20. Esteban V. Escalante, "Arcady Boytler, un director de fuste," *Revista de Revistas*, November 19, 1933, 28–29.

21. Ibid., 28.

22. Ibid.

23. Ibid., 29.

24. Ibid.

25. Phillips also helmed Boytler's shorts *Un espectador impertinente* (An Impertinent Spectator, 1932), *Joyas de México* (Gems of Mexico, 1933), and *Revista musical* (Musical Review, 1934).

26. That said, it is clear from contemporaneous film periodicals that Boytler intentionally cultivated an image that connected him to Eisenstein.

27. Negrete, 111–12.

28. In *Hollywood Lighting from the Silent Era to Film Noir*, Keating argues "The right-mood-for-the-story theory encourages cinematographers to vary the lighting to suit the changing moods of the story" (160). Keating discusses how this adage became a theory that would come to frame how cinematographers practice their craft in specific historical contexts.

29. "Mano a mano," Advertisement, December 11, 1932, 6 (first section). "Los grandes programas que presentan hoy los cines del primer circuito," *Excélsior*, December 11, 1932, 8 (first section). An earlier advertisement also notes the film was to appear at the Alcazar, Majestic, Mundial, and Parisiana theaters. "Mano a mano," Advertisement, *El Universal*, December 8, 1932, 8 (first section). Among

others, Amador and Ayala Blanca claim the film premiered at the Cine Palacio on December 10, 1932. *Cartelera cinematográfica, 1930–1939* (Mexico City: Filmoteca UNAM, 1980), 73. Numerous film histories claim *Mano a mano*'s production company as Producciones Alcayde; however, contemporaneous reporting and the film's credits list it as México Nuevo Studio. Compañía Nacional Productora de Películas' studios burned down in 1933 during the filming of *El pulpo humano* (*The Human Octopus*, dir. Jorge Bell, 1933). García Riera *Historia documental del cine mexicano*. Vol. 1 (Guadalajara: Universidad de Guadalajara, 1993), 76.

30. "Nueva Producción Nacional MANO A MANO," *Filmográfico*, October 5, 1932, 18.

31. "'Mano a Mano' . . . hemos quedado," *Filmográfico*, November 5, 1932, 26.

32. "Hoy el 'Monumental Cinema' repite su enorme triunfo 'Mano a mano,' *Excélsior*, December 12, 1932, 7 (first section).

33. "Cine Goya" (Mexico City: Cine Goya, February 16, 1933), n.p. Including the film *Diablos de mar* (*Sea Devils*, dir. Joseph Levering, 1931) and a lecture by Boytler entitled "El Cinema Vanguardista" ("Avant-Garde Cinema"), the program for *Mano a mano*'s rerelease is held by the Centro de Documentación of the Cineteca Nacional in Mexico City. Boytler's lecture, which seems much more a performance, is described in the program as "Something that will excite and intrigue everyone who sees it. Intangible figures of the screen, materializing and descending from the canvas makes the audience and, after being among it, returns to the screen to become animated silhouettes once again."

34. Plot summaries of Mexican films are, perhaps inescapably, influenced by various volumes of Emilio García Riera's *Historia documental del cine mexicano* and David E. Wilt's *The Mexican Filmography, 1916 through 2001* (Jefferson and London: McFarland, 2004).

35. A recording on "Discos Peerless" of the title song, appearing with the *bambuco* "Pálida princesa," was sold. This is merely one example of an often employed cross-promotional marketing strategy that began in the early sound period and continues to today. A. Wagner y Levien, Advertisement, *Filmográfico*, December 5, 1932, 19.

36. Patrick Keating, "The Volcano and the Barren Hill: Gabriel Figueroa and the Space of Art Cinema," in *Global Art Cinema: New Theories and Histories*, ed. Rosalind Galt and Karl Schoonover (Oxford and New York: Oxford University Press, 2010), 202.

37. *El Exhibidor*, October 1932, qtd. in Eduardo de la Vega, *Arcady Boytler* (Guadalajara: Universidad de Guadalajara, 1992), 38.

38. Denegri (Roberto Cantú Robert), "Arcady Boytler Realizador de 'La mujer del puerto,'" *Filmográfico*, December 1933, 14.

39. More specifically, it was produced by Warner Bros.' Mexico City office. Now presumed lost, it was also shot by Alex Phillips.

40. "Una película mexicana que sienta escuela," *Filmográfico*, February 1934, 7.

41. Carlos de Nájera, "Nueva estrella en el cielo fílmico nacional," *Filmográfico*, December 1933, 6; "Una película mexicana que sienta escuela," *Filmográfico*, February 1934, 7. The so-called Soler dynasty—Fernando, Andrés, Domingo, Julián, and Mercedes—were children of actors Domingo Díaz García and Irene Pavia Soler, Spanish actors who migrated to Mexico.

42. "'La Mujer del Puerto' es una excelente película mexicana," *Mundo cinematográfico*, February 1934, 10.

43. "'La mujer del puerto despierta entusiasmo," *El Universal*, February 13, 1934, 1.

44. "Películas nacionales por A.F.B.," 4.

45. Esteban V. Escalante, "Del cine nacional," *Filmográfico*, January 1935, 40.

46. "Reporteando," *Cinema Reporter*, August 14, 1942, 2.

47. Agustín Jiménez had spent time working with Phillips, among others.

48. Esteban V. Escalante, "Del cine nacional," *Filmográfico*, January 1935, 40.

49. Antonio Acevedo V., "La mujer del puerto," *Filmográfico*, March 1934, 13.

50. Eduardo de la Vega, *Arcady Boytler*, 108.

51. Eugenia Meyer, "Andrea Palma," in *Testimonios para la historia del cine mexicano Vol. I*, ed. Meyer (México, D.F.: Cineteca Nacional; Instituto Nacional de Antropología e Historia, 1975), 45–62.

52. Arcady Boytler contract with Eurindia Films, undated, Casefile Number A-00252, Cineteca Nacional de México Centro de Documentación, Mexico City, Mexico.

53. In the piece, Boytler quickly touches upon edits to tighten *La mujer del Puerto* and preparation for a new film with Eurindia (which would never get made) before directing his attention to the issue of collaboration. "Boytler el gran realizador," *Filmográfico*, March 1934, 26.

54. Santini Publicista (Miguel Santini Ávila), *La primera guía cinematográfica mexicana para el año de 1934* (Mexico City: Cía. "La Mexicana" Elaboradora de Películas, 1934), 6, 8.

55. Coincidentally, *El tesoro de Pancho Villa* was reviewed in the same issue of *Mundo cinematográfico* as *El primo Basilio*. "Porcentaje taquillero de las siguientes películas," *Mundo cinematográfico*, July 1935, 16. According to the note, the films ran more or less concurrently (*El tesoro de Pancho Villa* from July 4–12 in Cine Principal and *El primo Basilio* from July 3–10 in the Cine Balmori). In the same issue, *El tesoro de Pancho Villa* was deemed as 60 percent in its *porcentaje taquillero* (compared to *El Primo Basilio*'s 55 percent). Meanwhile, the French film *El jorobado* (*Le bossu*, dir. René Sti, 1933) and the Hollywood film *Contra el imperio del crimen* (*G Men*, dir. William Keighley, 1935) got 95 percent and 90 percent respectively. Both films were played with subtitles in Spanish.

56. Best known for his work with Cecil B. DeMille, Wyckoff was most active in the silent period. Keating discusses their collaborations in *Hollywood*

Lighting: From the Silent Era to Film Noir, 84–88. He shot two films in Mexico: *El primo Basilio* and *María Elena* (dir. Raphael J. Sevilla, 1936).

57. "Cuentos animados del cine nacional," *Jueves del Excélsior*, October 18, 1934, 10.

58. "Cerca de nuestras estrellas," *Filmográfico*, April 1935, 10. It is claimed that the director, cinematographer, and production manager will take on more risk in the agreement, but also work under better conditions and receive better guarantees. Mier, of course, would eventually become one of the most important producers in the Mexican film industry in the classical period.

59. According to *Revista de Revistas*, filming on *El tesoro de Pancho Villa* was to begin on May 15. Hugo del Mar (Esteban V. Escalante), *Revista de Revistas*, May 12, 1935. Quoted in de la Vega, *Arcady Boytler* (Guadalajara: Universidad de Guadalajara, 1992), 72.

60. In several reviews contemporaneous to the film's premiere, *El tesoro de Pancho Villa* is deemed to be a Western (using the English term) and is compared with the Hollywood genre. One states, "The best *western* produced until now by national cinema." Expediente hemerográfico de El tesoro de Pancho Villa, A-03303, Centro de documentación e información, Cineteca Nacional de México.

61. De la Vega writes, "*Cronistas* and commentators from almost all of the capital papers heaped praise on Boytler's new film." *Arcady Boytler*, 73. Despite this, the film appears to have only run for a week in Mexico City. María Luisa Amador and Jorge Ayala Blanco, *Cartelera cinematográfica, 1930–1939* (Mexico City: Filmoteca UNAM, 1980), 140. Quite curiously, this odd advertisement for a metal detector appeared in mid-1939: "Pancho Villa's treasure (El tesoro de Pancho Villa). There are many great treasures lost by the sudden death of their owners. Explore the earth with the Fisher metal detector (*el metaloscopio Fisher*), formidable machine for underground exploration, locate hidden treasures, veins of gold, mineral streaks, and buried riches." Compañía Panamericana Metaloscopio Fisher advertisement, *Jueves de Excélsior*, April 20, 1939, 16.

62. *Revista de Revistas*, July 7, 1935. Quoted in de la Vega, *Arcady Boytler*, 72. Del Mar also notes that it is the Miers' first production.

63. Interestingly, Boytler's direction is criticized, largely due to a parallel draw with *Mano a mano*. "De cine en cine," Expediente hemerográfico de El tesoro de Pancho Villa, A-03303, Centro de documentación e información, Cineteca Nacional de México.

64. Here, I use *expressive* not to refer to German expressionism but rather a melodramatic style prevalent at the time. For lengthier discussions, see Keating's *Hollywood Lighting from the Silent Era to Film Noir*.

65. Victor Milner, "Creating Moods with Light," *American Cinematographer*, January 1935, 7. Keating examines the essay in *Hollywood Lighting: From the Silent Era to Film Noir*, 124.

66. It is for this reason that de la Vega sees *Celos* as a precursor to Buñuel's *Él* (1952), which was shot by Gabriel Figueroa (110).

67. Negrete, 126. De la Vega, 109–10.

68. "Cuentos animados del cine nacional," *Jueves del Excélsior*, October 18, 1934, 10. In a later note published in *Jueves del Excélsior*, Luis de Garmendia reports that Felipe Mier would produce *Celos*, on whose production plan he was already working. "México cinema," November 14 1935, 28.

69. "Boytler, el artista de alma poliforme," *Filmográfico*, July 1935, 13.

70. De la Vega discusses Boytler's desire, using Escalante's interview with the director. It is claimed that it appears in *Filmográfico*, but it seems more likely to have been published in *Revista de Revistas*. De la Vega, *Arcady Boytler*, 75–76.

71. *La mujer del puerto*, *El tesoro de Pancho Villa*, *¡Así es mi tierra!*, *Águila o sol*, and *El capitán aventurero* were all shot at México-Films, Jorge Stahl's studios.

72. Quoted in de la Vega, *Arcady Boytler*, 86. Described as "a week later," the issue of *Revista de Revistas* to which de la Vega refers is almost certainly February 2, 1936.

73. De la Vega, *Arcady Boytler*, 121.

74. "Felipe Mier ofreció una comida," *Cinema Reporter*, August 12 1938, 2.

75. "Reporteando," *Cinema Reporter*, October 7 1938, 7. "Reporteando," *Cinema Reporter*, November 25 1938, 25. García Riera incorrectly dates filming from October 7 to November 5, 1938, an error frequently repeated in Mexican film historiography. *Historia documental del cine mexicano*. Vol. 2 (Guadalajara: Universidad de Guadalajara, 1993), 215. Several reports were published regarding the film's production costs. "Reporteando," *Cinema Reporter*, October 21 1938, 2. "Reporteando," *Cinema Reporter*, November 25 1938, 25. Based loosely on Émile Zola's *Pot-Bouille* (serialized in 1882 and published as book in 1883), *La casa del ogro* was directed by Fernando de Fuentes and helmed by Gabriel Figueroa.

76. *Cine* rated the film as a *caballo* (horse), signifying "excellent." "Sinopsis fílmico del mes," *Cine*, March 1953, 53.

77. Capitalization is original to the quote. Manuel Horta, "Tropiezos y aciertos del séptimo arte," *Cinema Reporter*, February 24, 1939, 1. Horta praises the acting but notes, "There is only one but, the slow progress of some scenes that would be borne in the theater, but are out of tune in cinematic technique. Adaptation and direction of Salvador Novo and Arcady Boytler deserve warm applause."

78. In one piece, Manuel Horta argues, "Praise has rained for 'El Capitán Aventurero.' That Mojica sings songs in a sublime way, that the script is very ingenious, that the panoramas enrapture, and that the actors shine. But something very transcendental has remained in the shadows: the direction of the period of which the great painter Montenegro was in charge. And we, to justify ourselves, send warm applause to the artist." "Tropiezos y aciertos del séptimo arte," *Cinema Reporter*, March 3 1939, 1.

79. De la Vega, 121.

80. Negrete, 131.

81. De la Vega, 99.

82. Qtd. in ibid.

83. Luis Orozco Jr., "¿Qué opina Ud. de la cinematografía nacional y *Filmográfico*?, *Filmográfico*, September 1933, 21.

84. "Nuestros técnicos y el porvenir de la cinematografía mexicana," *Revista de Revistas*, October 15 1933, 44–46.

85. Ibid., 44.

86. Ibid. Similar stories are told of Argentine director Luis Moglia Barth, who edited U.S. companies' films for local tastes. Subtitles would play a role in *Allá en el Rancho Grande*'s eventual success. "In his distribution contract with United Artists, Fernando de Fuentes retained rights to *Allá en el Rancho Grande* for distribution in the United States. An indication of the film's broad appeal was de Fuentes's decision to add English subtitles, a first for a Mexican film." Desirée J. García, *The Migration of Musical Film: From Ethnic Margins to American Mainstream* (New Brunswick: Rutgers University Press, 2014), 82. García cites "Most U.S. Companies Setting Plans for Features for Latin Countries," *Motion Picture Herald*, January 7, 1939, 14.

87. Ibid.

88. "Producciones 'Fesa' ha iniciado sus actividades . . . ," *Filmográfico*, September 1933, 16. "Pajaritas de nuestro cine," *Filmográfico*, Noviembre 1933, 38. In this note, Phillips's late-October marriage to Alicia Bolaños is reported.

89. Esteban V. Escalante, "Una orientación mexicanista en nuestra cinematografía," *Revista de Revistas*, November 5, 1933, 24–25.

90. "Vox Populi," *Filmográfico*, Noviembre 1933, 42.

91. Luz Alba in *Ilustrado* (November 30, 1933), as quoted in Emilio García Riera, *Fernando de Fuentes (1894/1958): trabajo colectivo*, 101.

92. Negrete, 150–55.

93. Ibid., 151.

94. For more on glamour and lighting strategies in the 1920s and 1930s, see Keating's *Hollywood Lighting from the Silent Era to Film Noir*, 50–52, 132–33.

95. Although it wrapped first, *El tigre de Yautepec*'s production schedule overlapped with that of *Enemigos*. It is not entirely clear if Phillips worked on both at the same time or, more likely, if his filming on *El tigre de Yautepec* ended before beginning *Enemigos*.

96. Esteban V. Escalante, "Migajas del Cine Nacional," *Filmográfico*, August 1934, 36. The note explains that Paul H. Bush will soon decide which script will be Impulsora Cinematográfica's first film. It was likely to be *Cruz Diablo*.

97. Esteban V. Escalante and Roberto Cantú Robert, "Migajas," *Filmográfico*, September 1934, 34; Esteban V. Escalante, "Migajas del Cine," *Filmográfico*, October 1934, 20–21. It states, "Sets constructed under the direction and design of Fernando A. Rivero are wonderful, as is the luxurious wardrobe, the photography of Alex Phillips, and the sound of the eighty thousand Rodríguez brothers,

not one more, not one less." Later in the column, it is written that "José Bohr is just waiting on Alex Phillips to become available after 'Cruz Diablo' in order to directly proceed to the filming of a drama that will be entitled 'Tu hijo.'" It would, in fact, be the cinematographer's next film. Roberto Cantú Robert, "Cuentos animados del cine," *Jueves del Excélsior*, November 11, 1934, 11. Report after a screening of "a great deal" of *Cruz Diablo.*

98. Roberto Cantú Robert, "Cuentos animados del cine," *Jueves del Excélsior*, October 25, 1934, 10. Paramount's representatives included Katherine De Mille, Francis Drake, Mary Boland, and Luigi Luraschi, "production chief at Paramount's studios."

99. "El Conde de Luna caracterizado por Ramón Pereda en 'Cruz Diablo,'" *El Universal*, November 20, 1934; "Un capitán de las tropas del virrey en el film 'Cruz Diablo," *El Universal*, November 21, 1934; "Un capitán de bandoleros en la película 'Cruz Diablo,'" *El Universal*, November 22, 1934; "Toparca, otro bandolero a quien se suponía que fuese Cruz Diablo," *El Universal*, November 23, 1934; "Lupita Gallardo, hija del Conde de Luna en la cinta 'Cruz Diablo,'" *El Universal*, November 26, 1934. These pieces are included in the film's folder in the Centro de Documentación at the Cineteca Nacional in Mexico City. These images almost certainly belong to Gabriel Figueroa, as he is credited by *Filmográfico* as photographer in the same images taken in shoots with Gallardo and Ramón Pereda. In one instance, it is the very same photo. Film Exchange, the distribution company, ran a prerelease contest "to see if anyone could correctly guess the identity of 'Cruz Diablo' before the film premiered." (This was reported upon earlier in *El Universal*—"'Cruz Diablo' se estrena mañana," November 27, 1934). Ten people did so successfully, and two hundred and fifty pesos were distributed among them.

100. Alfonso de Icaza in *El Redondel* (December 2, 1934), as quoted in Emilio García Riera, *Fernando de Fuentes (1894/1958): trabajo colectivo* (México: Cineteca Nacional, 1984), 116.

101. Bertha Elena Castañeda, "Tercer Premio. 'Cruz Diablo,'" *El Universal*, December 9, 1934.

102. "'Cruz Diablo' seguirá en programa dos días," *El Universal*, December 4, 1934. Farkas's *La bataille* is a remake of Édouard-Émile Violet and Sessue Hayakawa's 1923 silent feature. Charles Boyer and Annabella appear in race drag, as neither Hayakawa nor his wife Tsuru Aoki were cast to reprise their roles.

103. Fernando Rondón in *Ilustrado* (December 6, 1934, as quoted in Emilio García Riera, *Fernando de Fuentes (1894/1958)*, 117. Rondón also notes its resemblance to the Douglas Fairbanks vehicles *El pirata negro* (*The Black Pirate*, dir. Albert Parker, 1926) and *Don Q* (*Don Q, Son of Zorro*, dir. Donald Crisp, 1925).

104. Esteban V. Escalante, "Del cine nacional," *Filmográfico*, January 1935, 38.

105. Rondón, 117. Emilio García Riera, *Historia documental del cine mexicano*, Vol. 1 (Mexico City: Ediciones Era, 1969), 79.

106. Fidel Solís, "La pantalla y sus artistas," *El Universal*, November 24, 1934.

107. Solís fails to mention another potential element: the sequel. In early 1935, the project *El hijo de Cruz Diablo* (*Cruz Diablo's Son*) was in development. It would not be produced until 1941. Vicente Oroná, who played Chacho in the original film, directed. In 1954, he also later directed another sequel, *La sombra de Cruz Diablo* (The Shadow of Cruz Diablo).

108. In addition to these genres, de Fuentes shot two contemporary melodramas—*El anónimo* (The Anonymous Letter, 1933), a lost film about which relatively little is known, and *La calandria* (*The Bunting*, 1934)—and the fantasy film *El fantasma del convento*.

109. Miguel de Zárraga, "Hollywood por radio," *Filmográfico*, October 1935, 29. An earlier piece reports Impulsora Cinematográfica's increased activities, noting that it was also producing English- and Spanish-language versions of *María Elena*, directed by Raphael J. Sevilla. "Cerca de nuestras estrellas," *Filmográfico*, May 1935, 8. The English-language version, *She-Devil Island*, was released by First Division in 1936. Wilt, *The Mexican Filmography, 1916 through 2001*, 27.

110. "Cerca de nuestras estrellas," *Filmográfico*, July 1935, 7.

111. "Actividades del cine nacional," *Mundo cinematográfico*, July–August 1935, 6.

112. Martinelli was a highly experienced cameraman whose career began in the mid-1910s with Rolfe Photoplays, a production company that filmed in New Jersey and New York, before he worked in Hollywood and, later, Europe. In the 1930s, he shot many minor films, including *White Zombie* (dir. Victor Halperin, 1932), the first zombie movie, as well as multilinguals such as *Sombras de gloria* (vers. *Blaze O' Glory*, dirs. Andrew L. Stone and Fernando C. Tamayo, 1930) and original *films hispanos* such as *Mis dos amores* (My Two Loves, dir. Nick Grinde, 1938), and *Verbena trágica* (Tragic Festival, dir. Charles Lamont, 1939) and the final Spanish-language film shot in the 1930s in Hollywood, *La inmaculada* (*The Immaculate One*, dir. Louis J. Gasnier, 1939). Martinelli shot three films in Mexico with Contreras Torres: *Juárez y Maximiliano, No matarás* (*Thou Shalt Not Kill*, 1935), and *La emperatriz loca* (The Mad Empress, 1939). Gómez Urquiza would have to wait until the 1950s to become a Director of Photography. He was a minor cinematographer, active in the 1950s–1970s. In *Águilas de América* (Eagles of America, dir. Manuel R. Ojeda, 1933), Phillips is credited with Julio Lamadrid, one of the *vieja guardia* who never broke into the sound film industry. Lamadrid, following the model of Salvador Toscano, shot documentaries for Pathé (García Riera, 51). Jorge del Moral shot songs on *Chucho el roto*.

113. Alfonso Patiño Gómez's piece in *Anuario 1938 de El Cine Gráfico*, as quoted in Emilio García Riera's *Fernando de Fuentes: trabajo colectivo* (México: Cineteca Nacional, 1984), 132.

114. Linder, "Películas del mes," *Filmográfico*, September 1935, 23. Roberto Cantú Robert, "La producción mexicana en 1935," *Filmográfico*, January 1936, 36.

115. This language mirrors a similar assessment Cantú Robert made earlier in "Cerca de nuestras estrellas," *Filmográfico*, August 1935, 7. I would like to thank Rafael Acosta and Ana M. López for assistance on this translation.

116. Luz Alba in *Ilustrado* (August 8, 1935), as quoted in García Riera, *Fernando de Fuentes (1894/1958): trabajo colectivo*, 131. Alba continues, somewhat strangely, "Our cinema is characterized, almost always, by a lack of masculinity [*varonilidad*]. It is a feminine cinema." One is left to wonder how much Phillips might have done to perpetuate this kind of cinema.

117. C. L. Ellis, "English Section," *Mundo cinematográfico*, July-August 1935, 12.

118. In *Excélsior* (August 2, 1935), as quoted in García Riera, *Fernando de Fuentes (1894/1958): trabajo colectivo*, 131. Roberto Cantú Robert, "La producción mexicana en 1935," *Filmográfico*, January 1936, 36.

119. Alfonso de Icaza in *El Redondel* (August 4, 1935), as quoted in García Riera, *Fernando de Fuentes (1894/1958): trabajo colectivo*, 131.

120. Negrete, 183.

121. Jorge Guerrero Suárez affirms that *La Zandunga* is not entirely de Fuentes's, as the director was forced to withdraw from production due to illness. Miguel M. Delgado, the assistant director on the film, finished the film. *Cuaderno de la Cineteca Nacional* n. 8 (1978), 23.

122. Somewhat tellingly, García Riera mistakenly attributes *La Zandunga*'s cinematography to Ross Fisher. Fisher worked with de Fuentes more regularly, but García Riera's error suggests a kind of sense of interchangeability regarding these cameramen from the north. *Historia documental del cine mexicano*. Vol. 1 (Guadalajara: Universidad de Guadalajara, 1993), 300.

123. Roberto Cantú Robert, "Cómo viven las artistas mexicanas en Hollywood," *Filmográfico*, April-May, 1937, 10–16, 112.

124. S. L. de Ortigosa Jr., in "Cinerías" in *La afición* (March 22, 1938), as quoted in García Riera, *Fernando de Fuentes (1894/1958): trabajo colectivo*, 145.

125. Curiously enough, *La Zandunga* was one of the films distributed by La Distribuidora Hispano-Mexicana to private exhibitors in Buenos Aires. "Películas mexicanas en privado," *Cinema Reporter*, July 23, 1939, 7.

126. "A" en *El Universal* (March 28, 1938), as quoted in García Riera, *Fernando de Fuentes (1894/1958): trabajo colectivo*, 145–46.

127. Ramón Navarro's first and only credit in Mexico was Julio Bracho's 1942 *La virgen que forjó una patria* (*Virgin that Forged a Country*). After her first appearance in Emilio Fernández's 1943 *Flor silvestre*, Dolores del Río was one the most important stars of the *época de oro*.

128. *Jarocho* refers to someone from Guadalajara, while *tehuano* refers to someone from the isthmus.

129. Luz Alba in *Ilustrado* (March 31, 1938), as quoted in García Riera, *Fernando de Fuentes (1894/1958): trabajo colectivo*, 146.

130. Mónica García Blizzard, ""Lupe Vélez's 'Whiteness' in Mexico: *La Zandunga* (1937)," Paper presented at SCMS 2019, Seattle, March 13–17, 2019.

131. Xavier Villaurrutia in *Hoy* (April 2 and 16, 1938), as quoted in García Riera, *Fernando de Fuentes (1894/1958): trabajo colectivo*, 146.

132. Luz Alba in *Ilustrado* (March 31, 1938), as quoted in García Riera, *Fernando de Fuentes (1894/1958): trabajo colectivo*, 146.

133. Some context: in this period, Phillips worked on more than twenty films and de Fuentes directed seven.

134. Arising out Maricruz Castro Ricalde and Robert McKee Irwin's collaborations, two excellent works explore the film's transnational horizons. "*Doña Bárbara* (1943): La mexicanización de la cultura venezolana," in *El cine mexicano "se impone." Mercados internacionales y penetración cultural en la época dorada* (Mexico City: Universidad Nacional de México, 2011), 69–87. Irwin, "Mexico's Appropriation of the Latin American Visual Imaginary: Rómulo Gallegos in Mexico," in *Global Mexican Cinema. Its Golden Age*, ed. Castro Ricalde and Irwin (London: Palgrave; British Film Institute, 2013), 89–105. Quote is from ibid., 93.

135. *La trepadora* was almost certainly an adaptation of Rómulo Gallegos's 1925 novel, which was originally to star Blanca de Castejón. It was later developed by CLASA (Cinematografía Latino Americanas, S.A.) and directed by Gilberto Martínez Solares in 1944. "Reporteando," *Cinema Reporter*, August 14, 1942, 2. De Fuentes would never direct de Castejón, but she did appear in a classic comedy he produced, *Escuela de vagabundos* (*School of Vagabonds*, dir. Rogelio González, 1955), which de Fuentes adapted from *Merrily We Live* (dir. Norman Z. McLeod, 1938). "Fernando de Fuentes Prepara una obra," *Cinema Reporter*, August 28, 1942, 6.

136. "María E. Márquez [*sic*] con de Fuentes," *Cinema Reporter*, December 4, 1942, 4. *El jorobado (Enrique de Lagardere)* is an adaptation of Paul Féval's serialized historical swashbuckler novel *Le Bossu* (1858).

137. "Lo que se filma, *Cinema Reporter*, March 19, 1943, 4. On March 27, 1943, the magazine notes that *Doña Bárbara* is in its second week of filming. "Segunda semana de 'Doña Bárbara,'" 1.

138. "Fue necesario darle una semana más a 'Doña Bárbara,'" *Cinema Reporter*, May 1, 1943, 1.

139. "'Doña Bárbara' es un barbaridad . . . ," *Cinema Reporter*, August 28, 1943, 20.

140. *Doña Bárbara* was also released in Guadalajara and Monterrey the day of its premiere in Mexico City. "'Doña Bárbara' en Nuevo León y Jal.," *Cinema Reporter*, September 11, 1943, 31. "Expectación ante el próximo estreno de 'Doña Bárbara," *Cinema Reporter*, September 4, 1943. Similar to other films whose heavy expectations came to weigh them down, *Doña Bárbara*'s premiere was postponed several times. Following private screenings, first in early May and later in mid-July and late August, it was announced that it would premiere the

first week of August at the Palacio. "Gustó 'Doña Bárbara' en su primer corte," *Cinema Reporter*, July 17, 1943, 5. "'Doña Bárbara' está a punto de estreno," *Cinema Reporter*, July 24, 1943, 3. "Vio la prensa 'Doña Bárbara,'" *Cinema Reporter*, August 28, 1943, 2.

141. "'Doña Bárbara,' los periodistas y los diplomáticos," *Cinema Reporter*, September 18, 1943, 31.

142. "Cartelera fílmica," *Cinema Reporter*, October 23, 1943, 30. More details of its run at the Palacio were published in "'Doña Bárbara' dio 230,072.00 en cinco semanas," *Cinema Reporter*, October 30, 1943, 30. Its box office receipts continued to be reported on after its first run ended.

143. "Noticiario CLASA Films," *Cinema Reporter*, May 1, 1934, 31. It notes that filming of Doña Bárbara has come to a happy ending.

144. It does, however, reveal sentiments prevalent even today: with Hollywood in the picture, Mexican cinema always seems to have something to prove. That said, by 1943, the Mexican film industry had already established itself as a force with which to be reckoned well beyond the country's borders.

145. "Lo estrenado hasta el miércoles," *Cinema Reporter*, September 25, 1934, 30.

146. "Lo estrenado hasta el miércoles," *Cinema Reporter*, October 2, 1934, 30.

147. Alfonso de Icaza in *El Redondel* (September 19, 1943), as quoted in García Riera, *Fernando de Fuentes (1894/1958): trabajo colectivo*, 169.

148. María Álvarez de Burgos, "'Doña Bárbara' según una gran escritora venezolana," *El Universal*, September 19, 1943, 11. Despite being described as Venezuelan, it seems likely that the author was the Spanish-born daughter of writer and women's rights activist Carmen de Burgos.

149. Alfonso de Icaza, "Nuestro mundo y el cine hispano," *Cinema Reporter*, December 31, 1943, 50.

150. "¡La mejor película del año!," *Cinema Reporter*, December 18, 1934, 29. Marta Elba, "Por fin se entregaron los premios de 1943," *Cinema Reporter*, February 19 (?), 1944, 8–11, 24.

151. Edmundo Báez, "Julio Bracho vs. El Indio Fernández," *Cinema Reporter*, December 4, 1943. 16. The article, including this passage, was translated by Rielle Navitski. We had hoped to include the piece in our coedited volume *Cosmopolitan Film Cultures in Latin America, 1896–1960*, but we were unable to secure its rights.

152. Marta Elba, "Por fin se entregaron los premios de 1943," *Cinema Reporter*, February 19, 1944, 8–11, 24.

153. Santini Publicista (Miguel Santini Ávila), *La primera guía cinematográfica mexicana para el año de 1934* (Mexico City: Cía. "La Mexicana" Elaboradora de Películas, 1934), 42–43.

154. Emilio García Riera, *Historia documental del cine mexicano*, Vol. 1 (Mexico City: Ediciones Era, 1969), 31–37. *Historia documental del cine mexicano*, Vol. 1 (Guadalajara: Universidad de Guadalajara, 1993), 59–74.

155. García Riera, *Historia documental del cine mexicano*, Vol. 1 (1969), 31.

Chapter 6

1. A motif throughout the film, Juan's physical reactions to reviews show increasing displeasure with his critical reception.

2. Translations of dialogue taken from English subtitles of *The Fantastic World of Juan Orol*, DVD, Directed by Sebastián del Amo, San Francisco: Global Film Initiative, 2012.

3. Orol had donated negatives of his films to the Cineteca Nacional, which suffered a massive fire on March 24, 1982. It is often said that the fire provoked a state of depression from which Orol would suffer until his death in 1988.

4. Orol's career was celebrated by the Dirección General de Cinematografía (the General Film Organization) during its Seventh Week of the Memory of Mexican Cinema (*Séptima semana del recuerdo del cine mexicano*), which took place in the Palacio Chino theater in Mexico City not in 1982, but from October 28 to November 1, 1972. The Madrid city council sponsored the *I Semana de la Crítica de Cine*, which centered on Spanish contributions to the development of Mexican cinema. "In said tribute, among others, Luis Buñuel, Luis Alcoriza, Emilio García Riera, José de la Colina, Jomí García Ascot, María Luisa Elío Octavio Alba, Pedro Miret, Julio Alejandro and Juan Orol were invited." Eduardo de la Vega, *Juan Orol* (Guadalajara: Universidad de Guadalajara, 1987), 96. The Filmoteca de la Universidad Nacional Autónoma de México presented a comprehensive film series of Orol's work from his first film, *Sagrario* (dir. Peón, 1933), to his last, *El tren de la muerte* (*The Train of Death*, dir. Orol, 1978). These are three of many tributes.

5. "Viewers began to refer to many movies made in Mexico as *churros* as early as 1950, comparing them to the machine-made crullers [a ring-shaped, deep-fried cake] for sale on many street corners: Like *churros*, Mexican movies were not nourishing, rapidly made, soon forgotten, identical to one another, and cheap." Anne Rubenstein, "Mass Media and Popular Culture in the Post Revolutionary Era," in *The Oxford History of Mexico*, ed. Michael C. Meyer and William H. Beezley (Oxford: Oxford University Press, 2000), 665.

6. Ignacio M. Sánchez Prado references Orol's 1946 film *Una mujer de Oriente* (A Woman of the Orient), which was first released in 1950 in the middle of the *Época de oro*, but the same can be said of his films in the early sound period. "The Golden Age Otherwise: Mexican Cinema and the Mediations of Capitalist Modernity in the 1940s and 1950s," in *Cosmopolitan Film Cultures in Latin America, 1896–1960*, ed. Rielle Navitski and Nicolas Poppe (Bloomington: Indiana University Press, 2017), 261.

7. Jorge Ayala Blanco, *La aventura del cine mexicano* (Ciudad de México: Universidad Autónoma de México, 2017), 121. Ayala Blanco concurs with García

Riera, claiming that "The title of great naif Mexican director" belongs to José Bohr. *Contrabandistas del Caribe* and *Antesala de la silla eléctrica* were Mexico-Puerto Rico coproductions starring Dinorah Judith.

8. García Riera's assessments of Orol's films are included in the "Filmography and Testimonies" ("Filmografía y testimonios") in Eduardo de la Vega's *Juan Orol* (Guadalajara: Universidad de Guadalajara, 1987), 109–90.

9. De la Vega, *Juan Orol*, 11. Also, Eduardo de la Vega, *El cine de Juan Orol* (Mexico City: Universidad Nacional Autónoma de México, 1985).

10. De la Vega describes his first Orol book as a *mini-libro-homenaje*. *Juan Orol*, 105. In addition to serving as a kind of rough draft of his later volume, *El cine de Juan Orol* contains a brief interview with the director. "Mis gustos cinematográficos (5 preguntas a Juan Orol)," 45–49.

11. Aurelio de los Reyes, *Cine y sociedad en México, 1896–1930: Sucedió en Jalisco o Los Cristeros (1924–1928)* (Mexico City: Universidad Nacional Autónoma de México; Instituto de Investigaciones Estéticas, 2013), 11.

12. Maricruz Castro Ricalde and Robert McKee Irwin, *El cine mexicano "se impone": mercados internacionales y penetración cultural en la época dorada* (Mexico City: Universidad Nacional Autónoma de México, 2011), 113–18. In addition to other references in *El cine mexicano "se impone,"* Orol is discussed throughout in Castro and Irwin's edited volume *Global Mexican Cinema: Its Golden Age* (New York: Palgrave Macmillan/British Film Institute, 2013). Francisco Peredo Castro, "Entre tradición y modernidad. El cine mexicano en su evolución y contradicciones discursivas (1896–1956)," in *Historia sociocultural del cine mexicano: aportes al entretejido de su trama (1896–1966)*, ed. Francisco Peredo Castro and Federico Dávalos Orozco (Mexico City: Universidad Autónoma de México, 2016), 299–304. Rosario Vidal Bonifaz, *Surgimiento de la industria cinematográfica y el papel del Estado de México, 1895–1940* (Mexico City: Miguel Angel Porrúa, 2011), 332–35. In both Pereda Castro and Vidal Bonifaz, Orol is cited throughout.

13. Ana M. López, "Before Exploitation: Three Men of Cinema in Mexico," in *Latsploitation, Exploitation Cinemas, and Latin America*, ed. Victoria Ruétalo and Dolores Tierney (London: Routledge, 2009), 13–33.

14. Ibid., 13.

15. Upon applying for a license to be shown in public, *El calvario de una esposa* and *Honrarás a tus padres* were originally translated as *A Wife's Cavalry* and *Honor Your Parents* by the Motion Picture Division of the Education Department of the State of New York. Rather than use these titles, I have chosen to use my own translations that better fit the themes of the films. Both were originally distributed in New York by Cinexport.

16. This list is not meant to be comprehensive in any way whatsoever, but rather to touch upon a few scholars whose work is ever present in interventions on Latin American melodrama. Peter Brooks's foundational book *The Melodramatic Imagination: Balzac, Henry James, Melodrama, and the Mode of Excess* (New

Haven: Yale University Press, 1976). Hermann Herlinghaus's edited collection *Narraciones anacrónicas de la modernidad: melodrama e intermedialidad en América Latina* (Santiago: Editorial Cuarto Propio, 2002). López's important meditation on melodrama includes "Tears and Desire: Women and Melodrama in the 'old' Mexican Cinema," in *Mediating Two Worlds: Cinematic Encounters in the Americas*, ed. John King, Ana M López, and Manuel Alvarado (London: BFI, 1993), 147–63. Carlos Monsiváis's work on melodrama is scattered, but several key essays are included in *Mexican Postcards*, trans. John Kraniauskas (London and New York: Verso, 2000). Also see "No te vayas, mi amor, que es inmoral llorar a solas," in *Narraciones anacrónicas de la modernidad: melodrama e intermedialidad en América Latina*, 105–23. Silvia Oroz, *Melodrama: o cinema de lágrimas da América Latina* (Rio de Janeiro: Funarte, 1999).

17. De la Vega, *Juan Orol*, 15–16.

18. Martín Fernández, "La vida exagerada de Juan Orol, cineasta mexicano oriundo de O Valadouro," *La Voz de Galicia*, December 31, 2016, 6.

19. Martín Fernández recounts that "[a]fter the [Spanish] Civil War, Juan Orol, the Mexican filmmaker, contacted his family in O Valadouro. He sent a letter to his father, Juan Orol Maseda, but it never reached him: he had died years before. Chance, which others call destiny, wanted the postmaster to be Prudencio Orol Balseiro, son of the deceased, who opened the missive. And that is how he found out that he and his sixteen siblings had a half-brother in Mexico who was triumphing as a director and actor in the cinema" (6). In *El fantástico mundo de Juan Orol*, Juan returns to El Ferrol to visit family. A childhood friend inadvertently convinces him to return to making movies.

20. Eugenia Meyer, "Juan Orol," in *Testimonios para la historia del cine mexicano Vol. II*, ed. Eugenia Meyer (Mexico City: Cineteca Nacional; Instituto Nacional de Antropología e Historia, 1976), 27.

21. De la Vega, however, unsuccessfully attempts to substantiate Orol's assertions about his bullfighting career. *Juan Orol*, 17.

22. Certificate of Marriage, Juan Orol to Amparo Moreno, 24 January 1924, Mexico City. Registro Civil del Distrito Federal, Matrimonios, 1861–1950.

23. In contrast to several of Amparo's siblings, I have been unable to find any record of Consuelo's birth to Moisés Moreno and Pilar Bañuelos, or her baptism.

24. Birth Certificate for Arnoldo Orol y Moreno, 15 February 1925, Registro Civil, Nacimientos, 1861–1934, Archivo Estatal de Distrito Federal.

25. Death Certificate for Amparo Moreno, 18 February 1931, Mexico City. Registro Civil, Defunciones, 1861–1987. According to baptism records, it appears likely that Amparo was thirty-one at the time of her death. Baptism Certificate for Amparo de los Ángeles Moreno, 2 December 1899, Toluca de Lerdo, México. México, Lista parcial de registros de bautismo, 1560–1950.

26. Fittingly, this period is also somewhat fuzzy in the history of the radio station. As J. Justin Castro notes, "The formal inauguration of XE-Partido

Nacional Revolucionario-XEO was on New Year's Day 1931, though proprietors of *Excélsior* had allowed to use its station since June 1929." *Radio in Revolution: Wireless Technology and State Power in Mexico, 1897–1938* (Lincoln: University of Nebraska Press, 2016), 184.

27. Meyer, "Juan Orol," 29.

28. Santini also notes that the film's rights had been sold to twenty-two areas for a percentage of box-office receipts. Santini Publicista (Miguel Santini Ávila), *La primera guía cinematográfica mexicana para el año de 1934* (Mexico City: Cía. "La Mexicana" Elaboradora de Películas, 1934), 14.

29. Meyer, "Juan Orol," 31.

30. In 1935, Pezet passed away due to peritonitis. Not yet forty years old, Pezet's company FESA (Films Exchange) produced two Fernando de Fuentes films: *El tigre de Yautepec* (1933) and *El fantasma del convento* (1934). FESA and its distribution company were formed with Jorge's brother Juan.

31. *Madre querida* and, most likely, *El calvario de una esposa* were distributed by Orol's Aspa Films. *Sagrario* and *Mujeres sin alma* had been distributed by Gonzalo Varela.

32. López, here, writes about *Madre querida*, but the same could easily be said of *El calvario de una esposa*. "Before Exploitation," 27.

33. De la Vega describes that Orol had written two or three novellas, which he took the precaution of registering at the copyright office. He later deposited copies of the manuscripts at the SOGEM (Sociedad General de Escritores Mexicanos/General Society of Mexican Writers). Its archives, however, were destroyed. *Juan Orol*, 30.

34. Mother's Day was officially celebrated for the first time in the United States in 1914, even though all states had adopted the holiday by 1911. In Mexico, Mother's Day was imported as a reactionary countermeasure to small advances in women's rights in the Yucatan Peninsula. It was instituted by Álvaro Obregón's government and heavily promoted by *Excélsior*. It did, however, come to have a quite different meaning by the mid-1930s both politically and culturally. Marta Acevedo, *El 10 de mayo* (Mexico City: Secretaría de Educación Pública, Dirección de Publicaciones y Bibliotecas; Martín Casillas Editores, 1982).

35. "'Madre querida' se estrena el 10 de mayo en once cines del primer circuito," *El Nacional*, May 5, 1935, 6 (primera sección). An advertisement on the same page includes the same information.

36. López cites De la Vega, who in turn cites Carlos Monsiváis's television series *Los que hicieron nuestro cine*. *Juan Orol*, 30. López also puts forth, "In a sense, given its carefully arranged promotional angle, *Madre querida* could be considered the first Mexican film to be marketed with the panache and hucksterism later associated with exploitation cinema." López, "Before Exploitation," 27.

37. Examples of early production reports include Roberto Cantú Robert, "Cuentos animados del cine," *Jueves de Excélsior*, November 29, 1934, 7; and Hugo

del Mar (Esteban V. Escalante), "Luces y sombras del cine nacional," *Revista de Revistas*, March 31, 1935, 6. In the first note, Orol's plans to act, direct, write, and produce his next film, "Honra del Destino." In the second, published less than six weeks before the film's premiere, it is announced that shooting of "Huérfanos del destino" is coming to a close in Industria Cinematográfica's studios in Lomas de Chapultepec.

38. "'Madre querida' se estrena el 10 de mayo en once cines del primer circuito," *El Nacional*, May 5, 1935, 6 (primera sección).

39. Alfonso de Icaza in *El Redondel* (May 12, 1935), as quoted in *Juan Orol*, 116.

40. In *Revista de Revistas* (May 26, 1935), as quoted in *Juan Orol*, 116–17.

41. Anonymous notes in *El Cine Gráfico* (June 2, 1935, and September 1, 1935), as quoted in *Juan Orol*, 116–17.

42. Orol cites Josué Mirlo (Genaro Robles Barrera)'s poem "Madre" ("Mother").

43. De la Vega and López note its parallels to the radio. *Juan Orol*, 29. López, "Before Exploitation," 27.

44. Ibid., 28.

45. *Madre querida*, Advertisement, *Filmográfico*, May 1935, 29.

46. Vidal Bonifaz, 185.

47. Ibid.

48. Initially focusing on Consuelo Frank's return to the movies, precipitated by marriage, the most interesting of these notes remarks that "Juanito Orol has a contract in his portfolio (*cartera*) to direct some movies for 'Selecciones Capitolio' from Barcelona. He is thinking of leaving soon, and he may possibly take Charlie Cabello [a director's assistant who did some acting] with him." Roberto Cantú Robert, "Cerca de nuestras estrellas," *Filmógrafico*, February 1936, 38.

49. Esteban V. Escalante, "Casos y Cosas del Cine Nacional," *Filmógrafico*, August 1936, 39.

50. Fidel Solís in *Ilustrado* (September 8, 1936), as quoted in *Juan Orol*, 120.

51. Luz Alba in *Ilustrado* (September 10, 1936), as quoted in *Juan Orol*, 120–22. For more on Cube Bonifant's film criticism, see Viviane Mahieux, "Una pequeña Marquesa de Sade en la crónica mexicana," in *Una pequeña Marquesa de Sade: crónicas selectas, 1921–1948*, ed. Viviane Mahieux (Mexico City: Dirección de Literatura, Universidad Nacional Autónoma de México, 2009), 41–44. Rocío del Consuelo Pérez Solano, "Cube Bonifant," in *Women Film Pioneers Project*, ed. Jane Gaines, Radha Vatsal, and Monica Dall'Asta (Center for Digital Research and Scholarship, New York: Columbia University Libraries, 2013).

52. Alfonso Medina in "Seis años de anécdotas del *Ilustrado*," in *Ilustrado*, May 17, 1934, 17, 38, as quoted in Cube Bonifant, *Una pequeña Marquesa de Sade*, 43.

53. Escalante, "Casos y Cosas del Cine Nacional," *Filmógrafico*, October 1936, 71–72. In the second note, Escalante also writes that "on this occasion, at the request of the public, Consuelo Moreno will not work."

54. Francisco Peredo Castro, "Entre tradición y modernidad. El cine mexicano en su evolución," in *Historia sociocultural del cine mexicano. Aportes al entretejido de su trama (1896–1966)*, ed. Peredo Castro and Federico Dávalos Orozco (Mexico City: Universidad Nacional Autónoma de México, 2016), 300–302.

55. Like the didactic introductions to *Madre querida* and *El calvario de una esposa*, Orol's foreignness remains uninterrogated, even though he is placed into a credible role as a *torero*.

56. The metacinematic reflexivity of *El calvario de una esposa* extends beyond Orol's Aspa productions: José Bohr is referenced both in Raulito's song and in conversation when the titular protagonist of *Luponini (el terror de Chicago)* [*Luponini (The Chicago Terror*, 1935] is mentioned as if he were a real person.

57. *El calvario de una esposa*, Advertisement, *Filmógrafico*, July, 1936, 77.

58. "El próximo viernes se estrena 'Honrarás a tus padres' en los cines del primer circuito," *El Nacional*, January, 31, 1937, 2 (tercera sección).

59. *Allá en los trópicos* was also destroyed in the fire at the archives of the SOGEM.

60. Alfonso de Icaza in *El Redondel*, February 7, 1937, as quoted in *Juan Orol*, 124.

61. Escalante, "Casos y Cosas del Cine Nacional," *Filmógrafico*, February 1937, 40.

62. Luz Alba in *Ilustrado*, February 18, 1937, as quoted in *Juan Orol*, 124. Hortensia Elizondo, "El cinema en México. La película 'Honrarás a tus padres," *La Opinión*, February 21, 1937, 6 (segunda sección). *La Prensa*, February 21, 1937, 3 (segunda sección).

63. A year later, Elizondo would be deemed an *enemiga del cine nacional*. Hortensia Elizondo, "Cine Nacional. ¿Enemiga del cine nacional?," *La Opinión*, April 20, 1938, 4. "El cinema en México. ¿Enemiga del cine nacional?," *La Prensa*, April 24, 1938, 3 (segunda sección).

64. She also notes its aspatiality (the film's setting is ambiguous) and atemporality (it seems to be somewhat contemporary, but there is a Count). Hortensia Elizondo, "El cinema en México. La película 'Honrarás a tus padres," *La Opinión*, February 21, 1937, 6 (segunda sección). *La Prensa*, February 21, 1937, 3 (segunda sección).

65. Several scenes in *Honrarás a tus padres* are cut from the copy of the film that I have viewed, but are included in the dialogue taken from screen that were included in paperwork submitted to screen the film in New York. "Honrarás a tus padres," March 18, 1937, Casefile Number 32696, Box 516, New York State Motion Picture Division License Application Case Files, New York State Archives, Albany, New York, United States.

66. Orol would establish other production companies such as España Sono Films and Producciones Juan Orol throughout the rest of his career.

67. In the piece, it is reported that "it is advertised to premiere in the Regis theater tomorrow, Tuesday," and, "This film was screened some time ago to a group of people when it still was not finished." Anonymous note in *El Universal* (March 21, 1938), quoted in *Juan Orol*, 126.

68. *Eterna mártir* was distributed by Caribe Films.

69. Anonymous note in *El Universal* (October 27, 1937), quoted in *Juan Orol*, 128.

70. This quote remains unchanged from its original version published in 1969. *Historia documental del cine mexicano*. Vol. 1 (Guadalajara: Universidad de Guadalajara, 1993), 261.

71. Alfonso de Icaza in *El Redondel* (January 30, 1938), quoted in *Juan Orol*, 125.

72. It is possible that de Icaza's review had some critical influence, but it is equally likely that a later note in *Excélsior* reflects the same critical discourse about *El derecho y el deber*. Anonymous note in *Excélsior* (March 24, 1938), quoted in *Juan Orol*, 126–27.

73. This is one of a number of instances in which a man of African descent is treated without curiosity in Orol's early films. In many ways, this distinguishes Orol not only from other Mexican directors of the time, but also those working in other film industries throughout the world.

74. In a moment of honesty, the two discuss the questionable parentage of Checha's son.

75. López, "A Cinema for the Continent," in *The Mexican Cinema Project*, ed. Chon A. Noriega and Steven Ricci (Los Angeles: UCLA Film and Television Archive, 1994), 7.

76. Alfonso de Icaza in *El Redondel* (October 31, 1937), as quoted in *Juan Orol*, 128.

77. Italics are original to the quote, as de Icaza uses the Anglicism "gross public."

78. Campos Ponce, "Boicot contra las malas películas," *La Prensa*, April 18, 1937, 2 (segunda sección).

79. "Noticias de los estudios mexicanos," *La Prensa*, September 13, 1936, 2 (segunda sección).

Chapter 7

1. "Debe fomentarse la cinematografía argentina por un sistema racional," *Film*, November 4–10, 1932, 1.

2. It is plausible that "Debe fomentarse la cinematografía argentina por un sistema racional" was written in response to the production of *Tango!*.

Competing studio Lumiton employed a very different industrial strategy: they contracted foreign technicians John Alton and Lazlo Kish. *Revista del Exhibidor* published an excellent profile of the studio in its December 20, 1932, issue. "Nuevos estudios argentinos," 5.

3. España, "El model institucional," in *Cine argentino industria y clasicismo, 1933–1956*, ed. Claudio España (Buenos Aires: Fondo Nacional de las Artes, 2000), 22–157.

4. Ibid., 34.

5. Carlos Borcosque, "No hay que hacer solo buenas películas; hay que saberlas distribuir, *Sintonía*, December 21, 1935, 33.

6. Other foreign-born performers active in the first five years of the talkies in Argentina were Enrique Arellano, Olimpio Bobbio, Ignacio Corsini, Pierina Dealessi, Alfredo Gobbi, Laura Hernández, Amelia Lamarque, Carmen Lamas, Choly Mur, Manolita Poli, Julio Traversa, and Juana Tressols.

7. Santiago Arrieta (aka Donadío), Fernando Borel, Paquito Busto, Antonio Daglio, Luis Díaz, María Esther Duckse, Isabel Figlioli, Roberto Fugazot, Pablo Lagarde, Perla Mary, Félix Mutarelli, Antonio Podestá, Arturo Podestá, Totón Podestá, Segundo Pomar, Atilio Supparo, Froilán Varela, and Paquita Vehil were other Uruguayans who acted in the early sound period in Argentina.

8. *Bodas de sangre* featured the Spanish actors Margarita Xirgu, Pedro López Lagar, Amelia de la Torre, Helena Cortesina, Amalia Sánchez Ariño, Alberto Contreras, Eloísa Vigo, Eloísa Cañizares, and Luisa Sala.

9. Some other foreign actors who were credited in these years were José Alfayate, Alicia Barrié, Esther Borja, Antonio Botta, Emperatriz Carvajal, Dolores Dardés, José Franco, Pilar Gómez, Ernesto Lecuona, Venturita López, Julián de Meriche, Inés Murray, Elvira Pagã, Rosina Pagã, Ilde Pirovano, María Santos, Satanela, Esteban Serrador, Teresa Serrador, Hilda Sour, Tania, Consuelo Velázquez, Pablo Vicuña, and Blanca Vidal.

10. Among this group of foreign directors are now nearly forgotten cineastes such as James Bauer and Emilio Kartulovich.

11. Nelo Cosimi and Isidoro Navarro were two other foreign-born Argentines who directed in the period.

12. Like Arniches and Botta, works by Spanish writers such as María Lejárraga and Luis Marquina were produced by Argentine studios. José Bustamante y Ballivián, writer of *Riachuelo*, is another notable foreign screenwriter who worked in the period.

13. The work of other foreign musicians such as Dajos Bela, Los Dixie Pals (Paul Wyer), Enrique Mario Casella, Manuel Jovés, Gerardo Matos Rodríguez, Eugenio Nóbile, Manuel Parada, and Rudolf Sachs also resounded.

14. Di Núbila discusses editing practices in the 1930s and 1940s at length in *Historia del cine argentino. Vol. 1* (Buenos Aires: Cruz de Malta, 1959), 217–22.

15. "No vengo a dirigir producto importado," *Radiolandia*, July 11, 1938, 57.

16. Juan Carlos Garate, "La industria cinematográfica argentina," doctoral dissertation, Universidad de Buenos Aires, 1944, 112.

17. "No todas son flores para las grandes películas argentinas que se exhiben en tierras extrañas," *Radiolandia*, November 26, 1938, 51. The piece references the reception of the 1937 Luis César Amadori movie *El pobre Pérez* (Poor Pérez) in Rio de Janeiro.

18. España, "El model institucional," 37. España is explicitly referencing Julio Joly's Cinematografía Julio Joly and Adolfo Z. Wilson's Cinematográfica Terra.

19. Garay, 32. An initial rise from 1938 to 1940, which saw 569, 668, and 776 workers plying their trades in the Argentine film industry, leveled off later. 1941, 1942, and 1943 saw 910, 950, and 990, respectively.

20. Many other foreign-born Argentines earned their first credits between 1939 and 1943. Some examples: Emilio Ariño, Ana Arneodo, Olga Casares Pearson, Juan Corona, Margarita Corona, Josefa Goldar, Marga Landova, Diana Maggi, Iris Marga, Felisa Mary, Arsenio Perdiguero, and Silvana Roth. Uruguayans such as Baby Correa, María Padín, Jesús Pampín, Celia Podestá, Mirtha Reid, and Carlos Tajes were also active, as was Cuba's Amelia Sinisterra. Elsa del Campillo, Rafael Frontaura de la Fuente, Casimiro Ros, and Enrique Vico Carré also appeared.

21. Mexicans Ana María González, Carlos Montalbán, and Elvira Ríos also appeared in Argentine films in the period.

22. Other Spanish actors who appeared in Argentine films include Consuelo Abad, Angelillo, María Antinea, Ricardo Canales, Mary Capdevila, Vicente Climent, Pura Díaz, Enrique Diosdado, Ricardo Galache, Eliseo Herrero, Marcial Manent, Herminia Mas, Diego Martínez, Alejandro Maximino, Manolo Perales, and Manuel Villegas López.

23. Enrique Jardiel Poncela, Last Reason, Armando Moock, Jaime Prades, Yamandú Rodríguez, César Tiempo also wrote or cowrote films produced in the late 1930s and early 1940s. Bombal freely adapted Colombian writer Jorge Isaac's classic romantic novel *María* (1867).

24. Working on films of the period were also composers such as Paco Aguilar, Francisco Balaguer, Mario Battistella Zoppi, Julián Bautista, Dajos Béla, Jacobo Ficher, and Jean Gilbert.

25. These technicians had a wide range of jobs on set, from assistant directors to production managers to equipment operators.

26. Claudio España, *Medio siglo de cine: Argentina Sono Film, S.A.C.I.* (Buenos Aires: Abril, 1984), 202.

27. "Reporteando," *Cinema Reporter*, March 19, 1943, 2. "Argentine Studio Destroyed in Fire," *Motion Picture Daily*, February 17, 1943, 1.

28. España, *Medio siglo de cine*, 206.

29. Much work is yet to be done on the decline of the Argentine film industry in the 1940s, but Nilo Couret provides a compelling summary in *Mock*

Classicism: Latin American Film Comedy, 1930–1960 (Berkeley: University of California Press, 2018), 165.

30. Italics serve to denote that the Anglicism *turning point* is original to the text. *Historia del cine argentino. Vol. 2* (Buenos Aires: Cruz de Malta, 1960), 35.

Chapter 8

1. Pablo Coll, "Opina Don Pablo Coll," *Heraldo del Cinematografista*, November 25, 1931, 87. Domingo Di Fiore and Sebastián Martínez, "Opinan Di Fiore y Martínez," *Heraldo del Cinematografista*, December 2, 1931, 91–92. Joaquín A. Lauraret and Pablo Cavallo. "Opinan Lautaret y Cavallo," *Heraldo del Cinematografista*, December 9, 1931, 95. Clemente Lococo, "Opina D. Clemente Lococo," *Heraldo del Cinematografista,* December 16, 1931, 99–100. Humberto Cairo, "Opina D. Humberto Cairo," *Heraldo del Cinematografista,* December 23, 1931, 103–104. Francisco Borrazas, "Opina D. Francisco Borrazas," *Heraldo del Cinematografista,* December 30, 1931, 107–108. The Sociedad Cinematográfica Argentina de Exhibidores was founded early that year, in July 1931. Its interests adjacent to other industry guilds, but at times quite distinct, the Sociedad Cinematográfica Argentina de Exhibidores allowed exhibitors a space to collectively work on issues central to their business.

2. (Israel) Chas de Cruz was a significant contributor to Argentine film culture until his death in 1968. Jason Borge discusses his importance in *Latin American Writers and the Rise of Hollywood Cinema* (New York: Routledge, 2008), 120–26.

3. Cairo, 103.

4. Di Fiore and Martínez, 91.

5. The piece argues, "If *Fruta amarga* managed to be decently successful when its English dialogues could not be understood by our audiences, there is room for hope that it will now be more liked with Spanish actors." "Se estrenó la versión española de 'Fruta amarga,'" *Revista del Exhibidor*, August 20, 1931, 21.

6. Coll, 87. Di Fiore and Martínez, 91. Starring John Boles Genevieve Tobin, and Lois Wilson, the cast of *Seed* also included a small part for Bette Davis. It was her second film.

7. Borrazas, 107. Cairo, 103.

8. Ibid.

9. Borrazas, 108.

10. Di Fiore and Martínez, 92.

11. Cairo, 104.

12. Coll, 87.

13. Lococo, 100.

14. Lautaret and Cavallo, 95.

15. Carmelo Santiago, "Carmelo Santiago no olvida a Don Ángel Mentasti," in *Medio siglo de cine: Argentina Sono Film, S.A.C.I.*, Claudio España (Buenos Aires: Abril 1984), 266–69.

16. "Hondo pesar causó la muerte de Don Ángel Mentasti," *Revista del Exhibidor*, June 30, 1937, 1–2.

17. In an interview, Atilio José Mentasti says, "But I do not know when exactly he came to Argentina; it was at the end of last century. I do not precisely know these pieces of information. I don't have them." Claudio España, *Medio siglo de cine: Argentina Sono Film, S.A.C.I.,* 13.

18. Dirección de inmigración de la República Argentina, *Resumen estadístico del movimiento migratorio en la República Argentina, 1857–1924* (Buenos Aires: El Gráfico, 1925), 4–5. In the period between 1898–1902, emigrants from Lombady constituted 8.78 percent of all Italian immigrants to Argentina (18,058 of 215,158), surpassed by those of the Marche (19,352), Abruzzi e Molise (22,403), Campania (30,732), Piedmont (34,286), and Calabria (37,404). *Annuario statistico dell'emigrazione italiana dal 1876 al 1925* (Rome: Commissariato Genérale dell'Emigrazione, 1926), 150.

19. Samuel L. Baily, *Immigrants in the Lands of Promise: Italians in Buenos Aires and New York City, 1870–1914* (Ithaca: Cornell University Press, 1999). Chapter 5, "Fare l'America," is particularly useful.

20. His obituary in *La Nación* incorrectly claims that he was born in 1874. "Falleció Don Ángel Mentasti," June 25, 1937, 13.

21. Ibid., 61. At some point in time, Ángel and Virginia would become estranged. José Atilio would later become a doctor. *Caras y caretas*, December 9, 1916, 66.

22. "En pocas palabras por el editor," *Heraldo del Cinematografista*, June 30, 1937, 79. "Con el fallecimiento del señor Ángel Mentasti, la Cinematografía Nacional pierde su más eficaz y tesonero elemento," *Imparcial Film*, June 25, 1937, 1.

23. In what may be telling work, especially given the parallels between Italian immigration to Argentina and the United States, Akcigit, Grigsby, and Nicholas explore aspects of the relationship between immigration and innovation and show that immigrant inventors were significantly more productive than their native-born counterparts in the context of the United States between 1880 and 1940. Ufuk Akcigit, John Grigsby, and Tom Nicholas, "The Rise of American Ingenuity: Innovation and Inventors of the Golden Age," NBER Working Paper #23047, 2017 and "The Rise of American Ingenuity" NBER Working Paper #23137, 2017.

24. "Una entrevista 'ad hoc' con Ángel Mentasti—Como [*sic*] se inició en la cinematografía—Recuerdos del tiempo viejo," *Imparcial Film*, September 20, 1932, 38. Domingo Di Núbila, *La Época de Oro: Historia del cine argentino I* (Buenos Aires: Jilguero, 1998), 74–75. España, *Medio siglo de cine*, 61.

25. In a 1910 advertisement published in at least two issues of *Caras y caretas*, "Ángel B. Mentasti—Donado, 170, Bahía Blanca (Buenos Aires)" is listed

as agent of a watch distributed by Manuel M. Casanova y Cia. in exchange for seven pesos or a variety of promotional slips. November 15, 1910, 124–25 (insert), and November 22, 1910, 105–106 (insert).

26. In another recurring ad published in *Caras y caretas*, which was reprinted for several years (at least between 1910–13), he is also listed as a distributor of Exterminador, "Mortal Enemy of Pests, Cockroaches, Ants, etc." October 26, 1910, 143. At some point, he also lived in Santa Fe, which is located north of Buenos Aires in the province of the same name. *Medio siglo de cine*, 61.

27. España, *Medio siglo de cine: Argentina Sono Film*, 62–63.

28. Hundreds of people died during the *Semana Trágica*, a week in January 1919 in which a workers' strike spun out of control. It was violently crushed by various elements of the government.

29. "Diversas notas de interés," *Excelsior*, March 17, 1932, 33.

30. It appears that Cosmos Film was formed as another one of Tucci's enterprises dissolved; Tucci, Mancini y Cia. distributed material in Argentina for the transnational film company Italux Film. Curiously, however, Cosmos Film's trademark was only registered in early September 1932. "Disolución de Sociedad." *Imparcial Film*. July 15 1932, 1. "Informaciones breves,"*Revista del Exhibidor*, September 10, 1932, 8.

31. "La primera novedad de Cosmos Film," *Revista del Exhibidor*, July 10, 1932, 14. Published a few days earlier, the distributor is mentioned as a subscriber to *Heraldo del Cinematografista* in what appears to be its first mention in a film periodical. "Gracias," July 6, 1932, 224.

32. "Cosmos Film cuenta con material interesante," *Revista del Exhibidor*, July 20, 1932, 17.

33. "La primera novedad de Cosmos Film," *Revista del Exhibidor*, July 10, 1932, 14.

34. "Pasó al Metropol Los falsificadores de Londres," *Revista del Exhibidor*, August 30, 1932, 6.

35. "Las próximas actividades de Cosmos Films," *Revista del Exhibidor*, September 30, 1932, 9.

36. "Notas sueltas," *La Película*, October 6, 1932, 5.

37. Perhaps because Mentasti and Moglia Barth increasingly dedicated themselves to film production, little news of Cosmos Film was published between late 1932 and mid-1933. On May 12, 1933, a note in *Film* announces that Mentasti has severed ties with Cosmos to fully dedicate himself to Argentina Sono Film. "Notas de interés," *Film*, May 12, 1933, 11.

38. "Argentina Sono Film," *Imparcial Film*, October 30, 1932, 1. "Argentina Sono Film es una nueva productora nacional," *Revista del Exhibidor*, October 30, 1932, 7.

39. "Argentina Sono Film," *Imparcial Film*, October 30, 1932, 1.

40. "Argentina Sono Film es una nueva productora nacional," *Revista del Exhibidor*, October 30, 1932, 19.

41. Nilo Couret, "Introduction," in *Mock Classicism: Latin American Film Comedy, 1930–1960* (Berkeley: University of California Press, 2018), 1–21.

42. "Producción nacional," *Heraldo del Cinematografista*, November 16, 1932, 317. "La filmación de la película nacional 'Tango' está a punto de terminarse," *Revista del Exhibidor*, November 20, 1932, 9. A month later, Argentina Sono Film moved production from the S.I.C.A. Voz workshops to Cinematografía Valle's recently set up studio, which incorporated "advances in modern sound technology." "Continuará filmando en otros estudios la Argentina Sono Film," *Revista del Exhibidor*, December 20, 1932, 7. A similar report made the front page of *Imparcial Film*. "'Tango' se filma en Cinematografía Valle," December 20, 1932, 1. An additional note in *Imparcial Film* reports that the film was soon to wrap. "Noticias diversas," January 20, 1933, 9.

43. Domingo Di Núbila, *Historia del cine argentino. Vol. 1* (Buenos Aires: Cruz de Malta, 1959), 53. Abel Posadas, "Argentina Sono Film. El cine como empresa," *Cine en la cultura argentina y latinoamericana* 2 (1983): 3. Ricardo Manetti, "Argentina Sono Film. Más estrellas que en el cielo," In *Cine argentino industria y clasicismo, 1933–1956*, ed. Claudio España (Buenos Aires: Fondo Nacional de las Artes), 162–64.

44. Initially, Cosmos Film was credited as *Tango!*'s production company. "'Tango,'" *Heraldo del Cinematografista*, January 25, 1933, 355. A similar conflation is made in news regarding Chilean distribution of the film. "La firma Weinstein adquirió producciones para Chile," *Imparcial Film*, February 25, 1933, 7. Curiously, in the same issue of *Imparcial Film*, it is reported that Cosmos Film will distribute "a new national film made by Argentina Sono Film." "'Tango' será distribuida por Cosmos Film," February 25, 1933, 16.

45. Argentina Sono Film, Advertisement, *Revista del Exhibidor*, August, 20, 1936, 7.

46. "Tengo plena fé en el éxito que obtendrá 'Tango' nos dice Angel Mentasti, director de la Argentina Sono Film," *Imparcial Film*, January 30, 1933, 8.

47. Ibid. Many of these same points were later repeated in a note appearing in *Revista del Exhibidor*. After stressing that the diegesis of *Tango!*, so connected to tango culture and its stars, is a sure hit, the note argues that "its announcement has awakened interest among exhibitors both in the capital and the interior, which shows a favorable environment for said movie and for all national production." "La producción argentina 'Tango,' figura entre los primeros estrenos de 1933," February 10, 1933, 6.

48. Claudio España argues that "*Tango!*'s plot was only a barely interesting excuse in order for the tangos and their performers to have a prominent dimension." *Medio siglo de cine*, 38. Di Núbila calls the film "a kind of festival

of our popular song." *Historia del cine argentino. Vol. 1*, 51). Finally, in my piece "Sounding Out Temporality in the Argentine Film Musical of the 1930s," I argue that "rather than being a film rooted in diegesis, it is a kind of musical cavalcade whose plot serves an almost secondary function. Its rather formulaic plot . . . is frequently relegated to the background while songs take center stage." *Arizona Journal of Hispanic Cultural Studies* 16 (2012): 214.

49. I examine the function of these songs in ibid., 213–15, 217.

50. "La producción argentina 'Tango,' figura entre los primeros estrenos de 1933," February 10, 1933, 6.

51. "La firma Weinstein adquirió producciones para Chile," *Imparcial Film*, February 25, 1933, 7. In this note, which repeats many of Mentasti's assertions in the February 10 interview, Cosmos Film is still referenced as the distributor of *Tango!*. "Noticias diversas," *Imparcial Film*, March 11, 1933, 9. "Noticias diversas," *Imparcial Film*, March 30, 1933, 14. Rights in Rosario were sold for a large sum to the owners of the Cine Teatro Nacional, J. and M. Mantovani. Rights in Santa Fe and San Juan were sold to Carbonell and Rodríguez, respectively.

52. These reports frequently contradict ones previously published. "'Tango' en Rosario," *Revista del Exhibidor*, June 10, 1933, 10. According to the note, rights belonged to Rosario (Pablo Aliseri); the rest of Santa Fe province (*Señores* Coronel and Corte); Julián Ajuria (Chile); Columbia Picture's representative, Teófilo Fiege (Peru); and Demetrio del Cerro (Uruguay). "Notas de interés," June 16, 1933, 11.

53. "Tiene un gran argumento con gran variedad de situaciones, la producción nacional 'Tango,'" *Imparcial Film*, March 30, 1933, 10.

54. "Hay gran espectativa [*sic*] por el estreno de 'Tango,'" *Imparcial Film*, April 20, 1933, 7.

55. *Revista del Exhibidor*, April 10, 1933, 12.

56. The original program is reproduced in a number of publications, including España's *Medio siglo de cine*, 14. It is likely that the *Paramount Sound News* short (listed as 59-33) refers to number 59, whose one reel was submitted for copyright on February 25, 1933. *Catalogue of Copyright Entries. Part 1, Group 3. Dramatic Compositions. Motion Pictures* (Washington, DC; United States Government Printing Office, 1933), 94. Even though it shares its name with the Barcelona-based *Paramount gráfico*, a self-proclaimed "Publicity Organ for Paramount Films," which was directed by the Galician journalist María Luz Morales, I have been unable to confirm any additional details about the newsreel beyond its existence. Finally, it would appear that *Fiesta alegre* is likely *Mickey's Beach Party*. It is described as "by Mickey" in *La Nacion*'s "Programa de los espectáculos" (November 10, 1933, 11) and, later, a part of the "Programa Ratón Mickey" shown at the Cine Astor on December 1, 1933 (*La Nación*, 12).

57. In "Premier en el Real," Horacio Ferrer writes that "Mentasti and his men know, moreover, other things: that there is a mass of spectators that is, potentially, the perfect clientele for a film of porteño inspiration. One that, grad-

ually, had been abandoning the exhaustive seats of the *sainete* and the *revista.*" In *El libro del tango. Historias e imágenes* (Buenos Aires; Ediciones Ossorio—Vargas, 1970), XLIII.

58. "Tango," *Film*, May 5, 1933, 3.

59. "En pocas palabras por el editor," *Heraldo del Cinematografista*, Mayo 10, 1933, 427.

60. "Tango," *Imparcial Film*, April 30, 1933, 9. "Tango," *La Prensa*, April 28, 1933, n.p. A typed photocopy of the review in *La Prensa* is held in the Biblioteca del Museo del Cine Pablo Ducrós Hicken, Folder *Tango* (1933).

61. More specifically, Lamarque and Sandrini were praised by *Heraldo del Cinematografista, Imparcial Film*, and *La Prensa*. Gómez was panned by *Heraldo del Cinematografista*, while Arias's diction was critiqued in *Imparcial Film*. Arias, who later would become one of the most important comic stars of early Argentine sound film, hit back at critics in an interview in which he discusses being miscast. "Querían que yo pusieran gracia que falta en 'Tango,'" *Film*, April 28, 1933, 4.

62. "En el Real Cine fué estrenada la producción nacional 'Tango,'" *Revista del Exhibidor*, April 30, 1933, 4.

63. Argentina Sono Film, Advertisement, *Film*, May 5, 1933, 7. Argentina Sono Film, Advertisement, *Revista del Exhibidor*, 6–7.

64. Argentina Sono Film, Advertisement, *Imparcial Film*, May 20, 1933, Insert. Many of these showings were also included in the ad published in *Revista del Exhibidor* before the film's premiere.

65. "Lo que vi anoche. En 'Tango' nos dan tangos por lujo," *El Mundo*, April 28, 1933. Folder *Tango* (1933), Biblioteca del Museo del Cine Pablo Ducrós Hicken.

66. "El patriotismo bien entendido en la producción nacional," *Imparcial Film*, Mayo 30, 1933, 5.

67. "Producción Nacional. Un paso adelante," *Imparcial Film*, April 10, 1933, 10.

68. One of many examples: "Alarmante Estadística. La Argentina es el país que tiene más cines en relación con el número de sus habitantes," *Film*, June 16, 1933, 9. This worry, of course, was also reflected in the questions posed to exhibitors by *Revista del Exhibidor* in late 1931.

69. "Argentina Sono Film distribuirá películas españolas," *Imparcial Film*, September 5, 1933, 1. "Argentina Sono Film instalará agencia directa en Barcelona," *Imparcial Film*, September 15, 1933, 3. "Iníciase un plan de intercambio cinematográfico," *Film*, September 29, 1933, 3.

70. "Argentina Sono Film instalará agencia directa en Barcelona," *Imparcial Film*, September 15, 1933, 3.

71. Ibid.

72. "Antonio Masetti has bought the distribution rights in France and Italy for *Dancing*. The film will also be immediately released in Spain." "El film argentina en el exterior," *Revista del Exhibidor*, October 10, 1933, 1.

73. "Argentina Sono Film instalará agencia directa en Barcelona," *Imparcial Film*, September 15, 1933, 3.

74. "'Tango' es un film de gran arrastre," *Imparcial Film*, May 20, 1933, 14. Here, the word *bordereaux* refers to financial statements that almost certainly demonstrate the film's box-office success.

75. "Se inició la filmación de 'Dancing,'" *Imparcial Film*, August 10, 1933, 5.

76. "Producción Nacional," *Film*, September 22, 1933, 5. "'Dancing' se estrenará en octubre. Hoy se dará termino a su filmación," *Imparcial Film*, September 25, 1933, 5. An earlier note prematurely announced the film's completion. "Se está ultimando el rodaje de 'Dancing,'" *Imparcial Film*, September 5, 1933, 4. "La S.I.D.E. ha realizado un buen trabajo técnico en 'Dancing,'" *Imparcial Film*, September 25, 1933, 11.

77. A continuation of models established in the silent period, intertextuality between media can also notably been seen in José Agustín Ferreyra's 1927 short *La vuelta al bulín*, which reimagines the 1917 tango "De vuelta al bulín" (Pascual Contursi and José Martínez) made famous by Carlos Gardel.

78. "Informaciones breves," *Revista del Exhibidor*, September 30, 1933, 2. "La producción cinematográfica nacional," *La Nación*, October 8, 1933, n.p.

79. "Aplazóse de nuevo el estreno del film local 'Dancing,'" *Film*, November 3, 1933, 6.

80. "Con el drtor. de 'Dancing,' Moglia Barth," *Imparcial Film*, November 5, 1933, 3.

81. "Estrenó anoche el teatro Porteño la cinta argentina 'Dancing,'" *La Prensa*, November 10, 1933. Folder *Dancing* (1933), Biblioteca del Museo del Cine Pablo Ducrós Hicken.

82. "Anoche se estrenó 'Dancing,'" *Film*, November 10–16, 1933, 1–2. "Dancing," *Heraldo del Cinematografista*, November 15, 1933, 567.

83. Mickey Mouse. "Yo, crítico," *Cinegraf*, November 1933, 39.

84. Ibid. *Cinegraf* consistently praises local productions as being superior to Hollywood's Spanish-language productions, even despite their many deficiencies. Reviewing the 1933 season, a piece published in the magazine states, "Productions like 'Tango' and 'Dancing' are in a higher plane than imports like 'Espérame.'" "Otras consideraciones de la temporada," Diciembre 1933, 46.

85. "Dancing," *Heraldo del Cinematografista*, November 15, 1933, 567.

86. "Anoche se estrenó 'Dancing,'" *Film*, November 10–16, 1933, 1–2. A longer review was to be published the next week.

87. Argentina Sono Film, Advertisement, *Revista del Exhibidor*, November 30, 1933, 7.

88. Screenwriters for *Tango!* and *Dancing* as well, Bustamante and Ballivián's work on *Riachuelo* is initially noted in "En pocas palabras por el editor," *Heraldo del Cinematografista*, March 21, 1934, 653. Filming of *Riachuelo* is reported by "Argentina Sono Film filma 'Riachuelo,'" *Revista del Exhibidor*, March 20, 1934,

2, and, later, "Nuevos studios," *Heraldo del Cinematografista*, May 23, 1934, 697. Finally, the conclusion of shooting and the beginning of postproduction is detailed in "'Argentina Sono Film' terminó el rodaje de 'Riachuelo' con Sandrini," *Imparcial Film*, June 5, 1934, 4.

89. "'Riachuelo' será una película que hará honor a la producción nacional, nos dice el señor Mentasti," *La Película*, May 31, 1934, 1.

90. *Imparcial Film* reveals "'RIACHUELO' WILL BE EXHIBITED in private within a few days. Coming ahead are excellent accounts of this new film by Argentina Sono Film." "Información general. Últimas noticias," June 15, 1934, 5. In its next issue, it reported not only that the film would premiere, but also it was a "film of which we have seen various *actos* (scenes), which allows us to assure that it is an excellent work, realized with careful appearance and performance." "Én estos días se estrenará 'Riachuelo,'" *Imparcial Film*, June 25, 1934, 3. *Heraldo del Cinematografísta* later made a similar observation, saying the film made a very good impression and "It can be affirmed that this production marks a step of progress by national cinema." "'Riachuelo,'" July 4, 1934, 734.

91. In addition to noting the success of the prerelease screening, *Giornale d'Italia* reports that the film will be presented at next August's Venice Biennale. "'Riachuelo' es un film interesante.'" Folder *Riachuelo* (1934), Biblioteca del Museo del Cine Pablo Ducrós Hicken.

92. "Riachuelo," *Heraldo del Cinematografista*, July 11, 1934, 737.

93. "'Riachuelo' (Nacional)," *Imparcial Film*, July 5, 1934, 4.

94. "'Riachuelo,' un triunfo de la Sono Film, en el cine Renacimiento," *La Bandera*. Folder *Riachuelo* (1934), Museo de Cine Pablo Ducrós Hicken.

95. "Fue estrenada ayer la película nacional titulada 'Riachuelo,'" *La Prensa*, July 5, 1934. Along with *Giornale d'Italia* and *La Bandera* reviews, this appears in the *Riachuelo* folder of the Museo del Cine Pablo Ducrós Hicken in Buenos Aires. Also included are reviews published in *Bandera Argentina*, *Crítica*, *Crónica*, *El Mundo*, *La Nación*, *Noticias Gráficas*, *El Pueblo*, *La Razón*, *La República*, *República Ilustrada*, and *Última hora*. Folder *Riachuelo* (1934), Biblioteca del Museo del Cine Pablo Ducrós Hicken.

96. "'Riachuelo' constituye un buen éxito de la cinematografía nacional," *La Razón*, Folder *Riachuelo* (1934), Biblioteca del Museo del Cine Pablo Ducrós Hicken.

97. "'Riachuelo,' una manifestación de potencia del cine nacional," *Cinegraf*, July 1934, 8.

98. Moglia Barth receives frequent praise for his work on the film, especially in *La Nacion*'s review. "Es una película animada y simpática 'Riachuelo.'" Folder *Riachuelo* (1934), Biblioteca del Museo del Cine Pablo Ducrós Hicken.

99. "'Riachuelo' (Nacional)," *Imparcial Film*, July 5, 1934, 4.

100. Néstor, "Lo que vi anoche," *El Mundo*, Folder *Dancing* (1933), Biblioteca del Museo del Cine Pablo Ducrós Hicken.

101. "Luis Sandrini, tartamudo por casualidad," Folder *Riachuelo* (1934), Biblioteca del Museo del Cine Pablo Ducrós Hicken.

102. "'Riachuelo,'" *Heraldo del Cinematografista*, July 11, 1934, 737.

103. Likely for reasons tied to its financial difficulties, indebtedness to Sandrini also led to his inclusion as a partner of Argentina Sono Film, as reported in "Luis Sandrini, tartamudo por casualidad."

104. "Algunos Intérpretes Principales de 'Riachuelo," Folder *Riachuelo* (1934), Biblioteca del Museo del Cine Pablo Ducrós Hicken.

105. "Fue estrenada ayer la película nacional titulada 'Riachuelo,'" *La Prensa*, July 5, 1934. "Es una película animada y simpática 'Riachuelo,'" *La Nación*. Folder *Riachuelo* (1934), Biblioteca del Museo del Cine Pablo Ducrós Hicken.

106. "Continúan los Estrenos. Tiene Aciertos Fotográficos la Película 'Riachuelo,'" *Noticias gráficas*, July 5, 1934. Folder *Riachuelo* (1934), Biblioteca del Museo del Cine Pablo Ducrós Hicken.

107. Manetti, 189–205.

108. "Es Halagüeño el Exito de 'Riachuelo,'" *Crítica*, July 10, 1934. Folder *Riachuelo* (1934), Biblioteca del Museo del Cine Pablo Ducrós Hicken.

109. "Información general. Últimas noticias," *Imparcial Film*, July 15, 1934, 5.

110. "El éxito de 'Riachuelo,'" *Imparcial Film*, July 15, 1934, 7.

111. "La S. de Exhibitors repudia las incorrecciones de la Argentina Sono Film," *Revista del Exhibidor*, July 30, 1934, 1. "En pocas palabras por el editor," *Heraldo del Cinematografista*, August 1, 1934, 754. "Protesta contra Argentina Sono Film," *La Película*, August 2, 1934, 7.

112. "Información general. Últimas noticias," *Imparcial Film*, August 5, 1934, 7.

113. "'Riachuelo' en el extranjero," *Imparcial Film*, August 15, 1934, 1. An agreement with Juan Robertson to distribute the film in Spain would have to wait a year after the film's release in Argentina. "En pocas palabras por el editor," *Heraldo del Cinematografista*, July 11, 1935, 735.

114. "'Riachuelo' triunfa en Nueva York," *Imparcial Film*, January 10, 1935, 7.

115. "Luis Sandrini será contratado por la Warner?" *La Película*, November 29, 1934, 6.

116. "Desarrollo de la producción local," *Cinegraf*, September 1934, 49.

117. "A propósito de un comentario sobre la cinematografía nacional," *Imparcial Film*, July 15, 1934, 8.

118. Ibid.

119. "D. Angel Mentasti hace interesantes aclaraciones," *Imparcial Film*, July 15, 1934, 1.

120. The editorial uses a variation of a well-known refrain in Spanish indicating wisdom comes with age: "Más sabe el diablo por viejo que por diablo" ("The devil knows more from old age than from being the devil"). "Don Ángel Mentasti, Veterano Cinematografista Argentino, Está Realizando una Labor Eficaz en Pro de la Producción Nacional," *La Película*, November 29, 1934, 2.

121. The other two films announced were *Monte criollo* and *El circo*. "La producción nacional el 1934," *Imparcial Film*, September 25, 1934, 24.

122. In addition to updates on *El alma del bandonéon* and *Monte criollo*, it also informs readers of the progress of two films that were never produced, *El novio de Mar del Plata* (The Boyfriend [or Groom] of Mar del Plata) and *El millonario* (The Millionaire). "Argentina Sono Film estrenará a partir de marzo, una película mensual," *La Película*, December 20, 1934, 6.

123. Ibid.

124. "40 Producciones en Castellano para 1935," *Imparcial Film*, January 20, 1935, 7.

125. Argentina Sono Film released three feature films in 1935: *El alma del bandoneón*, *Monte criollo*, and *La barra mendocina* (whose previous title was almost certainly *La conquista de Buenos Aires*). It also released the short *Pibelandia*. Like many other projects, *El circo* was eventually abandoned. Curiously, *El alma del bandoneón* and *Monte criollo* were reportedly going to be released in March and April, respectively. "Los dos primeros estrenos de Argentina Sono Film," *Imparcial Film*, January 30, 1935, 1. The following year, *Puerto Nuevo* and a Sandrini film (a project initially known as *Los reseros* [The Herdsmen], which later become *Loco lindo*) were released. It also appears to have been named *El pampa Andrade* for a time. "'El pampa Andrade' se titulará la obra que filmará Sandrini," *Imparcial Film*, March 3, 1935, 7.

126. "En pocas palabras por el editor," *Heraldo del Cinematografista*, January 30, 1935.

127. While this was similar to the period between *Dancing* and *Riachuelo*, a similar lapse would not happen again until the film studio's decline in the late 1960s.

128. "'Tango' es un film de gran arrastre," Imparcial Film, May 20, 1933, 14. Numerous notes are published, including an anecdote about her weight in the film. Don X, "En voz alta," *Imparcial Film*, June 15, 1935, 9.

129. "Varios," *Heraldo del Cinematografista*, July 25, 1934, 746.

130. *El alma del bandonéon* was categorized as an *espectáculo familiar* by the Comisión Honoraria de Contralor Cinematográfico (Honorary Comission of Film Inspection). "Actividades de la censura," *Heraldo del Cinematografista*, March 20, 1935, 889.

131. An anecdote about the final scene in the Teatro Colón is related in an October 1934 issue of *Imparcial Film*. Don X, "En voz alta," October 25, 1934, 7.

132. "En pocas palabras por el editor," *Heraldo del Cinematografista*, February 20, 1935, 871.

133. "El alma del bandoneon, *Heraldo del Cinematografista*, February 27, 1935, 879.

134. "Ultimas noticias," *Imparcial Film*, March 5, 1935, 5. "'El alma del bandoneón' triunfa en España," *Imparcial Film*, October 15, 1935, 3.

135. "Sobre producción nacional. Se dice que . . ." *Imparcial Film*, November 5, 1935, 8.

136. "El alma del bandoneón," *Cinegraf*, February 1935, 42.

137. César F. Marcos, "A través de un año de películas nacionales. ¡Dinero!, palabra de orden en el cine argentino," *Cinegraf*, December 1935, 36, 46.

138. "En pocas palabras por el editor," *Heraldo del Cinematografista*, March 20, 1935, 889.

139. *Sparta* asserts that *Riachuelo* would be the first Argentine film to appear in Spain, but its release would come after *El alma del bandoneón*. "Notas gremiales," March 25, 1935, 21.

140. "En pocas palabras por el editor," *Heraldo del Cinematografista*, May 15 1935, 929.

141. "Argentina Sino [*sic*] Film instala agencia directa en Brasil," *Revista del Exhibidor*, May 15, 1935, 1.

142. "En pocas palabras por el editor," *Heraldo del Cinematografista*, August 14, 1935, 993.

143. "Visita de un productor argentino," *La Época*, October 19, 1935, 5.

144. "Visita del director del Sono Film," *La Libertad*. October 19, 1935, 8.

145. "Monte criollo," *Imparcial Film*, March 25, 1935, 3. "Al margen del estreno de 'Monte criollo,'" *Imparcial Film*, May 5, 1935, 3.

146. "Se prepara una demostración a D. Angel Mentasti y Arturo S. Mom," *Imparcial Film*, June 5, 1935, 7.

147. "El 19 del corriente tendrá lugar la demostración a Don Ángel Mentasti y Arturo S. Mom," *Imparcial Film*, June 15, 1935, 5.

148. "Se exhibió en privado 'Monte criollo,'" *Imparcial Film*, May 5, 1935, 1.

149. Categorized as *especial*, *Monte criollo* was given the following scores out of a possible five by *Heraldo del Cinematografista*: three and a half (commercial value), three (artistic value), and two (plot value). "Monte criollo," May 29, 1935, 941.

150. Athos, "Monte criollo," *Imparcial Film*, May 25, 1935, 5.

151. César F. Marcos, "A través de un año de películas nacionales. ¡Dinero!, palabra de orden en el cine argentino," *Cinegraf*, December 1935, 46.

152. Following a model used in previous films, Argentina Sono Film printed reviews of *Monte criollo* as part of an advertisement that also promotes the premieres of *La barra mendocina* (listed as July 4, it was released on August 2) and *Los raseros* (whose August 7 premiere never happened; *Loco lindo* made its way into theaters on May 13, 1936). Argentina Sono Film, Advertisement, *Imparcial Film*, May 25, 1935, 5. The film was such a hit with audiences, in fact, that interesting anecdotes regarding the theft of a print of the film were published in several film periodicals including "Industria local," *Heraldo del Cinematografista*, June 5, 1935, 943, and "¿Existe una organización dedicada al robo de copias de películas?" *Imparcial Film*, June 5, 1935, 4.

153. A note published in the *Heraldo del Cinematografista* claims the film is complete and will premiere July 4 in the Monumental. "En pocas palabras por el editor," May 29, 1935, 939. A later note in *Imparcial Film* (following a two-page advertisement) claims a July 24 premiere. "'La barra mendocina' irá el 24 de julio en el Monumental," *Imparcial Film*, June 25, 1935, 9.

154. "La barra mendocina," *Heraldo del Cinematografista*, August 7, 1934, 991.

155. A still accompanies the piece in *Caras y caretas*. "Cinco minutos de intervalo," July 27, 1935, 167. "En pocas palabras por el editor," *Heraldo del Cinematografista*, September 19, 1934, 783. In this report, the short "En el maravilloso país de Pibelandia" ("In the Marvelous World of Pibelandia") is described as being acted by children.

156. "Programa de los espectáculos cinematográficos," *La Nación*, October 4, 1935, 12.

157. "En pocas palabras por el editor," *Heraldo del Cinematografista*, August 14, 1935, 993. In addition to Mexican and Spanish films, a later note also includes French material. "Ultimas noticias," *Imparcial Film*, November 5, 1935, 8.

158. "La visita del director de Sono Films, de Buenos Aires, a los Estudios Ballesteros," *Heraldo de Madrid*, October 19, 1935, 5. "En los estudios Ballesteros. Visita del director de Sono Film," *La Libertad*, October 19, 1935, 8. "Un editor cinematográfico argentino visita nuestros estudios y juzga nuestra producción," *Cinegramas*, October 27, 1935, 21. "Ultimas noticias," *Imparcial Film*, October 25, 1935, 8.

159. "En pocas palabras por el editor," *Heraldo del Cinematografista*, November 20, 1935, 1063.

160. "Informaciones breves," *Revista del Exhibidor*, December 15, 1935, 8.

161. *Puerto Nuevo* and *Loco lindo* are in production. "La actividad de las productoras nacionales," *Imparcial Film*, September 25, 1935, 21. In preparation are *La virgen del valle* (Virgen of the Valley) and *Petróleo* (Oil), among others. A month later, *Imparcial Film* publishes more information on these developing projects. "Argentina Sono Film en 1936," *Imparcial Film*, October 15, 1935, 5. By late 1935, it is known that Argentina Sono Film has completed *Puerto Nuevo* and *Loco lindo* and is preparing *Petróleo, La virgen del valle*, and an untitled film directed by Daniel Tinayre that will be the first in the country to use RCA's high fidelity sound. "Algo de la producción nacional para 1935–1936," *Imparcial Film*, October 25, 1935, 2. A very kind piece was published in *Imparcial Film* about Argentina Sono Film's upcoming 1936 program. "Argentina Sono Film en 1936," December 10, 1935, 2.

162. Argentina Sono Film, Advertisement, *Imparcial Film*, December 15, 1935, 4.

163. At its height in the 1940, 1941, and 1942 seasons, Argentina Sono Film produced twelve feature films per annum. It regularly produced four to

eight films a year until the mid-1960s, when it began to shift more toward film distribution.

164. "Nuevas actividades de la productora local Argentina Sono Film," *Imparcial Film*, March 25, 1936, 5.

165. Ibid. Details of the Bulnes studio were originally reported in the magazine's previous issue. "Instaló Estudios Propios Argentina Sono Film," *Imparcial Film*, March 15, 1936, 1.

166. In the article "Argentina," published in the November issue of *Cinelandia*, Carlos Borcosque writes that "the Argentine film industry has entered into a very interesting momento of technical advance. Good studios are being built, and what is more praiseworthy, better laboratories. The Estudios Cristiani already possess an automatic laboratory, with developing machines designed and constructed in Argentina, a true pride of modern cinema and the same thing is happening, utilizing American equipment, in the Laboratorios Tecnofilm. This assures better photography and better sound reproduction," 60.

167. Alicia Vignoli, for example, was signed to a three-movie deal, in which she was to support Pepe Arias twice. "En pocas palabras por el editor," *Heraldo del Cinematografista*, April 29, 1936, 1163.

168. Originally, six films were announced for 1936. Of these, *Cadetes de San Martín* would wait another year for its premiere, while *El circo* and *La virgen gaucha* (The Gaucho Virgen) would never be completed. *¡Goal!*, the final release of the year, was not promoted early in the season. "Películas argentinas cuyo estreno se anuncia para la temporada de 1936," *Anuario Cinematográfico Argentino*, Buenos Aires: Argos, 1936, 24.

169. "Sucursales, Agencias y Representaciones de Empresas Distribuidoras y Productoras en el Interior," *Anuario Cinematográfico Argentino*, Buenos Aires: Argos, 1936, insert. Sporadically, news from these branches is reported. One example: the opening of the office in General Pico, a city in the province of La Pampa. "En pocas palabras por el editor," *Heraldo del Cinematografista*, March 11, 1936, 1131.

170. Evincing the ways in which different aspects of Argentina Sono Film's business dealings were enmeshed, it was announced in the same column that the studio's 1937 premieres will occur in the Gran Cine Monumental in Buenos Aires. "En pocas palabras por el editor," *Heraldo del Cinematografista*, December 23, 1936, 1319.

171. "Conoceremos pronto 'Chucho el Roto,'" *Revista del Exhibidor*, February 15, 1936, 4.

172. "Intercambio cinematográfico hispano-argentino," *Mundo gráfico*, March 25, 1936, 36.

173. "Argentina Sono Film," *Cine Sparta*, April 11, 1936, 7.

174. Slated to premiere earlier, *Puerto Nuevo* was screened on February 12, 1936, and *Loco lindo* was finally released on May 13, 1936. *Loco lindo* had been promoted throughout 1935, and was even reported to have been scheduled

to have an August 7, 1935, premiere as *Los reseros*. "Últimas noticias," *Imparcial Film*, May 15, 1935, 5. Late that same month, a publicity photo was published in *Imparcial Film* that stated that it would soon be released. "El celebrado cómico Luis Sandrini reaparecerá en 'Loco lindo,'" *Imparcial Film*, August 25, 1935, 5.

175. "En pocas palabras por el editor," *Heraldo del Cinematografista*, Mayo 29, 1935, 929. "En pocas palabras por el editor," *Heraldo del Cinematografista*, June 12, 1935, 949.

176. "Últimas noticias," *Imparcial Film*, July 25, 1935, 5. "Últimas noticias," *Imparcial Film*, August 5, 1935, 8.

177. "Puerto nuevo," *Heraldo del Cinematografista*, February 15, 1936, 1122.

178. "'Puerto Nuevo' sigue dando grandes entradas," *Imparcial Film*, March 25, 1936, 1.

179. "'Loco lindo' señala una ágil realización," *La Nación*, May 14, 1936, 14. "'Loco lindo,'" *Heraldo del Cinematografista*, May 20, 1936, 1182.

180. "'Un estreno: 'Loco lindo,'" *Cinegraf*, June 1936, 40.

181. Tabú, "El cine nacional es un juego de azar," Folder *Amalia* (1936), Biblioteca del Museo del Cine Pablo Ducrós Hicken.

182. Marmol's *Amalia* was first serialized in 1851 in *La semana*, a newspaper Marmol had founded in exile in Montevideo. Its narrative would only be completed years after its writing was suspended, when it was published as a novel by Imprenta Americana. Beatriz Curia examines the two versions her "Problemas textuales de Amalia de José Mármol," contending that effectively there are two *Amalias*. *Incipit* II (1982: 61–83). By foundational fictions, I refer to Doris Sommer's book and, more specifically, the chapter "*Amalia*: Valor at Heart and Home." *Foundational Fictions: The National Romances of Latin America* (Berkeley: University of California Press, 1991), 83–113.

183. In a note reporting the end of *Amalia*'s filming, R*evista del Exhibidor* mentions that "350 extras take part, 70 of them being people of color." "Terminó la filmación de 'Amalia,'" June 10, 1936, 3. In my "John Alton in Argentina, 1932–1939," I examine the cinematographer's work on the film. In *Cosmopolitan Film Cultures in Latin America*, 1896–1960, ed. Rielle Navitski and Nicolas Poppe (Bloomington: Indiana University Press, 2017), 225–226. Tecnofilm's involvement in the movie, as well as its impending installation of ultramodern laboratories allowing the company to develop a wide range of negatives (panochromatic, sound, etc.) is noted in "En pocas palabras por el editor," *Heraldo del Cinematografista*, July 29, 1936, 1226.

184. "De Vuelta en la Sono Film Moglia Barth Prepara 'Amalia,'" *La Nación*, Folder *Amalia* (1936), Biblioteca del Museo del Cine Pablo Ducrós Hicken.

185. "¡Alerta, Productores Argentinos," *Heraldo del Cinematografista*, July 1, 1936, 1204.

186. Soon after the publication of "¡Alerta, Productores Argentinos," perhaps reacting to the attention *Amalia* was receiving, *Revista del Exhibidor* reminds its readers that the cinematic conventions must be respected in adaptations of

works of literature or theater. "Es peligroso desdeñar los convensionalismos del cinematográfo," *Revista del Exhibidor*, July 10, 1936, 2.

187. "Amalia," *Heraldo del Cinematografista*, July 15, 1936, 1220.

188. The film was reviewed throughout Argentina in newspapers such as *Tribuna* (Rosario), *La Razón* (Chivilcoy), *La Capital* (Mar del Plata), *Noticias Gráficas* (Buenos Aires), *La Prensa* (Buenos Aires), *Crónica* (Buenos Aires), *La Razón* (Buenos Aires), *El Pueblo* (Buenos Aires), *La Capital* (Rosario), *El Atlántico* (Bahia Blanca), *Il mattino d'Italia* (Buenos Aires), and *La Comuna* (Tres Arroyos). One of the few bad reviews was titled "'Amalia' Is a Well-Intentioned but Absolutely Anti-Cinematic Film." "'Amalia' es una película bien intencionada pero absolutamente anti-cinematográfica," *El Diario* (Buenos Aires), July 9, 1936. Folder *Amalia* (1936), Biblioteca del Museo del Cine Pablo Ducrós Hicken.

1189. Mary Mar, "La 'Première' de AMALIA en el Monumental," *Imágenes*, July 17, 1936. Folder *Amalia* (1936), Biblioteca del Museo del Cine Pablo Ducrós Hicken.

190. Carmelo Santiago, "'Amalia' es la mejor película argentina presentada hasta la fecha," *Sintonía*, July 25, 1936, 60–61.

191. Signed on August 30, 1936, Moglia Barth's contract stipulates that he was to be paid five thousand pesos to direct the film, previously titled *Destinos* (Destinies), and oversee its editing. Payment, per the contract, would be made within thirty days of the film's premiere. Folder *¡Goal!* (1936), Biblioteca del Museo del Cine Pablo Ducrós Hicken.

192. *El cañonero de giles* is reported to be completed a month after initial reports surface. "Lumitón hará otra película con Luis Sandrini," *Revista del Exhibidor*, May 10, 1936, 6. "Informaciones breves," *Revista del Exhibidor*, June 10, 1936, 3.

193. "Los discos del cine," *Cinegraf*, November 1936, 42.

194. Despite receiving a two out of four for artistic value and one and one-half out of four for its plot value, it receives a three our of four (but, notably, "para populares" or for "popular theaters"). "¡Goal!," *Heraldo del Cinematografista*, October 21, 1936, 1279.

195. "Los dos últimos estrenos nacionales," *Cinegraf*, November 1936, 46.

196. "Argentina Sono Film en la temporada 1937," *Revista del Exhibidor*, November 30, 1936, 1, 7. "En pocas palabras por el editor," *Heraldo del Cinematografista*, December 9, 1936, 1311. Of these films, *Cadetes de San Martín*, *Pobre Pérez*, *Palermo*, *Melgarejo*, *¡Segundos afuera!*, *Los Ranqueles* (as *Viento norte*), and, eventually, *Fragata Sarmiento* were made. *La palanca*—along with another project written by Arturo S. Mom, *La novia de Mar del Plata*—was never made. "En pocas palabras por el editor," *Heraldo del Cinematografista*, July 22, 1936, 1221. *El cantar de los tangos* also never appeared, despite being reported on later. *El fantasma de Mar del Plata* and *El curita* appear to have been abandoned at earlier stages of development.

197. "Prodigieux Essor de la Production Argentine," *La cinématographie française*, January 16, 1937, 12.

198. Preproduction news include hiring Amadori as director ("En pocas palabras por el editor," *Heraldo del Cinematografista*, May 20, 1936, 1179), completion of filming ("'El Pobre Pérez' y 'Los cadetes de San Martín,'" *Revista del Exhibidor*, November 30, 1936, 8), and a quickly dismissed lawsuit brought by Óscar R. Beltrán regarding Mentasti and Argentina Sono Film's use of the title ("No exist lesión moral ni material en el pleito por el título 'El Pobre Pérez,'" *Imparcial Film*, May 25, 1937, 7). *Revista del Exhibidor* reported on its pre-premiere screening. "La 'premiére' [*sic*] de 'El pobre Pérez,'" February 15, 1937, 2.

199. "El pobre Pérez," *Heraldo del Cinematografista*, February 17, 1937, 1354. Its ratings: commercial value, four and one-half out of five (*para populares* or for popular theaters); artistic value, three; and plot value, three. Its character is listed as a *comedia dramática.*

200. Di Núbila, *Historia del cine argentino*. Vol. 1, 86.

201. Pertiné is credited in the film's initial sequence. Later, as mayor of Buenos Aires, he would be considered to be "the most outstanding pro-Nazi in the Government." Cordell Hull, *Foreign Relations of the United States Diplomatic Papers 1944, Vol. VII, The American Republics* (Washington, DC: Government Printing Office, 1967), 304.

202. "Primer plano," *Cinegraf*, July 1936, 1.

203. "'El Pobre Pérez' y 'Los cadetes de San Martín,'" *Revista del Exhibidor*, November 30, 1936, 8. Advertisement of Argentina Sono Film, *Revista del Exhibidor*, August 20, 1936, 7.

204. "Cadetes de San Martín (Nacional)," *Imparcial Film*, March 5, 1936, 5.

205. "Cadetes de San Martín (Nacional) Para satisfacer las exigencia [*sic*] del público . . . ," *Imparcial Film*, March 5, 1937, 5.

206. "'Melgarejo' irá el 19 en el Monumental," *Imparcial Film*, May 15, 1937, 3.

207. "Melgarejo," *Heraldo del Cinematografista*, May 26, 1937, 56. In the review, the film receives a four out of four for its commercial value, but "para populares."

208. "Ha tenido éxito en el Monumental 'Melgarejo,'" *Revista del Exhibidor*, May 30, 1937, 2.

209. "Noticias de Argentina Sono Film," *Revista del Exhibidor*, October 20, 1937, 2.

210. "Intensifica su Producción la Argentina Sono Films," *Imparcial Film*, June 5, 1937, 7.

211. Parsing out Ángel Mentasti's work on these films is difficult, but Soffici's *Viento norte* is generally considered to be the first film fully developed

and produced by Atilio and Luis Ángel. In its credit sequence, an epitaph appears, "To the unforgettable memory of Ángel Mentasti, who permitted the beginnings of this film with his efforts."

212. "Angel Luis Mentasti asumió la dirección general de Argentina Sono Film," *Imparcial Film*, July 5, 1937, 1. "En pocas palabras por el editor," *Heraldo del Cinematografista*, July 7, 1937, 85.

213. "Palermo," *Heraldo del Cinematografista*, June 30, 1937, 82.

214. "Noticias de Argentina Sono Film," *Revista del Exhibidor*, October 20, 1937, 2.

215. Various obituaries indicate that Mentasti's condition, initially thought to be minor, quickly deteriorated, which may explain why the only report of his sickness appeared in "Nos han soplado que . . . ", a regular gossip column in *Revista del Exhibidor*. June 20, 1937, 4.

216. "Hondo pesar causó la muerte de Don Ángel Mentasti," *Revista del Exhibidor*, June 30, 1937, 1–2. The obituary in *Revista del Exhibidor* also recounts scenes from his funeral. "En pocas palabras por el editor," *Heraldo del Cinematografista*, June 30, 1937, 79. "Con el fallecimiento del señor Ángel Mentasti, la Cinematografía Nacional pierde su más eficaz y tesonero elemento," *Imparcial Film*, June 25, 1937, 1. "Falleció Don Ángel Mentasti," *La Nación*, June 25, 1937, 13.

217. "Obituaries," *Variety*, July 21, 1937, 70.

218. "Falleció Don Ángel Mentasti," *La Nación*, June 25, 1937, 13.

219. "Con el fallecimiento del señor Ángel Mentasti, la Cinematografía Nacional pierde su más eficaz y tesonero elemento," *Imparcial Film*, June 25, 1937, 1.

220. Ibid.

221. In early 1937, a series of complaints about Mentasti's business practices were published in *Revista del Exhibidor*. Altoparlante, "Linternazos," March 15, 1937, 8. "Linternazos," April, 10, 1937, 2. Altoparlante claims that Mentasti is a hypocrite who criticizes the films of other production companies, but promotes the national film industry.

222. "Ángel Luis Mentasti asumió la dirección general de Argentina Sono Film," *Imparcial Film*, July 5, 1937, 1.

223. "En San Isidro se levantarán los estudios de la A. Sono Film," *Revista del Exhibidor*, October 10, 1937, 2. A note about the ceremony was also published in *Heraldo del Cinematografista*. "En pocas palabras por el editor," October 6, 1937, 157.

224. Mentasti was remembered with some regularity in periodicals after his death, even in the United States. A few examples: "A un año de la muerte de D. Angel Mentasti," *Imparcial Film*, June 15, 1938, 1. "El Gremio Recordó a D. Angel Mentasti," *Imparcial Film*, June 25, 1938, 9. "Noticias del cine nacional," *Imparcial Film*, June 15, 1939, 7. "Multiples Rule in Argentina," *Film Daily*. August 9, 1940, 4.

Chapter 9

1. The other themes were sovereignty and national identity, education, information, culture and recreation, social engagement, technological development, legal and economic frameworks, and decentralization and regionalization.

2. Tito Davison, "Preparación profesional cinematográfica," *Comunicación social* no. 6 (1983): 158–59. Davison's assessment, of course, says more about his perspective than it does about the importance of films schools such as the Centro Universitario de Estudios Cinematográficos (CUEC) of the Universidad Nacional Autónoma de México (UNAM). Of the many important figures who studied at the CUEC, Latin America's oldest film school, are Alfonso Cuarón, Fernando Eimbcke, Jorge Fons, Issa López, Emmanuel Lubezki, and María Novaro.

3. Many foundational figures of the Mexican film industry, including Juan Orol, participated in this project.

4. María Isabel Souza. "Tito Davison." In *Testimonios para la historia del cine mexicano Vol. 7*, ed. Eugenia Meyer (México, D.F.: Cineteca Nacional; Instituto Nacional de Antropología e Historia, 1976), 139–53.

5. Peter Wollen, *Signs and Meaning in the Cinema*, rev. ed. (Bloomington: Indiana University Press, 1972), 105. Christopher Beach makes a similar point to mine in *A Hidden History of Film Style: Cinematographers, Directors, and the Collborative Process* (Oakland: University of California Press, 2015), 2–3.

6. In one of the few scholarly works to seriously examine Davison's work, Dana Zylberman studies his career in Mexico. Dana Zylberman, "Intercambio de directores entre las cinematografías argentina y mexicana en el período clásico-industrial: el caso de Tito Davison," in *Pantallas transnacionales*, ed. Ana Laura Lusnich, Alicia Aisemberg, and Andrea Cuarterolo (Buenos Aires: Imago Mundi, 2017), 19–32.

7. Appropriately, Anchou makes this assessment in a footnote to his "Veinticinco años de producción independiente. Las fronteras ignoradas," in *Cine argentino: industria y clasicismo, 1933/1956*, vol. 1, ed. Claudio España (Buenos Aires: Fondo Nacional de las Artes, 2000), 488.

8. Davison continues, "But perhaps it was something related a bit with the proximity of my homeland [*mi tierra*] and I went to Buenos Aires, where after a short time an opportunity to direct presented itself to me." María Isabel Souza, "Tito Davison," in *Testimonios para la historia del cine mexicano Vol. 7*, ed. Eugenia Meyer (México, D.F.: Cineteca Nacional; Instituto Nacional de Antropología e Historia, 1976), 139–53.

9. The anglicism "miss" is original to the report. "Tito Davison, casado," *Ecran*, February 9, 1937, 20.

10. *Radiolandia* published reports on the project, which does not not appear to have been commercially distributed. "Glorias marinas. Una película dirigida

por José María Reynal que regresa el 2 de febrero," January 23, 1937, 58. "Reynal regresa satisfecho y con ansias de volver," February 27, 1937. In addition to lacking page numbers or a table of contents, the copy of the latter issue held by the Biblioteca Nacional Mariano Moreno is missing its first few pages.

11. Souza, 139. There is some confusion, however, about his description of his mother's roots as being English or Scottish.

12. In his interview with Souza, Davison refers to Carlos Borcosque as "a relative of mine." Ibid. I have been unable to identify to my satisfaction their exact relationship, but the pair were undoubtedly close. In his *Botica de turnio*, Jorge Délano (or "Coke," as he was known) describes Davison as being Borcosque's "*aprovechado discípulo*" (whose double entendre translates both to "resourceful disciple" or "free-loading disciple") (Santiago: Zig-Zag, 1963), 166. In that same interview, Davison states that he arrived at San Pedro, Los Angeles' port, "exactly the day in which the city paid homage to Charles Lindbergh" (140). Various reports in the *San Pedro Daily News* confirm the date (but not, of course, Davison's arrival) as September 20, 1927. "Tuesday Set Aside as Lindbergh Day," September 17, 1927, 1. Memory is, however, untrustworthy. *Cinelandia* notes that he arrived on September 19, 1927. "Las nuevas caras del cine hispano," March 1931, 30. That said, at times, so is reporting.

13. Souza, 141. In this interview, Davison claims he met Mexicans such as Emilio Fernández, Alfonso and Luis Sánchez Tello, Chano Urueta, and René Cardona through working as an extra. Tito Davison, "La vida de los extras," *Aconcagua*, January 1935, 90, 109.

14. Ibid., 90. So as to signal that it originally appeared in English, italics here are mine.

15. Ibid., 109.

16. Felipe de Leiva (Agustín Aragón Leiva), "Memoirs of an Extra," translated by Rielle Navitski, in *Cosmopolitan Film Cultures in Latin America, 1896–1960*, ed. Rielle Navitski and Nicolas Poppe (Bloomington: Indiana University Press, 2017), 101–11. It originally appeared in *Cinelandia* as "Memorias de un extra," November 1927, 56, 61 and "Memorias de un extra, jornada dos" December 1927, 39, 61.

17. Souza, 141.

18. Tito Davison, "Extras ayer . . . ," *Ecran*, May 12, 1936, 37.

19. "La vida de los extras," 90. *Sombras de gloria* was the Spanish-language version of Renaud Hoffman and George J. Crone's 1929 *Blaze O'Glory*.

20. According to Juan B. Heinink and Robert G. Dickson's *Cita en Hollywood*, Davison appeared in the following Spanish-language films produced in Hollywood: *Así es la vida* (Spanish-language version of *What a Man* [dir. George J. Crone], dir. Crone, 1930), *La fuerza del querer* (Spanish-language version of *The Big Fight* [dir. Walter Lang, 1930], dir. Ralph Ince, 1930), *Los que danzan* (Spanish-language version of *Those Who Dance* [dir. William Beaudine], dir.

William McGann, 1930), *El presidio* (Spanish-language version of *The Big House* [dir. George Hill], dir. Ward Wing, 1930), *La gran jornada* (Spanish-language version of *The Big Trail* [dir. Raoul Walsh], dir. David Howard, 1931), *Cheri-Bibi* (dir. Borcosque, 1931), *Granaderos del amor* (dir. John Reinhardt, 1934), and *Rosa de Francia* (dir. Gordon Wiles, 1935). He also made uncredited appearances in the English-language films *Laughing Boy* (dir. W. S. Van Dyke, 1934), *Stamboul Quest* (dirs. Sam Wood and Jack Conway, 1934), and *Under the Pampas Moon* (dir. James Tingling, 1935).

21. "Chile tiene un Astro en Hollywood" is cited in Wolfgang Bongers and María José Torrealba, and Ximena Vergara, *Archivos i letrados: escritos sobre cine en Chile: 1908–1940* (Providencia; Santiago: Editorial Cuarto Propio, 2011), 148–49. A similar, but more reserved note was published in the *Cinelandia* series "The New Faces of the *cine hispano*." "Las nuevas caras del cine hispano," March 1931, 30.

22. Coinciding with taking on other kinds of film work, Davison contributed little to the magazine in 1935.

23. Disentangling Davison's unattributed contributions from their publications, much less understanding how his work interacted with that of other contributors, would seem to be an impossibility.

24. I have been unable to access issues of *Ecran* from 1931 (numbers 21–53). Consequently, it is possible that Davison began writing slightly earlier. Tito Davison, "Una 'panne' una estrellita y un tío novelista," January 5, 1932, 8–9. "En Hollywood, donde los proverbios se invierten: 'La suerte de la bonita, la fea la desea," *Ecran*, March 22, 1932.

25. Tito Davison, "Una gran actriz ingenua," *Ecran*, January 10, 1933, 1–3. "La múltiple personalidad de Chester Morris," *Ecran*, April 5, 1932, 5–7. "Un hombre que prestigia a Chile en Hollywood: Carlos Borcosque," *Ecran*, March 20, 1934, 15. "Los caballeros prefieren las rubias . . . ," *Ecran*, April 19, 1932, 2–4. "La falange extranjera de Hollywood," *Ecran*, June 23, 1936, 26. "Escribiendo a las estrellas," *Ecran*, March 7, 1933, 1–3. "El 'amaneramiento' del intérprete cinematográfico," *Ecran*, May 2, 1933, 8–9. "La belleza se fabrica," *Ecran*, Abril 26, 1937, 18–19.

26. I have not been able to verify who wrote under the playful pseudonym of "Galo Pando [Gallo Ping]." An example in which Davison filled in: "Chismes y cuentos," *Cinelandia*, July 1936, 10–12, 56–57.

27. "Gary Cooper—lancero de Bengala," *Cinelandia*, June 1935, 11, 50–51. "Franchot Tone," *Cinelandia*, July 1935, 16, 45–47. "Jean Harlow," *Cinelandia*, September 1935, 11, 52–53. "Robert Montgomery," *Cinelandia*, October 1935, 27, 44–45. "Claudette Colbert," *Cinelandia*, November 1935, 10, 44–46. "Carol Lombard," *Cinelandia*, December 1935, 11, 50–52. "Bette Davis," *Cinelandia*, January 1936, 11, 52–54. "Kay Francis," *Cinelandia*, February 1936, 29, 45–47. "Shirley Temple," *Cinelandia*, March 1936, 12–13, 50–51.

28. "Estrellas de 1940 (?)," *Cinelandia*, April 1936, 22–23, 35–36, 41. On Griffith, he wrote "Un 'pioneer' cinemático," *Cinelandia*, July 1936, 34–35.

29. In his interview with Souza, Davison claims that he wrote for *Sintonía*, *Fémina*, and *Aconcagua* (142). Of the three, his work appeared credited only in *Aconcagua*. Pieces such as "Hollywood Salad" in *Fémina* were possibly composed by Davison. "Salpicón Hollywoodense," May 14, 1934, 18.

30. "Vida privada de los artistas de cine," November 1934, 94–95, 112, 161. "La vida de los extras," January 1935, 90, 109. "Son ellas las que mandan," May 1935, 124–126. "Lo que 'Aconcagua' ve en Hollywood," July 1935, 128–129.

31. "Lo que Shirley Temple piensa del cine," *Aconcagua*, December 1934, 48–49. In the same issue, he provides photographs for the spread "Carole Lombard." He did the same for a number of other photo spreads in *Aconcagua*.

32. "Lo que prepara Fanchon Royer," 539. Fanchon Royer, described as "the only woman film producer" by *Cine-Mundial*, independently produced her own films. Associated with production companies such as Mascot, Mayfair, and Sono-Art World Wide, Royer's work on Poverty Row is briefly discussed in Michael R. Pitts's *Poverty Row Studios, 1929–1940* (Jefferson: McFarland, 2005), 329–34. "Titi Davidson [*sic*]," *Cine-Mundial*, December 1935, 783.

33. Souza, 141.

34. Chas de Cruz, "El cine es talento, experiencia y dinero," July 8, 1942 (número extraordinario), n.p. Lamarque, "Las estrellas tenemos vida limitada," July 8, 1942 (número extraordinario), n.p. Soffici, "El error del 'yo' en cine," July 8, 1942 (número extraordinario), n.p. Davison, "Deben buscarse mejores argumentos," July 8, 1942 (número extraordinario), n.p.

35. Notably, its unstable noun form also does not have a direct translation in English.

36. Ďurovičová, "Translating America: The Hollywood Multilinguals, 1929–1933," in *Sound Theory/ Sound Practice*, ed. Rick Altman (New York: Routledge, 1992), 145.

37. Di Núbila, *Cómo se hace un film* (Buenos Aires: Abril, 1948), 12.

38. "Preguntas y respuestas," *Radiolandia*, November 1, 1941, 40.

39. " 'El haragán de la familia' nos devuelve a un astro: P. Arias," *Radiolandia*, March 2, 1940, 54. The well--known critic Calki makes a similar argument—that the real Pepe Arias returns after the previous failure in *El loco Serenata* (*The Crazy Man*, dir. Luis Saslavsky, 1939)—in his review in *El Mundo*. "Gran Eficacia Cómica Tiene 'El Haragán de la Familia,'" Museo de Cine Pablo Ducrós Hicken. "Producción argentina," *Heraldo del Cinematografista*, December 6, 1939, 193.

40. For more on Niní Marshall, see Nilo Couret, "The Call of the Screen: Niní Marshall and the Radiophonic Stardom of Argentine Cinema," *Mock Classicism: Latin American Film Comedy, 1930–1960* (Berkeley: University of California Press, 2018), 68–110.

41. Davison is credited with the *encuadre* on both of Martínez Sierra's films, which "like many others were lost in a fire." Rosa Peralta Gilabert, *La escenografía en el exilio de Gori Muñoz* (Valencia: Ediciones de la Filmoteca; Instituto Valenciano de Cinematografía Ricardo Muñoz Suay, 2002), 43. On *Locos de verano*, Davison was credited as "encuadre y colaborador." In a note published in *Heraldo del Cinematografista*, he is described as the film's "ayudante de dirección" ("assistant in direction"). "Producción argentina," April 30, 1941, 59.

42. A copy of *En el viejo Buenos Aires*' shooting script is held by the Museo del Cine Pablo Ducrós Hicken.

43. As Anchou remarks, little is known of Carlos Lucantis. Performed by the Cicarelli-Sapelli theater company, Vaccarezza's *sainete* premiered on April 3, 1936, in the Teatro Mayo in Buenos Aires. It would also appear later that year in *Nuestro Teatro*, a periodical published by the Argentine Authors' Circle (Círculo argentino de autores). A *sainete* or *sainete criollo* is "a one-act play popular in the South American River Plate region (1890–1930). Derived from nineteenth-century Spanish *sainetes* ('tasty morsels,' more or less) and *zarzuelas*, the *sainete criollo* was characterized by the encounter of local creole and immigrant cultures, resulting in a Babel of dialects, picturesque characters, songs, and celebrations, and melodramatic, often violent plots." Jean Graham-Jones, "*Sainete criollo*," in *The Oxford Encyclopedia of Theatre and Performance*, ed. Dennis Kennedy (Oxford: Oxford University Press, 2003), 1174.

44. A film's technical script would eventually revert to the control of the director (and the director's assistant). As I discussed in the previous section, there was a period in which these duties fell to the person in charge of a film's *encuadre*. Here, "film script" is in quotations to signal that it did not fully correspond to how we might understand that term today.

45. Owned by a company headed by powerful exhibitor Clemente Lococo, the Cine Opera was one of Buenos Aires' largest movie palaces with 2,530 seats. César Maranghello, "El cine Opera" in *Cine argentino: industria y clasicismo, 1933/1956*, vol. 2, ed. Claudio España (Buenos Aires: Fondo Nacional de las Artes, 2000), 536–37. *Murió el Sargento Laprida* was distributed by British Films Distributors (often used by fleeting production companies) in Argentina and Gerry Manes in the United States. It was rereleased several times soon after its initial arrival on screen. The film was approved by the Motion Picture Division of the Education Department of New York on March 16, 1939. I have been unable to find details concerning its exhibition in New York City. Casefile Number 36607, Box 694, New York State Motion Picture Division License Application Case Files, New York State Archives, Albany, New York, United States.

46. In the July 14, 1937, issue of *Heraldo del Cinematografista*, Davison was announced as the director of the new production company's first film, *Murió el Sargento Laprida*. "En pocas palabras por el editor," *Heraldo del Cinematografista*,

July 14, 1937, 93. A month later, *Radiolandia* reported that filming had begun. "Lo que se filma . . . ", *Radiolandia*, August 21, 1937, 50. Though ultimately not the case, *Revista del Exhibidor* revealed that an accelerated shooting schedule would lead to an October release. "'Murió el Sargento Laprida' para octobre," September 30, 1937, 12. In the recurring column "Light, Camera, Sound!" several additional brief notes were published, including the (ultimately unrealized) contracting of Paul Ellis, a peripatetic Argentine actor who previously acted in Hollywood and Mexico. "Luz, cámara, sonido! 'Lucantis Films' contrató a Paul Ellis," *Radiolandia*, October 16, 1937, 16. Suggestive of a drawn-out production, Lucantis Film celebrated the film's wrap with a cocktail party on October 27, 1937. "En pocas palabras por el editor," *Heraldo del Cinematografista*, November 3, 1937, 180.

47. "Murió el Sargento Laprida," *Heraldo del Cinematografista*, December 29, 1937, 224. Out of four, the film was given a commercial value of three "para populares," an artistic value of three, and a plot value of two.

48. It should come of little surprise, therefore, that Davison and the film's cast took to the radio to promote *Murió el Sargento Laprida* "Gente de cine en Radio Splendid," *Radiolandia*, 9. López develops the idea of the radiophonic imaginary in "Film and Radio Intermedialities in Early Latin American Sound Cinema," in *The Routledge Companion to Latin American Cinema*, ed. Marvin D'Lugo, Ana M. López, and Laura Podalsky (Abingdon; New York: Routledge, 2018), 316–28, as well as conference papers.

49. As the radio broadcaster in the film later announces, the tango's music is composed by Julio de Caro, its lyrics by Carlos de la Púa, and its refrain by Pedro Laura.

50. Michel Chion, *Audio-Vision: Sound on Screen* (New York: Columbia University Press, 1994), 48. I explore this idea in greater detail in "Sounding Out Temporality in the Argentine Film Musical of the 1930s," *Arizona Journal of Hispanic Cultural Studies* n. 16 (2012), 211–26.

51. Suggestively, as the viewer soon discovers, the dialogues taken from screen to satisfy New York's Motion Picture Division mistake "con motivo de su condecoración" ("for his award") with "con motivo de su corazón" ("for his heart's sake"). Dialogues taken from screen by Gerry Manes, March 15, 1939, Casefile Number 36607, Box 694, New York State Motion Picture Division License Application Case Files, New York State Archives, Albany, New York, United States.

52. La Tigra, in fact, laments that Laprida is too good.

53. Curiously, given his later work in the Argentine film industry, Davison was not in charge of the film's *encuadre* (J. J. Bolla was credited). PAF's six films were *Bajo la Santa Federación* (Under the Holy Federation, dir. Daniel Tinayre, 1934), *Sombras porteñas* (dir. Tinayre, 1935), *Una porteña optimista* (dir. Tinayre, 1936), the remake *Nobleza gaucha* (*Gaucha Heart*, dir. Sebastián Naón, 1937), *Las de Barranco*, and *El hombre que nació dos veces* (The Man Who Was Born Twice, dir. Oduvaldo Vianna, 1938). For more on the production company, see Gregorio

Anchou, "Producción independiente en el amanecer del clasicismo (1932–1935)," in *Cine argentino: industria y clasicismo, 1933/1956*, vol. 1, ed. Claudio España (Buenos Aires: Fondo Nacional de las Artes, 2000), 473, 477–80.

54. Ibid., 473.

55. "Para 'Las de Barranco' se reprodujo un típico patio de principios de siglo," *Film*, June 5, 1938. Reports on the film adaptation of Laferrère's play began appearing in mid-1937. A handful of other articles reference its production in periodicals such as *Film*, *Heraldo del Cinematografista*, *Radiolandia*, and *Revista del Exhibidor*.

56. "'Las de Barranco' es un film ennoblecido de emoción," *Radiolandia*, July 9, 1938, 68. In its final section, "A Hit Film," it is stated that "the Argentine public will feel the desire to contemplate this film as a way of satisfying the yearning of evocation that moves the spirit of our people [*pueblo*]."

57. "El consejero del exhibidor," *Proyecciones*, July 1938, 14.

58. "Las de Barranco," *Heraldo del Cinematografista*, July 6, 1938, 108. The film received a commercial value of three, an artistic value of two, and a plot value of two out of a possible four.

59. "Medio año de la temporada cinematográfica argentina," July 23, 1938, 49. The failure of adaptations like *Las de Barranco* would continue to be a topic of discussion into the 1940 in piece such as Carlos Borcosque's "Adaptors and Performers." "Adaptadores e intérpretes, *Heraldo del Cinematografista*, July 8, 1942 (número extraordinario), n.p.

60. "Medio año de la temporada cinematográfica argentina," July 23, 1938, 49.

61. Patoruzú has increasingly become an object of academic study. Judith Gociol and Diego Rosemberg, *La historieta argentina: Una historia* (Buenos Aires: Ediciones de la Flor, 2000). Ana Merino, "Fake Nostalgia for the Indian: The Argentinean Fiction of National Identity in the Comics of Patoruzú," in *No Laughing Matter: Visual Humor in Ideas of Race, Nationality, and Ethnicity*, ed. Angela Rosenthal, David Bindman, and Adrian W. B. Randolph (Hanover: Dartmouth, 2016), 149–75.

62. Raúl Manrupe, *Breve historia del dibujo animado en la Argentina* (Buenos Aires: Libros del Rojas, 2004), 26. "Detrás de las cámaras," *Sintonía*, September 20, 1939, 59. However, as the note remarks, the war precluded its production in Germany.

63. Ostuni et al reassemble some of this merchandise in their *Patoruzú, vera historia no oficial del grande y famoso cacique tehuelche* (Buenos Aires: Ediciones La Bañadera del Comic, 2001).

64. "Producción argentina," *Heraldo del Cinematografista*, October 14, 1942, 182.

65. The Columbia Pictures comedy *De buena familia* (*Hello, Annapolis*, dir. Charles Barton, 1942) rounded out the program that night. *Upa en apuros* screened privately in the Ambassador the daily before its premiere. "Producción argentina," *Heraldo del Cinematografista*, November 18, 1942, 209.

66. "Upa en apuros," *Heraldo del Cinematografista*, November 25, 1942, 217. Indicative of its unusualness, the film's review lacks typical ratings.

67. These animators included Director of Animation, Tulio Lovato; Principal Collaborators, Óscar Blotta and Jaime Romeu; and Scenery Director, Gustavo Goldschmidt.

68. "Patoruzú se inicia en cine," *Sintonía*, November 25, 1942, 85.

69. In a brief note, it is reported that "On November 23 in EFA's studios, Carlos Gallart will begin a production with María Duval. Enrique Amorim and Tito Davison will collaborate." "Producción argentina," *Heraldo del Cinematografista*, October 28, 1942, 195. It does seem, however, that filming started later. "En los estudios Pampa comenzó a rodarse 'Casi un sueño,' protagonizado por la Duval," *Radiolandia*, December 19, 1942, 40. "'Casi un sueño' filma la Duval," *Radiolandia*, December 26, 1942, 44.

70. At the very least, *Casi un sueño* arrived on screens in Argentina, Mexico, Peru, United States, and Uruguay.

71. *Canción de cuna* was a coproduction with an even more fleeting independent production company, Generalcine.

72. For more on *ingénue* cinema of the 1940s, see Alejandro Kelly Hopfenblatt's "Un modelo de representación para la burguesía: La reformulación de identidades y espacios en el cine de ingenuas," *Imagofagia* 10 (2014): 1–60.

73. "Producción argentina," *Heraldo del Cinematografista*, September 7, 1942, 178.

74. "'Casi un sueño' se titula la producción de Gallart para la E.F.A. que rodarán en Pampa," *Radiolandia*, December 5, 1942, 44.

75. "Por nuestros 'sets,'" *Film*, December 12, 1942.

76. "Producción argentina," *Heraldo del Cinematografista*, December 16, 1942, 229. "Producción argentina," *Heraldo del Cinematografista*, December 30, 1942, 234.

77. "Casi un sueño," April 28, 1943, 59. Out of a possible four, the film was assessed to have a commercial value of three "para familiares," an artistic value of two and a half, and a plot value of two.

78. Ray (Josephs), "Casi un sueno ('Almost a Dream') (Argentine-Made)," *Variety*, May 19, 1943, 8. In his five years in Buenos Aires, Josephs worked as a regular contributor for the *Buenos Aires Herald*, as well as a correspondent for the *New York Herald*, *Time*, and *Variety*. Shortly before the publication of *Argentine Diary: The Inside Story of the Coming of Fascism* (New York: Random House, 1944), which warned of the consequences of the rise of Peronism, he left Argentina.

79. I borrow this wording from a conversation with Alejandro Kelly Hopfenblatt about the film. His exact wording: "*Casi un sueño* es la cumbre de lo que podía ser el cine de ingenuas"

80. Davison, 159.

81. Nilo Couret, *Mock Classicism: Latin American Film Comedy, 1930–1960* (Berkeley: University of California Press, 2018), 165.

82. María Isabel Souza. "Tito Davison." In *Testimonios para la historia del cine mexicano Vol. 7*, edited by Eugenia Meyer (México, D.F.: Cineteca Nacional; Instituto Nacional de Antropología e Historia, 1976), 142–43.

83. "Noticioso," *Heraldo del Cinematografista*, May 5, 1943, 63.

84. Contract with Paramount Pictures, February 29, 1944, Paramount Pictures Contract Summaries, Folder 598, Margaret Herrick Library, Academy of Motion Picture Arts and Sciences, Los Angeles, California, United States.

Chapter 10

1. The film was also known contemporaneously as *Cousas Nossas*.

2. Byington & Cia. advertisement, *Cinearte*, December 2, 1931, 4.

3. "Cinema brasileiro," *Cine Arte*, February 17, 1932, 7. Paulo Amarante, "Um novo ponto de partida no cinema nacional, *A Scena Muda*, July 9, 1946, 3. Antônio Moreno, *Cinema brasileiro: história e relações com o estado* (Niterói: EDUFF, 1994), 83.

4. Jurandyr Noronha, *Dicionário Jurandir Noronha de cinema brasileiro. Os que vieram de outras terras* (Rio de Janeiro: EMC Edições, 2015), 177.

5. Downey was not the first American to impact Brazilian cinema—actors Antonia Denegri and Olivette Thomas and directors William Jansen and Eugênio Kerrigan were involved in its silent period to varying degrees—but he may be the most important until David Zing in the 1960s and '70s or more recent figures such as Roberto Gevirtz and Alan Langdon.

6. Nilo Couret, *Mock Classicism: Latin American Film Comedy, 1930–1960* (Berkeley: University of California Press, 2018), 156. In the chapter "Fictions of the Real: The Currency of the Brazilian Chanchada," Couret provides a historical analysis of the *chanchada*, arguing that genre definition and medium specificity are intrinsic to the creation of an idea of national cinema, 153–91.

7. Rafael de Luna Freire traces the evolution of the term in "Descascando o abacaxi carnavalesco da chanchada: A invenção de um gênero cinematográfico nacional." *Contracampo* 23 (2011): 66–85. Foreign film workers discussed subsequently have entries in Norohna's volume *Os que vieram de outras terras*.

8. Many Portuguese or Portuguese-born actors worked in Brazilian cinema in the period, including Roberto Acácio, Alice Archamleau, Eduordo Arouca, Ernani Augusto, João de Deus, Alma Flora, Armando Nascimento, Sarah Nobre, Abel Pêra, Manuel Pêra, and Manoel Rocha. Joining them on set were other foreign performers such as Gina Bianchi, Pepita Cantero, Corita Cunha, Augusta Guimarães, Conchita Moraes, Heriberto Muraro, Pablo Palitos, Carlos Ruel, and Afonso Stuart.

9. A Spanish-language version of the film, *El grito de la juventud*, was produced as well. A few productions leaned heavily on foreign talent: for example,

Noites cariocas (Rio Nights, dir. Enrique Cadícamo, 1935) included Argentines María Luisa Palomero, Carlos Perelli, and Carlos Viván, while *A sedução do garimpo* (Seduction of Prospecting, dir. Luiz de Barros, 1941) featured U.S. actors Nan Bower, Dianne Dreene, Joya Matten, and Frank Mazzone. The Italian Gita de Barros worked as a writer on the film.

10. João Tinoco de Freitas was also born in Portugal, while Julien Mandel, Bob Chust, and Leo Marten were from France, Paraguay, and Poland, respectively.

11. Among the other cinematographers working at this time were the Argentine Roque Funes and the Hungarian Adalberto Kemeny. They were joined on set by foreign cameramen Ignio Bonfioli, Victor Ciacchi, Carlos Felten, Ramón García, Rudolph Lustig, Hikoma Udihara, and Serge Uzum.

12. Noronha, 109. Many other European technicians worked in Brazilian cinema at the time. These include William Gericke, Lazlo Meitner, Fritz Lucien Mellinger, and Luiz Seel.

13. Paulo Antonio Paranaguá, "Brésil," in *Les Cinémas de l'Amérique latine*, ed. Guy Hebelle and Alfonso Gumucio-Dagrón (Paris: Nouvelles Editions Pierre L'Herminier, 1981), 122.

14. An Argentine of Basque descent, Juan Etchebehere worked primarily as a film editor. *Dos destinos* was his only credit as director. His brother Alberto was a prolific cinematographer who shot films such as *Hay que educar a Niní* (dir. Luis César Amadori, 1940), *Nacha Regules* (*Saint and Sinner*, dir. Amadori, 1950), and *Deshonra* (*Dishonor*, dir. Daniel Tinayre, 1952). An Italian who immigrated to Argentina, Emilio Peruzzi was *Dos destino*'s cinematographer. Like Alberto Etchebehere, he shot many films. Its sound was charged to an Argentine: Ramón Ator. The film's talent, however, was Uruguayan: for example, its star Pepe "El Parisino" Corbi was a radio singer and its screenwriter Edmundo Bianchi composed plays and tangos.

15. José Carlos Álvarez, *Breve historia del cine uruguayo* (Montevideo: Cinemateca Uruguaya, 1957), 11.

16. Peter B. Schumann, *Historia del cine latinoamericano* (Buenos Aires: Legasa, 1987), 285.

17. With Isidoro Navarro, Alberto Roca established the production company NIRA film in Santa Fe. NIRA produced two films directed by Navarro: *Viejo barrio* (Old Neighborhood, 1935), *El casamiento de Chichilo* (Chichilo's Wedding, 1938).

18. Raimondo Souto, *Una historia del cine en Uruguay: memorias compartidas* (Montevideo: Planeta, 2010), 45.

19. Often coproductions, these films employed local actors such as Mirta Torres and Juan Carlos Mareco, as well as largely Argentine foreign talent like Armando Bó (who would later direct sexploitation films with Isabel Sarli) and Roberto Airaldi. Their crew also brought together Uruguayans and foreigners, from Austrian director Land to cinematographers such as American Bob Roberts.

Moving from the late 1940s to the early 1950s, they were made by increasingly Uruguayan casts and crews.

20. Ricardo Bedoya, *El cine sonoro en el Perú* (Lima: Fondo Editorial Universidad de Lima, 2015), 20. My reading of the early sound period in Peru is heavily indebted to Bedoya's scholarship.

21. In the 1930s, Hollywood dominated Lima's movie theaters, constituting 2693 of the 3698 (73.6 percent) of films shown. Peaking in 1931, its 145 Spanish-language films made up 3.8 percent of all movies. Argentine films, eventually totaling 112 (3 percent), began to arrive in larger numbers in 1936 and continued to grow into the 1940s. Despite closing the decade with few films, 167 Mexican imports amounted to 4.5 percent. Violeta Núñez Gorritti, *Cartelera cinematográfica peruana, 1930–1939* (Lima: Universidad de Lima, Fondo de Desarrollo Editorial, 1998), 375.

22. Bedoya, 40.

23. Jeffrey Middents, *Writing National Cinema: Film Journals and Film Culture in Peru* (Hanover: Dartmouth College Press, 2009), 17. The points are quoted in Bedoya, 3 and Middents, 17.

24. Bedoya, 34.

25. Peter H. Rist, *Historical Dictionary of South American Cinema* (Lanham: Rowman and Littlefield, 2014), 22.

26. Other Spanish actors include Trini Delor, Esperanza Ortiz de Pinedo, Armando Guerrini, María Manuela, and Carmen Paradillo.

27. December 19, 1937. Qtd. in Bedoya, 48.

28. Bedoya, 52–53.

29. Ibid., 54.

30. November 21, 1938. Qtd. in ibid., 62.

31. Ibid., 77.

32. Middents, 18–19. Sporadic feature-length activity continued, as did more regular production of newsreels and documentaries, which provided regular employment for local film workers. Bedoya, 92–96.

33. María Paz Peirano, "Chilefilms, el proyecto nacional y los discursos sobre el cine chileno durante la década de 1940," in *Chilefilms, el Hollywood criollo: aproximaciones al proyecto industrial cinematográfico chileno (1942–1949)*, ed. María Paz Peirano, Catalina Gobantes, Luis Horta, and Alonso Machuca Serey (Santiago: Editorial Cuarto Propio, 2015), 41.

34. Jacqueline Mousca and Carlos Orellana note that the sound equipment was built by local representatives of RCA. *Breve historia del cine chileno* (Santiago: LOM Ediciones, 2010), 57.

35. Ibid., 60.

36. After his birth in Bonn, Germany, Bohr's family moved to Bahía Blanca, Argentina. Soon thereafter they moved to Chile, first to Puerto Porvenir and, later, to Punta Arenas.

37. Some exceptions included the Spanish actors Conchita Buxón, Alberto Closas, Olvido Leguía, and Agustín Orrequia; the Peruvian actor Lucho Córdoba; and the German cinematographer Egidio Heiss. Others were born in different countries. Peruvian-born brothers Eugenio and Rogel Retes worked on several films, while Argentine-born Pablo Petrowitsch also directed five films from 1942 to 1950.

38. "Producción en Chile," *Heraldo del Cinematografista*, December 10, 1941, 237.

39. "Argentine's Sono Sets Pact with Chilean Co. on Prod. Organization," *Variety*, January 7, 1942, 90.

40. Additionally, it would coproduce four (1949–1951) and collaborate on six more (1945–1951). *Chilefilms, el Hollywood criollo*, 253–73.

41. Even though they enjoyed long careers in Argentina, Andreani (credited as Jorge Andriani in Chile) and Testi were from Poland and Italy, respectively. With the notable exception of Spanish actor Ernesto Vilches, the casts of these films were Chilean.

42. Mario (Vieyra) Lugones had only helmed one film before directing *El último guapo* (The Last Tough Guy, 1947). He would go on to direct more than a dozen more movies in his native Argentina. In various film histories, Roberto de Ribón is described as Argentine, Spanish, and even Chilean. He was of Colombian nationality. Born in Paris to a Colombian father and Argentine mother, he led a peripatetic life. In Rome, he directed with Edgar Neville the fascist Spanish/Italian co-production *Santa Rogelia* (1940), a Spanish-language version of *Il peccato di Rogelia Sanchez* (The Sin of Rogelia Sanchez, dir. Carlo Borghesio). His wife was the Austrian actress Trude von Molo, a brief star in late Weimar-era cinema. Roberto Germán de Ribón and Gertrudis de Molo de Germán Ribón Immigration Cards, November 9, 1946, "Rio de Janeiro Brazil, Immigration Cards, 1900–1965," FamilySearch, Salt Lake City, UT.

43. Nilo Couret, *Mock Classicism: Latin American Film Comedy, 1930–1960* (Berkeley: University of California Press, 2018), 221.

44. Alonso Machuca Serey, "Chilefilms, un capítulo ignorado. Imaginario expuesto en las producciones íntegras de la empresa chilena entre 1944 y 1947," in *Chilefilms, el Hollywood criollo*, 234.

Bibliography

Acevedo, Marta. *El 10 de mayo.* Mexico City: Secretaría de Educación Pública, Dirección de Publicaciones y Bibliotecas; Martín Casillas Editores, 1982.

Ackcigit, Ufuk, John Grigsby, and Tom Nichols. "The Rise of American Ingenuity: Innovation and Inventors of the Golden Age," NBER Working Paper #23047, 2017.

Álvarez, José Carlos. *Breve historia del cine uruguayo.* Montevideo: Cinemateca Uruguaya, 1957.

Amador, María Luisa, and Jorge Ayala Blanco. *Cartelera cinematográfica, 1930–1939.* Mexico City: Filmoteca UNAM, 1980.

Anchou, Gregorio. "Producción independiente en el amanecer del clasicismo (1932–1935)." In *Cine argentino: industria y clasicismo, 1933/1956.* Vol. 1, edited by Claudio España. Buenos Aires: Fondo Nacional de las Artes, 2000.

———. "Veinticinco años de producción independiente. Las fronteras ignoradas." In *Cine argentino: industria y clasicismo, 1933/1956.* Vol. 1, edited by Claudio España. Buenos Aires: Fondo Nacional de las Artes, 2000.

Armero, Álvaro. *Una aventura americana: españoles en Hollywood.* Madrid: Compañía Literaria, 1995.

Ayala Blanco, Jorge. *La aventura del cine mexicano.* Mexico City: Universidad Autónoma de México, 2017.

Baily, Samuel L. *Immigrants in the Lands of Promise: Italians in Buenos Aires and New York City, 1870–1914.* Ithaca: Cornell University Press, 1999.

Beach, Christopher. *A Hidden History of Film Style: Cinematographers, Directors, and the Collborative Process.* Oakland: University of California Press, 2015.

Bedoya, Ricardo. *El cine sonoro en el Perú.* Lima: Fondo Editorial Universidad de Lima, 2015.

Berg, Charles Ramírez. *The Classical Mexican Cinema.* Austin: University of Texas Press, 2015.

Blanco, Jorge Ayala, *La aventura del cine mexicano.* Mexico City; Universidad Autónoma de México, 2017.

Bongers, Wolfgang, María José Torreabla, and Ximena Vergara. *Archivos i letrados: escritos sobre cine en Chile: 1908–1940.* Providencia; Santiago: Editorial Cuarto Propio, 2011.

Borge, Jason. *Latin American Writers and the Rise of Hollywood Cinema.* New York: Routledge, 2008.

Bourdieu, Pierre. *Outline of a Theory of Practice.* Cambridge: Cambridge University Press, 1977.

Cagle, Chris. "Classical Hollywood, 1928–1946." In *Cinematography,* edited by Patrick Keating. New Brunswick: Rutgers University Press, 2014.

Castro, J. Justin. *Radio in Revolution: Wireless Technology and State Power in Mexico, 1897–1938.* Lincoln: University of Nebraska Press, 2016.

Castro Ricalde, Maricruz, and Robert McKee Irwin. *El cine mexicano "se impone": mercados internacionales y penetración cultural en la época dorada.* Mexico City: Universidad Nacional Autónoma de México, 2011.

———, eds. *Global Mexican Cinema. Its Golden Age.* London: Palgrave; British Film Institute, 2013.

Catalogue of Copyright Entries. Part 1, Group 3. Dramatic Compositions. Motion Pictures. Washington, DC: United States Government Printing Office, 1933.

Chion, Michel. *Audio-Vision: Sound on Screen.* New York: Columbia University Press, 1994.

Commissariato Genérale dell'Emigrazione. *Annuario statistico dell'emigrazione italiana dal 1876 al 1925.* Rome: Commissariato Genérale dell'Emigrazione, 1926.

Couret, Nilo. *Mock Classicism: Latin American Film Comedy, 1930–1960.* Oakland: University of California Press, 2018.

Davison, Tito. "Preparación profesional cinematográfica." *Comunicación Social* no. 6 (1983).

De las Carreras, María Elena, and Jan-Christopher Horak, eds. *Hollywood Goes Latin: Spanish-Language Cinema in Los Angeles.* s.l.: FIAF/UCLA Film & Television Archive, 2019.

De la Vega, Eduardo. *Arcady Boytler.* Guadalajara: Universidad de Guadalajara, 1992.

———. *El cine de Juan Orol.* Mexico City: Universidad Nacional Autónoma de México, 1985.

———. *Juan Orol.* Guadalajara: Universidad de Guadalajara, 1987.

De los Reyes, Aurelio. *Cine y sociedad en México, 1896–1930: Sucedió en Jalisco o Los Cristeros (1924–1928).* Mexico City: Universidad Nacional Autónoma de México Instituto de Investigaciones Estéticas, 2013.

Díez Martín, José. *Memorias del ídolo José Mojica.* Madrid: Alco, 1975.

Di Núbila, Domingo, *Historia del cine argentino.* Vol. 1. Buenos Aires: Cruz de Malta, 1959.

———. *Historia del cine argentino.* Vol. 2. Buenos Aires: Cruz de Malta, 1960.

———. *La Época de Oro: Historia del cine argentino I.* Buenos Aires: Jilguero, 1998.

Dirección de Inmigración de la República Argentina. *Resumen estadístico del movimiento migratorio en la República Argentina, 1857–1924.* Buenos Aires: El Gráfico, 1925.

Ďurovičová, Nataša. "Translating America: The Hollywood Multilinguals, 1929–1933." In *Sound Theory/Sound Practice*, edited by Rick Altman. New York: Routledge, 1992.

Dyer, Richard. *Stars.* London: British Film Institute, 1998.

España, Claudio. *Medio siglo de cine: Argentina Sono Film, S.A.C.I.* Buenos Aires: Abril, 1984.

———. "El model institucional." In *Cine argentino industria y clasicismo, 1933–1956*, edited by Claudio España. Buenos Aires: Fondo Nacional de las Artes, 2000.

Fein, Seth. "Myths of Cultural Imperialism and Nationalism in Golden Age Mexican Cinema," In *Fragments of a Golden Age: The Politics of Culture in Mexico, 1940–2000*, edited by Gilbert Joseph, Anne Rubenstein, and Eric Zolov. Durham: Duke University Press, 2001.

———. "Transnationalization and Cultural Collaboration: 'Mexican' Cinema and the Second World War." *Studies in Latin American Popular Culture* 17 (1998).

Ferrer, Horacio. "Premier en el Real." *El libro del tango. Historias e imagines.* Buenos Aires: Ediciones Ossorio-Vargas, 1970.

Fleeger, Jennifer. *Sounding American: Hollywood, Opera, and Jazz.* Oxford: Oxford University Press, 2014.

Fulguiera, María Alba. "Alex Phillips." In *Testimonios para la historia del cine mexicano.* Vol. 1, edited by Eugenia Meyer. Mexico City: Cineteca Nacional; Instituto Nacional de Antropología e Historia, 1975.

Garate, Juan Carlos. "La industria cinematográfica argentina." PhD diss. Universidad de Buenos Aires, 1944.

García, Desirée J. *The Migration of Musical Film: From Ethnic Margins to American Mainstream.* New Brunswick: Rutgers University Press, 2014.

García de Dueñas, Jesús. *¡Nos vamos a Hollywood!* Madrid: Nickel Odeon, 1993.

García Riera, Emilio. *Breve historia del cine mexicano.* Zapopan: Ediciones Mapa, 1998.

———. *Fernando de Fuentes (1894/1958): trabajo colectivo.* Mexico City: Cineteca Nacional, 1984.

———. *Historia documental del cine mexicano*, Vol. 1. Mexico City: Ediciones Era, 1969.

———. *Historia documental del cine mexicano.* Vol. 1. Guadalajara: Universidad de Guadalajara, 1993.

———. *Historia documental del cine mexicano.* Vol. 2. Guadalajara: Universidad de Guadalajara, 1993.

Gledhill, Christine. "Signs of Melodrama." In *Stardom: Industry of Desire*, edited by Christine Gledhill. London; New York: Routledge, 1991.

Gociol, Judith, and Diego Rosemberg. *La historieta argentina: Una historia.* Buenos Aires: Ediciones de la Flor, 2000.

Goulart, Isabella. "Perdidos na tradução: as representações da latinidade e as versões em espanhol de Hollywood no Brasil (1929–1935)." PhD diss. Universidade de São Paulo, 2018.

Graham-Jones, Jean. "*Sainete criollo.*" In *The Oxford Encyclopedia of Theatre and Performance*, edited by Dennis Kennedy. Oxford: Oxford University Press, 2003.

Green Quintana, Roberto. "Buried in the Vault: The Restoration of Hollywood's Spanish-language Films." In *Hollywood Goes Latin: Spanish-Language Cinema in Los Angeles*, edited by María Elena de las Carreras and Jan-Christopher Horak. s.l: FIAF/UCLA Film & Television Archive, 2019.

Gunckel, Colin. *Mexico on Main Street: Transnational Film Culture in Los Angeles Before World War II.* New Brunswick: Rutgers University Press, 2015.

———. "The War of the Accents: Spanish Language Hollywood Films in Mexican Los Angeles," *Film History* 20 (2008).

———, Jan-Christopher Horak, and Lisa Jarvinen, eds. *Cinema Between Latin America and Los Angeles: Origins to 1960*, New Brunswick: Rutgers University Press, 2019.

Hake, Sabine. *Popular Cinema of the Third Reich.* Austin: University of Texas Press, 2001.

Heinink, Juan B., and Robert G. Dickson. *Cita en Hollywood: antología de las películas norteamericanas habladas en castellano.* Bilbao: Mensajero, 1990.

Hernández Girbal, Florentino. *Los que pasaron por Hollywood*, edited by Juan B. Heinink and Robert Dickson. Madrid: Verdoux, 1992.

Horak, Jan-Christopher. "Cantabria Films and the LA Film Market, 1938–1940." In *Cinema Between Latin America and Los Angeles: Origins to 1960*, edited by Colin Gunckel, Jan-Christopher Horak, and Lisa Jarvinen. New Brunswick: Rutgers University Press, 2019.

Hull, Cordell. *Foreign Relations of the United States Diplomatic Papers 1944, The American Republics.* Washington, DC: U. S. Government Printing Office, 1967.

Irwin, Robert McKee. "Mexico's Appropriation of the Latin American Visual Imaginary: Rómulo Gallegos in Mexico." In *Global Mexican Cinema. Its Golden Age*, edited by Maricruz Castro Ricalde and Robert McKee Irwin. London: Palgrave; British Film Institute, 2013.

Jarvinen, Lisa. *The Rise of Spanish-Language Filmmaking: Out from Hollywood's Shadow, 1929–1939.* New Brunswick: Rutgers University Press, 2012.

Josephs, Ray. *Argentine Diary: The Inside Story of the Coming of Fascism.* New York: Random House, 1944.

Kanellos, Nicolás. *A History of Hispanic Theatre in the United States: Origins to 1940.* Austin: University of Texas Press, 1990.

Keating, Patrick. *Hollywood Lighting from the Silent Era to Film Noir*. New York: Columbia University Press, 2010.

———. "The Volcano and the Barren Hill: Gabriel Figueroa and the Space of Art Cinema." In *Global Art Cinema: New Theories and Histories*, edited by Rosalind Galt and Karl Schoonover. Oxford and New York: Oxford University Press, 2010.

Kelly Hopfenblatt, Alejandro. "Un modelo de representación para la burguesía: La reformulación de identidades y espacios en el cine de ingenuas." *Imagofagia* 10 (2014).

Key, Pierre V. R., and Bruno Zirato. *Enrico Caruso: A Biography*. Boston: Little, Brown, 1922.

King, John, Ana M López, and Manuel Alvarado, eds. *Mediating Two Worlds: Cinematic Encounters in the Americas*. London: British Film Institute, 1993.

Koegel, John. "Mexican Musicians in California and the United States, 1910–50." *California History* 84, no. 1 (2006).

López, Ana M. "A Cinema for the Continent." In *The Mexican Cinema Project*, edited by Chon A. Noriega and Steven Ricci. Los Angeles: UCLA Film and Television Archive, 1994.

———. "Before Exploitation: Three Men of Cinema in Mexico." In *Latsploitation, Exploitation Cinemas, and Latin America*, edited by Victoria Ruétalo and Dolores Tierney. London: Routledge, 2009.

———. "Early Cinema and Modernity in Latin America," *Cinema Journal* 40, no. 1 (2000): 48–78.

———. "Film and Radio Intermedialities in Early Latin American Sound Cinema." In *The Routledge Companion to Latin American Cinema*, edited by Marvin D'Lugo, Ana M. López, and Laura Podalsky. Abingdon; New York: Routledge, 2018.

Luna Freire, Rafael de. "Descascando o abacaxi carnavalesco da chanchada: A invenção de um gênero cinematográfico nacional." *Contracampo* 23 (2011).

Machuca Serey, Alonso. "Chilefilms, un capítulo ignorado. Imaginario expuesto en las producciones íntegras de la empresa chilena entre 1944 y 1947," In *Chilefilms, el Hollywood criollo: aproximaciones al proyecto industrial cinematográfico chileno (1942–1949)*, edited by María Paz Peirano, Catalina Gobantes, Luis Horta, and Alonso Machuca Serey, Santiago: Editorial Cuarto Propio, 2015.

Mahieux, Viviane. "Una pequeña Marquesa de Sade en la crónica mexicana." In *Una pequeña Marquesa de Sade: crónicas selectas, 1921–1948*, edited by Viviane Mahieux. Mexico City: Dirección de Literatura, Universidad Nacional Autónoma de México, 2009.

Manetti, Richard. "Argentina Sono Film. Más estrellas que en el cielo." In *Cine argentino industria y clasicismo, 19331956*. Vol. 1, edited by Claudio España. Buenos Aires: Fondo Nacional de las Artes, 2000.

Manrupe, Raúl. *Breve historia del dibujo animado en la Argentina*. Buenos Aires: Libros del Rojas, 2004.

Maranghello, César. "El cine Opera." In *Cine argentino: industria y clasicismo, 1933/1956*. Vol. 2, edited by Claudio España. Buenos Aires: Fondo Nacional de las Artes, 2000.

Martin, José Diez. *Memorias del ídolo José Mojica*. Madrid: Alco, 1975.

Merino, Ana. "Fake Nostalgia for the Indian: The Argentinean Fiction of National Identity in the Comics of Patoruzú." In *No Laughing Matter: Visual Humor in Ideas of Race, Nationality, and Ethnicity*, edited by Angela Rosenthal, David Bindman, and Adrian W. B. Randolph. Hanover: Dartmouth College Press, 2016.

Meyer, Eugenia. "Andrea Palma." In *Testimonios para la historia del cine mexicano*. Vol. 1, edited by Eugenia Meyer. Mexico City: Cineteca Nacional; Instituto Nacional de Antropología e Historia, 1975.

———. "Juan Orol." In *Testimonios para la historia del cine mexicano*. Vol. 2, edited by Eugenia Meyer. Mexico City: Cineteca Nacional; Instituto Nacional de Antropología e Historia, 1976.

Middents, Jeffrey. *Writing National Cinema: Film Journals and Film Culture in Peru*. Hanover: Dartmouth College Press, 2009.

Mojica, José. *I, A Sinner*. Chicago: Franciscan Herald Press, 1963.

Monsiváis, Carlos. "Mexican Cinema: Of Myths and Demystifications." In *Mediating Two Worlds: Cinematic Encounters in the Americas*, edited by John King, Ana M. López, and Manuel Alvarado. London: British Film Institute, 1993.

Mora, Carl J. *Mexican Cinema: Reflections of a Society, 1896–1980*. Berkeley: University of California Press, 1982.

Morin, Edgar. *The Stars*. Minneapolis: University of Minnesota Press, 2005.

Mousca, Jacqueline, and Carlos Orellana. *Breve historia del cine chileno*. Santiago: LOM Ediciones, 2010.

Negrete Álvarez, Claudia. "Historias narradas con luz. Tres décadas de labor cinematográfica de Alex Phillips." PhD diss. Universidad Nacional de México, 2009.

Noronha, Jurandyr. *Dicionário Jurandir Noronha de cinema brasileiro. Os que vieram de outras terras*. Rio de Janeiro: EMC Edições, 2015.

Núñez Gorritti, Violeta. *Cartelera cinematográfica peruana, 1930–1939*. Lima: Universidad de Lima, Fondo de Desarrollo Editorial, 1998.

———. *Cartelera cinematográfica peruana, 1940–1949*. Lima: Self-published, 2006.

———. "Hollywood's Spanish-Language Movies in Buenos Aires, Lima, Montevideo, and Mexico City." In *Hollywood Goes Latin: Spanish-Language Cinema in Los Angeles*, edited by María Elena de las Carreras and Jan-Christopher Horak. s.l: FIAF/UCLA Film & Television Archive, 2019.

Ostuni, Hernán, Fernando García, Andrés Ferreiro, Mario Fermosa, and Norberto Rodríguez Van Rousselt. *Patoruzú, vera historia no oficial del grande y famoso cacique tehuelche*. Buenos Aires: Ediciones La Bañadera del Comic, 2001.

Paranaguá, Paulo Antonio. "Brésil." In *Les Cinémas de l'Amérique latine*, edited by Guy Hebelle and Alfonso Gumucio Dagrón. Paris: Nouvelles Editions Pierre L'Herminier, 1981.

———. *Cinema na América Latina: longe de Deus e perto de Hollywood.* Porto Alegre: L & PM Editores, 1985.

Peirano, María Paz. "Chilefilms, el proyecto nacional y los discursos sobre el cine chileno durante la década de 1940." In *Chilefilms, el Hollywood criollo: aproximaciones al proyecto industrial cinematográfico chileno (1942–1949)*, edited by María Paz Peirano, Catalina Gobantes, Luis Horta, and Alonso Machuca Serey. Santiago: Editorial Cuarto Propio, 2015.

Peralta Gilabert, Rosa. *La escenografía en el exilio de Gori Muñoz*. Valencia: Ediciones de la Filmoteca; Instituto Valenciano de Cinematografía Ricardo Muñoz Suay, 2002.

Peredo Castro, Francisco. *Alejandro Galindo, un alma rebelde en el cine mexicano.* Mexico City: Editorial Miguel Ángel Porrúa, 2000.

———. "Entre tradición y modernidad. El cine mexicano en su evolución." In *Historia sociocultural del cine mexicano. Aportes al entretejido de su trama (1896–1966)*, edited by Peredo Castro and Federico Dávalos Orozco. Mexico City: Universidad Nacional Autónoma de México, 2016.

———, and Federico Dávalos Orozco, eds. *Historia sociocultural del cine mexicano: aportes al entretejido de su trama (1896–1966).* Mexico City: Universidad Autónoma de México, 2016.

Pérez Solano, Rocío del Consuelo. "Cube Bonifant." In *Women Film Pioneers Project*, edited by Jane Gaines, Radha Vatsal, and Monica Dall'Asta. Center for Digital Research and Scholarship. New York: Columbia University Libraries, 2013.

Pitts, Michael R. *Poverty Row Studios, 1929–1940.* Jefferson: McFarland, 2005.

Poppe, Nicolas. "John Alton in Argentina, 1932–1939." In *Cosmopolitan Film Cultures in Latin America, 1896–1960*, edited by Rielle Navitski and Nicolas Poppe. Bloomington: Indiana University Press, 2017.

———. "Made in Joinville: Transnational Identitary Aesthetics in Carlos Gardel's Early Paramount Films." *Journal of Latin American Cultural Studies* 21, no. 4 (2012).

———. "Sounding Out Temporality in the Argentine Film Musical of the 1930s." *Arizona Journal of Hispanic Cultural Studies* 16 (2012).

———. "Tito Guízar on Radio Row: Intermediality, Latino Identity, and Two Early 1930s Vitaphone Shorts." In *The Routledge Companion to Gender,*

Sex, and Latin American Culture, edited by Frederick Luis Aldama. New York: Routledge, 2018.

Posadas, Abel. "Argentina Sono Film. El cine como empresa." *Cine en la cultura argentina y latinoamericana* 2 (1983).

Pulido Islas, Alfonso. *La industria cinematográfica de México*. Mexico City: Editorial México Nuevo, 1939.

Rist, Peter H. *Historical Dictionary of South American Cinema*. Lanham: Rowman and Littlefield, 2014.

Rubenstein, Anne. "Mass Media and Popular Culture in the Post Revolutionary Era." In *The Oxford History of Mexico*, edited by Michael C. Meyer and William H. Beezley. Oxford: Oxford University Press, 2000.

Sánchez Prado, Ignacio M. "The Golden Age Otherwise: Mexican Cinema and the Mediations of Capitalist Modernity in the 1940s and 1950s." In *Cosmopolitan Film Cultures in Latin America, 1896–1960*, edited by Rielle Navitski and Nicolas Poppe. Bloomington: Indiana University Press, 2017.

Schumann, Peter B. *Historia del cine latinoamericano*. Buenos Aires: Legasa, 1987.

Serna, Laura Isabel. *Making Cinelandia: American Films and Mexican Film Culture Before the Golden Age*. Durham and London: Duke University Press, 2014.

Shingler, Martin. *Star Studies: A Critical Guide*. London: Palgrave Macmillian; British Film Institute, 2012.

Soloman, Aubrey. *The Fox Film Corporation, 1915–1935*. Jefferson and London: McFarland, 2011.

Sommer, Doris. *Foundational Fictions: The National Romances of Latin America*. Berkeley: University of California Press, 1991.

Souto, Raimondo. *Una historia del cine en Uruguay: memorias compartidas*. Montevideo: Planeta, 2010.

Souza, María Isabel. "Tito Davison." In *Testimonios para la historia del cine mexicano*. Vol. 7, edited by Eugenia Meyer. México, D.F.: Cineteca Nacional; Instituto Nacional de Antropología e Historia, 1976.

Valentine, Maggie. *The Show Starts on the Sidewalk*. New Haven: Yale University Press, 1994.

Vincendeau, Ginette. "Hollywood Babel: The Coming of Sound in the Multiple-Language Version." *Screen* 29, no. 2 (1988).

Vidal Bonifaz, Rosario. "José Mojica: The Tenor from Jalisco, Mexico, Who Conquered Hollywood." In *Hollywood Goes Latin: Spanish-Language Cinema in Los Angeles*, edited by María Elena de las Carreras and Jan-Christopher Horak. s.l: FIAF/UCLA Film & Television Archive, 2019.

———. *Surgimiento de la industria cinematográfica y el papel del Estado de México, 1895–1940*. Mexico City: Miguel Angel Porrúa, 2011.

Waldman, Harry. *Hollywood and the Foreign Touch: A Dictionary of Foreign Filmmakers and Their Films from America, 1910–1995*. Lanham; London: Scarecrow Press, 1996.

Wollen, Peter. *Signs and Meaning in the Cinema*. Rev. ed. Bloomington: Indiana University Press, 1972.

Wilt, David E. *The Mexican Filmography, 1916 through 2001*. Jefferson and London: McFarland, 2004.

Zylberman, Dana. "Intercambio de directores entre las cinematografías argentina y mexicana en el período clásico-industrial: el caso de Tito Davison." In *Pantallas transnacionales*, edited by Ana Laura Lusnich, Alicia Aisemberg, and Andrea Cuarterolo. Buenos Aires: Imago Mundi, 2017.

Index

Note: page numbers followed by *f* refer to figures.

www.ingramcontent.com/pod-product-compliance
Lightning Source LLC
LaVergne TN
LVHW050147080826
844660LV00002B/101

* 9 7 8 1 4 3 8 4 8 5 0 3 4 *